BALANCING HUMAN RIGHTS, ENVIRONMENTAL PROTECTION AND INTERNATIONAL TRADE

This book explores the means by which economic liberalisation can be reconciled with human rights and environmental protection in the regulation of international trade. It is primarily concerned with identifying the lessons the international community can learn, specifically in the context of the WTO, from decades of EC and EU experience in facing this question.

The book demonstrates first that it is possible to reconcile the pursuit of economic and non-economic interests, that the EU has found a mechanism by which to do so and that the application of the principle of proportionality is fundamental to the realisation of this. It is argued that the EU approach can be characterised as a practical application of the principle of sustainable development. Second, from the analysis of the EU experience, this book identifies fundamental conditions crucial to achieving this 'reconciliation'. Third, the book explores the implications of lessons from the EU experience for the international community. In so doing, it assesses both the potential and limits of the existing international regulatory framework for such reconciliation.

The book develops a deeper understanding of the inter-relationship between the legal regulation of economic and non-economic development, adding clarity to the debate in a controversial area. It argues that a more holistic approach to the consideration of 'development', encompassing economic and non-economic concerns—'sustainable' development—is not only desirable in principle but also realisable in practice.

Studies in International Trade Law: Volume 16

Studies in International Trade Law
Recent titles in this series:

Balancing Human Rights, Environmental Protection and International Trade

Lessons from the EU Experience

Emily Reid

·H A R T·
PUBLISHING
OXFORD AND PORTLAND, OREGON
2015

Published in the United Kingdom by Hart Publishing Ltd
16C Worcester Place, Oxford, OX1 2JW
Telephone: +44 (0)1865 517530
Fax: +44 (0)1865 510710
E-mail: mail@hartpub.co.uk
Website: http://www.hartpub.co.uk

Published in North America (US and Canada) by
Hart Publishing
c/o International Specialized Book Services
920 NE 58th Avenue, Suite 300
Portland, OR 97213-3786
USA
Tel: +1 503 287 3093 or toll-free: (1) 800 944 6190
Fax: +1 503 280 8832
E-mail: orders@isbs.com
Website: http://www.isbs.com

Hart Publishing is an imprint of Bloomsbury Publishing plc.

British Library Cataloguing in Publication Data
Data Available

ISBN: 978-1-84113-826-8

Typeset by Compuscript Ltd, Shannon
Printed and bound in Great Britain by
CPI Group (UK) Ltd, Croydon CR0 4YY

Acknowledgements

This book developed from doctoral research undertaken at the University of Southampton. Its seeds were sown, however, during a period I spent as a research assistant at the Durham European Law Institute. I am particularly grateful to Rosa Greaves, Holly Cullen and Colin Warbrick for the support I received during that time and thereafter. Holly and Colin are among those to whom I am grateful for comments on early drafts of parts of this book.

The Law Faculty at the University of Southampton funded the period of doctoral research from which this book has developed. Thanks are due to Takis Tridimas for his supervision, in particular for the time and freedom which he gave me to develop this research, and for his ongoing support since the completion of the doctoral stage of the project. My period as a postgraduate researcher in Southampton was one which was enriched by the warmth with which I was welcomed: other members of the Faculty were generous with their enthusiasm and time, not least Elizabeth Fisher and Jenny Steele. They, together with Takis and others, provided a rich, intellectually stimulating and inspiring environment in which to work. I am also grateful to the examiners of my doctoral thesis, Marise Cremona and Nick Hopkins, who saw the potential for, and encouraged, its further development.

I subsequently spent a period in Sussex Law School and I remain grateful to Malcolm Ross for his generous practical and intellectual support in the early years of my academic career, and for his comments on early drafts of work related to this book.

Following my return to Southampton, I found myself fortunate once again. Ed Bates, Andrew Serdy and Mark Telford are among the many people who read early drafts of parts of this book, as was Gerrit Betlem. In the final stages, however, I have been overwhelmed by the support of colleagues who have willingly read and discussed drafts at very short notice: Ed, Andrew and Mark again, and also Marta Iljadica and Paul Scott, who have been incredibly generous with their time and support in the final stages. While any errors remain absolutely my own, there are fewer of them and the argument is undoubtedly stronger as a consequence of their insight.

I presented an early draft of the part of the conclusions of this book at the *Symposium on Socio-Legal and Theoretical Perspectives on International Economic Law*, held at UCL and organised by Fiona Smith and Lisa Toohey in November 2013. The positive response of participants there eased the path to completion of the manuscript, as did discussions with Matthew Nicholson, which contributed to the development of that paper.

Natalie Lee, as Head of the School of Law, supported a period of research leave at a crucial stage. I am also grateful to the contribution of students on Globalisation and Law who, in the autumn of 2013, engaged enthusiastically with the ideas underpinning this research.

In addition to those already mentioned, I am grateful to Antonis Antoniadis for reading drafts of early work related to this book and to Fiona Smith, with whom I have had a number of insightful discussions at significant times. I am also grateful to the anonymous referees for their comments on the original book proposal. This project has been a long time in development and I have had many occasions on which to value the patience of Richard Hart and Rachel Turner at Hart Publishing.

And finally, my family: my parents, Alison and David, have been a steadfast source of support. Their enthusiasm for the completion of this project possibly contributed to their willingness to proofread almost the entire final manuscript. I am immensely grateful for their goodwill regarding this task, but even more so for their support and inspiration over the years. I also want to thank my children, Verity and Keir: without them, there is no doubt that this book could have been completed sooner, but they have ensured that I have maintained a sense of balance. They are also a constant, and very real, reminder of the imperatives underpinning this research—the nature of contemporary global challenges and our responsibility to future generations. Thank you also, especially, to Mark, who has provided endless practical and emotional support throughout this project, and has shown tremendous understanding of the pressures it has brought, particularly in the final months. I look forward to spending more time with all of you.

Contents

Table of Cases

Numerical

General Court Cases prefixed T- are tabled at the end of each year

European Court of Human Rights

International Court of Justice

National Courts

WTO Decisions

GATT Decisions

Tables of Legislation

International Treaties and Conventions

GATT and World Trade Organisation Agreements

EC and EU Treaties

EC and EU Secondary Legislation

Regulations

Directives

Decisions

National

United States

1

Introduction: The Purpose and Frame of this Inquiry

I. INTRODUCTION

THE ACCELERATION OF globalisation through the later stages of the twentieth century, bringing new forms of governance operating at different levels (regional and international/transnational) and accompanied by the emergence of new, specialised, increasingly sophisticated and demanding legal regimes, gives rise to a pressing range of challenges for the international community. How does the international community[1] give effect to varying, potentially conflicting objectives? How do these legal orders interact? How can the diverse requirements of these new legal orders and governing entities be met and, in particular, how can commitments which are traditionally presented as conflicting be simultaneously fulfilled? For a variety of reasons, these challenges are particularly acute in the context of legal regulation of international trade.

The international community has in one context developed a highly sophisticated regime pursuing the liberalisation of trade, originally the General Agreement on Tariffs and Trade (GATT) and latterly under the auspices of the World Trade Organization (WTO). In other contexts the international community has committed itself to the protection of (for example) the environment and human rights, and has given substance to those commitments through the creation of international declarations and obligations. Relatively little attention has been paid (including where commitments are entered into) to the question of how diverse international regimes and commitments interact, yet there are instances in which they do collide. This book is particularly concerned with how trade liberalisation regimes (specifically that of the European Union (EU) and the WTO) interact with obligations concerning the protection of 'non-economic' interests.

---

[1] In some contexts 'international community' is presented as a loaded term, suggesting the inclusion of some and the exclusion of other states. In this book the term 'international community' is used simply to represent the collective of international actors, primarily states, but including international organisations such as the WTO itself and the United Nations (UN).

The question of how to reconcile the pursuit and protection of economic and non-economic interests in the context of international trade is one of the great challenges facing the international community in the twenty-first century. On the one hand, neoliberalism gathered force as the dominant orthodoxy in the last decades of the twentieth century—driving the trade liberalisation agenda. At the same time, non-economic interests, including environmental and human rights protection, emerged as significant policy and popular concerns. Economic interests (pursued, inter alia, through trade liberalisation) and non-economic interests (including human rights and environmental protection) are frequently presented as inherently conflicting. This book contests this characterisation, recognising that contemporary global challenges, such as climate change, ask new questions of the existing legal architecture and require integrated responses that challenge traditional regulatory approaches. It is argued in this book that far from being essentially inherently conflicting, economic, environmental and social objectives are ultimately inter-related objectives, as is manifest in the concept of sustainable development.

In the global context, the relationship between environmental protection and free trade has provoked vigorous academic debate as well as public protest. Similarly, the relationship between WTO law and human rights has attracted increasing attention: from the question of whether the WTO should provide for, or permit, the exception of labour standards from its standard rules, to more recent questions concerning whether the relationship with 'human rights' per se should be addressed within the WTO legal framework.

The immediate prima facie conflict between these interests is clear: any national (or international) regulatory measure aimed at either human rights or environmental protection carries with it the capacity to restrict international trade. Similarly, the pursuit of trade liberalisation, carrying, as it does, obligations to remove barriers to trade, can restrict the freedom of states to regulate in order to protect non-economic priorities. A fundamental difficulty arises from the fact that international environmental law, human rights law and trade law have all developed in parallel with relatively little connection between them, despite evident overlap in application. Dealing with these issues is not straightforward, yet the impact of WTO dispute settlement rulings, combined with growing popular concern, requires that the international community engage with these questions.

A. The Objectives of this Book

This book seeks, pragmatically, to facilitate a deeper understanding of the regulatory inter-relationship between economic and non-economic interests per se, in order to better equip the international community to address this set of very real challenges. The EU is an organisation which has moved from a primary focus upon market rules and liberalisation to a broadly based constitutional order, embracing a wide range of economic and non-economic concerns and pursuing a diverse range of, as it acknowledges, integrated objectives. Recognising this, the core of this book comprises an examination of the EU experience regarding both the emergence of non-economic interests within its legal order and the relationship between those new non-economic interests and its original economic objectives. The purpose of this examination is to identify what may be learnt from that experience, which may be of relevance for the broader international community. The analysis carried out raises many questions regarding the institutional and conceptual framework through which the international community can work towards achieving balance in the pursuit of economic and non-economic objectives.

B. Why Human Rights and the Environment?

In exploring the relationship between economic and non-economic interests, this book focuses upon the protection of human rights and the environment. This selection of interests requires explanation. Primarily, human rights and the environment were the most celebrated and pursued non-economic interests of the late twentieth century. The significance of these interests remains undisputed—indeed, it has arguably grown: the imperative to address climate change is one of the most pressing challenges facing local, national and international communities. This is a challenge which undoubtedly engages environmental, social and economic interests.

Yet, in spite of the broad consensus as to their significance, the pursuit of both human rights and environmental protection has always been controversial. Despite this controversy, however, the EU has developed the protection of each of these interests, both internally and externally, in its relations with third states. Furthermore, environmental protection and social interests (including human rights) are tied together with economic interests in the principle of sustainable development.[2]

It is argued that a more holistic approach to the consideration of 'development', encompassing economic and non-economic concerns, that is, 'sustainable' development, is not only desirable in principle but also realisable in practice. Crucially, no single interest can or should have absolute prioritisation: balance must be found.

---

[2] Discussed further below.

C. The Significance of the EU Experience

The EU has developed a deeper level of integration than any other regional trading bloc, not only in economic but also in political terms. Traditionally recognised as an economically powerful and politically influential organisation, its actions may be significant in the international progress towards balancing and resolving the potential conflict between economic growth and trade liberalisation on the one hand, and the protection of non-economic interests on the other. In addition, the EU has a history, as an economically and politically powerful actor, of actively seeking to pursue these interests in its external relations and thus actively seeking to influence other states in pursuit of these interests. Regardless of future EU developments (and the direct impact or not of EU policy in this field), the experience of the EU to date provides a case study worthy of further analysis. Having developed internal policies pursuing the reconciliation and integration of economic and non-economic interests, and having subsequently sought to export this integrative approach by including the protection of certain non-economic interests as elements (and indeed as conditions) of its cooperation with third states, the EU experience can provide a wealth of insight regarding the interrelationship between these interests. Consequently, the progress the EU has made, and the factors which have facilitated this progress, have relevance for the wider international community. At the very least, a systematic engagement with these issues, comparing and contrasting their development in the EU, identifying certain common elements but substantial differences and extrapolating from this can inform the discussion, debate and policy making in addressing this issue in the international community. This is the case notwithstanding that the reconciliation of economic and non-economic interests is, of course, not static, but dynamic: it evolves over time and also differs according to context. At the very least, the achievement of simultaneous pursuit of these interests demonstrates that they are not inherently in conflict. This indicates that the pursuit of these diverse interests could also be reconciled globally, although, crucially, not necessarily to the same effect.

The comparative analysis of the emergence of human rights as an EU concern (and now objective) and environmental protection as an EU objective allows breadth as well as depth of analysis. Triangulating the conclusions as to how the EU has responded to the tension between economic and non-economic interests in one context (economic liberalisation and human rights) by comparison with another (economic liberalisation and environmental protection) allows both the identification of key common elements for the reconciliation of distinct instances of conflict, such as consensus as to the value to be protected, and the exclusion of certain factors which do not apply in both contexts. This analysis includes an exploration of the particular institutional and legal conditions which have contributed to the emergence of these interests in the EU context. It also facilitates the 'cross-fertilisation' of lessons arising from the experience of different approaches in the different contexts.[3] Building on this, it is also constructive to apply a joined-up approach to unpacking the relationships with the third element of sustainable development, economic development.

The conclusions from the analysis of the EU experience are as follows. First, it *is possible* to reconcile the *pursuit* of both economic and non-economic interests, that the EU has found a mechanism by which to do so and that the application of the principle of *proportionality* is fundamental to the realisation of this. It is argued that the EU approach can be characterised as a practical application of the principle of *sustainable development*. Second, certain conditions are identified as crucial to achieving this 'reconciliation' in the EU context. These conditions are identified through the examination of relevant policy emergence in the EU.

i. The Relevance of the EU Experience for the WTO

With these conclusions in mind, it is possible to evaluate the extent to which the lessons of the EU experience may inform the approach utilised in the international context. This raises the question of whether the conditions identified as crucial to the EU approach are present in the international context and also whether absent conditions may be realised. In addition, it requires an examination of the existing international legal architecture and its capacity to respond to contemporary global challenges. The nature of this existing international institutional and regulatory framework is such that the focus in the second part of this book (chapters six to nine) inevitably falls upon the institutions and legal order of the WTO.

A factor of crucial significance to any comparison between the EU and WTO approaches concerns the very basis, the fundamental purpose, of each organisation. In the EU context there is a clear underlying objective: the development of economic inter-dependency as a means of maintaining international security and enhancing welfare. In pursuing these objectives the EU has developed a deep level of integration and in this a very tangible developing polity is apparent. As will be seen below, a comparison of the

---

[3] The link between the environment and human rights is also reflected at the EU level in the inclusion of 'the environment' in the Charter of Fundamental Rights for the European Union. Although there is growing acceptance of rights relating to the environment, this book does not explore this in detail, but instead focuses upon a comparison of the approaches adopted for environmental and human rights protection, linking them where it is necessary or helpful to do so. This reflects both the fact that the EU has pursued each of these through different means and with different levels of intensity, and that this differential approach is also apparent in the context of international law. Consequently, the reasons for, and implications of, the different approaches are explored, as is whether anything can be learnt from either approach for the other interest. While valuable in its own right, the concept of the 'right to the environment' blurs this particular distinction to some extent.

development and the approaches taken to the environment and human rights in the EU exposes the significance of this polity. The EU has developed a level and range of governance that is absent from other international organisations, including the WTO. Together, these have the capacity to bestow legitimacy upon decision making that may otherwise be lacking. This polity and range of governance approaches is dependent upon a consensus as to certain fundamental values; there can be little doubt that this consensus reflects the relative homogeneity of EU Member States. As such, the EU is a unique organisation and its approach may not be replicable, and is certainly not directly transferable to any other organisation.

The purpose of the WTO has arguably been more contested. While the GATT emerged in the same post-Second World War context, sharing the EU's objective of securing peace and stability, there is no doubt that in the second half of the twentieth century, neoliberalism became the driving, dominant orthodoxy.[4] The implications of this regarding the potential role of the WTO in the reconciliation of the pursuit of economic and non-economic interests are significant. Whether the objectives of the WTO can be reclaimed from neoliberalism, and to what end, will inevitably shape its future role. When exploring these issues, the starting point must be the recognition that the WTO, as a trade organisation, is by definition a much narrower organisation than the EU and therefore cannot develop in the same way that the EU has. At the same time, its membership is far broader and more diverse. Lacking the relative homogeneity of the EU Member States, it also lacks the consensus of values that shaped the evolution of the EU.[5] However, it should be recognised that the international legal context and architecture is such that outcomes within the WTO legal order have the capacity to spill over and carry effects into the wider international legal order.

This research therefore does not propose to identify an EU 'model' which can be transferred to the international context or applied by the WTO. Rather, an examination is undertaken of the way in which the EU, and in particular the Court of Justice of the European Union (European Court of Justice), has dealt with the tension arising in specific instances from its pursuit of trade liberalisation, as manifested in the rules relating to the regulation of the internal market, while also seeking to respect human rights or protect the environment.[6] Lessons concerning the means by which the EU has tackled this issue are derived from this practical experience. This is distinct from the question of the extent to which the EU approach can be directly transferred to the international context, which would depend, among other factors, upon the extent to which conditions which

---

[4] Discussed in ch 9.

[5] See ch 2.

[6] See chs 2 and 3. In particular, the European Court of Justice has considerable experience of determining the legitimacy (or not) of national regulatory measures that constitute a restriction of trade.

have led the EU to handle this tension in a particular way also apply in the international context.

D. The Starting Point for this Inquiry: Pragmatism Rather than Ideology

As indicated above, the subject matter of this book emerges from the observation of a practical and imperative challenge facing the international community, that is, how to manage the relationship between, and pursuit of, diverse commitments and agreed objectives. This particular challenge is a consequence of the 'fragmentation' of international law. Responses to it may clearly be ideologically driven. However, in line with its foundation in the observation of this challenge, this book looks to pragmatic responses. Yet it must be acknowledged that in criticising or applauding certain approaches, decisions and developments, judgments are made which inevitably reflect a particular worldview.

The starting point for the present work is a rejection of a view that either economic or non-economic objectives should automatically and absolutely prevail in every circumstance: such a dogmatic approach would compromise the achievement of the other interests. This cannot be satisfactory unless the commitment to these other interests were explicitly secondary. The international community could choose to make it so, but has not, at this point, done so; indeed, in embracing the principle of sustainable development, the international community has done the reverse.

Recognising that contexts vary internationally, an answer or approach which is appropriate in one context may not be applicable in another (being dependent, for example, upon the state of economic development or the mandate of the particular decision maker). A crucial measure of the integrity of the decision maker concerns the manner in which it approaches its dual obligations. However, this too is tempered by the limits placed upon the decision maker. Accordingly, it is worth reiterating that what is learned from and understood of the EU experience, that is the 'lessons' from that experience, do not provide a prescriptive model to be applied in other contexts. They are instead lessons concerning the nature of a particular experience, in a particular context, the understanding of which may inform decision making in the international context, having regard to particular institutional and legal conditions and characteristics.

E. Framing the Inquiry: Sustainable Development and Proportionality

At the heart of the present analysis are two principles that emerge as significant early on and that are subsequently referred to, relied upon and drawn from: these are the principles of sustainable development and proportionality. Neither of these is uncontested; indeed, each is renowned for its vagueness. Therefore, it is worth spending a little time setting these out and delimiting their scope in this particular context.

i. Sustainable Development

It is argued in this book that sustainable development can be used as a conceptual lens through which to view the relationship between economic and non-economic interests. This perspective facilitates a joined-up, integrative approach to development. Although the content and scope of sustainable development remain controversial,[7] the Brundtland Commission Report of 1987[8] clearly embraces the environment and humans and their needs.[9] Sustainable development is seminally defined therein as 'development that meets the needs of the present without compromising the ability of future generations to meet their own needs'.[10] The foreword to the Report emphasises that to have concentrated only on environmental problems would have been erroneous since the environment is inherently inter-related with human actions, and that to attempt to focus exclusively upon the environment creates, in certain contexts, a connotation of naivety.[11] The

---

[7] For discussion of 'sustainable development', see: J Wetlesen, 'A Global Ethic of Sustainability?' in W Lafferty and O Langhelle (eds), *Towards Sustainable Development: On the Goals of Development and the Conditions of Sustainability* (New York, St Martin's Press, 1999); P Sands, 'Sustainable Development: Treaty, Custom and the Cross-fertilization of International Law' in A Boyle and D Freestone (eds), *International Law and Sustainable Development: Past Achievements and Future Challenges* (Oxford, Oxford University Press 1999); V Lowe, 'Sustainable Development and Unsustainable Arguments' in A Boyle and D Freestone (eds), *International Law and Sustainable Development: Past Achievements and Future Challenges* (Oxford, Oxford University Press 1999); K Lee, 'Global Sustainable Development: Its Intellectual and Historical Roots' in K Lee, A Holland and D McNeill, *Global Sustainable Development in the 21st Century* (Edinburgh, Edinburgh University Press, 2000); A Holland 'Sustainable Development: The Contested Vision' in K Lee, A Holland and D McNeill, *Global Sustainable Development in the 21st Century* (Edinburgh, Edinburgh University Press, 2000); P Birnie, A Boyle and C Redgwell, *International Law and the Environment* (3rd edn, Oxford, Oxford University Press, 2009) ch 3; J Ellis, 'Sustainable Development as a Legal Principle: A Rhetorical Analysis', http://papers.ssrn.com/sol3/papers.cfm?abstract_id=1319360; Geert van Calster, 'The Law(s) of Sustainable Development' http://papers.ssrn.com/sol3/papers.cfm?abstract_id=1147544; Alhaji BM Marong, 'From Rio to Johannesberg: Reflections on the Role of International Legal Norms in Sustainable Development' (2003–04) 16 *Georgetown International Environmental Law Review* 21; Opinion of Vice-President Weeramantry, *Case Concerning the Gabcikovo-Nagymaros Project (Hungary v Slovakia)* [1998] 37 ILM 162, 204–13.

[8] *Report of the World Commission on Environment and Development: Our Common Future* (1987) (hereinafter referred to as the Brundtland Report), available at: www.un-documents.net/wced-ocf.htm.

[9] It has, however, been argued that sustainable development is a purely physical concept: see Wetlesen (n 7).

[10] Brundtland Report, at 43 (a consideration known as 'Social equity').

[11] ibid xi.

Report subsequently dismisses the purely physical concept of sustainable development on the grounds that the protection of this may not be achieved without consideration of issues such as *access* to resources.[12] It is crucial to note that sustainable development does not prioritise any interest over the others, but instead requires consideration of each in relation to development issues. This was subsequently made explicit in the 2002 Johannesburg Declaration, which recognised:

> [A] collective responsibility to advance and strengthen the interdependent and mutually reinforcing pillars of sustainable development—economic development, social development and environmental protection—at the local, national, regional and global levels.[13]

Yet, accepting the benefits of considering the environment and basic needs together does not explain why a link should be made between the environment and human rights (or even social interests). The Brundtland Report, however, states as a pre-requisite to the fulfilment of everyone's needs that everyone has 'the opportunity to satisfy their aspirations for a better life'. The fulfilment of aspirations may not easily be separated in practice from the enjoyment of fundamental human rights, yet it is recognised that *collective* needs for the 'fulfilment of aspirations' may be quite different from the requirements for absolute protection of *individual* rights: there is thus a tension between the protection of collective and individual rights. Similarly, the particular human rights protected or prioritised may give rise to quite different results regarding the 'fulfilment of aspirations' or welfare gain. For example, the prioritisation of a 'right to trade' as the fundamental guarantor of human dignity may give rise to quite a different set of consequences from the protection of labour rights.[14]

This raises an issue which is worth highlighting. When the relationship between economic and non-economic interests or between trade, environment and human rights is discussed, there can be a tendency to treat this in binary terms: trade versus human rights; trade versus environment. In fact, human rights and environmental protection may themselves come into conflict (for instance, protecting biodiversity might require a restriction upon an individual's enjoyment of his or her property). Similarly, as noted above, specific human rights can be in opposition. These tensions, including the disjuncture between individual and collective interests, must be addressed. That there are fundamental political choices to be made in this regard should be openly acknowledged. Therefore, balancing the protection

---

[12] ibid 43.

[13] Article 5 of the Johannesberg Declaration on Sustainable Development, www.un-documents.net/jburgdec.htm.

[14] See discussion in ch 8.

of these interests is very much a process that should be undertaken on a case-by-case basis.

Much ink has been spilt over the question of the status of 'sustainable development': what the commitment to it means; whether it is a legal principle; whether it is too vague to be meaningful. However, in the present context the focus with regard to sustainable development is upon what it is and offers rather than what it lacks. Thus, the significance of sustainable development lies in its integrated approach and its recognition that development requires a holistic approach. Sustainable development is therefore used as a lens through which the question of the relationship between economic and non-economic interests can be examined, a perspective from which this question, at the heart of a complex set of global challenges, can be approached.

a. Sustainable Development and the EU

The EU (then the EC) adopted 'sustainable development' as a guiding principle in the 1990s[15] and, in so doing, appears to have adopted the Brundtland[16] definition of the concept. It has explicitly recognised the role of human rights in sustainable development:

> Respect for all human rights and fundamental freedoms, including respect for fundamental social rights, democracy based on the rule of law and transparent and accountable governance are an integral part of sustainable development.[17]

Despite the common suggestion that sustainable development is so vague as to have little practical application or utility, analysis of the EU experience of ensuring the fulfilment of environmental and human rights obligations within the framework of the requirements of the internal market will demonstrate a practice which appears to have the characteristics of practical application of sustainable development.[18] This supports the emphasis in this book upon what sustainable development is and thus has to offer rather than what it lacks.

---

[15] See ch 2.

[16] The Brundtland Report was the report of an independent body established by the UN in 1983. It articulated what has become the most commonly accepted definition of sustainable development, which sought to integrate apparently conflicting interests and identify a common goal for these.

[17] Article 9 of the Cotonou Convention, signed 23 June 2000, available at: http://ec.europa .eu/europeaid/where/acp/overview/documents/devco-cotonou-consol-europe-aid-2012_en.pdf.

[18] See the discussion of Case C-112/00 *Schmidberger, Internationale Transporte und Planzuge v Austria* [2003] ECR I-5659 and subsequent case law in ch 3. In *Schmidberger* the protection of fundamental rights, specifically the rights to protest and freedom of assembly, collided with the internal market requirement of the free movement of goods. In this case, the Court of Justice required not only that the measure undertaken to ensure the enjoyment of fundamental rights was the least trade-restrictive, but also that the enjoyment of the right to the free movement of goods was achieved through the least possible encroachment upon the enjoyment of fundamental rights.

b. Sustainable Development and the WTO

The preamble to the WTO Agreement includes reference to the 'objective of sustainable development':

> Recognizing that their relations in the field of trade and economic endeavour should be conducted with a view to raising standards of living, ensuring full employment and a large and steadily growing volume of real income and effective demand, and expanding the production of and trade in goods and services, while allowing for the optimal use of the world's resources in accordance with the objective of sustainable development, seeking both to protect and preserve the environment and to enhance the means for doing so in a manner consistent with their respective needs and concerns at different levels of economic development.[19]

This statement is, however, unquestionably ambiguous: does it mean that sustainable development is thus a WTO objective? Or is it a reference simply to the wider, general commitment of the international community? Since the reference is made in the context of use of the world's resources, referencing environmental protection, is sustainable development here conceived of as a purely environmental principle? The latter would seem unlikely; the first paragraph of the Preamble to the WTO Agreement is, in its entirety, consistent with the principle of sustainable development. The requirement that trade and economic endeavour should be directed towards goals clearly concerned with improvements in welfare, social development and the expansion of trade, while taking account of environmental considerations and levels of economic development, could have been explicitly shaped by the principle of sustainable development.

The very 'vagueness' for which sustainable development is criticised is a reflection of the fact that it is not a principle which can provide single, definitive substantive answers. Fundamentally, at its most pared-down level, in view of the relativity of the contexts and the consequent specificity of responses to particular given situations, the application of sustainable development must concern process rather than substantive outcomes.[20]

Sustainable development provides a lens through which the interdependence of social, environmental and economic development can be conceptualised and consequently managed. Adopting the three-pillar characterisation of the Johannesburg Declaration, it requires that each pillar (social, environmental and economic) is considered and that action pursuing one pillar of development takes account of the impact upon the others. This does not prescribe particular outcomes, giving rise to the charge of

---

[19] Paragraph 1 of the Preamble to the Marrakesh Agreement Establishing the World Trade Organization.

[20] This is characterization of sustainable development is a key element of Weeramantry's Opinion in *Case Concerning the Gabcikovo-Nagymaros Project* (n 7). For further discussion see Ellis; Van Calster; Marong, n 7.

vagueness. However, this process of consideration ensures that where the interests represented by these pillars prima facie conflict, a balance is struck between them. This is what the ECJ achieved in *Schmidberger*.[21] The particular balance to be struck will vary according to the circumstances. As such, sustainable development does not provide an answer to the balancing exercise—it does not determine the decision to be reached—rather, it provides a structure for that process.

ii. The Principle of Proportionality

Having recognised the potential contribution of the principle of sustainable development in terms of managing the relationship between economic liberalisation and the pursuit of other interests, a means must be found through which to make a decision in particular instances of conflict. There is a risk that any such decision may be, or may be perceived to be, partial. A crucial measure of the integrity of the decision-making system is the manner in which it approaches its 'conflicting' obligations. Yet this is tempered by the limits placed upon the decision maker. As noted above, criticism of, or praise for, particular developments can reflect both a particular standpoint and the specific context. In analysing the pursuit and reconciliation of economic and non-economic interests, a key question concerns the criteria by which successful reconciliation may be measured. At the simplest level, the criterion for success is whether conflicting interests are being 'effectively' balanced against one another, with due regard for costs and benefits in the instances in which one must make concessions for the other. Similarly, the starting point for criteria to assist the judicial inquiry in dealing with an economic/non-economic conflict must be this same condition: there must be due consideration for each interest where they come into conflict, with the prioritisation of one being weighed against the restraining effect upon the other. Such an approach, which may be characterised as based on 'proportionality', avoids the danger arising from the prescription of specific approaches which could lack sensitivity to particular contexts and values.

In this context it is therefore proposed that 'proportionality' is used as an instrument to assist the decision maker (administrative or judicial) in finding the appropriate balance for the particular circumstances. The open-endedness of proportionality means that it offers considerable flexibility as a basis for judicial review of decision making. However, this same open-endedness means that the test must be clearly defined in order to ensure that it can provide the desired legitimacy.

---

[21] Above n 18.

a. Defining Proportionality

Tridimas characterises proportionality 'at its most abstract level [as requiring] that action undertaken must be proportionate to its objectives'.[22] This definition can be elaborated upon with reference to the application of the principle of proportionality. The application of the principle has been traditionally described, in the EU context, as a three-part test.[23] Thus, the court assesses whether a measure is: first, appropriate to achieve the desired aim; second, whether it is necessary (defined as requiring that there is no less restrictive alternative); and, third, whether it is proportionate *strictu sensu*—that there is no overly restrictive effect. The application of this third element of the test is rather thin: Tridimas observes that in its analysis the court does not distinguish between the second and the third elements. Furthermore, he highlights that:

> In some cases the Court finds that a measure is compatible with proportionality without searching for less restrictive alternatives or even where such alternatives seem to exist. The essential characteristic of the principle is that the Court performs a balancing exercise between the objectives pursued by the measure in issue and its adverse effects on individual freedoms.[24]

Proportionality has been a key element of the review of the compatibility of national regulatory measures with the economic integration provisions in the context of the EU internal market.[25] Under Article 34 of the Treaty on the Functioning of the European Union (TFEU) (formerly Article 30 European Community Treaty (TEC), state measures restricting the free movement of goods between Member States are prohibited, subject to limited grounds of derogations that are listed in Article 36 TFEU. A national regulatory measure pursuing one of the Article 36 derogations is subject to a test of 'proportionality'. In this context, proportionality has been used as an instrument of market integration, of economic liberalisation, while at the same time it has been used as an instrument ensuring the protection of the fundamental rights set against economic liberalisation.[26] Maduro has explicitly characterised the Court of Justice's approach in the seminal *Dassonville* and *Cassis de Dijon* cases as 'establishing the foundations of a cost/benefit analysis (a balance test)' under Article 30 (now Article 34 TFEU).[27]

---

[22] T Tridimas, *The General Principles of EU Law* (2nd edn, Oxford, Oxford University Press, 2006) 136.

[23] See, for example, ibid 139.

[24] ibid.

[25] See further ch 3.

[26] See further ch 3.

[27] Maduro goes on to explain that 'the costs of the measure are to be assessed according to their effect on trade under the *Dassonville* formula and the *Cassis de Dijon* mutual recognition principle; the benefits of the measure are to be assessed under the mandatory requirements and Article 36 tests': MP Maduro, *We the Court: The European Court of Justice and the*

Flexibility in the notion of proportionality allows the Court to use it for a variety of purposes, including the imposition of a relatively rigorous scrutiny where there is a clear indication of policy consensus at the EU level. On the other hand, where the Court does not want to substitute its view for that of the national decision maker, it can apply a relatively light touch. However, this flexibility requires transparency in order to ensure the integrity and legitimacy of the process, and this includes teasing out the interests at stake and the nature of the balancing process. Jans concludes that:

> The proportionality principle is an instrument which allows the Court of Justice to make a balanced assessment of the legality of national restrictions of free movement and, in doing so, to take account of the sensitive nature of the division of powers between judiciary and legislature and between the EC and its Member States.[28]

b. The Approach Adopted in this Book

One of the observed difficulties regarding the application of 'proportionality' concerns the challenge posed by measuring, or quantifying, the benefit and/or cost attributed to a particular policy interest. Thus, whereas it might be relatively straightforward to identify the cost or benefit to trade associated with a particular regulatory measure, it is much more difficult to quantify the cost or benefit of that same measure to social policy. There is a common-sense argument for considering 'costs' and 'benefits' of particular regulatory measures. However, equally, there is something fundamentally discomfiting about attributing a quantitative, monetary value (or cost) to, for example, human life or environmental goods and then weighing that in the balance against the costs to trade of a particular regulation. As Ackerman and Heinzerling put it:

> The basic problem with narrow economic analysis of health and environmental protection is that human life, health and nature cannot be described meaningfully in monetary terms; they are priceless.[29]

Thus, the arguments for a 'cost-benefit' analysis drawn from classical economics should be handled with caution.[30] Because of its associated economic connotations, I therefore eschew both the language and the form of 'cost-benefit' analysis, preferring the more flexible, less economically loaded language of 'proportionality'.

European Economic Constitution: A Critical Reading of Article 30 of the EC Treaty (Oxford, Hart Publishing, 1999) 52.

[28] Jan H Jans, 'Proportionality Revisited' (2000) 27(3) *Legal Issues of Economic Integration* 239, 264.

[29] Frank Ackerman and Lisa Heinzerling, *Priceless: On Knowing the Price of Everything and the Value of Nothing* (New York, New Press, 2004) 8.

[30] See Cass Sunstein, *The Cost-Benefit State: The Future of Regulatory Protection* (Chicago, American Bar Association, 2002) 26.

The fact that the Court of Justice has tended not to provide a detailed economic analysis, preferring a broader balancing approach, can in this regard be viewed as a strength. In their unbridled, and persuasive, critique of the economic emphasis of cost-benefit analysis, Ackerman and Heinzerling demonstrate by reference to the 1970 US Clean Air Act that 'it is sometimes possible to make very good decisions without benefit of intricate economic analysis, and even without noticeable attention to market mechanisms'. They highlight one of the fundamental problems with cost-benefit analysis: it 'frequently turns out to be "complete cost-incomplete benefit" analysis'. Consequently, they seek a means of decision making that 'reflect[s] values without prices'.[31]

Consistent with this approach, in the present context, proportionality is to be understood by reference to its meaning in the EU internal market context and as applied by the Court of Justice (which will be explored in chapter three), but which crucially, as noted above, does not engage in forensic unpacking of the interests at stake or in any attempt to apply monetary values to interests or values which are priceless; rather, the focus is upon a broad balancing process. One question which will be considered is the extent to which it should be left to the 'judicial' decision maker to perform this function, or not. These issues will be examined in greater detail below with reference to the case law of both the Court of Justice and the WTO Dispute Settlement Body.

II. STRUCTURE OF THE BOOK

The first part of this book (chapters two to five) examines the extent to which the EU has indeed succeeded in reconciling the pursuit of economic and non-economic interests, and the extent to which non-economic objectives are integrated into the EU legal order. To this end, chapter two examines the emergence of human rights and environmental protection as concerns of and within the EU. In doing so, the development of human rights and environmental protection in the EU is traced through treaty provision, the contribution of the Court of Justice and secondary legislation. In considering the contribution of the Court of Justice, the role of the national courts cannot be ignored. The significance of the relationship between the Court of Justice and the national courts, and between EU law and national law, has repercussions for any attempt to compare the development of protection of non-economic interests in the EU with this potential process in the WTO. Chapter three examines the enforcement and protection of non-economic interests in the EU and the balance that has been struck between

---

[31] Ackerman and Heinzerling (n 29) 206–08.

the economic and non-economic interests assessed. Despite the rhetoric and the very tangible progress in the context of the internal market, it appears that the mechanisms for the enforcement of both environmental protection and human rights are not yet altogether satisfactory.

In chapter four, the focus moves to the EU's external actions. The nature and extent of the EU's general external competence is examined first, with subsequent specific analysis of its competence to pursue environmental protection and human rights externally. Particular attention is paid to the development of implied powers and analysis of the relationship between concurrent and 'complementary'[32] powers. The effect of international agreements concluded by the EU is also examined. The reason for this consideration of the EU's external action is straightforward: alongside their emergence as internal EU concerns, the EU has actively pursued both human rights and environmental protection in its relations with third states. This is significant in terms of establishing what the EU is empowered to do (from an internal perspective). However, it is also significant in view of the capacity for EU action to influence the international approach to managing the relationship between pursuit of economic and non-economic interests. To what extent is the EU setting the agenda in this context? Chapter five examines the development and substance of clauses protecting human rights and the environment in the EU's external agreements, and compares the relative force given to each interest in the EU's relations with third states. This presents a curious paradox when compared with the nature and extent of the EU's internal competence and action. The manifestation of these clauses is not the whole story, however, and this chapter also explores questions concerning their application and potential difficulties regarding their enforcement, as well as other instruments such as the Generalised System of Preferences.

An examination of these questions leads into the crucial question of what may be extrapolated from the EU experience to inform the approach adopted at the global level. In the second part of this book (chapters six to nine) the focus therefore shifts to the interaction between economic and non-economic interests in the international context, and in particular within the WTO, where the relationship between economic and non-economic interests is currently being developed. In the WTO, the differences between the approach to environmental protection and to the debate surrounding 'human rights' issues are even more pronounced than in the EU. Consequently, a detailed examination will be made of each of these

---

[32] Although not generally recognised as a term of art, the notion of 'complementary' powers arises, from the expression of Community competence in relation to, inter alia, development cooperation (Article 177 (ex 130u) EC): 'Community policy in the sphere of development cooperation, which shall be complementary to the policies pursued by the Member States, shall foster....'

individually, before drawing conclusions on an appropriate international approach.

Chapter six presents a brief analysis of the relationship between WTO law and 'international law' and of the potential for the WTO legal order to accommodate non-economic interests under the current rules. Chapter seven specifically analyses the potential for protection of the environment under WTO law, focusing primarily upon the GATT, although some consideration is given to the other WTO Agreements. In so doing, it compares the balance achieved under the original GATT dispute settlement process with that under the WTO. In this analysis questions are raised as to whether the rulings of the dispute settlement panels and the Appellate Body are consistent with what might have been the intention of the Members in formulating the GATT public policy exceptions. This is particularly significant given the developing normativity of the panel findings. There has been a perceptible shift in the rhetoric of WTO panels and the Appellate Body in particular with regard to the environment, notably in relation to extra-territorial action. This shift, which is manifested in the recognition in principle of the potential legitimacy of an extra-territorial, unilateral environmental measure as an exception to the rules of the GATT,[33] is examined, as are its practical implications. The approaches of the WTO dispute settlement panels and the Appellate Body are compared to that of the Court of Justice in the resolution of disputes—analysing the application of different tests in each jurisdiction.

Chapter eight explores the relationship between international human rights law and international trade law. It examines the two levels upon which this relationship has developed: exploring on the one hand a case study relating to labour standards (or, more recently, labour rights) and on the other hand exploring the relationship between international human rights law per se and the WTO. This chapter examines the significance of the centrality of labour standards to the human rights/international trade discourse, which is in sharp contrast to the EU approach.[34] It continues to highlight, in particular, the incoherence in international law, which leads into an exploration of the conceptual framework for the international trading system, which is raised in the concluding chapter.

---

[33] See discussion of the *Shrimp Turtle* dispute in ch 7 below; Appellate Body Report in *United States-Import Prohibition of Certain Shrimp and Shrimp Products*, AB-1998-4 WT/DS58/R (98-0000) (1998) 38 ILM 121, 12 October.

[34] It is submitted that the development of labour standards in the EU occurred originally as a means of removing competitive distortions rather than as a 'rights' issue and has only relatively recently grown into a 'rights' issue. In contrast, 'labour standards' and 'labour rights' in the WTO context have from the outset ostensibly been pursued as a 'rights-based' issue rather than a means of levelling the economic playing field. However, there has been considerable suspicion from developing states that this is a manifestation of protectionism. Consequently, this thesis focuses on the WTO debate, but does not explore the development of social rights in the EU in any detail.

In chapter nine, some consideration is given to the potential roles of both the WTO and the EU in the development of international law, and additionally in the normative process towards reconciling economic and non-economic interests. The conclusions to chapters six to eight raise the question whether the current legal and institutional framework is capable of achieving the legitimate reconciliation of economic and non-economic interests. In light of this, chapter nine proposes that a different conceptual approach to the legal regulation of international trade, reframed through the lens of sustainable development, might help to resolve some of the apparent incoherence between different international legal systems.

Assessing the potential role of the WTO requires a consideration of the different bases for the respective approaches of the Court of Justice and WTO, and whether lessons from the former could mitigate some of the legitimacy questions raised by the latter's 'balancing' of economic and non-economic interests. In considering the question of the role and appropriateness of the WTO in developing a balance between economic and non-economic interests, it is interesting to return to the question of what motivates the EU's considerable action and achievements in this field. To what extent is this transferred into its external policy and, potentially, international law? Does this give us any insight into how the WTO may act?

Part I

The EU Experience

2

The Emergence of Human Rights and Environmental Protection in the EU

INTRODUCTION

THE CONTEMPORARY EUROPEAN Union is an organisation far removed from the original European Economic Community, both in membership and purpose. It has grown from the original six to now 28 members. From the original economic focus of the Community, the Union has evolved to now recognise and protect a range of non-economic concerns (including human rights and environmental protection) which received little or no consideration during the early period of European integration. The emergence of interests and objectives in these fields raises certain questions including, fundamentally, how these may be balanced against and interact with the Union's original economic objectives, particularly where these come into conflict (or are perceived to conflict).

This experience, including how the European Community (EC) and latterly European Union (EU) has responded to such questions, is directly relevant to the contemporary global challenges facing the international community. An analytical study of the emergence of non-economic objectives and their relationship with economic liberalisation has the potential to offer insight into the inter-relationship between these interests, which can inform the policy and decision-making process in the international context. The first two sections of the chapter therefore provide a chronological narrative account of the history of the emergence of, in turn, human rights (section I) and environmental protection (section II). This permits the identification of the key conditions which required and facilitated the development of policy in respect of each of these interests. Taking this chronological approach allows parallel developments in the Court of Justice[1] the Member States and the institutions to be seen together, and exposes their mutual influence: this is key to understanding the evolution of the economic Community into the contemporary Union. The second section of Part II (section II.B) departs

---

[1] 'Court of Justice' is used to refer to both the Court of Justice of the European Union (CJEU) and its predecessor the European Court of Justice (ECJ).

from the narrative chronological approach, examining the fundamental governing principles which emerged originally in environmental policy, but which have subsequently been given cross-cutting application. This is significant: it demonstrates the increasingly integrated approach of the EU to the manner in which it views its various, emerging and evolving objectives. However, this part of the chapter also looks forward, exploring the significance of the emergence of sectoral environmental policy and highlighting the significance of new approaches to governance which again are initially particularly evident in the development of EU environmental policy.[2]

A number of points about the emergence of EU human rights and environmental policy are worth noting from the outset. As will be seen in the first section of the chapter, the emergence of EU human rights protection has been essentially reactive; it arose as a consequence of the need to secure the (then) EC legal order. It was (and largely remains) premised upon the integration of existing legal obligations rather than the creation of new or autonomous obligations. In this respect it can be said to have emerged through the roots of the EU legal order, informing and shaping it. The legitimacy of this development is secured by its reliance upon pre-existing rules and obligations. It is only very recently, under the Lisbon Treaty (2007), that the EU has been given a general objective regarding the pursuit of human rights protection, and this is in its relations with third states.

In contrast, while the development of EU environmental policy was also originally reactive, it was, even in its early stages, identifiably a discernible European policy: the active development of EU environmental policy has been pursued since the adoption of the first Environmental Action Programme in 1973, notwithstanding that there was no competency in the Treaty for the pursuit of environmental policy until the Single European Act (1986).[3] Initially at least it was also top-down: a declaration by the Heads of State that 'economic expansion is not an end in itself ... particular attention will be given ... to protecting the environment'[4] was clearly significant. This distinction between the reactive emergence of EU human rights protection (signalling the receptivity to existing law derived from other legal orders) and the more autonomous (although still reactive) development of environmental policy explains the emphasis in this chapter upon the principles shaping and governing EU environmental policy. There is no equivalent with regard to human rights policy, except to the extent that these originally environmental principles have subsequently been given cross-cutting effect, which will be examined.

---

[2] The scope of this chapter is such that the intention here is to provide an overview; the analysis does not purport to be exhaustive and the reader is referred to footnote sources for more detail.

[3] See section II.

[4] EC Commission, Sixth General Report (EC Brussels, 1972); see also the Declaration of the Heads of State and Government of 19/20 October 1972 at the Paris Summit about collaboration in environmental policy [1972] EC Bulletin (No 10) 21, discussed in section II.

The comparative analysis of environmental and human rights protection allows for a triangulation through which more generalised conclusions may be reached regarding the emergence of non-economic interests than would be apparent from focus upon one single field.[5] This proper understanding of the key conditions shaping the emergence of human rights and environmental policy in the EU is fundamental to the assessment of what lessons may be drawn from the EU experience for potential application in other contexts.

I. THE PROTECTION OF HUMAN RIGHTS IN THE EU

A. The Emergence of EU Human Rights Protection: A Chronological Account

i. The Treaty of Rome (1957)

When examining the evolving status of and respect accorded to 'human rights' within the EU legal orders, it is important to recognise that understandings of human rights themselves have evolved over the last 60 years. So, for example, when the Treaty of Rome was drafted, 'human rights' were generally understood in the European context to comprise civil and political rights.[6] This was a rather narrower conceptualisation than the contemporary one, which would generally include socio-economic rights.

Thus, there is a significant temporal contextual issue at play which partly explains the early belief that 'the essentially economic character of the Communities ... makes the possibility of their encroaching upon fundamental human values, such as life, personal liberty, freedom of opinion, conscience etc, very unlikely'.[7] Even allowing for that temporal consideration, however, the distinction between different categories of rights has always been blurred: for example, the right to property, itself a classic liberal value, was not referred to in the Treaty of Rome, or indeed in the

---

[5] Respecting the historic position, for clarity, for the parts of this chapter which deal with the European (Economic) Community period, reference will be made to 'EC' (or 'Community') rather than European Economic Community or EU. General (non-period specific) reference will be to the European Union (EU).

[6] As exemplified in the European Convention on Human Rights (ECHR). It is worth recognising that economic and social rights had been recognised in Article 22 of the UDHR. They were internationally recognised in a binding treaty in the 1966 International Covenant of Economic, Social and Cultural Rights (ICESCR), prior to which they had been recognised in the 1961 European Social Charter. The ICESCR only entered into force in 1976, in the same year as the International Covenant on Civil and Political Rights (ICCPR). See further J Harrison, *The Human Rights Impact of the World Trade Organisation* (Oxford, Hart Publishing, 2007) ch 3.

[7] A Toth, 'The Individual and European Law' (1975) 24 *ICLQ* 659.

European Convention on Human Rights (ECHR).[8] Yet, unsurprisingly, in light of its obvious economic implications, it has been the subject matter of many cases before the Court of Justice.[9]

The question of the inclusion of fundamental rights within the Treaty did arise during its negotiation, but was ultimately rejected. While certain socio-economic rights were included in the Treaty of Rome, for example, in Articles 117, 118 and 119,[10] these were included on economic grounds to ensure the proper functioning of the market rather than with the intention of conferring fundamental human rights per se. Without the market consideration, it appears unlikely that they would have been included. The other key provisions which confer rights, those relating to the four freedoms,[11] are conditional upon the status of the individual as a national of an EU Member State, and are therefore not generally viewed as fundamental human rights. Thus, although certain rights were conferred in the Treaty, it would be misleading to describe them as human rights provisions.[12]

The role of the Court of Justice in the development of human rights protection in the EU has been greatly discussed.[13] In the early cases the Court was exploring and defining the limits of its power. Human rights had recently been expressly omitted from the Treaty and judicial activism at that time in that field would have been rash, if not fatal to the authority of the Court. In the first attempt to bring 'fundamental rights' before it, in the late 1950s, both the Court and the Advocate-General avoided consideration

---

[8] It was added, subject to many qualifications, in the First Protocol.

[9] See, inter alia, Case 44/79 *Hauer v Rheinland Pfalz* [1979] ECR 3927 [1980] 3 CMLR 42; Case 5/88 *Wachauf v Germany* [1989] ECR 2609 [1991] 1 CMLR 328.

[10] Now Articles 151, 153 and 157 TFEU.

[11] The free movements of goods, persons (including establishment), services and capital are set out in Articles 34, 45, 49, 56 and 63 TFEU.

[12] See E Reid, 'Protecting Non-economic Interests in the European Community Legal Order: A Sustainable Development?' 24 (2005) *Yearbook of European Law* 385 regarding the classification of rights.

[13] See, among others, M Mendelson, 'The European Court of Justice and Human Rights' (1982) *Yearbook of European Law* 125; R Lawson, 'Confusion and Conflict? Diverging Interpretations of the European Convention on Human Rights in Strasbourg and Luxembourg' in R Lawson and M de Blois (eds) *The Dynamics of the Protection of Fundamental Rights in Europe: Essays in Honour of Henry G Schermers Vol III* (Dordrecht/London, Nijhoff, 1994); M Dauses, 'The Protection of Fundamental Rights in the Community Legal Order' (1985) 10 *EL Rev* 389; HG Schermers, 'The European Communities Bound by Fundamental Human Rights' (1990) 27 *CML Rev* 249; J Coppel and A O'Neill: 'The European Court of Justice: Taking Rights Seriously?' (1992) 29 *CML Rev* 669; J Weiler and S Lockhart, '"Taking Rights Seriously" Seriously: The European Court and its Fundamental Rights Jurisprudence—Part I' (1995) 32 *CML Rev* 51, and Part II (1995) 32 *CML Rev* 579; F Jacobs, 'Human Rights in the European Union' in N Emiliou and D O'Keefe (eds), *Legal Aspects of Integration in the European Union* (London, Kluwer Law International, 1997); Bruno de Witte, 'The Past and Future Role of the European Court of Justice in the Protection of Human Rights' in P Alston (ed), *The EU and Human Rights*, (Oxford, Oxford University Press, 1997); D Spielmann, 'Human Rights Case Law in the Strasbourg and Luxembourg Courts: Conflicts, Inconsistencies and Complementarities' in Alston (ed), *The EU and Human Rights*.

of the rights question and confined themselves to interpretation of the Treaty.[14] The applicant sought to rely on rights under the (West) German Grundgesetz (to freely develop his own personality and to choose his own trade or occupation) to have decisions taken by the High Authority annulled. He described these rights, which exist under the constitutions of 'virtually all' the Member States, as 'fundamental'. The Court, however, refused to allow reliance upon these rights and ruled that its competence only allowed it to apply EC law in annulling a decision. This approach was confirmed in *Geitling*.[15] In *Humblet* in 1960, the Court recognised the need for the 'effective enforcement' of rights conferred by EC law, but emphasised the separation of powers and the responsibility of the Member States for enforcement. Thus, the Court held that it had no power to annul a national measure.[16] In *Sgarlata*,[17] the applicant attempted to overturn an EC regulation on the basis of 'fundamental principles shared by all the Member States'. The Court, however, simply invoked the supremacy of EC law to refuse to annul the regulation. This was significant: in so ruling, the Court created a risk that a national constitutional court would refuse to apply EC law on the grounds that it was constitutionally unlawful. This would have had serious implications for the uniformity and supremacy of EC law.

It is worth recalling in this context that the principles of direct effect and supremacy had at this point only recently (and controversially) been established by the Court of Justice.[18] The establishment of each had been premised upon the need to secure the uniform application of EC law. Clearly, the Court of Justice was going to be reluctant to risk sacrificing this. Yet the national constitutional courts were legitimately concerned that EC law might conflict with national constitutional provisions and demonstrated resistance to this. The Italian[19] and German constitutional courts in particular made it clear that they would not accept the supremacy of EC law at the expense of their constitutional rights and principles, thus threatening the very uniformity of application of EC law that supremacy, and also direct effect, had been intended to secure. The Court began to address this threat in *Stauder*[20] when it acknowledged that fundamental human rights

---

[14] Case 1/58 *Stork v High Authority* [1959] ECR 7.

[15] Joined Cases 36-38, 40/59 *Geitling v High Authority* [1959] ECR 7.

[16] Case 6/60 *Humblet v Belgium* [1960] ECR 559.

[17] Case 40/64 *Sgarlata and Others v Commission* [1965] ECR 215.

[18] The principle of direct effect, that Community law can be enforced directly in the national courts, had been established in Case 26/62 *Van Gend en Loos* [1963] ECR 13. The supremacy of EC law was established in the case of Case 6/64 *Costa v ENEL* [1964] ECR 585. Under this principle, EC law takes precedence over conflicting national law.

[19] *Frontini v Ministero delle Finanz Giurisprudenza Constitutionale* [1974] CMLR 372.

[20] Case 29/69 *Stauder v City of Ulm* [1969] ECR 419.

were principles of EC law.[21] In *Internationale Handelsgesellschaft*,[22] the Court finally confirmed that respect for human rights was 'an integral part of the general principles of law protected by the Court of Justice' and must be protected within the 'framework of the structure and objectives of the Community'.

What emerges clearly from this sequence of cases is that faced with a direct threat to the unity of the EC legal system and to the supremacy of EC law, the Court had little option but to reassure the uneasy national constitutional courts that their rights would not be limited or restricted by EC law. Consequently, it framed the rights to be protected in terms of those 'inspired by the constitutional traditions common to the Member States'. The Court may be described as activist in its assertion of the principle of protection of fundamental rights: it could have stuck with its initial approach, applying EC law as written, without referring to fundamental or human rights. Had it done so, it would have required the Member States themselves to resolve any friction between EC law and their other obligations. But this would have cost the Court both the supremacy of EC law and the uniformity of application of EC law, each of which it was going to strongly resist. Significantly, therefore, the Court's undertakings with respect to fundamental rights are directly related to the EC's unique legal system, which distinguishes the EU from other international legal systems, including the World Trade Organization (WTO). The initial expression of the then EC's relationship with fundamental rights was clearly driven by a need to reassure the Member States that their fundamental rights would not be limited by the EC. Seen in this light, the stance of the Court was anything but activist: the national constitutional courts had essentially reminded the Court of Justice that the Member State governments could not confer upon the EC competence which they did not themselves possess. They had no competence to transfer any power which could give rise to a violation of their constitutional rights. Consequently, EC law, which emerged from the creation of those states, could not require a breach of national constitutional rights. The recognition of fundamental rights as part of EC law was therefore less the assertion by the Court of an EC competence over fundamental rights than recognition of the limits imposed upon EC action by the requirement to respect fundamental rights. Thus, the original emergence of EU human rights policy is essentially reactive.

Having recognised the limitations of EC competence, the question which followed was how far-reaching the implications might be. It is worth highlighting that in *Internationale Handelsgesellschaft*, while recognising that 'respect for fundamental rights forms an integral part of the general

---

[21] On the facts, the Court ruled that the relevant breach occurred at national law.

[22] Case 11/70 *Internationale Handelsgesellschaft v Einfuhr und Vorratstelle für Futtermittel und Getreide* [1970] ECR 1125.

principles of law protected by the Court of Justice', the Court held that 'the protection of such rights ... must be ensured within the framework of the structure and objectives of the Community'. This indicates that the recognition of fundamental rights was limited to the context of achievement of the EC objectives, notably economic integration, and could not bring into question the validity of an EC act, as this would question the legal basis of the EC itself.[23]

In subsequent cases the Court and its Advocates-General expanded the sources from which EC-protected 'fundamental rights' would be drawn.[24] However, the Court was for a long time ambiguous concerning the status of international conventions, referring to them initially as 'providing guidance'.[25] In *National Panasonic*,[26] there was a change of emphasis: the Court recognised that fundamental rights were an integral part of the general principles of EC law, which it would ensure in accordance with international treaties to which the Member States were signatories. This could reflect the adoption by the Institutions of the Joint Declaration on Human Rights in 1977.[27]

This, however, was not without its problems, central to which was, first, the question of the relationship between the EC and the ECHR,[28] then, second, what fell within the scope of EC law (and therefore under the jurisdiction of the Court of Justice). On the question of the scope of EC law, the Court initially declared in *Cinéthèque* that it was not competent to deal with matters falling within the jurisdiction of the national legislator.[29] This position, as will be seen, was to be the subject of subtle yet significant evolution over the following years.

ii. The Single European Act (1986)

The Preamble to the Single European Act (SEA)[30] introduced the first explicit reference to human rights in the EC Treaties:

---

[23] *Internationale Handelsgesellschaft* (n 22) [3] and [4].

[24] For example, Advocate-General Warner in Case 17/74 *Sadolin & Holmblad A/S, Members of the Transocean Marine Paint Association v Commission* [1974] ECR 1063 recognised the shared principles of the Member States; principles of international law were recognised by the Court in Case 41/74 *Van Duyn v Home Office* [1974] ECR 1337.

[25] See, inter alia, Case 4/73 *Firma J Nold v Commission* [1974] ECR 491; and Case 44/79 *Hauer v Rheinland-Pfalz* [1979] ECR 1207. In this context it is worth noting that this development is consistent with the fact that since 1974, all members of the EU have also been signatories to the ECHR.

[26] Case 136/79 *National Panasonic (UK) Ltd v Commission* [1980] ECR 2057 [1980] 3 CMLR 169.

[27] OJ [1977] C103/1.

[28] See, inter alia, Lawson (n 13); Spielmann (n 13).

[29] Joined Cases 60 and 61/84 *Cinéthèque SA and Others v Fédération Nationale des Cinémas français* [1985] ECR 2605.

[30] [1987] OJ L169/1.

Determined to work together to promote democracy on the basis of the fundamental rights recognised in the constitutions and laws of the Member States, in the Convention for the Protection of Human Rights and Fundamental Freedoms and the European Social Charter, notably freedom, equality and social justice.[31]

It continued with reference to the EC's commitment to the international human rights standards endorsed by its members. This significant commitment was reaffirmed by the EC foreign ministers when they met later that same year.[32]

During this period, the Court was faced with the questions left unresolved by its ruling in *Cinéthèque* that it was not competent to rule on matters falling within the jurisdiction of the national legislators.[33] In *Demirel* it ruled that it had no power to rule on matters falling outside the scope of EC law.[34] This is significant because whereas *Cinéthèque* could be interpreted as meaning that a matter which fell within the scope of both national and EC law would be beyond the jurisdiction of the Court, *Demirel* suggests that it would be subject to the review of the Court of Justice. This was explicitly confirmed by the Court in *Grogan* when it ruled that if a national rule has effects upon an area of EC law and requires justification under EC law, that matter is a matter within the jurisdiction of the Court of Justice.[35] Significantly, the Court subsequently declared itself bound not merely to respect the principles and rights arising from the ECHR, but also to review the acts of national legislatures in accordance with the ECHR when implementing EC law which itself protects a fundamental right. Thus, the Court would ensure, within the sphere of EC law, the respect of such rights by the Member States.[36] The implementation of EC law by Member States therefore fell within the scope of EC law. The question which logically followed concerned whether derogation from EC law would be held to be within the scope of EC law. In *ERT* the Court held that it would,[37] and this departure from *Cinéthèque*[38] was subsequently confirmed in *Familiapress*.[39]

---

[31] Preamble.

[32] Statement of 21 July 1986, meeting in the framework of European Political Co-operation.

[33] *Cinéthèque*, (n 29).

[34] Case 12/86 *Demirel v Stadt Schwäbisch Gmünd* [1987] ECR 3719 [28].

[35] Case 159/90 *Society for the Protection of the Unborn Children (Ireland) Ltd (SPUC) v Stephen Grogan and Others* [1991] ECR I-4685.

[36] Case 5/88 *Wachauf v Germany* [1989] ECR 2609 [1991] 1 CMLR 328. This was confirmed by the ECJ in relation to agricultural policy in *Karlsson*, where the Court held that fundamental rights must also be protected by the Member States in their implementation of EC law. See Case C-292/97 *Karlsson* [2000] ECR I-2737 [37].

[37] Case 260/89 *Elliniki Radiophonia Tileorassi AE v Dimotiki Etairia Pliroforissis and Sotirios Kouvelas* [1992] ECR I-2925. The derogation in question was from EC provisions on freedom of provision of services.

[38] *Cinéthèque*, (n 29).

[39] Case C-368/95 *Vereinigte Familiapress Zeitungsverlags-und Vertriebs GmbH v Heinrich Bauer Verlag* [1997] ECR I-3689.

These developments are consistent with the provisions of the SEA, as well as with the Court's position that it would act in the pursuit of EC law and that where EC law impinged on matters concerning the ECHR, this must be respected as part of the EC's legal order. There was as yet no conclusive answer to the question of what fell within the scope of EC law, raising concerns about the Court's apparent expansion of its jurisdiction.

iii. The Treaty on European Union (1992)

In the preamble to the Treaty on European Union (TEU), the Member States confirmed their 'attachment to the principles of liberty, democracy and respect for human rights and fundamental freedoms and the rule of law'. The most significant provision of the TEU in relation to human rights was Article 6, which stated:

> The Union shall respect fundamental rights, as guaranteed by the European Convention for the Protection of Human Rights and Fundamental Freedoms ... and as they result from the constitutional traditions common to the Member States, as general principles of Community Law.

This rather traditional reference to human rights, with no mention of social rights, may be said to be a step back from the SEA. Article 11 provided that one objective of the *Union* was 'to develop and consolidate democracy and the rule of law, and respect for human rights and fundamental freedoms'. The means by which these objectives could be pursued, joint actions and common positions, were placed exclusively within the framework of the EU. The general provision on human rights was also placed within the EU rather than the EC Treaty, and, significantly, was excluded from the jurisdiction of the Court.[40] There was thus no provision for autonomous action by the EC within this context.

This exclusion demonstrated a lack of political will to bring human rights protection to the same level as the achievement and enforcement of the economic objectives of the Treaty. A rather different picture was presented in the specific context of development cooperation, which was stated to be indivisible from the promotion of respect for human rights and with regard to which it was explicitly provided that EC policy must contribute to the objective of respect for human rights.[41] The TEU thus empowered the EC to make respect for human rights a condition of an agreement within the context of development cooperation. Beyond this specific context, however, there appeared to be no conferred power. This is consistent with the reservation of foreign policy to the inter-governmental EU. It is also consistent

[40] Article L (now Article 46) TEU.
[41] Articles 130w 130x and 130y (subsequently Articles 179, 180 and 181) EC (now Articles 209, 210 and 211 TFEU) gave the EC the competence to adopt measures necessary to the attainment of the objectives, where necessary in cooperation with other third countries.

with the view of human rights within the EC as principles and standards that the EC was bound to uphold, rather than empowered to pursue and promote.

During this same period, the Court finally clarified to some extent what falls within the scope of EC law. In *Konstantinidis*, Advocate-General Jacobs had suggested that the scope of EC law with regard to human rights was very wide indeed: that any fundamental rights violation should be able to be opposed by a 'civis europeus' under EC law.[42] The Court, however, adopted a strict reading of the extent of the EC's competence and ruled accordingly, resisting the invitation of the Advocate-General to widen the application of the general principle of fundamental rights protection.[43] Subsequently in *Kremzow*,[44] the Court clarified that it has no jurisdiction outside the scope of EC law. Consequently, it refused in that case to interpret the ECHR, as the matter was not genuinely within the scope of EC law.

The Court thus considered it to be its responsibility to ensure both its and the Member States' respect of the principles and provisions of the ECHR within the scope of EC law. It endeavoured, however, to reassure the Member States that it was doing this only in the pursuit of EC law and that national law would not be interfered with where a matter does not impinge on EC law. During this period, the Court also ruled that the EC itself had no competency to accede to the ECHR.[45] Accession had originally been proposed by the Commission in 1979, but in *Opinion 2/94* the Court ruled that there was no general EC competence in relation to fundamental rights, and consequently accession would not be possible without amendment to the Treaty. This ruling was the subject of some scepticism, including the criticism that the key issue instead concerned the constitutional implications of accession.[46] Setting aside such cynicism, the question could be asked where competence could have been found for accession by the EC.

iv. The Treaty of Amsterdam (1997)

The Treaty of Amsterdam brought significant developments in this field, although no amendment to the Treaty regarding accession to the ECHR. First, the Preamble reverted to some extent to the concerns of the SEA,

---

[42] Case 1168/91 *Konstantinidis v Stadt Altensteigstandesamt* [1993] ECR I-1191 [46].

[43] See below for further discussion on this issue.

[44] Case C-299/95 *Kremzow v Austria* [1997] ECR I-2629.

[45] *Opinion 2/94 Re the Accession of the Community to the European Human Rights Convention* [1996] ECR I-1759.

[46] See P Eeckhout, 'The EU Charter of Fundamental Rights and the Federal Question' (2002) 39 *CML Rev* 945, 982–83; JHH Weiler and S Fries, 'A Human Rights Policy for the European Community and Union: The Question of Competences' in Alston (n 13); N Burrows, 'Question of Community Accession to the European Convention Determined' (1997) 22 *EL Rev* 58.

referring once again to the European Social Charter as well as to the EC Charter of Fundamental Social Rights of Workers. Second, Article 6 TEU declared that: 'The Union is founded on the principles of liberty, democracy, respect for human rights and fundamental freedoms and the rule of law, principles which are common to the Member States'.[47] Article 7 confirmed this by providing for the possibility of a determination by the Council of a 'serious and persistent breach of fundamental rights by a Member State' and for the *suspension* of rights deriving from the application of the Treaty where such a determination is made.[48] In addition, Article 49[49] imposed respect for the Principles enshrined in Article 6(1) as a pre-condition for any state wishing to accede to the EU. Article 46(d) conferred jurisdiction upon the Court of Justice with respect to actions of the EC institutions in relation to Article 6(2), thereby enhancing both the Court's role in respect of human rights, but also, significantly, clarifying the obligation upon the institutions to respect these standards and removing what had been a lacuna.[50]

The Treaty also made provision for EC action: thus, Article 13 (now Article 19 TFEU) provided that the 'Council ... *may take appropriate action* to combat discrimination based on sex, racial or ethnic origin, religion or belief, disability, age or sexual orientation'.[51] Further possibilities for action arose under Articles 2 and 3 in relation to positive discrimination to promote the equality of men and women, *for the achievement of all its objectives*.[52] It should be noted that although these last provisions were only *facilitative* of the adoption of relevant legislation, the EC acted upon Article 13 (now Article 19 TFEU) in the adoption of the Race Directive[53] and the Framework Directive on equal treatment in employment and occupation.[54]

v. *The Treaty of Nice (2001) and the Charter of Fundamental Rights for the European Union*

The most significant development in relation to human rights within the Treaty of Nice (ToN) was the extension of the powers of the EU in relation

---

[47] Now Article 6 TEU
[48] Now Article 7 TEU.
[49] Now Article 49 TEU.
[50] This provision is repealed by the Treaty of Lisbon, reflecting inter alia the removal of the EU's pillar structure. The jurisdiction of the Court in respect of human rights post-Lisbon will be explored below.
[51] Emphasis added. This again perhaps reflected a desire to integrate EC policies and objectives. See now Article 8 TFEU.
[52] Emphasis added.
[53] Council Directive 2000/43/EC of 29 June 2000 implementing the principle of equal treatment between persons irrespective of racial or ethnic origin [2000] OJ L180/22.
[54] Council Directive 2000/78/EC of 27 November 2000 establishing a general framework for equal treatment in employment and occupation [2000] OJ L303/16.

to the breach of fundamental rights by a Member State. Whereas under the Treaty of Amsterdam this provision had referred to a 'persistent and serious breach' of fundamental rights, Article 7 ToN (now Article 7 TEU) permitted the Council to act if there is a 'clear risk of a serious breach by Member State of principles mentioned in Article 6(1) [Article 6(1) TEU)]'. This provision closed a lacuna in EU rights protection whereby the EU could do little proactively to *prevent* a breach of fundamental rights by one of its Member States; it could only act reactively in the event that a breach was committed.[55] A second significant development of the ToN arose under the new title of 'Economic, financial and technical cooperation with third countries'. Article 181(a)(1) provided that 'Community policy ... shall contribute to the general objective of developing and consolidating democracy and the rule of law, and to the objective of respecting human rights and fundamental freedoms'.[56] This is significant in that it created a new general human rights objective in relations with third states. Previously, such an objective existed only in relation to development cooperation.

a. The Approval of the Charter of Fundamental Rights
   for the European Union

Under the ToN, the Member States also approved the Charter of Fundamental Rights for the European Union which had been solemnly proclaimed by the Commission, the Council and the Parliament.[57] Formally, the Charter was declaratory of the rights already existing and protected within the EU.[58] There were, however, some new substantive rights within the Charter, including the prohibition of discrimination on grounds of sexual orientation,[59] which, although provided for under the Treaty of Amsterdam, had not yet at that time been acted upon. Similarly, the prohibition on reproductive human cloning[60] was altogether new. A further notable feature of the Charter was the inclusion of recognition of some individual interest in environmental protection. However, this is formulated

---

[55] This limitation had been exposed when the far right Freedom Party became part of the Austrian Government: the EU found itself powerless to act, despite fears that a serious violation of human rights would ensue. This particular event has also been attributed with having added urgency to the adoption of the Race Directive (n 53). See N Whitty, T Murphy and S Livingstone *Civil Liberties Law: The Human Rights Act Era* (Oxford, Oxford University Press, 2001) at 396.

[56] See now Article 212 TFEU.

[57] See [2000] OJ C364/1.

[58] The sources from which these were to be drawn were specified as: the ECHR, the common constitutional traditions of the Member States, the provisions of the European Social Charter and the Community Charter of Fundamental Social Rights of Workers: Conclusions of the Cologne European Council, June 1999.

[59] Article 21.

[60] Article 3, Right to Integrity of the Person.

as a principle rather than as a right:[61] this genuinely declaratory provision was therefore more significant for its very inclusion in this context than for its substantive force.

The Proclamation of the Charter raised a number of issues, particularly regarding its status and effect. Before returning to these, however, it is worth first noting developments under the Treaty of Lisbon.

vi. The Treaty of Lisbon (2007)

Following the Treaty of Lisbon, accession to the ECHR is now an EU objective,[62] as is the promotion and protection of fundamental rights in its relations with third states.[63] Furthermore, the Charter of Fundamental Rights is now formally stated to have equivalent legal status to that of the Treaties themselves.[64]

B. The Coming of Age of EU Human Rights: 2000–

Observing the chronology of the emergence of EU human rights, a shift in the tempo and nature of commitment to human rights can be observed post-2000. The starting point for this is the declaration of the Charter, the evolving status of which is reflected in both the Lisbon Treaty and the jurisprudence of the Court of Justice and the (then) Court of First Instance (CFI).[65] It will be seen below that alongside this development there has also been, in *Kadi*,[66] a significant active positioning of the EU legal order within the international legal order. Before examining EU fundamental rights in the international legal order, however, there are a number of issues concerning the Charter of Fundamental Rights which should be considered.

i. Issues Raised by the Charter of Fundamental Rights

The Charter of Fundamental Rights carries substantial symbolic significance, not least in that it reinforces the development of the EU as a constitutional order. However, as noted above, most of the rights contained within

---

[61] Article 37: 'A high level of environmental protection and the improvement of the quality of the environment must be integrated into the policies of the Union and ensured in accordance with the principle of sustainable development.'

[62] Article 6(2) TEU.

[63] Article 3(5) TEU.

[64] Article 6(1) TEU.

[65] Discussed below.

[66] Joined Cases C-402/05P *Kadi v Council and Commission* and C-415/05 P *Al Barakaat International Foundation v The Council and Commission* [2008] ECR I-6351.

it were indeed already protected in the EU, so its substantive significance was limited.[67]

Article 51(1) of the Charter provides that it is addressed to the institutions and bodies of the EU and to the Member States only when they are implementing EU law, raising the question whether it also applies to the Member States when they seek to derogate from EU law. The Explanations to the Charter clarify this:

> As regards the Member States, it follows unambiguously from the case law of the Court of Justice that the requirement to respect fundamental rights defined in the context of the Union is only binding on the Member States when they act in the scope of Union law.[68]

This clarification, referring as it does to the existing case law, indicates that the Charter applies to Member States when derogating from EU law and anything within the scope of EU law.[69] As Barnard observes, however, even a narrow interpretation of 'implementation' would in any case be mitigated by the fact that the general principles of EU law, including fundamental rights, continue to be relevant and binding upon the Member States.[70]

A further question arising from Article 51 of the Charter, particularly concerning the *scope* of the Charter, was highlighted by both McDonagh[71] and Eeckhout:[72] that is, whether incorporation of the Charter could have the unintended effect of expanding the competence of the EU in relation to fundamental rights. Article 51(1) bound the EU to 'promote the application' of the Charter rights. This was a significant development as it created an active obligation. Until the Charter was adopted, the EC was subject to a passive obligation not to infringe such rights in its activities rather than an obligation to promote them.

Yet Article 51(2) stated that the Charter creates no new tasks or powers for the EC. Thus, there remained some confusion as to the nature of the EU's obligation in relation to fundamental rights. The Charter appears to

---

[67] See, for example, 'Human Rights in the EU: The Charter of Fundamental Rights', House of Commons Research Paper 00/32.

[68] Explanations relating to the Charter of Fundamental Rights, prepared under the authority of the Praesidium of the Convention which drafted the Charter [2007] OJ C303/17. Regarding the status of the Explanations, it is stated in the Preamble that: 'They do not as such have the status of law, they are a valuable tool of interpretation intended to clarify the provisions of the Charter.'

[69] *ERT* (n 37); *Familiapress* (n 39).

[70] See Case C-555/07 *Kücükdeveci v Swedex GmbH & Co KG*, Judgment of 19 January 2010; C Barnard, 'The EU Charter of Fundamental Rights: Happy 10th Birthday?' (2011) 24 *European Union Studies Association Review* 5.

[71] European Convention Working Group II, Modalities and consequences of incorporation into the Treaties of the Charter of Fundamental Rights and accession of the Community/Union to the ECHR, Working Document I, Contribution by Bobby McDonagh, 24 June 2002.

[72] Eeckhout (n 46).

suggest that the then EC's power to 'promote' fundamental rights already existed, but this is by no means beyond dispute.

The Charter was amended when it was given legal effect under the Lisbon Treaty. Perhaps in response to the uncertainty regarding the scope of rights guaranteed, Article 51(2) now states:

> The Charter does not extend the field of application of Union law beyond the powers of the Union or establish any new power or task for the Union, or modify powers and tasks as defined in the Treaties.

This appears to set clear limits upon the competences of the EU and the Member States. However, both the Czech Republic and Poland have seen fit to emphasise explicitly that the Charter does not compromise or curtail national competence in this field.[73] Article 53 remains unchanged post-Lisbon: it provides that the Charter is not intended to have the effect of limiting or detrimentally affecting fundamental rights protection as provided for 'in their respected fields of application' by inter alia EU law, international law and the Member States' constitutions. This indicates that the Charter was not intended to extend the jurisdiction of the Court of Justice; it was suggested, however, that Article 53 could detrimentally affect the operation of the supremacy of EC law.[74]

The establishment of the Charter did not end the debate on the EU's accession to the ECHR. In its discussion paper the Secretariat emphasised that the development of the Charter and accession to the ECHR are complementary rather than being alternatives. The Convention and the Charter should support and strengthen each other rather than create divergence in the protection of fundamental rights in the EU.[75] This responded to the concern raised during the drafting of the Charter that a legally binding charter might undermine the ECHR system, which of course would have serious implications for the wider Europe. Under Article 6(2) TEU, accession to

---

[73] See *Declarations annexed to the final act of the Inter-Governmental Conference which adopted the Treaty of Lisbon*, 53, *Declaration by the Czech Republic on the Charter of Fundamental Rights of the European Union*, '2. The Czech Republic also emphasises that the Charter does not extend the field of application of Union law and does not establish any new power for the Union. It does not diminish the field of application of national law and does not restrain any current powers of the national authorities in this field' and '61. *Declaration by the Republic of Poland on the Charter of Fundamental Rights of the European Union* 'The Charter does not affect in any way the right of Member States to legislate in the sphere of public morality, family law, as well as the protection of human dignity and respect for human physical and moral integrity'. This latter is in addition to Protocol 30, discussed below.

[74] J Liisberg, 'Does the EU Charter of Fundamental Rights Threaten the Supremacy of Community law?' (2001) *CML Rev* 1171. See Eeckhout (n 46) 954–56 for discussion of the drafting history of Article 51 and the consequent ambiguity as to its extent. See also G De Búrca, 'The Drafting of the EU Charter of Fundamental Rights' (2001) 26 *EL Rev* 126.

[75] CONV 116/02 Modalities and consequences of incorporation into the Treaties of the Charter of Fundamental Rights and accession of the Community/Union to the ECHR Secretariat's Discussion paper 18 June 2002, at 17.

the ECHR is now formally an objective of the European Union.[76] In this context it should be noted that under Article 344 TFEU, Member States must, for matters within the scope of EU law, submit disputes to the EU dispute settlement processes (the Court of Justice) rather than any other dispute settlement body (so they cannot go to the ECHR regarding fundamental rights matters within the scope of EU law).

a. The Status of the Charter

The initial approval of the Charter by the Member States was significant in another respect: while approving the proclamation of the Charter, the Member States, as noted above, deliberately did not accord the Charter binding legal status, therefore the question of the legal effect or status of the Charter was also originally contentious.[77] One argument was that a legally binding Charter would put human rights on a firmer footing within the EU, possibly facilitating their development as a policy objective of the Union.[78] However, although the European Parliament was broadly in favour of a binding charter, the European Council, the Commission, most representatives of national Parliaments and the Council of Europe had reservations about this. In the light of these concerns, it was unsurprising that it was decided at Nice that the Charter would not, at that time, be legally binding. This did not, however, prevent reliance upon it in a similar manner to the ECHR.[79]

b. The Approach of the Courts to the Charter

The Court of Justice, the CFI and the Advocates-General initially gave the Charter varying degrees of respect and attention. Unsurprisingly, in light of the controversy regarding its initial status, the Charter was initially treated with considerable caution by both Courts and the Advocates-General. Even after the CFI[80] and certain Advocates-General[81] had referred to it, the Court

---

[76] The draft accession Agreement was finalised on 5 April 2013. In July 2013 the Commission requested an Opinion from the Court of Justice under Article 218(11) TFEU on the legality of the Accession Agreement; the hearing in these proceedings (*Opinion 2/13*) took place on 5 May 2014. The draft Accession Agreement is available at: www.coe.int/t/dghl/standardsetting/hrpolicy/Accession/Meeting_reports/47_1%282013%29008rev2_EN.pdf.

[77] See, inter alia, K Lenaerts and E de Smijter, 'A Bill of Rights for the European Union' (2001) 38 *CML Rev* 273, Liisberg (n 74); AJ Menendez, 'Chartering Europe: Legal Status and Policy Implications of the Charter of Fundamental Rights for the European Union' (2002) 40 *Journal of Common Market Studies* 471. This is a question which has not entirely been answered by developments under the Treaty of Lisbon, notwithstanding Article 6(1) TEU.

[78] House of Commons Research Paper 00/32 at 9. This raises comparisons to the underlying objective of environmental protection (discussed below).

[79] The status of the Charter was, as noted above, revisited in the Treaty of Lisbon and is now declared to have the same legal value as the Treaties (Article 6(1) TEU).

[80] See, for example, Case T-112/98 *Mannesmannröhren-Werke v Commission* [2001] ECR II-729; Case T-54/99 *max.mobil Telekommunikation Service v Commission* [2002] ECR II-313; Case T-177/01 *Jégo Quéré v Commission*, Order of the Court of First Instance [2002] ECR II-2365; Case T-211/02 *Tideland Signal v Commission*, Order of the Court of First Instance [2002] ECR II-3781; Case T-377/00 *Philip Morris International v Commission* [2003] ECR II-1.

[81] See, for example, AG Geelhoed in Case C-313/99 *Mulligan and Others v Minister of Agriculture and Food, Ireland and the Attorney General* [2002] ECR I-5719 [28]: 'I also note

of Justice for a long time declined to do so. Advocate-General (AG) Tizzano in *BECTU* argued that although the Charter had no binding effect, it could be used as 'a point of reference' confirming the existence of a right in the EC context.[82] The initial response of the CFI to an attempt by a plaintiff to invoke the Charter was to reject this.[83] In *max.mobil Telekommunikation Service*,[84] the CFI did, however, recognise the significance of the Charter, describing Articles 41 and 47 as being declaratory of general principles of law common to the Member States. In *Jégo Quéré*,[85] the CFI went further still when it relied upon Article 47 to justify a shift away from the narrow test for standing which had previously been developed by the Court.[86] Eventually, in *Viking Line*,[87] the Court of Justice recognised the Charter as a source of rights.

Article 37 of the Charter[88] refers to the *principle* of environmental protection, which initially raised some questions concerning its status or effect. However, since Lisbon, Article 52(5) provides that:

> The provisions of this Charter which contain principles may be implemented by legislative and executive acts taken by institutions, bodies, offices and agencies of the Union, and by acts of Member States when they are implementing Union law, in the exercise of their respective powers. They shall be judicially cognisable only in the interpretation of such acts and in the ruling on their legality.

Therefore, the 'principles', including Article 37, unequivocally do not have direct effect. Article 37 may be used to reinforce the importance of

that Article 17 of the Charter of Fundamental Rights of the European Union recognises the principle of respect of the right to property. As Community law currently stands, however, the Charter does not have any binding effect'; Opinion of AG Tizzano in Case C-173/99 *BECTU v Secretary of State for Trade and Industry* [2001] ECR-I 4881; Opinion of AG Mischo in Joined Cases C-20/00 and C-64/00 *Booker Aquaculture Trading as Marine Harvest McConnell and Hydro Seafood GSP Ltd v The Scottish Ministers* [2003] ECR I-7411 [126] and also in Cases C-122 and 125/99P *D and Sweden v Council* [2001] ECR I-4319; Opinion of AG Jacobs in Case C-377/98 *The Netherlands v European Parliament and Council of the European Union* [2001] ECR I-7079 [197]; Opinion of AG Léger in Case C-353/99 P *Council of the European Union v Heidi Hautala* [2001] ECR I-9565.

[82] Opinion of AG Tizzano, in *BECTU*, ibid. This was a view expressed also by AG Mischo in *Marine Harvest McConnell* (n 81); Jacobs in *The Netherlands v European Parliament* (n 81) and Leger in *Hautala* (n 81). Similarly, AG Alber, in Case C-63/01 *Samuel Sidney Evans* [2003] ECR I-14447, recognised the Charter as a 'standard of comparison, at least insofar as it reflects general principles of Community law'.

[83] *Mannesmannröhren-Werke* (n 80) [15]–[16].

[84] *max.mobil Telekommunikation Service* (n 80).

[85] *Jégo Quéré* (n 80).

[86] Such a development was subsequently rejected by the Court of Justice, which held that a change in the test for locus standi would require treaty amendment: Case C-50/00P *Union de Pequeños Agricultores v Council* [2002] ECR I-6677. The impact of this judgment in relation to the protection of non-economic interests in EU law is discussed below.

[87] Case C-438/05 *International Transport Workers' Federation (ITF) and Finnish Seamen's Union (FSU) v Viking Line ABP and OÜ Viking Line Eesti* [2007] ECR I-0779.

[88] 'A high level of environmental protection and the improvement of the quality of the environment must be integrated into the policies of the Union and ensured in accordance with the principle of sustainable development.'

environmental protection and to ensure its integration with other policies, but it does not create a justiciable right. However, the ambiguity does not end there, for while it is clear that Article 52(5) applies to Article 37 of the Charter, it is by no means entirely clear which other provisions contain 'principles' and which provide rights.

Despite the eager anticipation which accompanied it,[89] the Charter initially added little, substantively, to human rights protection within the EU. The rulings of the Court had already made it quite clear that, within the scope of EC law, it would ensure that fundamental rights obligations are fulfilled. Although the Charter was intended to be declaratory of rights recognised and protected within the EU, there are, as noted above, certain rights included within it which were not protected in other contexts—for example, the right to non-discrimination on grounds of sexual orientation.[90] The *D* case[91] highlighted this anomaly, as it concerned what could have been viewed as discrimination on grounds of sexual orientation—it dealt with the non-payment of a family relocation allowance to the unmarried (registered) partner of a Council official. The allowance was payable only to a 'spouse'. The Court of Justice and the Advocate-General rejected the argument that this was discrimination on the grounds of sexual orientation and dealt with the matter solely on the basis of the definition of marriage, holding that this extended only to marriage in the 'traditional sense' (between a man and a woman), regardless of the fact that a same-sex partner may not meet this condition.[92] Adopting this approach, the Court and the Advocate-General avoided ruling on the protection of the right to non-discrimination on grounds of sexual orientation. If it had been established that a right declared in the Charter was not in fact protected within the EU, this would damage the credibility of the EU's human rights protection, thus weakening the perception of the overall scheme of human rights protection in the EU.

When contemplating possible reasons for the Court's initial reluctance to refer to the Charter, sensitivity towards the Member States is clearly relevant. This manifests itself in two quite different ways: on the one hand, substantively, in instances in which the right at issue might be viewed as controversial (either as a consequence of uncertainty regarding its source,

---

[89] Lenaerts and de Smijter (n 77) 273. See also 'The EU Charter of Fundamental Rights Still Under Discussion' (2001) 38 *CML Rev* 1 (editorial).

[90] Article 21, Charter of Fundamental Rights of the European Union, 'Non-Discrimination 1. Any discrimination based on any ground such as sex, race, colour, ethnic or social origin, genetic features, language, religion or belief, political or any other opinion, membership of a national minority, property, birth, disability, age or sexual orientation shall be prohibited.'

[91] *D and Sweden v Council* (n 81).

[92] For further comment on the *D* case, see E Caracciolo di Torella and E Reid, 'The Changing Shape of the European Family and Fundamental Rights' (2002) 27 *EL Rev* 80.

or by virtue of its specific content, as in *D v Sweden*);[93] And, on the other hand, the Member States had explicitly declared the Charter not to have legal effect, which could have driven recognition of, and sensitivity to, the limits of the Court's own powers.

In the account so far, which highlights the gradual recognition of the Charter, parallels can clearly be seen with the Court's incremental recognition of the ECHR. However, a significant caveat should be applied to any attempt to make too much of these parallels: ultimately the Court referred to fundamental rights and to the ECHR, as a response to the position of the Member States' constitutional courts. As seen above, the early Court of Justice judgments relating to fundamental rights responded to concerns expressed by the national constitutional courts, safeguarding the integrity of the (then) EC legal order. Recognition of the requirement to respect the ECHR was in fact essentially a necessary recognition of the limits of the competence of the EC. In contrast, as regards the early cases relating to the Charter, the Member States had explicitly declared the Charter not to be legally binding; thus, there was no equivalent pressure upon the Court of Justice to refer to it and to explicitly give effect to it.

The initial development of fundamental rights protection by the Court was a political response to the pressure of the Member States concerning the protection of their constitutional rights and principles, including their fundamental rights. In drawing on fundamental rights, the Court of Justice effectively bolstered national constitutional rights. In contrast, the binding Charter transfers ultimate protection of those same rights to this supranational body, the Court of Justice. This was controversial, particularly for Poland and the UK. Yet, an effective means of protecting human rights is essential in the increasingly powerful system of governance which the EU is undoubtedly developing. The current position (post-Lisbon) is, as already noted, that the Charter is legally binding upon the EU and the Member States in the implementation of EU law; Article 6(1) now provides that it has the 'same legal value as the Treaties'.

With regard to the relationship between the EU law and the ECHR, the general approach to be adopted is characterised by the Court of Justice judgment that:

> It is clear that the said Article 7 [of the EU Charter] contains rights corresponding to those guaranteed by Article 8(1) of the ECHR. Article 7 of the Charter must therefore be given the same meaning and the same scope as Article 8(1) of the ECHR, as interpreted by the case-law of the European Court of Human Rights.[94]

---

[93] It is worth noting that concerns about substantive content, particularly with regard to, for example, gay marriage, are indeed a driver in the Polish opt-out. See Barnard (n 70).

[94] Case C-400/10 *PPU J McB v LE* [2010] ECR I-8965 [53].

As O'Neill observes, this will reinforce the impression of the EU legal order and ECHR law as part and parcel of one single legal system. However, he concludes from his survey of the Charter case law that:

> [T]he express provisions of the Charter are not seen as confining the Court of Justice. Instead the Luxembourg Court maintains its 'dynamic' approach, with the express rights set out in the Charter being seen as the starting point of any consideration of EU law, rather than an end-point of discussions as to the nature, extent and effect of EU law.[95]

In the context of an examination of the current status and effect of the Charter, it cannot be ignored that the UK and Poland negotiated what is commonly referred to as an 'opt-out' under Protocol 30 of the Lisbon Treaty.[96] Yet the practical value of this protocol as an 'opt-out' may be questioned, given that the rights contained within the Charter are almost exclusively rights which are also protected in other contexts. The protocol does, however, succeed in avoiding the political sensitivity of explicitly passing jurisdiction on human rights to a supranational body, which is not insignificant.[97]

As previously noted, the Charter now, under Article 6(1) TEU, has the same legal value as the Treaties, it is binding upon the Member States, and even Protocol 30 (relating to the UK and Polish 'opt-out') confirms its binding effect.[98] This reinforces, if any doubt remained, the status and significance of human rights within the contemporary EU legal order.

ii. The Significance of the Role of the Court of Justice

The discussion so far has traced the emergence of the internal regime for the protection of human rights within the EU legal order. It has been seen that this development was initially reactive, driven by the particular characteristics of that legal order.

The role of the Court of Justice in the development of fundamental rights protection in Europe must not be understated, yet through the 1990s there

---

[95] Aiden O'Neill, 'How the CJEU Uses the Charter of Fundamental Rights', *EUtopia Blog*, 4 April 2012, http://eutopialaw.com/tag/aidan-oneill.

[96] '1. The Charter does not extend the ability of the Court of Justice of the European Union, or any court or tribunal of Poland or of the United Kingdom, to find that the laws, regulations or administrative provisions, practices or action of Poland or of the United Kingdom are inconsistent with the fundamental rights, freedoms and principles that it reaffirms.

2. In particular, and for the avoidance of doubt, nothing in Title IV of the Charter creates justiciable rights applicable to Poland or the United Kingdom except in so far as Poland or the United Kingdom has provided for such rights in its national law.'

[97] On the function of the opt-out, see further Barnard (n 70); and the Opinion of the Advocate General and Judgment of the Court in Case C-411/10 *NS v Secretary of State for the Home Department*, Opinion of the Advocate General at points 169–70, Judgment of the Court (Grand Chamber) of 21 December 2011 (nyr).

[98] ibid.

was some indication of judicial restraint both as regards the development of EC law and the protection offered by the Court to fundamental rights. This may be seen in *Opinion 2/94*,[99] *Konstantinidis*[100] and in the strict response of the Court in *Kremzow*.[101] It is also apparent in the Court's approach to the scope of EC law generally, for example, in its judgments in the *Tobacco Advertising Directive*[102] case (concerning EC competence to enact harmonisation legislation relating to improving the functioning of the internal market), and in *UPA* (concerning the standing of natural and legal persons to bring an action for judicial review of acts of the EU institutions).[103] However, while this restraint apparently contrasts with what is perceived to be the Court's earlier more active role with regard to fundamental rights, that contrast is based upon a misunderstanding concerning the Court's earlier motives. The analysis presented above highlights the influence of both the national constitutional courts and EU legislative developments upon the development of fundamental rights' protection by the Court. Rather than viewing the Court's rulings as being activist or comprising the unilateral acquisition of a competence, they are more accurately viewed as being a product of the interaction between the Court of Justice and national constitutional courts, and between the national and EU legal orders. These limits flowed from the requirements of Member States' constitutions, and the Court ruled as necessary, in the light of these, in order to secure the EU legal order. A further factor contributing to the Court's apparent enthusiasm for and subsequent reservation in relation to fundamental rights is the development and consequent recognition of relevant legislation. This removes the need to rely upon fundamental rights as a principle, but should provide alternative grounds of action, for example, the Framework Directive on Equality.

It has only been since the Declaration of the Charter in 2000 that a more active EU identity to its human rights protection can be discerned. However, given that the Charter was explicitly declaratory of rights already protected in the EU, any sense of autonomous identity remained limited. The Lisbon Treaty, however, added substance both as regards the legal status of the Charter and the establishment of a general EU objective to pursue fundamental rights and democracy in its relations with third states.[104]

---

[99] *Opinion 2/94 on the Accession of the European Community to the European Convention on Human Rights* [1996] ECR I-1759.

[100] *Konstantinidis* (n 42).

[101] *Kremzow* (n 44).

[102] Case C-376/98 *Germany v Parliament and Council* [2000] ECR I-8419.

[103] See above, n 86, although, strictly, *UPA* also concerned protection of fundamental rights, being again concerned with the right to an effective remedy (Article 47 of the Charter), which manifested itself in relation to the appropriate interpretation to be given to Article 230(4) EC.

[104] This is important; it will be seen below that the EU introduced obligations relating to human rights in its relations with third states in the context of development cooperation in the 1980s, as seen above the Maastricht Treaty explicitly gave it the power to do so (see the

C. EU Human Rights Protection and the International Legal Order

Attention now turns to a slightly different, albeit connected topic: while the status of human rights within the EU legal order is clearly of great significance, it is also important, in the present context, to consider the relationship between the EU human rights regime and the international legal order.

i. *EU Law in the International Legal Order: The* Kadi *Case*

The approach of the Court of Justice and the CFI to the relationship between the EU legal order and the wider international legal order, as manifested in the *Kadi* cases, has been a source of substantial controversy.[105] *Kadi* concerned a binding UN Security Council Resolution in the field of counter-terrorism (so-called 'listing'). EU implementation of the Resolution was successfully challenged on the grounds, inter alia, that it breached the appellants' fundamental rights.[106]

a. The Approach of the CFI

The EU Council and Commission argued that the EU was bound by the UN Security Council Resolution. Similarly, the CFI held that the EU is, pursuant to the EC Treaty, indirectly bound by the obligations of the UN Charter and indeed that it is bound 'to adopt all the measures necessary to enable its Member States to fulfil those obligations'.[107] In an unexpected move, the CFI held itself competent to review the Security Council measures for compatibility with *jus cogens*, and controversially included the right to property among these. As a question of international law, there is no doubt that, like the UN Charter, UN Security Council resolutions take precedence over national law. The approach of the CFI was to recognise the EU legal order as squarely within the international legal order and, within that international legal order, as subordinate to UN law.

b. The Approach of the Court of Justice

In sharp contrast to the approach of the CFI, however, the approach of the Court of Justice was premised upon a view that the effect of international

---

text accompanying n 41). It has, however, systematically pursued the protection of human rights in its broader relations with third states since the 1990s, although its competency to do this was by no means certain: the Nice Treaty conferred a competency to pursue human rights protection in its economic, financial and technical cooperation with third states in Article 181(a) EC, now 212 TFEU (see the text accompanying n 56). EU and EC competency regarding human rights is further discussed in ch 4 and ch 5, which specifically examines the manifestation of the human rights clause in the EC's relations with third states.

[105] *Kadi v Council* and *Al Barakaat International Foundation* (n 66).
[106] Including the rights to be heard and to enjoyment of property, both of which are protected within the framework of the ECHR.
[107] *Kadi v Council and Commission* (n 66) [204].

obligations within the EU legal order is determined by EU law and that pursuant to Article 6 TEU, fundamental rights are non-derogable. Consequently, the Court of Justice held that the Council Regulation implementing the Security Council Resolution was invalid, for breach of fundamental rights.

Unsurprisingly, this ruling has proved controversial. Tridimas and Gutierrez Fons characterised it as '[entrenching] the constitutional credentials of the EC Treaty asserting the autonomy of the Community legal order vis-à-vis the UN and also the European Convention for the Protection of Fundamental Rights'.[108] De Búrca, however, sounds a more sceptical note, highlighting the EU-centric character of the ruling[109] and that:

> [T]he decision sits uncomfortably with the traditional self-presentation of the EU as a virtuous international actor ... as well as with the broader political ambition of the EU to carve out a distinctive international role for itself as a 'normative power' committed to effective multilateralism under international law.[110]

It is worth recalling that the image of the EU as a 'virtuous international actor' is not only 'self-presented'; it was recognised by the ECHR in its ruling in *Bosphorus*.[111]

ii. The View of the ECHR Regarding EU Fundamental Rights

The view of the ECHR was clearly indicated in its judgment in *Bosphorus*. This case concerned an aircraft which was impounded in 1993 by the Irish authorities under an EC Regulation which gave effect to UN sanctions against the Federal Republic of Yugoslavia. The key question in this instance concerned the *state* responsibility for human rights violation as a consequence of acts flowing from its membership of an international organisation. Significantly, the European Court of Human Rights declared a presumption that as long as an international organisation 'is considered to protect fundamental rights ... in a manner which can be considered at least equivalent to that for which the Convention provides', then, where a member of that organisation had no discretion in implementing the legal obligations flowing from its membership, the Court will presume that the State has acted in compliance with the Convention. The Court was explicit that this presumption 'could not be final and would be susceptible to review

---

[108] T Tridimas and JA Gutierrez-Fons, 'EU Law, International Law and Economic Sanctions against Terrorism: The Judiciary in Distress?' (2008) 32 *Fordham International Law Journal* 660–730.

[109] See, inter alia, G de Búrca, 'The International Legal Order after *Kadi*' (2010) 51 *Harvard International Law Journal* 1–49.

[110] ibid 3.

[111] *'Bosphorus Airways' v Ireland* (Application No 45036/98), Grand Chamber judgment, 30 June 2005.

in the light of any relevant change in fundamental rights protection'. It also went on to state that this is a rebuttable presumption.[112]

With these caveats in place, the Court of Human Rights held that this presumption applied to the EU and that the EU 'is considered to protect fundamental rights ... in a manner which can be considered at least equivalent to that for which the Convention applies'.[113] One interesting question which is raised by the prospect of EU accession to the ECHR concerns what will happen to this presumption at that point.[114] However, this outstanding question does not detract from the fact that the EU's internal evolution concerning human rights protection has been recognised and endorsed by the ECHR. It remains to be seen how this will play out post-accession.

iii. The Impact of Kadi and Kadi II

Since the *Kadi* ruling is precisely directed towards ensuring the protection of Convention rights, it does not undermine the presumption in *Bosphorus*. However, the pluralist approach of the Court of Justice in *Kadi* has the potential to undermine the international legal order more widely, a consequence of considerable significance in an increasingly globalised world. Furthermore, in undermining its role as 'virtuous international actor', the Court of Justice damages the credibility of the EU as an actor pursuing an active role in the protection of international law (including fundamental rights) in its relations with third states.

Following this ruling, the Commission adopted a new regulation,[115] which *Kadi* also challenged. In *Kadi II*[116] the General Court[117] held that the reasons provided to Kadi (the UN Sanctions Committee Summary of reasons) were insufficient to justify his listing and therefore annulled the Regulation insofar as it applied to Kadi. On appeal, the Court of Justice held that provision of the UN Sanctions Committee Summary of Reasons was sufficient communication of reasons for listing Kadi. It held, however, that the reasons therein were not substantiated and therefore it upheld the General Court's annulment of the regulation, but on narrower grounds.

---

[112] ibid [155]–[156].

[113] ibid [165].

[114] I would like to acknowledge Ed Bates for raising this question with me. Since the presumption applies in respect of organisations which are not subject to the jurisdiction of the ECHR, presumably EU accession will render this presumption inapplicable insofar as it applies to the EU, as the EU will itself be brought under the jurisdiction of the ECHR.

[115] Regulation EC 1190/2008 of 28 November 2008 amending for the 101st time Council Regulation (EC) No 881/2002 imposing certain specific restrictive measures directed against persons and entities associated with Usama bin Laden, the Al-Qaida network and the Taliban [2008] OJ L322, 25.

[116] Case T-85/09 *Kadi v Commission* [2010] ECR II-5177.

[117] The General Court is the post-Lisbon Treaty successor to the CFI.

The key issue emerging from *Kadi II* concerns the nature and intensity of judicial review of measures implementing a UN Security Council resolution. Criticising the ruling of the General Court, AG Bot argued that the Court of Justice's reference in *Kadi* to 'in principle [a] full review' of EU acts implementing Security Council resolutions, specifically envisaged exceptions to full review. In Bot's view it would be appropriate that counter-terrorism measures (such as were in issue in *Kadi II*) would fall within such an exception.[118] Bot's approach was very deferential: he questioned the appropriateness of intensive review of the evidence upon which counter-terrorism measures are based, highlighting their adoption by 'competent national authorities' following and upon the basis of an assessment of the 'existence, the reliability and the sufficiency of evidence or serious and credible clues of the involvement of the person concerned in terrorist activities'.[119]

The Court of Justice, however, observed that:

> European Union measures implementing restrictive measures decided at international level enjoy no immunity from jurisdiction ... that, without the primacy of a Security Council resolution at the international level thereby being called into question, the requirement that the European Union institutions should pay due regard to the institutions of the United Nations must not result in there being no review of the lawfulness of such European Union measures, in the light of the fundamental rights which are an integral part of the general principles of European Union law.[120]

In line with this, the Court of Justice held that there should be a review of both the process and the substance of the measure, including the extent to which the reasons justifying the measure were in fact substantiated.[121] In so doing, the Court affirmed that the effect of international obligations is determined by EU law, thus reaffirming the pluralistic approach and the autonomy of the EU legal order which it had asserted in *Kadi I*. Viewed in the context of the pragmatic explanation of the Court's earlier approach to the recognition of fundamental rights, for which the necessity to ensure the integrity and strength of the EU legal order was a fundamental driver, the Court's approach in *Kadi* is perhaps less surprising. The Court's rulings are consistently characterised by an evident focus upon securing the strength and primacy of the EU legal order.

---

[118] Opinion of AG Bot in Joined Cases C-584/10 P, C-593/10 P and C-595/10 P *Commission and Others v Kadi*, 19 March 2013 at [61].

[119] ibid [66], referring to Joined Cases C-539/10 P and C-550/10 P *Al-Aqsa v Council* and *The Netherlands v Al-Aqsa* [2012] ECR I-0000 [69].

[120] Joined Cases C-584/10 P, C-593/10 P and C-595/10 P, judgment of 18 July 2013, at [67], referring to Joined Cases C-399/06 P and C-403/06 P *Hassan and Ayadi v Council and Commission* [2009] ECR I-11393 and Case C-548/09 P *Bank Melli Iran v Council* [2011] ECR I-0000 in support of this.

[121] Joined Cases C-584/10 P, C-593/10 P and C-595/10 P, judgment of 18 July 2013 (nyr).

D. Human Rights in the EU: Conclusions

The current position in relation to human rights is that the EU demands and ensures the respect of human rights, as expressed in international conventions and the shared constitutional principles of the Member States in matters arising under EU law. It is now a condition of entry to the EU that a state must respect fundamental rights and principles and ensure them. In the event that a Member State seriously violates this requirement or poses a threat of serious violation, the privileges of its membership of the EU may be suspended. In none of this, until the Charter, did 'human rights' become more than a set of principles underlying EC action. The pursuit of 'human rights' was not an objective of the EC, except for in the context of development cooperation and economic and technical cooperation. The Charter suggested there was already an EC competence to promote fundamental rights, yet, until Lisbon, this appeared only to exist in certain explicitly provided-for contexts. This left the status of human rights and the external competence of the EU in this field open.[122]

It is evident from the case law that the tension between EU and Member States, and between the Court of Justice and national courts, and between (then) EC law and national law was also crucial to the emergence of the EU Charter of Fundamental Human Rights. The post-Lisbon status of the Charter indicates that after a long and not particularly direct journey, human rights are now of equal legal standing with the treaties. The implications of this regarding the relative status of the EU's economic objectives and human rights will be explored below.[123]

The preceding analysis demonstrates that there are a number of factors which have facilitated, demanded and shaped the development of fundamental human rights protection in the EU legal order. First, the specific characteristics of the EU legal order have clearly been fundamental, notably the principles of supremacy and direct effect of EU law which exacerbated a natural tension between the Court of Justice and the national constitutional courts. Second, the interpretative role of the Court of Justice was central to the resolution of this tension. Third, it was crucially important that there existed a set of common human rights standards and values to which all the Member States were party, so there was consensus regarding both the significance of human rights protection and the substance of human rights. Connected to this, there has been an evolution in the understanding and status of human rights and alongside that, an evolution of the EU itself. Each of these factors has made a crucial contribution to both the very fact

---

[122] See ch 3.
[123] See ch 3.

of the development of human rights protection in the EU legal order, and the nature and shape of that protection.

II. THE PROTECTION OF THE ENVIRONMENT IN THE EU

Having explored the emergence and development of human rights protection in the EU, it is time to examine the emergence and development of environmental protection.

A. The Emergence of EU Environmental Protection: A Chronological Account

i. The Treaty of Rome (1957)

As was the case with human rights, there was no reference to environmental protection in the Treaty of Rome. However, continuing the similarity, it could not be said that environmental protection had no impact or role in EC policy during the life of that Treaty.[124] Progress on the emergence and development of environmental protection was rather quicker, however, than that of human rights protection. At the Paris Summit in 1972, the Heads of State and Government of the then six Member States and applicant countries decided that the EC should pursue an environmental policy. In a declaration which dismissed any suggestion that the development of such a policy would require treaty amendment, they stated:

> Economic expansion is not an end in itself: its first aim should be to enable disparities in living conditions to be reduced ... It should result in an improvement in the quality of life as well as in standards of living. As befits the genius of Europe, particular attention will be given to intangible values and to protecting the environment so that progress may really be put at the service of mankind.[125]

This section is worth quoting in full as, by tying the economic objective together with improvement in quality of life and environmental protection, it contains the key elements of what would now be recognisable as the principle of sustainable development. Following this declaration,

---

[124] For discussion of the development of EU environmental law and policy, see D Chalmers, 'Inhabitants in the Field of European Community Environmental Law' (1998–99) 5 *Columbia Journal of European Law* 39 (also in Craig and de Búrca, The Evolution of EU Law, (Oxford, Oxford University Press, 1999) at 653–92.; McGillivray and Holder 'Locating EC Environmental Law' *YEL* (20) 2001, 139–71; Jan H Jans and Hans HB Vedder, *European Environmental Law: After Lisbon* (4th ed, Groningen, Europa Law Publishing, 2012).

[125] EC Commission, Sixth General Report (EC Brussels, 1972); see also the Declaration of the Heads of State and Government of 19–20 October 1972 at the Paris Summit about collaboration in environmental policy [1972] EC Bulletin (No 10) 21.

the first European Community Action Programme on the environment was published in 1973 and declared that, despite the fact that the Treaty had not been amended, the task of the EC required action in relation to various environmental issues.[126] The fact that the Treaty had not been amended, however, raises questions and doubts as to the legality of this early EC environmental policy, in the light of its lack of a clear legal base. Notwithstanding such uncertainty, the first Action Programme was succeeded by a second in 1977 and then five subsequent programmes, the most recent of which was adopted in November 2013 and will run until 2020.[127]

Alongside the developing views and policies of the Member States, the EC institutions were also involved in the development of environmental protection. The Commission acknowledged in 1980 that environmental protection was a potential limitation on Article 30 EC.[128] Article 30[129] provides for free movement of goods, which is one of the EU fundamental freedoms: recognition that this could be restricted on environmental grounds, even before environmental protection was written into the Treaty, was significant. The European Parliament established an environmental committee in 1973 and included a title on the Environment in its Draft Act of European Union in 1984. It is relevant to note that the powers of the Parliament were limited during this period and the resources of the Commission to deal with the environment were stretched. Outside actors did not participate at that stage in the development of EC environmental law. Despite the Environment Action Programme, this developed through response to crises rather than developing itself as a coherent entity.[130]

Between 1967 and 1986, the EC adopted over 150 pieces of environmental legislation. These were predominantly based upon Articles 100 and 235 EC, both of which required unanimity.[131] The Member States could therefore

---

[126] [1973] OJ C112/1. This was the first of now seven Environment Action Programmes, each of which sets out the environmental policy priorities for a number of years. The current (seventh) Environment Action Programme (see n 127 below) will shape environmental policy until 2020.

[127] Second Environment Action Programme [1977] OJ C139/1; Third Environmental Action Programme [1983] OJ C46/1; Fourth Environment Action Programme [1987] OJ C328/1; Fifth Environment Action Programme [1993] OJ C138/1; Sixth Environmental Action Programme, 'Our Future; Our Choice' [2002] OJ L242; Seventh Environment Action Programme, DECISION 1386/2013/EU of the European Parliament and of the Council of 20 November 2013 on a General Union Environment Action Programme to 2020: 'Living well, within the limits of our planet'. See http://ec.europa.eu/environment/newprg/index.htm.

[128] [1980] OJ L256/2.

[129] Now Article 34 TFEU.

[130] For a comprehensive discussion of the actors involved in the development of European environmental law, see Chalmers (n 124).

[131] Article 100 (now Article 114 TFEU) provided for the approximation of laws relating to the establishment or functioning of the internal market' and Article 235 (now Article 352 TFEU) provides for action necessary to achieve the objectives of the Community. This is discussed further below. The Wild Birds Directive [1979] OJ L103/1 was notable in being adopted under Article 235 alone.

remain confident that they would not lose power involuntarily, despite the fact that this was legislation in a field for which they had not, explicitly, given the EC competence. The existence of 'EC policy' and the non-exercise of the veto by the Member States in this field led the EC to be seen as the natural forum for developing environmental protection; consequently, the EC became involved in international developments and activities.

By the late 1970s, there was recognition from the founding director of the Institute for European Environmental Policy, Konrad Moltke, of the need for three things: first, a clear legal basis for environmental legislation; second, that Article 2 EEC should be amended to reflect the need for sustainable growth rather than 'continuous expansion';[132] and, third, that all EC policies should take the environment into account (an early enunciation of the principle of environmental integration).[133] It was recognised that unless these could be established, the development of an autonomous environmental policy would be impossible. It would remain reactive rather than proactive, subservient to the single market and economic forces, regardless of the 1972 declaration.[134] Notwithstanding these limitations, it is evident that it was recognised and accepted at a fairly early stage that environmental protection impacted upon the objectives of the Treaty, despite not being an EC objective per se.

a. The Contribution of the Court of Justice

As with the protection of fundamental rights, the approach of the Court of Justice was crucial in the determination of the development of EC environmental policy. In 1976, in *Handerskwekerij Bier*,[135] the Court ruled for the first time on an explicitly environmental issue.[136] In 1985, the Court ruled that environmental protection was 'one of the Community's essential objectives'.[137] Given that this was not stated in the Treaty, this could be

---

[132] Article 2 EEC provided: 'It shall be the aim of the Community, by establishing a Common Market and progressively approximating the economic policies of Member States, to promote throughout the Community a harmonious development of economic activities, a continuous and balanced expansion, an increased stability, an accelerated raising of the standard of living and closer relations between its Member States.'

[133] These ideas were expounded by Konrad Moltke, founding Director of the Institute for European Environmental Policy in 1977 and before the House of Lords Committee in 1979–80.

[134] During this period, only incidences of market failure were addressed by European 'environmental' legislation, as it was only these which were within the scope of EC law; for example, whereas unfair competition arising from disparate environmental standards would be resolved, the expansion of activity causing environmental degradation was outside the scope of EC action and therefore was not addressed.

[135] Case 21/76 *Handerskwekerij JG Bier v Mines de Potasse d'Alsace SA* [1976] ECR 1735.

[136] Concerning the proper interpretation of 'where the harmful event took place' in the Convention on Jurisdiction and the enforcement of judgments in Civil and Commercial matters, concluded at Brussels on 27 September 1968.

[137] Case 240/83 *Procureur de la République v Association de Défence des Bruleurs de l'Huiles Usagées* [1985] ECR 531 [13].

interpreted as a clear example of judicial activism, yet in view of the 1972 Declaration (of Heads of State and Government), any other position would have been in conflict with the expressed intentions of the Member States.

ii. The Single European Act (1986): The Foundations of a More Proactive Environmental Policy

The 1970s can be characterised as a period during which there was EC recognition of environmental issues, but the response to this was limited to action within the scope of EC law. In contrast, in the 1980s the EC began to develop a more proactive environmental policy. In the SEA, the Member States, having recognised the growing importance of environmental protection itself and its role in EC policy, introduced a title on the environment.[138] This set out the principles of EC environmental policy that already applied in the Environment Action Programmes,[139] giving them the authority they were previously lacking as a consequence of the absence of a clear legal base. Article 130s conferred concurrent power upon the EC to act in this field, with unanimity in Council. Article 100a, however, provided for both the adoption of measures according to the cooperation procedure and for decisions by qualified majority (with only a few exceptions under Article 100a(2)). This led to a tendency by the Commission (and the Parliament) to adopt measures on the basis of Article 100a.[140] Significantly, a requirement was laid down that environmental consequences be considered in the development of other EC policies.[141] This was an early articulation of what would become the duty of environmental integration. A further significant development was the introduction of qualified majority voting for certain elements of environmental legislation, notably that concerning standards for traded products.

The SEA thus gave a clear legal basis for both discrete environmental legislation and its integration into the EC's other policies. However, the third requirement of environmental policy identified by Moltke at the end of the 1970s, that Article 2 EEC should be amended to reflect the need for sustainable growth rather than 'continuous expansion',[142] had not been addressed: no satisfactory replacement had been found for the Article 2 task of 'continuous expansion'.

---

[138] Articles 130r–t (now Articles 174–76).
[139] See text accompanying n 126 above.
[140] See Case C-300/89 *Commission v Council* [1991] ECR I-2867.
[141] Article 130r(2).
[142] Above, n 125.

iii. The Treaty on European Union (1992)

The amendment of the EC task of 'continuous expansion' was achieved in the TEU (also known as the Maastricht Treaty): the new task of the EC was to achieve 'sustainable and non-inflationary growth respecting the environment ... the raising of the standard of living and quality of life'.[143] 'Continuous expansion' was thus tempered and the new task became something approaching, although not quite, 'sustainable development' per se. The concept of sustainable development had gathered credibility and strength following the Brundtland Commission report in 1987.[144] To have explicitly included sustainable development as the EC task, however, would have required a compromise of economic and monetary interests which proved unattainable at that time. A second significant change under the TEU was the adoption of qualified majority voting as the norm for the adoption of environmental legislation, whether according to the co-decision or cooperation procedures. The third significant development was in Article 130r(2) EC, which provided that 'Community policy on the environment shall aim at a high level of protection' and that 'Environmental protection requirements *must be integrated* into the definition and implementation of other Community policies'.[145]

Furthermore, Article 100a(4) EC (now Article 114 TFEU) provided that a Member State may rely on national environmental legislation, provided this had been notified to the Commission, on the grounds of major needs as referred to in Article 36 EC (now Article 36 TFEU). This raised the question of whether Member States may introduce new, more stringent standards, or only continue to apply such standards as existed pre-harmonisation.[146] Macrory and Hessian observed that as a consequence of its lack of definition,[147] the difficulty in reconciling economic and non-economic goals, and the questions it leaves concerning competence, the TEU 'tends to compound rather than resolve difficulties inherent in designing a comprehensive and consistent Community policy concerning the environment'.[148]

---

[143] Article 2 EC.

[144] *Report of the World Commission on Environment and Development: Our Common Future* 1987 (Hereinafter referred to as The Brundtland Report), available at: http://www.un-documents.net/wced-ocf.htm. Sustainable Development had been defined therein as 'development which meets the needs of the present without compromising the ability of future generations to meet their own needs'. See Chapter 1, Introduction.

[145] Emphasis added.

[146] See R Macrory 'The Amsterdam Treaty: An Environmental Perspective' in D O'Keefe and P Twomey, *Legal Issues of the Amsterdam Treaty* (Oxford, Hart Publishing, 1999), at 179–80.

[147] See also McGillivray and Holder (n 124).

[148] R Macrory and M Hessian 'Maastricht and the Environmental Policy of the Community: Legal Issues of a New Environmental Policy' in D O'Keefe and P. Twomey, *Legal Issues of the Maastricht Treaty* (Wiley, Chancery, 1994) at 151.

The weight given to sustainable growth in the TEU enabled the Commission to name the EC's Fifth Action Programme on the Environment 'Towards Sustainability', demonstrating a clear direction in the Commission's priorities. However, it has been observed that certain of the official languages of the EU lack a consistent, equivalent translation of 'sustainable'. Thus, in German, for example, the different treaties (EC, TEU and European Economic Area (EEA)) each use a different word for 'sustainable'. Notably, in Article 2 EC, the word used was 'beständig', which is closer in meaning to the traditional intention of the article, continuous economic growth, than to the new broader intention of sustainability.[149] Such differences demonstrate the work which had to be done to achieve the compromise necessary to bring sustainability into the Treaty.[150]

iv. The Treaty of Amsterdam (1997)

The Maastricht approach to environmental protection was consolidated under the ToA, which included the promotion of a high level of environmental protection and improvement of the quality of the environment as a new EC task.[151] In addition, the concept of sustainable development was finally explicitly introduced into the treaties.[152] However, there was no definition of sustainable development, prompting Macrory to observe that the concept remained of greater political than legal significance.[153]

The fact that the task of sustainable and non-inflationary growth was maintained in Article 2 (repealed by the Treaty of Lisbon) but no longer linked to the requirement to respect the environment may well be explained by the inclusion of the principle of environmental integration in Article 6 EC (now Article 11 TFEU) rather than Article 130r(2) EC as it was under the TEU (now Article 174 TFEU). While the legal effect of the duty of environmental integration remained unchanged, it was politically significant that it was moved out of the Title on Environment and into the general provisions of the Treaty. This gave it more prominence, putting it squarely among the EC's objectives. A further potentially significant change was that

---

[149] N Haigh, 'Introducing the Concept of Sustainable Development into the Treaties of the European Union' in T O'Riordan and H Voisey (eds), *The Transition to Sustainability: The Politics of Agenda 21 in Europe* (London, Earthscan, 1998).

[150] The Sixth Action Programme continued the pursuit of the Fifth Action Programme targets and the Seventh Action Programme is situated explicitly in the context of the Europe 2020 Strategy for Smart, Sustainable and Inclusive Growth.

[151] Article 2 EC.

[152] See Preamble: 'Determined to promote economic and social progress for their peoples, taking into account the principle of sustainable development'; Article 2 TEU: 'The Union shall set itself the following objectives: to promote economic and social progress and a high level of employment and to achieve balanced and sustainable development'; Article 6 EC: 'Environmental protection requirements must be integrated into the definition and implementation of the Community policies and activities referred to in Article 3, in particular with a view to promoting sustainable development.'

[153] Macrory (n 146).

it referred to 'policies and activities', whereas under Maastricht the duty referred only to the *policies* of the EC.

The ToA also explicitly permitted Member States to derogate from harmonised EC standards, in order to apply more stringent environmental provisions, on the basis of scientific evidence.[154] This contrasted with the position under the TEU, whereby such measures could only be applied in relation to standards which had been adopted by qualified majority voting, and only by the Member States which had not supported them. Measures adopted by both the Council and the Commission could be derogated from under the ToA.

a. The Significance of the Duty of Integration

It has been suggested that the significance of the duty of environmental integration was tempered to some extent by the fact that there were a growing number of similar duties within the Treaty.[155] With respect to human health, for example, the requirement under the TEU that 'Health protection requirements shall form a constituent part of the Community's other policies'[156] was developed in the ToA in the same manner as that of environmental integration. It was required that 'a high level of human health protection shall be ensured in the definition and implementation of all EC policies and activities'.[157] Similar obligations were introduced in the context of employment[158] and consumer protection,[159] and already existed in relation to the EC's industrial objectives.[160] Measures adopted under Article 175 (ex 130s) (now 192 TFEU) had to be adopted pursuant to co-decision procedure, but those requiring unanimity continued to require unanimity. The duty of integration was supported, following the ToA, by Declaration 12, which provided that the Commission consider the environmental impact of its proposals and the principle of sustainable growth, and that the Member States also consider these in implementing EC policies. Yet, following all the effort to move from the concept of growth to development, the return to 'sustainable growth' at this point appeared regressive.

v. The Treaty of Nice (2001)

The Treaty of Nice introduced no substantive changes to environmental protection within the EU. However, in the Charter of Fundamental Rights, there was, as seen above, a symbolically significant development in that

---

[154] Article 95(5) EC; this evidence should be specific to the member state concerned. The derogation must be approved by the Commission, which must assess whether to amend the existing harmonisation measure (Article 95(8) EC).

[155] Macrory (n 146). See also McGillivray and Holder (n 124).

[156] Article 129(1) EC.

[157] Article 152(1) EC.

[158] Article 127 (ex 109p) EC.

[159] Article 153(2) (ex 129a) EC.

[160] Article 157(3) (ex130) EC.

Article 37 includes a provision relating to the place of environmental protection within the EU, although it does not provide for it as a right.

vi. The Treaty of Lisbon (2007)

Article 3(3) TEU, post-Lisbon, provides that:

> The Union shall establish an internal market. It shall work for the sustainable development of Europe based on balanced economic growth and price stability, a highly competitive social market economy, aiming at full employment and social progress, and a high level of protection and improvement of the quality of the environment. It shall promote scientific and technological advance.

Jans and Vedder observe the significance of this in that under the old Article 2 TEU, reference was made to the 'sustainable development of economic activities'. The new Article 3(3) reference to 'sustainable development *of Europe*' broadens the scope of the commitment to sustainable development beyond economic development, explicitly referencing as it does employment, social progress and environmental protection.[161] Lee also notes a shift in emphasis in the reference to the promotion of 'scientific and technological advance'.[162] However, it is also striking that sustainable development remains premised upon economic *growth*: there is no evidence here of questions concerning the sustainability of continued growth:

> 'Sustainable development' is also now explicitly incorporated into Article 3(5) relating to the EU's external relations:

> 'the Union shall uphold and promote its values and interests and contribute to the protection of its citizens. It shall contribute to peace, security, the sustainable development of the Earth … free and fair trade, eradication of poverty and the protection of human rights…'

The duty of environmental integration is itself substantively unchanged under the Lisbon Treaty, but remains one of many integration principles. Therefore, the potential for that loss of distinction to render environmental integration less significant is certainly compounded under the Lisbon Treaty. Indeed, Article 7 TFEU has been described by Jans and Vedder as a 'super-integration clause in that it requires the Union to ensure consistency between all its policies and activities.'[163] This supports the interpretation that there is no inherent hierarchy of interests. Thus, while environmental protection must be considered in all the EU's activities, it has no inherent priority over other interests. In the event of conflict, these must be weighed

---

[161] Jans and Vedder (n 124).
[162] Maria Lee, 'The Environmental Implications of the Lisbon Treaty' (2008) 10 *Environmental Law Review* 133.
[163] Jans and Vedder (n 124) 11. See also Lee (n 162).

up and balanced. The significance of the principle of proportionality in effecting this is clear.[164]

Examination of the emergence of environmental protection in the EU thus demonstrates clearly the mutual dependency of economic and environmental interests. This is evident both in the case law and also in the terms in which the commitment to environmental protection is made and contextualised in the Treaties.

B. Fundamental Principles in EU Environmental Law and Policy

While there is little evidence that pursuit of economic *growth* per se might be questioned in the treaties, we have seen recognition that growth must be sustainable and that environmental sustainability is crucial to this.[165] In addition to the explicit commitment to sustainable growth, the commitment to the principle of sustainable development itself reinforces this. It is also evident in the duty of integration which, in its non-hierarchical approach, is in turn instrumental in the realisation of sustainable development. The principle of proportionality plays a similar instrumental role in delivering sustainable development by determining the appropriate relationship between environmental protection and other EU objectives where these interact.

European environmental policy and action has been based upon a number of fundamental principles: sustainability, integration, proportionality and also the precautionary principle. These have not been developed as a coherent body: there have been a number of initiatives to develop each, but there are increasing signs of them being drawn together, as in the Seventh Environment Action Programme. Before examining these principles, the role of subsidiarity in developing EU environmental legislation will be briefly considered.

i. Subsidiarity

The principle of subsidiarity was introduced into the EU by the TEU and is now contained in Article 5 TEU.[166] It applies in any context in which the EU does not have exclusive competence to act and limits EU action to instances in which the desired objective can be better achieved by action at the EU level than the Member State level. Thus, subsidiarity limits EU action, requiring that objectives be pursued, and decisions taken, as close

---

[164] Further discussed in ch 3 below.
[165] It might however be questioned whether economic *growth* is sustainable.
[166] This will be discussed further in ch 4.

to the citizen as possible.[167] The significance of subsidiarity in the development of environmental law and policy is demonstrated in the complementary nature of EU environmental competence. It is also evident in the 1997 Council Resolution on the drafting, implementation and enforcement of EC environmental law.[168] The Resolution referred to the shared responsibility in the implementation and enforcement of EC environmental policy. In the 2000 proposal for a Directive on public access to environmental information,[169] the Commission considered subsidiarity and explained the rationale for an EC dimension to environmental policy. This was based upon both the transfrontier nature of environmental problems and the fulfilment of the EC's international commitments. This was reinforced in the Commission's roadmap for the Seventh Environmental Action Programme:

> Improving the EU's environmental performance requires the adoption of a coordinated policy by the Commission across areas of shared and exclusive competence and given the trans-boundary dimension of many environmental challenges. Such an approach will ensure synergies and coherence between EU policies and across the economy. Given the relevance of environmental legislation for many business sectors, a coherent EU environmental policy will also ensure a level playing [sic] for EU businesses and a functioning internal market.[170]

The Seventh Action Programme emphasises the key role of subsidiarity in relation to the development of environmental policy. This underscores measures designed to engage stakeholders, including citizens.

ii. Sustainability: The Sustainable Development Strategy

The sustainable development strategy was adopted at the Gothenburg Summit in June 2001.[171] This recognised that economic growth and social cohesion are inter-dependent with environmental protection. Essentially the strategy required that all future major legislative proposals must include an assessment of economic, environmental and social costs. It also emphasised the need for the pricing of goods to reflect environmental and social externalities as a means by which to change consumers' behaviour. In addition, the 2001 Council highlighted the need to develop a global strategy, to

---

[167] This is expressed in the Preamble to the Treaty. The protocol on the application of the principles of subsidiarity and proportionality requires that all EU legislation includes a statement setting out the reasons justifying action at the EU rather than the Member State level, and that these reasons are supported by evidence pointing to the conclusion that the objectives of the legislation will be better achieved by EU than Member State action.

[168] [1997] OJ C321/1.

[169] COM (2000) 402 final.

[170] http://ec.europa.eu/governance/impact/planned_ia/docs/2012_env_013_7th_environmental_action_programme_en.pdf at A.

[171] 'A Sustainable Europe for a Better World: A European Union Strategy for Sustainable Development' COM (2001) 264 final.

which the Commission responded in 2002 in its Communication 'Towards a global partnership for sustainable development'.[172] This was essentially the external part of the EC's policy and followed the internal strategy's elements of sustainable development: recognising the inter-relationship between economic, social and environmental development, but emphasising the requirement for greater coherence in EU policies and improved governance at all levels.[173] To this end the EU undertook to ensure consistency in its international undertakings, to use its bilateral and multilateral relations to underpin sustainable development and to support closer cooperation between the WTO, international environmental bodies and the International Labour Organization (ILO). Among the priorities identified in the Global Partnership Communication was a need for better governance at all levels. The EU approach to governance was based upon 'openness, participation, accountability, effectiveness and coherence', which apply to internal and external actions alike. It included in its list for action the improvement of the global capacity to enforce ILO Conventions on labour standards, encouraging the ILO to promote social governance.

Central to the EU's plans in the Sustainable Development Strategy was recognition of the need to build upon existing international structures, including the ILO and the United Nations Environment Programme (UNEP), to ensure sustainable development and the need to develop global governance to facilitate this. The development of global governance is a thorny issue, however, as it requires both a common vision of what constitutes good governance and a political will to achieve that. In the EU's renewed Sustainable Development Strategy, the EU Heads of State and Government welcomed 'civil society initiatives which aim at creating more ownership for sustainable development and will therefore intensify dialogue with relevant organisations and platforms'.[174] This renewed strategy identified seven priority areas for the implementation of sustainable development.[175] Significantly, it highlighted the imperative need for cooperation with the Member States and also with civil society and business.[176] The 2007 Progress report on the sustainable development strategy concludes that 'progress on the ground is modest but that policy development at both

[172] 'Towards a Global Partnership for Sustainable Development' COM (2002) 82 final.
[173] ibid 3.
[174] Renewed EU Sustainable Development Strategy, as adopted by the EU Council, 15–16 June 2006, EU Council Doc 10917/06, 26 June 2006, at 26, para 32.
[175] Climate Change and Clean Energy, Sustainable Transport, Sustainable Consumption and Production, Conservation and Management of Natural Resources, Public Health Social Inclusion, Demography and Migration, and Global Poverty.
[176] See 'Progress Report on the Sustainable Development Strategy' COM (2007) 642 final {SEC(2007) 1416}.

EU and MS level has progressed significantly in many areas, notably on climate change and clean energy'.[177]

The 2009 Review of the Sustainable Development Strategy highlights that the EU has progressively 'mainstreamed the objective of sustainable development (SD) into a broad range of policies', while simultaneously recognising that 'unsustainable trends persist in several areas, despite a whole host of positive policy developments'. Areas of concern include a decline in biodiversity, the continuing rise in energy consumption in transport and the persistence of global poverty. This report was clearly influenced by the existing economic context and highlights the necessity that 'measures to support the real economy and reduce the social impact of the current crisis are compatible with long-term sustainability goals'. To this end, green measures should be pursued as a means to initially stimulate the economy and in the longer term to stimulate technological innovation. While recognising the continued rise in energy consumption in transport, the report identifies climate change and energy policies as providing 'evidence of the impact that sustainable development strategy has had upon the political agenda'.[178] The report notes the challenge posed in carrying sustainable development forward and, in particular, questions concerning the relationship between the sustainable development strategy and other cross-cutting strategies, including the Lisbon Strategy, and the potential for streamlining the sustainable development strategy as a consequence of clarification of this relationship.[179] One option identified is to focus upon the overarching nature of the sustainable development strategy, in particular upon its framework potential.

iii. Duty of Integration

At the heart of sustainable development is recognition of the mutual dependence and inter-relationship between the three pillars of economic, social and environmental development. The duty of integration, which is instrumental in achieving the application of sustainable development, has been observed emerging in the Treaties. In addition, the 1997 Resolution on the drafting, implementation and enforcement of EC environmental law[180] noted the particular challenges implicit in environmental protection which should be recognised in its development,[181] and the factors which distinguish it from other fields. These include the dynamic nature of the environment, the relationship between scientific and technical development

---

[177] 'Progress Report on the Sustainable Development Strategy', ibid, Conclusion at p 14, 6.
[178] 'Mainstreaming Sustainable Development into EU policies: 2009 Review of the European Union Strategy for Sustainable Development' COM (2009) 400 final.
[179] ibid 14.
[180] Council Resolution of 7 October 1997 on the drafting, implementation and enforcement of Community environmental law [1997] OJ C321/1.
[181] ibid Article 1.

and the environment, the different levels of public action impacting upon the environment and that the environment is generally represented by universal rather than private interests.[182] The Resolution prevailed upon the Commission and Member States to ensure, in the drafting of legislation, the coherence of EC and national legislation, and in particular coherence with international environmental instruments, recalling the duty of integration of environmental interests in EC actions and policies.

This may be a direct response to the situations which have arisen in which the Commission has approved funding to projects which have not complied fully with EC or Member State environmental requirements and yet which have escaped challenge as a consequence of gaps in the procedure for judicial review.[183] The possibility that this was under consideration is supported by Article 25.[184]

In a number of measures during the late 1990s and early 2000s, the Commission recognised the challenge of sustainable development; that is, as it observed, the challenge of developing policies in such a way as meets all its objectives, rightly recalling that this is not purely environmental but also concerns social development. The strategy for environmental integration proposed by the Commission in 1998[185] was a key element of this, as was the subsequent development of a number of soft law sectoral measures.[186]

The critical factor identified by the Commission in this context for the successful integration of environment into other EU policy is partnership: both inter-institutional and with and among the Member States. Notably, for its achievement, the decision-making procedure required a new cooperation, as policies can no longer be sectorally developed.[187] The Cologne Report on *Environmental Integration, Mainstreaming of Environmental Policy* recognised that there were many sectors in which the environment had not yet been successfully integrated, including transport, energy,

---

[182] Article 3.

[183] See Case C-321/95P *Greenpeace and Others v Commission* [1998] ECR I-165, discussed in ch 3 below.

[184] The Council 'stresses the importance that, in order to settle environmental disputes more efficiently (i.e. more speedily and at low cost) and with greater ease for citizens and national authorities alike, all Member States consider appropriate mechanisms at the appropriate levels to deal with complaints of citizens and NGOs regarding non-compliance with environmental legislation and make available information regarding the opportunities for complaints to be dealt with at the Member State level'.

[185] COM (1998) 333 final.

[186] Including, inter alia, Council Resolution for a strategy for integrating environmental aspects and sustainable development into energy policy, Council Document Env 185, adopted 30 April 2001; Commission proposal for a Council directive on the effect of certain plans and programmes on the environment [1999] OJ C83/13.

[187] The document then focuses on two particular individual policy areas: Agenda 21 (which will be discussed in ch 3) and the Kyoto Protocol which are viewed as being particularly urgent.

industry, internal market or development cooperation.[188] On the adoption
of the report, Commissioner Bjerregaard recognised the enormous challenge facing the EC, and in particular the Council, in the pursuit of environmental integration.[189] Advocate-General Léger has described integration as
'a mechanism whereby the linkages between the social, economic and environmental spheres may be acted upon'.[190] The expression of the perceived
need to focus on integration in the development process came despite the
existence of measures pursuing precisely that aim[191] and was followed by
further measures and opinions on that same subject.[192]

The duty of environmental integration is, as noted above, now contained
in Article 11 TFEU. It is worth recalling at this point that this now applies
to all the EU's 'policies and activities' and is tied explicitly to the promotion
of sustainable development. This expression not only strengthens the duty
of integration, as compared with its earlier manifestations, but, as observed
by Jans and Vedder, 'has given the concept of "sustainable development"
some legal "weight" and therefore cannot be seen merely as a policy objective to be achieved'.[193] However, questions may be raised with regard to the
meaning and scope of the duty of environmental integration. This can be
seen in the Commission's recent consultation document relating to the 2015
International Climate Change Agreement,[194] which requires that 'climate
change policy ... must support economic growth and the broader sustainable development agenda'. This suggests that notwithstanding its desired
'mainstreaming', climate change policy is subordinate to economic growth.
This is problematic, not least as it may be argued that economic growth
is not infinitely sustainable. The suggested subordination highlights that
if integration or mainstreaming requires only that environmental interests

---

[188] SEC (99)777.

[189] IP/99/348, http://europa.eu/rapid/press-release_IP-99-348_en.doc.

[190] Case C-371/98 *R v Secretary of State for the Environment, Transport and the Regions ex parte First Corporate Shipping Ltd* [2000] ECR I-9235.

[191] See, for example, COM (95) 294 final Proposal for a Council Regulation on environmental measures in developing countries in the context of sustainable development; Council Regulation (EC) No 722/97 of 22 April 1997 on environmental measures in developing countries in the context of sustainable development [1997] OJ L108/1. Proposal for a Council Regulation (EC) on measures to promote the full integration of the environmental dimension in the development process of developing countries [1999] OJ C47/06 (the amended proposal, Community preparatory acts 500PC0055, was delivered on 21 February 2000).

[192] See inter alia The Communication from the Commission to the Council and the European Parliament—Integrating environmental and sustainable development into economic and development co-operation policy—Elements of a Comprehensive Strategy COM (2000) 264 final lists the legal texts on Integration of Environment and Sustainable Development into EC Economic and Development Co-operation (Annex I), and into Selected EC Economic and Development Co-operation Policy Documents Since 1992 (Annex 2). See also text accompanying n 171 for discussion of the EU Sustainable Development Strategy.

[193] Jans and Vedder (n 124) 22–23.

[194] 'The 2015 International Climate Change Agreement: Shaping International Climate Policy Beyond 2020' COM (2013) 167 final.

(for example, climate change implications) are 'considered', this is unlikely to bring real results in environmental protection (or, in the instance, combating climate change). On the other hand, an automatic prioritisation of environmental interests would be equally as problematic in terms of its impact upon the EU's economic and social objectives.

This observation reinforces the significance of the commitment to sustainable development, which requires 'consideration' of all three interests, and explicitly eschews an automatic prioritisation for any single interest. But in so doing, it highlights the need for clarity regarding how the interests are to be 'considered' and, crucially, balanced against each other.[195]

The existence of a number of other interests to which a duty of integration also applies emphasises that the duty of environmental integration should not be seen as giving rise to a primacy for environmental protection: there is no hierarchy of interests flowing from the existence of this duty. This itself is of course consistent with the principle of sustainable development and reinforces the significance of how the potentially conflicting interests should be balanced against one another.

iv. Proportionality

The principle of proportionality has also been built squarely into environmental protection, as is evident in Article 114 TFEU (formerly Article 95 EC).[196] In this context proportionality requires that EU action does not go beyond what is necessary to achieve the desired objective. The application of proportionality has been developed through case law—thus, for example, a state wishing to derogate from the obligations of the Wilds Birds Directive,[197] in line with the derogations provided in the Directive,[198] may only do so to the extent that there is 'no other satisfactory solution'. The Court has held that exercise of the derogation must 'be proportionate to the needs which justify it'.[199] Similarly, with regard to the authorisation for renewable energy plants, the Court has held that the prohibition of 'the location of wind turbines not intended for self-consumption ... without any requirement for a prior assessment of the environmental impact of the project' is not precluded 'on condition that the principles of

---

[195] This is an issue which will be considered further in ch 3.

[196] The application of the proportionality test, as it has manifested itself as a means by which to manage the relationship between environmental protection and the EU's economic objectives, will be discussed in ch 3.

[197] Council Directive 79/409/EEC of 2 April 1979 on the conservation of wild birds [1979] OJ L103/1 and 2006/105/EC of 20 November 2006 [2006] OJ L363/368.

[198] Article 9: 'Member States may derogate from the provisions of Articles 5,6,7 & 8, *where there is no other satisfactory solution*, for the following reasons...' (emphasis added).

[199] Case C-76/08 *Commission v Malta* [2009] ECR I-8213 [49]–[57].

non-discrimination and proportionality are respected'.[200] Furthermore, in a number of cases the Court has concluded that flexibility in the provisions of a directive facilitates the observance of the proportionality principle by Member States in their implementation of EU environmental obligations.[201] Proportionality has also played a crucial role in the management of the relationship between environmental protection and the fundamental freedoms—that is, in delivering 'sustainable development'.[202]

v. The Precautionary Principle

The significance of consensus as to values and principles to be protected has been highlighted in the context of the development of EU human rights protection, and it is relevant with regard to the significance of the precautionary principle in the context of environmental protection. While the precautionary principle is crucial to the EU's environment policy, having been the basis of EU environmental policy since the TEU, it is not recognised as having reached the status of a General Principle of international law (notwithstanding its recognition in Principle 15 of the Rio Declaration).[203] This divergence in its status and recognition has caused problems at the international level.[204]

The Commission Communication on the Precautionary Principle[205] provides guidance on its application[206] and the complexities arising have not been confined to the international context.[207] The principle is applied to protect human health and the environment, and essentially means that the mere fact that there is no certainty over the nature of threats to these interests should not be used to prevent action being taken to protect those interests. Thus, the precautionary principle, which may be invoked without certainty as to the nature of risk, is distinct from a policy of prevention,

---

[200] Case C-2/10 *Azienda Agro-Zootecnica Franchin Sarl Eolica di Altamura Srl v Regione Puglia* [2011] ECR I-5031 [75].

[201] Case C-293/97 *Standley* [1999] ECR I-2603; Case 165/09-167/09 *Stichting Natuur en Milieu and Others*, judgment of 26 May 2011 (nyr). See further Jans and Vedder (n 124) 19–20.

[202] See ch 3 below.

[203] 'In order to protect the environment, the precautionary approach shall be widely applied by States according to their capabilities. Where there are threats of serious or irreversible damage, lack of full scientific certainty shall not be used as a reason for postponing cost-effective measures to prevent environmental degradation.'

[204] *European Communities-Measures Affecting Meat and Meat Products (Beef Hormones)*, Report of the Panel WT.DS26/R; Report of the Appellate Body WT/DS26/EB/R. See below for discussion.

[205] COM (2000) 1 final.

[206] See N Notaro and S Poli, 'Environmental Law 2001–2002' (2001) 21(1) *Yearbook of European Law* 489–534.

[207] For an overview of the principle, see E Fisher, 'Is the Precautionary Principle Justicable?' (2001) *JEnvL* 315–34.

which may be invoked where risks are known and established.[208] The Communication emphasised, however, that the precautionary principle cannot be used to justify arbitrary decisions: as well as the identification of possible adverse effects, available scientific data must be evaluated with due regard to the extent of scientific uncertainty.[209]

Exercise of the precautionary principle essentially requires an assessment of acceptable risk, but its application requires consideration of proportionality and non-discrimination, as well as the costs and benefits of inaction. These do not necessarily combine to provide the best level of environmental or health protection. They are also susceptible to protectionism, or the fear of protectionism. While there were early questions concerning the justiciability of the precautionary principle, the Court of Justice has applied it in a number of cases, describing it as a 'fundamental principle' of environmental protection.[210] It is also noteworthy that the restrictive effects ensuing from the invocation of the precautionary principle must be proportionate.

C. Looking Forward: The Emerging Significance of Sectoral Environmental Objectives (post-2007)

The Lisbon Treaty and recent policy developments indicate that while environmental protection is entrenched as an EU objective cutting across all its activities and policies (and sustainable development itself is also now explicitly recognised as an EU objective), the focus of action and policy on environmental protection is narrowing: climate change and energy have been identified as key target areas.[211] At the same time, however, there is continued recognition of the need to integrate environmental policy as a whole into other policy areas, and for policy development to involve all stakeholders both 'upwards', that is, international actors, and 'downwards', including individual citizens. The manifestation of this will be considered before attention turns to an assessment of its implications for environmental governance.

---

[208] See ibid 318.

[209] This two-stage approach has been endorsed by the Court in Case 333/08 *Commission v France* [2010] ECR I-757 [92]. The application of the precautionary principle requires two elements: 'first, identification of the potentially negative consequences for health of the proposed [risk factor] and, secondly, a comprehensive assessment of the risk to health based on the most reliable scientific data available and the most recent result of international research'. This was affirmed in Case 77/09 *Gowan Comercio Internacional e Servicos*, judgment of 22 December 2010 [75].

[210] Case C-121/07 *Commission v France* [2008] ECR I-9159 [74].

[211] See II.C.ii, below.

i. The Seventh Environmental Action Programme (2013)

In its Roadmap for the Seventh Environmental Action Programme,[212] the Commission was explicit that its objectives—'To bring about improvements to the EU's and the global environment whilst contributing to the EU's objectives of a smart, sustainable and inclusive economy for 2020 and beyond'—will focus upon certain priority areas. On the other hand, the provisions of the Lisbon Treaty, and indeed the 2020 Strategy, recognise very clearly the inter-related nature of economic, environmental and social development. Sustainable use of resources is viewed as essential to the economic growth strategy. The key elements of this will be to deepen the integration of environmental considerations into other policy areas, to increase policy coherence, to develop a more reliable knowledge base, to improve the implementation of existing environmental legislation, to renew the international dimension to the EU's environmental policy and to provide a longer-term vision.

The Commission was explicit in its roadmap that there was no intention to expand the range of environmental policy, but rather to focus attention upon particular priority areas. It was envisaged that the Seventh Action Programme would be more 'outcome oriented' than its predecessors and it does indeed set out measurable objectives in its priority areas, together with a framework of action to support their achievement and provision for monitoring progress towards this.[213] Throughout the programme there is recognition of the global dimension to combating environmental challenges, and the link to integrated strategies[214] and subsidiarity.[215]

Consistent with subsidiarity's roots in ensuring that decision making is undertaken as close to the citizen as possible, there is recognition of a need to develop common ownership of shared goals and objectives, requiring 'a sense of direction and predictable framework for action'. Recognising the need to increase the benefits of EU environment legislation (recognising weaknesses in the implementation of environmental acquis), the programme envisages increased citizen engagement, both as regards access to justice, but also the dissemination of information, enhancement of environmental governance through increased cooperation and dissemination of good practice between professionals working in the field.

---

[212] See n 127 above.

[213] Proposal for a General Union Action Programme, 'Living Well, Within the Limits of Our Planet', http://ec.europa.eu/environment/newprg/proposal.htm. The thematic priorities of the Seventh Action Programme are: first, to protect, conserve and enhance the EU's natural capital; second, to turn the EU into a resource-efficient, green and competitive low carbon economy; and, third, to safeguard EU citizens from environment-related pressures and risks to health and well-being. The remaining six priority areas provide the enabling framework intended to support their achievement.

[214] Paragraph 12.

[215] Paragraph 15.

It is recognised in the action plan that:

Achieving many of the priority objectives of this programme will demand even more effective integration of environmental and climate considerations into other policies, as well as more coherent, joined up policy approaches that deliver multiple benefits.[216]

To this end, the programme requires environmental integration in both new policy initiatives and review of existing policy and the completion of environmental impact assessment at both the Member State and the EU levels.

Consistent with the UN Human Development Report,[217] the Programme recognises that: 'Environmental sustainability is key to reducing poverty and ensuring quality of life and economic growth.' The Programme further highlights the recognition in Rio+20 of the significance of the inclusive green economy for the pursuit of sustainable development and the role of a healthy environment in ensuring food security and reducing poverty. In this context the Programme emphasises the need for global approaches and international cooperation, and, in order to secure EU credibility in this regard, the necessity that the Member States ensure ratification of those multilateral environmental agreements to which they are signatories. The action programme is squarely located in the context of both the international commitment to sustainable development and the EU's wider 2020 strategy. There is an express commitment to engagement in international environmental processes and fora.[218] Monitoring progress on the action plan is to be carried out through the 2020 Strategy process.

This Seventh Action Programme is heavily integrationist, not only in its emphasis upon the duty of integration as regards substantive policy development but also in that it is contextualised within the broader 2020 strategy and the EU's commitment to smart regulation. This latter reflects a concern for efficiency in regulation. However, through its emphasis upon subsidiarity and citizen ownership and participation, the Action Programme also confirms an approach to governance which seeks to distance itself from top-down decision making. In order to engage with global environmental challenges, it is crucial that all stakeholders are brought on board; the Environmental Action Programme clearly seeks to do this.

There can be little doubt from the nature of its development that environmental policy has been mainstreamed into EU law and is now central to the governance of the EU, although it does not hold a 'priority' position. Yet, following the ToA, McGillivray and Holder questioned the coherence of the European concept of environment.[219] There can be little doubt that

---

[216] At para 93.
[217] UNDP 2011.
[218] Proposal for a General Union Action Programme (n 213) para 100.
[219] McGillivray and Holder (n 124).

the fact that European environmental policy developed initially through its relationship to economic interests has been central to determining the shape of the European idea of 'environment'.[220] On the one hand, EU environmental policy appears to demonstrate recognition of a broad concept of environment: founded upon the 'shared commons'. This can be seen both in the judgment of the Court in *Lappel Bank*[221] (in relation to wild bird species) and in the content of the Sixth Action Programme.[222] On the other hand, increasing focus upon particular issues including climate change, explicitly provided for once again in the Seventh Action Programme, may, as Lee fears, undermine 'efforts to take a more holistic, integrated and sophisticated approach to environmental governance'.[223]

ii. Climate Change and Energy

Article 191(1) TFEU provides that:

> Union policy on the environment shall contribute to pursuit of the following objectives: preserving, protecting and improving the quality of the environment, protecting human health, prudent and rational utilization of natural resources, promoting measures at international level to deal with regional or worldwide environmental problems, and in particular combatting climate change.

The focus upon climate change is significant here and the importance attached to it by its explicit recognition in the Treaty has been reinforced by the creation, in 2010, of a separate Directorate General for Climate Change. This new Directorate General incorporates activities from the Directorates General for Environment, External Relations and Enterprise and Industry. EU environmental policy has also been reinforced by a new energy title, Article 194 TFEU, which includes the aims to 'promote energy efficiency and energy saving and the development of new and renewable forms of energy'. These aims are to be pursued 'with regard for the need to preserve and improve the environment'. The focus upon climate change is a key element of the Europe 2020 strategy and has been supported by the adoption of the EU Climate and Energy Package.[224] The Europe 2020

---

[220] There is a significant view, expressed inter alia by McGillivray and Holder, that the 'environment' in EU law is essentially 'anthropocentric ... [its] focus ... is on protecting the health of humans and certain 'useful' or valued animals... rather than protecting the environment for its own sake' *ibidem* at p 4.

[221] Case C-44/95 *R v Secretary of State for the Environment ex parte RSPB* [1996] ECR I-3805.

[222] The Sixth Action Programme focused upon four areas: climate change, biodiversity, environment and health, and sustainable management of resources and wastes. See further Notaro and Poli (n 206).

[223] Maria Lee, 'The Environmental Implications of the Lisbon Treaty' (2008) 10 *Environmental Law Review* 133.

[224] [2009] OJ L140: Directive 2009/28/EC of the European Parliament and of the Council of 23 April 2009 on the promotion of the use of energy from renewable sources and amending

Strategy, adopted by the European Council in 2010, is itself the follow-up to the Lisbon Strategy for growth and jobs, which was launched in 2000 and aimed to make 'Europe more dynamic and competitive to secure a prosperous, fair and environmentally sustainable future for all citizens'.[225] There are five key objectives of the 2020 Strategy, including energy and climate (the other four being employment, innovation, education and poverty reduction). The inter-relationship between economic, social and environmental interests in these priority areas is particularly apparent.

iii. The Emergence of New Approaches to Governance

While questions may be raised about potentially negative implications of focusing upon particular environmental areas, the EU's approach to environmental governance has evolved over the years. As noted above, the Seventh Action Programme emphasises the need for citizens' engagement with, and participation in, environmental decision making. This indicates a commitment to a mode of governance which is far removed from the original top-down development of European environmental policy. It is, however, an approach which reflects experience of environmental governance.

One of the challenges in developing environmental policy concerns the disjuncture between short-term (economic) interests and long-term interests. Recognition of this has implications for the conceptualisation of 'mainstreaming' environmental policy; it also has implications for

---

and subsequently repealing Directives 2001/77/EC and 2003/30/EC (Renewables Directive) [2009] OJ L140/16. Directive 2009/29/EC of the European Parliament and of the Council of 23 April 2009 amending Directive 2003/87/EC so as to improve and extend greenhouse gas emission allowance trading scheme of the Community (hereinafter EU ETS Directive) [2009] OJ L140/63; Directive 2009/30/EC of the European Parliament and of the Council of 23 April 2009 amending Directive 98/70 as regards the specification of petrol, diesel and gas-oil and introducing a mechanism to monitor and reduce greenhouse gas emissions and amending Council Directive 1999/32/EC as regards the specification of fuel used by inland waterway vessels and repealing Directive 93/12/EEC (Fuel Specification Directive) [2009] OJ L140/88; Directive 2009/31/EC of the European Parliament and Council of 23 April 2009 on the geological storage of carbon dioxide and amending Council Directive 85/337/EEC, European Parliament and Council Directives 2000/60/EC, 2001/80/EC, 2004/35/EC, 2006/12/EC, 2008/1/EC and Regulation (EC) No 1013/2006 (CCS Directive) [2009] OJ L140/114; Regulation (EC) No 443/2009 of the European Parliament and of the Council of 23 April 2009 setting emission performance standards for new passenger cars as part of the Community's integrated approach to reduce carbon dioxide emissions from light-duty vehicle (Passenger Car Regulation) [2009] OJ L140/1; Decision No 406/2009/EC of the European Parliament and of the Council of 23 April 2009 on the effort of Member States to reduce their greenhouse gas emissions to meet the Community's greenhouse gas emission reduction commitments up to 2020 (Effort-sharing Decision) [2009] OJ L140/136. See further K Kulovesi, E Morgera and M Munoz, 'Environmental Integration and Multi-faceted International Dimensions of EU Law: Unpacking the EU's 2009 Climate and Energy Package' (2011) 48 *CML Rev* 829.

[225] See http://ec.europa.eu/europe2020/index_en.htm; www.lisboncouncil.net/initiatives/eu2020.html.

effective governance. This disjuncture presents a regulatory challenge which is more easily met through bottom-up than top-down approaches: through approaches which engage and involve stakeholders. As observed by Shrivastava and Goel, there is a weight of evidence indicating that commitments are more likely to be met if they originate locally and where those affected participate in their development.[226] In the context of EU energy policy, Oettinger has observed the significance of engagement of all stakeholders for the realisation of progress on the first EU-wide Network Code on allocation of transport capacity in gas pipelines.[227] It is worth noting that there is a distinction between stakeholder participation in decision making and policy development and stakeholder engagement in policy delivery.

iv. The Benefits of Participatory, Deliberative Approaches: The Kosterhavet National Park

A particularly striking example of the significance of participatory, deliberative processes may be seen in the context of the Kosterhavet National Park. The area is of significant interest in terms of its marine environment, but it suffers from a number of environmental challenges. In addition to pollution, overfishing has impacted severely upon several key fish stocks. The Swedish Government had previously attempted to designate this area first a 'marine reserve' (1979) and second a marine national park (1989). However, both of these initiatives were unsuccessful following opposition from the local community, including fishermen. Both attempts were characterised by a lack of local consultation.

The subsequent attempt to establish a national park, in 2003, involved significant local consultation and participation, representing a range of interests including the fishing community, marine research, local government and planning. Where the original top-down proposals had failed, this initiative, building on existing dialogue and partnership between conservationists and fishermen, led to the establishment of the Kosterhavet National Park in 2009. A key element in the success of this project was clearly the education of both the fishing community, relating to conservation, and also, crucially, of local researchers and decision makers regarding the

---

[226] MK Shrivastava and N Goel, 'Shaping the Architecture of Future Climate Governance: Perspectives from the South' in F Biermann, P Pattberg and F Zelli (eds), *Global Climate Governance Beyond 2012: Architecture, Agency and Adaptation* (Cambridge, Cambridge University Press, 2010).

[227] G Oettinger, 'EU Energy Policy Beyond 2014', Speech/13/432, European Commission, available at: http://ec.europa.eu/commission_2010-2014/oettinger/headlines/speeches/index_en.htm.

fishing community's experience and lifestyle.[228] There was a clear tension here between environmental and social as well as economic interests. This dialogue and exchange of information led to a level of understanding and participation which could shape subsequent proposals and facilitate agreement on fishing and conservation.

Following the establishment of the National Park, this cooperation has not stopped: the Park's management, development and budget are overseen by a special body, the Koster Sea Delegation, which is comprised of representatives of local communities, interest groups, non-governmental organisations (NGOs), fisheries organisations, the Marine Centre, a Norwegian observer and the county administration. It is striking that through the participatory, deliberative process, an outcome has been achieved in which the local community are pursuing diversification of activity and resource management in pursuit of sustainability.[229]

This experience is consistent with Shrivastava and Goel's observations above as well as Oettinger's observations regarding the crucial significance of the involvement of stakeholders. There is a substantial body of research from a range of perspectives which confirms the significant benefits of participatory, deliberative democracy. This research is particularly clearly borne out by the experience of Kosterhavet.[230] The emphasis upon stakeholder engagement, public consultation and participation, together with the application of subsidiarity, highlights the new approaches to governance that the EU is adopting in this field. Such approaches are also likely to prove to be the key to international progress on environmental protection and sustainability.

D. EU Environmental Policy: Conclusions

i. The Development of Secondary EU Environmental Legislation

The EU's environmental policy has been developed according to the framework laid down under the action programmes and comprises literally hundreds of measures. There has been a gradual evolution in the means and context through which environmental protection policy has developed:

---

[228] Having participated in a course offered by the local Marine Science Centre, the fishermen themselves organised further courses educating local researchers and politicians on their interests.

[229] See further 'Nets, Nature and National Parks', European Environment Agency, www.eea.europa.eu/publications/nets-nature-and-national-parks.

[230] E Fisher, *Risk Regulation and Administrative Constitutionalism* (Oxford, Hart Publishing, 2007); J Steele, 'Participation and Deliberation in Environmental Law' (2001) 21 *OJLS* 415; E Reid and J Steele, 'Free Trade: What is it Good for? Globalisation, Deregulation and Public Opinion' (2009) 36(1) *Journal of Law and Society* 11.

while it was originally developed in the context of harmonisation measures[231] which were intended to create a 'level playing field' and thus ensure the proper functioning of the market, environmental policy is now developed as an objective in its own right. The emergence of a wave of integrative proposals and measures (ranging from agriculture to the development process in developing countries, and development policy itself) is of particular interest here, as are the emerging forms of governance, focusing upon stakeholder engagement and participatory decision making, as exemplified above.

ii. Legal Basis for Measures Including an Environmental Element

The implications of the choice of legal basis for a measure are significant. As the integration duty demonstrates, environmental protection is an inherent element of different EU policies and activities, rather than being exclusively a discrete policy in itself. Under the TEU, many areas of environmental policy were governed by qualified majority voting and the cooperation procedure under Article 130s. Others, however, were governed by the co-decision procedure under Article 189b, in accordance with Article 100a. These different legislative procedures provoked inter-institutional disputes as to the appropriate legal basis for individual measures.[232]

In *Commission v Council* the Court of Justice ruled that the selection of the legal basis for any measure having an environmental impact requires a judgment to be made as to the primary purpose of the measure.[233] It ruled that measures pursuing mixed aims, one of which is the environment, could be based upon Article 100a rather than Article 130s EC,[234] consequently permitting the adoption of legislation by qualified majority voting rather than by unanimity. The Court, however, has also ruled that it may be necessary to adopt a measure on the basis of both objectives pursued.[235] The ToA alleviated this problem by replacing the cooperation procedure with the co-decision procedure for the majority of environmental measures. The shift to the Ordinary Legislative Procedure under the Treaty of Lisbon confirms this.

A further significant development concerned the increasing use of soft law initiatives in relation to environmental protection.[236] The importance of this should not be underestimated as it indicates a shift towards a consensus on underlying environmental objectives per se, seen and defined

---

[231] Such as product standard regulation.
[232] See *Commission v Council* (n 140); Case C-70/89 *European Parliament v Council* [1991] ECR I-4529; Case C-155/91 *Commission v Council* [1993] ECR I-939; Case C-233/94 *Germany v Parliament and Council* [1997] ECR I-2405.
[233] Case C-300/89 *Commission v Council*, above, n 140.
[234] *Commission v Council* (n 140) at para. 23.
[235] Case 165/87 *Commission v Council* [1987] ECR 5545.
[236] Holder and McGillivray (n 124); Notaro and Poli (n 206).

as free-standing objectives rather than being defined only in relation to economic interests.[237] It is also consistent with the shift to emerging forms of governance which has become increasingly apparent.[238]

III. HUMAN RIGHTS AND ENVIRONMENTAL PROTECTION IN THE EU: CONCLUSIONS

The development of both human rights and environmental protection were both initially driven by economic issues. In the case of environmental protection, the driving force was the distortive market impact of varying national environmental standards. In relation to human rights, it was recognition that trade liberalisation impacted upon the enjoyment of fundamental rights upheld by the Member States: there was no absolute dividing line between these and the pursuit of the EU's economic objectives. The emergence of both EC human rights and environmental policy has thus been seen to have been essentially reactive in its early phases.

Yet notwithstanding its reactive nature, EC environmental policy inevitably had a more identifiably EC character than recognition of fundamental rights in the EC legal order. This can be seen in the adoption of the initial Environment Action Plan, in contrast to the early recognition that the EC was bound by (external) existing human rights standards. EC environmental policy, albeit initially similarly reactive and tied to its economic foundations, was more identifiably autonomous even during its early phase.

Following the TEU, the difference in approach to the protection of human rights as an EC issue on the one hand and environmental protection on the other became increasingly more apparent. The rhetoric in relation to each was stepped up, and clearly both were of growing importance to the Member States, yet quite different approaches were being adopted. Environmental protection was being pursued and developed as an objective in its own right, whereas the broad commitment to human rights was consolidated as the obligation to ensure observance of human rights obligations as they already existed within the Member States. Initially it was only within the narrow context of development cooperation that any power was conferred for the pursuit of human rights protection as an EC objective per se. The differences in approach to the protection of human rights and the environment, apparent in the Treaty since the SEA, had originally been borne out in the longstanding development of secondary environmental legislation and the lack of secondary human rights legislation applying to the internal EC context.[239] However, the adoption of the Charter of

---

[237] See Chalmers (n 124).
[238] See above.
[239] There is considerable secondary legislation relating to the protection of human rights in third countries which will be examined in ch 5.

Fundamental Rights for the European Union[240] and the enactment of secondary legislation under Article 13 EC[241] indicate a change in this. More recently, the explicit status of fundamental human rights and the status of the Charter itself under the Lisbon Treaty confirm this shift.

The development of both EU human rights and environmental protection has come about through a combination of Member State and Court of Justice action, followed by EU institutional action and amendment to the Treaty. It has been observed that the fact that environmental protection developed much earlier as an objective in itself distinguished it from human rights protection, which developed for a long time as an underlying set of standards to be applied to the activities and policies of the EC and subsequently the EU. With respect even to environmental protection, however, an assessment of the implementation and enforcement of EC environmental law concluded that after three decades of environmental legislation, the state of the environment was not improving (although it did not define how that was measured).[242] One of the perceived reasons for this was a lack of implementation of existing environmental legislation. The integrative approach to environmental protection was consolidated in the Sixth Environment Action Programme, but the direction pursued was the creation of more ownership in and responsibility for the environment.[243] This is reinforced in the Seventh Environment Action Programme. Such an objective cannot be achieved without a corollary extension of rights of access to the Court of Justice to the people and groups who are to take responsibility. The extent to which this has been achieved will be explored in chapter three in light of both Article 47 of the Charter (providing a right to access to justice) and the commitments of the Aarhus Convention regarding participatory democracy.[244]

While the early expression of the duty of environmental integration reflected its significance across EC activity, the subsequent development of 'super-integration' reins in the suggestion that 'environmental protection' is special in this regard. Environmental protection is only one of a range of interests to be taken into consideration across all EU action and policy. Thus, environmental protection is not automatically prioritised over other interests, but is to be pursued as part of an integrated approach. The existence and pursuit of environmental policy provided space for the development of a holistic approach which in turn pulled environmental protection

---

[240] Above, n 57.

[241] Above, nn 53 and 54.

[242] Second Annual Survey on the implementation and enforcement of Community environmental law, January 1998–December 1999, Working Document of the Commission Services.

[243] The 2020 Strategy (see above, text accompanying n 225) may prove significant in this context as it sets specific targets relating to its priority areas.

[244] See ch 3.

back within an integrated legal order. This regulatory space also provided one context for the development of new approaches to governance, including involving citizen and stakeholder participation. This could in turn contribute to the more effective implementation of environmental legislation.

Such citizen and stakeholder engagement is also consistent with the drive to bring the EU closer to its citizens and facilitate individuals' sense of engagement with and stake in the EU. A further element of this is reflected in turn in the development of the Charter of Fundamental Rights. Thus, these issues, despite their distinct approaches, are all connected, and a sense of the emerging polity of the EU is redolent throughout.

The existence of a pre-existing common consensus with regard to values has been crucial to the development of EU fundamental rights protection itself and to the requirement that these be observed both in the derogation from and application of EU law. However, there has been no equivalent mechanism by which to enforce fundamental rights before the Court, other than in relation to economic interests.

The comparative analysis undertaken has demonstrated the fundamental role played by consensus regarding the rights and values to be protected in the development of protection of non-economic interests. This extends both to the substantive nature of the interests to be pursued and as regards the means through which they should be protected. This has been expressed in relation to human rights in the adoption of the Charter, the development of secondary legislation and the case law of the Court. In relation to environmental protection, this manifests itself more as an issue of process: there is explicit acknowledgement of the importance of governance and participatory democracy in sustainable development.[245]

It is worth recognising the significance of a fundamental difference in the nature of cases reaching the Court of Justice. Fundamental rights cases have traditionally tended to involve individuals seeking to invoke their fundamental human rights against EU law measures. In contrast, in respect of environmental protection, it is the breach of EU law by national regulatory measures which has traditionally tended to be at issue.

Yet, despite the progress made with regard to the emergence of both human rights and environmental protection, questions remain regarding the status of non-economic interests in the EU. Recognising the integrated approach and the inter-connectedness of the interests under examination, the question to which consideration now turns concerns the manner in which these interests and objectives are managed when they come into contact, and also the extent to which rights arising under these newer EU objectives may be protected as free-standing interests, rather than where they arise in opposition to the traditional EU economic objectives.

---

[245] This will be discussed in ch 3.

3

The Standing of Human Rights and Environmental Protection in the EU Legal Order

INTRODUCTION

IN THE PREVIOUS chapter it has been shown that both human rights and environmental protection have now been recognised as EU objectives. Therefore, the question of how the relationship between these new objectives and the EU's traditional (economic) objectives is managed must be addressed. Profoundly significant issues then arise regarding the extent to which it is possible to enjoy and enforce the rights derived from these new objectives, independently of their relationship with the internal market rules: to what extent is it possible to enforce these rights as 'free-standing' objectives? The argument at the heart of this book concerns how to balance what appear prima facie to be competing objectives: how is the pursuit of economic liberalisation to be reconciled with the pursuit of human rights and environmental protection? Having recognised objectives relating to human rights and environmental protection, is the EU successful, and can it be, in pursuing non-economic interests and protecting these objectives? In the present context this has two levels of significance. First, what lessons can be drawn from the EU experience regarding the reconciliation of pursuit of economic and non-economic interests? Second, the EU has sought to pursue the protection of these non-economic interests in its relations with third states, particularly in the context of its trade and economic cooperation.[1] In thus adopting an agenda-setting role, the EU inevitably invites questions about the extent to which it successfully protects these interests domestically.

The first section of this chapter therefore examines the way in which the EU manages the interface between human rights and environmental protection[2] and the objectives of the internal market. The second section addresses the extent to which it is possible to enforce protection of these

---

[1] See ch 5 below.
[2] For shorthand, these will be referred to as 'non-economic interests'.

non-economic interests as free-standing objectives, where they arise independently of the EU's economic objectives. The final section draws conclusions relating to the nature and extent of protection of non-economic interests in the EU. It will be demonstrated that while the EU has found a means by which to balance the pursuit of non-economic interests with its traditional internal market objectives, the protection offered to these outside the internal market context is less than satisfactory.

I. REGULATING THE INTERFACE BETWEEN ECONOMIC AND NON-ECONOMIC INTERESTS: THE RULES OF THE INTERNAL MARKET

The EU's economic and non-economic interests traditionally come into conflict in the regulation of the internal market. The internal market rules include prohibition of restrictions on the free movement of goods (Article 34 TFEU), persons (Article 45 TFEU), establishment (Article 49 TFEU), services (Article 56 TFEU) and capital (Article 63 TFEU). A key question concerns the relationship between these 'fundamental freedoms' and Member State domestic regulation, in particular how to distinguish between legitimate national regulation which happens to restrict movement and unjustified unlawful barriers to trade.

Any national regulation may constitute a barrier to trade—for example, the introduction of a new (high) standard relating to car exhaust emissions would restrict imports if it imposed a new standard on imported goods which they would not be subject to in another state. The exhaust emissions standard may have been adopted as an environmental measure: the question is how this measure relates to the EU internal market rules. The TFEU provides for exceptions to the fundamental freedoms,[3] but the application of these has proved to be a complex issue which has raised some deep-seated questions about the nature of the right of free movement and the extent of national regulatory autonomy.[4] Central to these is the question of whether the EU rules are intended to remove all nationality-based barriers to trade arising from national regulation or whether they seek to ensure unfettered access to the market. The implications of the distinction are profound: a prohibition of nationality-based discrimination permits national regulation that does not discriminate on grounds of nationality. This would thus permit the car exhaust emissions standard referred to above, as long as it did not discriminate (directly or indirectly) against imported goods. In contrast,

---

[3] Article 36 TFEU (relating to goods), Article 52 TFEU (establishment and services) and Article 65 TFEU (capital).

[4] See E Reid, 'Regulatory Autonomy in the EU and WTO: Defining and Defending its Limits' (2010) 44 *Journal of World Trade* 877.

a right of unfettered access to the market would prima facie prohibit any national regulation, that restricts access to the market whether or not it is discriminatory, (unless such restriction can be justified). The car emissions standard would prima facie be prohibited and require justification. The Treaty does not specify whether a market access or discrimination-based approach applies and despite decades of engaging with this underlying question, there is still no decisive answer.[5]

The EU, unlike other trade organisations such as the World Trade Organization (WTO), has the competence to pursue regulatory harmonisation as a means by which to remove barriers to trade. However, harmonisation has proved complex and time-consuming, and in its absence the ECJ developed the principle of mutual recognition,[6] which was subsequently adopted by the Commission in the 1980s in the White Paper on the Completion of the Internal Market.[7] The principle of mutual recognition requires that a product which has been lawfully manufactured and marketed in one state should be permitted access to the market in the other Member States, thus facilitating the free-flow of goods in the absence of harmonisation. Mutual recognition derives from a presumption that the standard applied in the exporting (partner) state provides a satisfactory level of protection for the importing state. Consequently, any restriction on access arising from an importing state's national regulatory standards must be justified by reference to public policy (or a mandatory requirement) and subject to a test of its proportionality. The principle of mutual recognition thus restrains Member States' exercise of national regulatory autonomy. In so doing, it renders an importing state's regulatory preferences subject to scrutiny that does not apply to the exporting state's regulation.

In exploring the EU approach to the fundamental freedoms, it must be recognised that the EU has applied a slightly different approach in respect of goods from that regarding movement of persons. Any measure which restrains access to the market in respect of free movement of persons, whether to take up employment, to be self-employed or to provide or receive services, is prima facie a breach of Article 45, 49 or 56 TFEU and requires justification. In contrast, the Court has given more weight to the issue of discrimination in the context of free movement of goods. Thus, a discriminatory (or distinctly applicable) measure will prima facie breach

---

[5] See Opinion of Advocate General Tesauro in Case C-292/92 *Hunermund v Landesapthekerkammer* [1993] ECR I-6787; Opinion of AG Maduro, Joined Cases C-158/04 and C-159/04 *Alfa Vita Vassiloulos AE, Formerly Trofo Super-Markets AE v Elliniki Dimosio, Nomarkhiaki Aftodiikisi Ioanninon and Carrefour Marinopoulos AE v Elliniki Dimosio, Nomarkhiaki Aftodiikisi Ioanninon*, [2006] ECR I-8135 [43]–[45]; Reid (n 4) 882.
[6] Case 120/78 *Rewe-Zentrale AG v Bundesmonopolverwaltung fur Branntwein (Cassis de Dijon)* [1979] ECR 649.
[7] COM (85) 310 final 'Completing the Internal Market', available at: http://europa.eu/documents/comm/white_papers/pdf/com1985_0310_f_en.pdf.

Article 34 TFEU and can only be justified by Article 36 (the Treaty-based exceptions). An 'indistinctly applicable' measure[8] constituting a 'measure equivalent to a quantitative restriction' (MEQR) will breach Article 34 unless it can be justified by a 'mandatory requirement' (an imperative of public policy).[9] The Court in *Dassonville* seminally defined MEQRs as: 'all trading rules ... which are capable of hindering, directly or indirectly, actually or potentially, intra-Community trade'.[10] This is essentially a market access-based approach rather than one based upon nationality discrimination. Furthermore, an indistinctly applicable measure which regulates 'certain selling arrangements' will be outside the scope of Article 34 TFEU altogether, subject to the condition that it creates an equal burden in law and in fact, including upon access to the market.[11] However, a selling arrangement will be within the scope of Article 34 if it fails to satisfy this discrimination -based proviso. If it is within the scope of Article 34, it will need to be justified in order to be legitimate.

The EU focus upon market access has proved somewhat problematic: experience has demonstrated that almost any national regulatory measure, whether car emissions standards or shop opening hours, for example, will impact upon access to the market and therefore require justification. This includes national measures whose purpose is entirely unconnected with the internal market, such as a ban on Sunday trading.[12] This reality led to what the ECJ seminally described as 'the increasing tendency of traders to invoke Article [34] as a means of challenging any rules whose effect is to limit their commercial freedom even where such rules are not aimed at products from other Member States'.[13]

Thus, a market access-based approach casts a wider net than a discrimination-based approach and is more restrictive of national regulatory autonomy. While any measure may be justified, the discrimination-based approach gives the Member State greater regulatory autonomy—more freedom in the protection of its own environmental or human rights values. The discussion above provides a basic outline of the context in which non-economic interests, pursued through national regulation, come into contact with the EU's internal market objectives. Attention now turns specifically

---

[8] An indistinctly applicable measure is one which applies to both domestically produced and imported goods without distinction.

[9] *Cassis de Dijon* (n 6) [8]. The Court recognised that in the absence of harmonisation, a Member State may choose to regulate to protect particular interests and that such national regulation may constitute a restriction upon trade. Any such restriction may be justified by reference to 'mandatory requirements' (imperatives of public interest), subject to a proportionality test.

[10] Case 8/74 *Procureur du Roi v Dassonville* [1974] ECR 837 [5].

[11] Joined Cases 267/91 and 268/91 *Bernard Keck v Daniel Mithouard* [1993] ECR I-06097 [16].

[12] See, inter alia, Case 145/88 *Torfaen BC v B&Q plc* [1989] ECR 3851.

[13] Above n 11. [14]. The Court's response to this phenomenon was the introduction of the 'certain-selling arrangements' distinction referred to above (see text accompanying n 11).

to the relationship which has developed between fundamental human rights and the fundamental freedoms of the internal marked.

A. Human Rights and the Fundamental Freedoms

The recognition of human rights protection as an EU objective is clearly of great significance.[14] However, even before human rights protection was so recognised, the question of its relationship with EU law, and in particular with the fundamental freedoms, arose. Indeed, it was the practical relationship between the operation of the internal market rules and the enjoyment of human rights which essentially drove human rights' emergence as an EU concern.[15] In this context, it is worth recalling the Court's judgment in *Internationale Handelsgesellschafte*, in which it stated that:

> [T]he law stemming from the Treaty, an independent source of law, cannot because of its very nature be overridden by rules of national law, however framed, without being deprived of its character as Community law and without the legal basis of the Community itself being called in question. Therefore the validity of a Community measure or its effect within a Member State cannot be affected by allegations that it runs counter to either fundamental rights as formulated by the constitution of that state or the principles of a national constitutional structure.[16]

Crucially, the Court continued:

> [A]n examination should be made as to whether or not any analogous guarantee inherent in Community Law has been disregarded. In fact, respect for fundamental rights forms an integral part of the general principles of law protected by the Court of Justice. The protection of such rights, whilst inspired by the constitutional traditions common to the Member States, must be ensured within the framework of the structure and objectives of the Community.[17]

Thus, reflecting the fact that human, or fundamental, rights protection[18] was not an objective of the EU, it appeared to be a secondary consideration which was subordinate to the objectives of the Treaty. It was not until the case of *Schmidberger*, in 2002, that the Court ruled directly upon the relationship between the fundamental rights and the economic freedoms.[19]

---

[14] See ch 2.

[15] See ch 2.

[16] Case 11/70 *Internationale Handelsgesellschaft v Einfuhr und Vorratstelle für Futtermittel und Getreide* [1970] ECR 1125 [3].

[17] Ibid [4].

[18] The terminology of the Court in referring to human rights has lacked clarity. See further E Reid, 'Protecting Non-economic Interests in the European Community Legal Order: A Sustainable Development?' (2005) 24 *Yearbook of European Law* 385.

[19] Case C-112/00 *Eugen Schmidberger Internationale Transporte Planzuge v Republik Österreich* [2003] ECR I-5659. See ch 2 regarding the emergence of human rights in the EU legal order.

i. Schmidberger: *Introducing a Sustainable Development-Based Approach*

The case of *Schmidberger* arose as a consequence of an Austrian decision not to ban an environmental demonstration which caused a key transit route to be closed for the duration of the protest (30 hours). This restricted the free movement of goods, putting the exercise of EU-recognised fundamental rights (the freedom of assembly and right to protest) in opposition to the free movement of goods.

As AG Jacobs observed in his Opinion, this case differed from the earlier cases involving the relationship between the fundamental freedoms (of movement of goods, persons, services, establishment and capital) and fundamental rights: whereas in *ERT*, for example, the Court held that a derogation from the Treaty must comply with fundamental rights, in *Schmidberger*, fundamental rights were invoked as the very reason for the derogation from the Treaty.[20] Consequently, this was a case of great significance as it was the first instance in which human rights and the fundamental freedoms were put into opposition.

Jacobs also observed that the relevant national fundamental rights were included in the Charter, as well as in the ECHR, and continued that Community law (concerning free movement of goods) cannot prevent a Member State from pursuing an objective 'which the Community itself is bound to pursue'.[21] This Opinion was controversial at the time,[22] notwithstanding that it was consistent with Article 51(1) of the Charter.[23] It was not entirely unprecedented, however: there had been some evidence of the Court giving priority to the moral rather than the economic issues in relation to a particular provision.[24] As the rights of freedom of assembly and to protest are not absolute, the Court held in *Schmidberger* that they can be restricted so long as such restriction does not, 'taking account of the aim of the restrictions, constitute disproportionate interference, impairing the very substance of the rights guaranteed'.[25]

---

[20] ibid, Opinion of AG Jacobs, at [92]–[94]. See also ch 2.

[21] ibid [102].

[22] See ch 4 for discussion of the extent of the EC's competence relating to fundamental rights.

[23] Article 51(1) provides: 'The provisions of this Charter are addressed to the institutions, bodies, offices and agencies of the Union with due regard to the principle of susbsidiarity and to the Member States only when they are implementing Union law. They shall therefore respect the rights, observe the principles and promote the application thereof in accordance with their respective powers and respecting the limits of the powers of the Union as conferred on it in the Treaties.' This is discussed in ch 2.

[24] See, for example, Case C-50/96 *Deutsche Telekom v Schröder* [2000] ECR I-743. In this case the Court focused on the individual's dignity as a human right rather than on the economic issues relevant to non-discrimination.

[25] Above n 19 [80].

The Court thereby held, consistent with its earlier case law, that any restriction on free movement of goods must be proportionate. However, in a departure from prior case law, the Court also tested the impact of the exercise of free movement upon the enjoyment of fundamental human rights and held that any restriction upon fundamental rights must also be proportionate. Fundamental rights and free movement of goods must therefore be balanced against each other, with each being subject to the other according to circumstance. This two-way application of the test of proportionality, balancing human rights and the free movement of goods, can be conceptualised as a practical application of 'sustainable development'. This is so in that sustainable development comprises three mutually dependents pillars, none of which takes automatic priority. The non-hierarchical nature of their relationship requires that where they come into conflict, they must be balanced against one another. The Court's two-directional use of proportionality in *Schmidberger* suggests just such a balancing exercise. Proportionality in this context is the means by which this balancing exercise is carried out and ensures a degree of transparency in the balancing exercise. The emphasis upon the first two elements of the proportionality test ensures a degree of objectivity in its application.

a. Applying Proportionality

As already noted, it has traditionally been possible for a state to justify a restriction on the exercise of the fundamental freedoms under certain circumstances, which are that the measure must be adopted in pursuit of a legitimate objective and must be proportionate. The fundamental freedoms are intended to secure market integration, and exceptions to this have traditionally been narrowly construed. A national measure derogating from Article 34 TFEU, for example, may be justified on the basis of one of the (exhaustive) list of derogations listed in Article 36 TFEU. Alternatively, a measure which applies without distinction to both domestically produced and imported goods (an 'indistinctly applicable' measure) may be justified on the basis of 'mandatory requirements'.[26] However, even if a measure is adopted in pursuit of a legitimate objective, it must also be proportionate. As discussed in chapter one, the proportionality test traditionally applied in this context has three elements. The first is that the state measure in question must be appropriate in that it contributes to the achievement of the legitimate objective, while the second is that the measure be 'necessary'— that it be the least trade restrictive means by which to pursue that objective (for example, the protection of human rights such as the enjoyment

---

[26] The mandatory requirements are not a closed class—it is for the Member State to establish the significance of the particular public policy value pursued and different Member States are able to invoke different mandatory requirements according to national values; see *Cassis de Dijon* (n 6). For further discussion, see Reid (n 4).

of freedoms of assembly and protest). The third element is proportionality 'stricto sensu', which requires that the measure not be 'excessively' restrictive when weighed against the aim being pursued.[27] The first two elements have a degree of objectivity in their application, whereas the third element is inherently subjective. Perhaps for this reason, the Court of Justice has rarely based a determination of proportionality upon this element, seemingly preferring to base its decisions upon the first two, although there are instances in which consideration of proportionality has been notable for its absence.[28]

b. *Omega-Spielhallen*: The Sustainable Development-Based, Balancing
   Approach Confirmed
In *Schmidberger*, the Court assessed the proportionality of the enjoyment of the human rights, manifested in the environmental protest, in respect of its impact upon the free movement of goods. It also required consideration of the proportionality of the exercise of the free movement of goods, in terms of its impact upon fundamental rights (freedom of assembly and protest). This questioning regarding the impact of exercise of the free movement of goods upon enjoyment of human rights was new and marked a potentially significant shift in the approach to the primacy of the fundamental freedoms.

Does the fact that a restriction of fundamental rights caused by exercise of the EU fundamental freedoms must be justified, just as a restriction on free movement must be justified, suggest that the basic priority of the fundamental freedoms of movement has been removed? It appears not: the starting point for the Court's analysis in *Schmidberger* was that the enjoyment of fundamental rights, the protest, constituted a measure equivalent to a quantitative restriction (a restriction on the exercise of a fundamental freedom) which must be justified. Thus, the starting point in balancing competing rights remained that the restriction on free movement must be justified. Because the rights at issue in *Schmidberger* happened to be ones which were protected in the ECHR, a question remained following the case regarding whether it was only common rights which could be protected in this manner.

In *Omega Spielhallen*,[29] the development of the two-way balancing process applied in *Schmidberger* was further explored by AG Stix Hackl.[30] Omega-Spielhallen owned and operated a 'Laserdome' relating to which it was subject to a ban of offering games in which people 'shot' at human

---

[27] See ch 1.

[28] This is discussed below.

[29] Case C-36/02 *Omega Spielhallen-und Automatenaufstellungs-GnbH v Oberburgermeisterin der Bundesstadt Bonn* [2004] ECR 1-9609

[30] ibid [52]–[53].

targets. Germany argued that such a simulation was a violation of human dignity. As Stix-Hackl observed, if a restrictive national measure is based upon EU-recognised fundamental rights, then the question, strictly, is not whether this can justify a restriction to free movement, but rather, following *Schmidberger*, 'how the requirements of the protection of fundamental rights in the Community can be reconciled with those arising from a fundamental freedom enshrined in the Treaty'.[31]

The Court emphasised that the specific circumstances which may give rise to an invocation of an exception to the fundamental freedoms vary from state to state and also according to era.[32] Furthermore, it held specifically that there is no pre-requisite of a common conception of a particular right in order that a state may rely on it to justify an exception to the fundamental freedoms.[33] In so doing, the Court responded to uncertainty which had been left from *Schmidberger* concerning the potential to uphold *national* fundamental rights as against EU freedoms, on the grounds of public policy. In its judgment, the Court reinforced the mutual balancing of the EU economic right (the EU fundamental freedom), as against the fundamental human right. It therefore affirmed the approach adopted in *Schmidberger*. As a result, it endorsed the sustainable development-based approach discussed above.

c. *Viking* and *Laval*: A Reversion to the Traditional Approach?

In *Viking* and *Laval*[34] the Court was required to return to the issue of the relationship between the fundamental freedoms and human rights. These cases concerned trade union members' right to engage in collective (industrial) action. Observing that this right is not absolute, the Court held that it does not render EU law inapplicable. The Court did not examine restrictions placed upon the right to collective action, but considered the right of collective action as a restriction upon the exercise of Articles 43 and 49 EC (now Articles 49 and 56 TFEU). Thus, the burden falls upon trade unions to prove that their collective action is legitimate and proportionate.[35] The Court held that the right to take collective action against social dumping, for the protection of the workers of the host state, may constitute an overriding reason of public interest within the meaning of its case law. Such overriding reason in principle justifies a restriction of one of the fundamental freedoms guaranteed by the Treaty.[36] The Court recognised

---

[31] ibid [72].
[32] *Omega Spielhallen-und Automatenaufstellungs-GnbH* (n 29) [31].
[33] ibid [36]–[38].
[34] Case C-438/05 *International Transport Workers' Federation (ITF) and Finnish Seamen's Union (FSU) v Viking Line ABP and OU Viking Line Eesti* [2007] ECR I-0779; Case C-341/05 *Laval un Partneri Ltd v Svenska Byggnadsarbetareforbundet and Others* [2007] ECR I-11767.
[35] *Laval* (n 34) [95]–[97].
[36] ibid [103].

that pursuant to Article 3(1)(c) and (j) EC, the activities of the EU include 'policy in the social sphere' and that Article 2 EC refers to the Community task of 'promotion of a harmonious, balanced and sustainable development of economic activities' and a 'high level of employment and of social protection'.[37] In light of this, the Court held that:

> [R]ights under the provisions of the EC Treaty on the free movement of goods, persons, services and capital must be balanced against the objectives pursued by social policy, which include ... improved living and working conditions ... proper social protection and dialogue between management and labour.[38]

In *Laval*, however, although the Court recognised that blockading action, aimed at ensuring that 'posted workers'[39] have their terms and conditions of employment set at a certain level, is within the scope of the objective of protecting workers, it held that the specific obligations which the trade unions sought to impose gave rise to a restriction which could not be justified. In *Viking* the Court accepted that collective action to preserve jobs was potentially justifiable, but held that if the employer could provide a convincing undertaking that neither jobs nor terms and conditions would be affected, unions would not be entitled to take action.

Significantly, in these cases the court subjected the enjoyment of fundamental rights to proportionality review regarding its impact upon internal market freedom, but did not consider the impact of exercise of the internal market freedom upon the fundamental right. In so doing, in *Viking* the Court held that:

> [I]t is for the national court to examine, in particular ... whether, under the national rules and collective agreement law applicable to that action, [the union] did not have other means at its disposal which were less restrictive of freedom of establishment in order to bring to a successful conclusion the collective negotiations entered into with Viking and on the other whether that trade union has exhausted those means before initiating action.[40]

The approach of the Court in *Viking* and *Laval* appeared to indicate a marked step backwards regarding the status of fundamental rights in the EU legal order compared with the approach applied in *Schmidberger*. In *Schmidberger*, even though the human rights at issue were (as in *Viking* and *Laval*) not absolute, the restriction placed upon their enjoyment by

---

[37] See now Articles 3–6 TFEU.

[38] *Viking* (n 34) [79].

[39] 'Posted workers' are workers employed in one state whose employment requires them to provide services, on a temporary basis, in another state. The use of 'posted workers' can be controversial, particularly where they are perceived to be used to undercut local workers, as in *Laval*, which concerned a blockade by Swedish worker unions after a Latvian company won a contract, largely due to its lower labour costs, enabling it to undercut local competition. The objective of the blockade was the establishment of a collective agreement with the employers.

[40] *Viking* (n 34) [87].

the exercise of the EU fundamental freedom was required to be tested for its proportionality: thus, the Court in *Schmidberger* applied a two-way balancing test. In *Viking* and *Laval*, however, the Court reverted to simply testing the proportionality of exercise of the fundamental (human) rights at issue, requiring justification of the restriction on the exercise of the EU fundamental freedom.

d. *Commission v Germany*: The Reassertion of the Two-Way Proportionality Test

AG Trstenjak recognised this shift in position in her Opinion in *Commission v Germany*,[41] observing that the approach of the Court in *Viking* and *Laval*:

[S]uggests the existence of a hierarchical relationship between fundamental freedoms and fundamental rights in which fundamental rights are subordinated to fundamental freedoms and, consequently may restrict fundamental freedoms only with the assistance of a written or unwritten ground of justification.[42]

This approach is reminiscent of the Court's approach in *Internationale Handelsgesellshaft*, when it first recognised fundamental rights in the EU legal order, but these were secondary to the achievement of the EU objectives. In echoing this, the hierarchical approach in *Viking* and *Laval* ignored the development of the two-way balancing test which had been applied in *Schmidberger*. Trstenjak rejected such a hierarchy, advocating instead an approach premised upon 'equal ranking for fundamental rights and fundamental freedoms and resolution of conflicts on the basis of the principle of proportionality'.[43] Pursuant to this approach, referencing *Schmidberger*, she identified the test of proportionality as being crucial to securing the 'optimum effectiveness of fundamental rights and fundamental freedoms'.[44]

The post-Lisbon status of the Charter of Fundamental Rights—that it is of equal legal value to the Treaties[45]—has the potential to prompt a re-evaluation of the relationship between economic rights and fundamental rights in the EU legal order; it arguably confirms the shift of fundamental rights from being a secondary consideration, subordinate to the primary economic focus of the EU, to being an equal consideration and objective of the EU legal order. That the EU is to promote its values,[46] of which respect for human rights is one,[47] supports this. This crystallises the question of the relationship between the protection of fundamental rights and the pursuit of the EU's economic objectives as being a question of the relationship

---

[41] Case C-271/08 *Commission v Germany* [2010] ECR I-70901
[42] ibid [184].
[43] ibid [183]–[199].
[44] ibid [191]–[199].
[45] Article 6(1) TEU.
[46] Article 3 TEU.
[47] Article 2 TEU.

between EU objectives. The new status of the Charter may have contributed to the subsequent recognition by the Court in *Commission v Germany* of the need for 'verification ... as to whether ... a fair balance was struck in the account taken of the respective interests involved'. In its judgment the Court explicitly referred by analogy to *Schmidberger*.[48] Thus, it appears that the Court's approach in *Viking* and *Laval* is an aberration and that it has reverted to the two-way balancing approach of *Schmidberger* in determining the line to be drawn between pursuit of human rights and of economic freedoms. Proportionality is clearly crucial to this determination and it is the application of the proportionality test which distinguishes this approach from a simple balancing test: it provides a mechanism for the balancing exercise.

B. Environmental Protection and the Fundamental Freedoms

Whereas the emergence of human rights in the EU arose as an obligation to respect existing human rights and there was no EU human rights policy as such until the Lisbon Treaty,[49] the existence of European 'environmental policy' potentially created a different paradigm for the determination of the relationship, and balance to be drawn, in the event of 'conflict' between environmental protection and the EU's economic objectives. The Court originally gave effect to environmental protection over economic objectives even before environmental policy or objectives were developed in the Treaty.[50] As already observed, the Court recognised environmental protection as an essential objective in 1985.[51] Following this recognition, it was only to be a matter of time before the pursuit of this objective would come into conflict with the fundamental freedoms. So it was that the Court ruled in 1988, in *Commission v Denmark*, that 'the protection of the environment is a mandatory requirement which may limit the application of Article 30 EC [now Article 34 TFEU]'.[52]

It has been established that the duty of integration of environmental protection does not imply that environmental protection overrides all other areas of policy, so how is conflict between environmental protection and the EU's economic objectives to be resolved? Under what conditions may exercise of the fundamental freedoms be limited by pursuit of environmental protection? As there is no hierarchy of interests, there is no single

---

[48] *Commission v Germany* (n 41) [52].
[49] See ch 2.
[50] Discussed in ch 2.
[51] Case 240/83 *Procureur de la République v Association de Défence des Bruleurs de l'Huiles Usagées* [1985] ECR 531 [13].
[52] Case 302/86 *Commission v Denmark* [1988] ECR 4067.

answer to this question: the conflicting interests must be weighed up and balanced against each other on a case-by-case basis. The application of the principle of proportionality, as discussed above in the context of human rights, is therefore crucial to determining the answer to this question in each individual case.

i. Environmental Protection as a Justification for Restriction of Movement

In *Danish Bees*[53] the Court ruled that a prohibition on keeping certain species of bee within a given territory constituted a measure equivalent to a quantitative restriction within the scope of Article 30 EEC (now 34 TFEU). However, it held that the measure was justified under Article 36 EEC (now 36 TFEU) on the grounds of the protection of the health and life of animals, particularly in view of the importance of the maintenance of biodiversity and hence the protection of the environment. Traditionally, the Court has interpreted Article 36 TFEU (which does not mention environmental protection per se) narrowly. This was therefore a highly controversial interpretation which could not, politically, have been advanced without the development of environmental protection as an objective in itself.

a. Muddying the Waters: The Mandatory Requirement of Environmental Protection and Distinctly Applicable Measures

Although environmental protection had been recognised as a mandatory requirement,[54] these have traditionally been held to apply only to indistinctly applicable measures.[55] Distinctly applicable measures, in contrast, can only be justified by the Article 36 TFEU exceptions. In *Commission v Belgium*,[56] however, the Court permitted the mandatory requirement of environmental protection to be used to justify a measure which prohibited the import of waste for disposal. It held that the special nature of environmental waste was such that it was necessary that it be disposed of locally; therefore, this was not a discriminatory measure and it could be justified by the mandatory requirement of environmental protection. This judgment was subject to no little criticism, particularly from AG Jacobs in his Opinion in *PreussenElektra*.[57]

PreussenElektra itself concerned a German scheme supporting the purchase of electricity from renewable energy sources. The case raised a

---

[53] Case 67/97 *Criminal Proceedings against Ditlev Bluhme* [1998] ECR I-8033.
[54] The mandatory requirements, deriving from *Cassis de Dijon* (n 6), are the imperatives of public policy which may be invoked by a Member State in order to justify an indistinctly applicable national regulatory measure.
[55] Those applying to both imported and domestically produced goods.
[56] Case C-2/90 *Commission v Belgium* [1992] ECR I-4431.
[57] Case C-379/98 *PreussenElektra AG v Schleswag AG* [2001] ECR I-2099.

number of issues, which included the ability of a Member State to enact national schemes promoting the use of renewable sources of energy. This particular scheme favoured German sources and thus restricted the operation of a Community electricity market. AG Jacobs characterised the measure as a discriminatory quantitative restriction, a distinctly applicable measure which thus breached Article 34 unless it could be justified by Article 36 TFEU. Jacobs further submitted that even if it were possible to justify a discriminatory measure, this one would fail the proportionality test. Jacobs refused to apply the Court's *Belgian Waste* approach on the grounds that it was faulty.

The CJEU did not refer to whether the measure was distinctly or indistinctly applicable, but simply held that it did not breach Article 34 TFEU. The failure to refer to the distinct or indistinct applicability of the measure is significant in the light of the fact that the scheme discouraged the purchase of electricity from renewable energy sources outside Germany, and therefore was clearly discriminatory. Normally, a distinctly applicable measure such as this breaches Article 34 TFEU and may only be justified by reference to one of the derogations included in the exhaustive list provided in Article 36 TFEU. However, since Article 36 does not include 'environmental protection' as a justification for a breach of Article 34, it would have been difficult for the Court to pursue this line of reasoning. Yet in permitting 'environmental protection' to justify the compatibility of a measure with Article 34 rather than using it as a derogation to justify a measure conflicting with Article 34, the Court applied the approach normally reserved for indistinctly applicable measures that may be justified by the open range of 'mandatory requirements'.[58] Given that the Court clearly wished to support the 'environmental' measure, it would have struggled to provide more detailed reasoning in support of its decision, which clearly ran counter to the existing understanding of the law relating to justification for trade restriction.[59] Poli has observed that it would perhaps have been more satisfactory had the Court acknowledged that it was changing the availability of mandatory requirements.[60] It is perhaps disappointing that the Member States did not, in the Lisbon Treaty, amend the derogations contained in Article 36 TFEU to explicitly include environmental protection.

---

[58] See text accompanying n 26.

[59] The established position is that a distinctly applicable measure may only be justified by the exceptions listed in Article 36 TFEU. The open category of mandatory requirement is traditionally only available for indistinctly applicable measures.

[60] S Poli, 'National Schemes Supporting the Use of Electricity Produced from Renewable Energy Sources and the Community Legal Framework' (2002) 14(2) *Journal of Environmental Law* 209, 228.

b. PreussenElektra: *Prioritising Environmental Protection— Lacking Proportionality*

Aside from the failure to clarify the basis for environmental protection justifying a discriminatory measure, *PreussenElektra* is also striking for the Court's lack of consideration of the proportionality of the measure (it simply held that it was compatible). As noted above, AG Jacobs was quite clear that this measure, even if potentially justifiable, would fail the proportionality test: it would have been possible for Germany to have pursued the legitimate objective through a less trade-restrictive means.[61] The Court thus permitted environmental protection to be used to partition the market. The failure to consider the proportionality of the measure gave rise to an unpredictable result. In so doing, the Court effectively prioritised environmental protection, suggesting a hierarchical approach to the relationship between environmental protection and market integration.

This is problematic: it is inconsistent with both the application of proportionality in the development of EU environmental policy itself[62] and with the proportionality-based balancing approach which was applied regarding fundamental rights and free movement in *Commission v Germany*. It is, furthermore, inconsistent with understanding of the relationship between environmental and economic interests within the conceptual framework of sustainable development.[63]

The Court's approach in *PreussenElektra* is also in sharp contrast to its approach to the enforcement of environmental interests outside the context of the internal market rules and it is to this issue, concerning the enforcement of non-economic interests as free-standing objectives, that attention now turns. Given the relatively recent recognition of a positive obligation in respect of human rights, it is unsurprising that the majority of the case law on this question has emerged in respect of environmental protection.

II. HUMAN RIGHTS AND ENVIRONMENTAL PROTECTION AS FREE-STANDING OBJECTIVES?

Up to now, the focus of this chapter has been upon the protection of non-economic interests in the specific context of the internal market, in particular, upon the relationship between national regulatory measures and the fundamental freedoms. It has been seen that in this context the Court has

---

[61] For example, a certificate of origin scheme would have allowed Germany to support the use of any renewable energy, regardless of its state of origin, not just German-sourced renewable energy thereby constituting a less trade restrictive means.

[62] See discussion of renewable energy and the Wild Birds Directive in ch 2.

[63] See ch 2.

been quite willing to recognise and give effect to the non-economic interests, including as exceptions to the fundamental freedoms. Attention now turns, however, to the extent to which the rights emerging from non-economic interests may be enforced directly against acts of the EU institutions.

A. Remedies and Case Law

i. The System of Remedies

Examination of the application and enforcement of environmental protection reveals some interesting issues. The TFEU provides for a number of remedies for breach of EU law by both the Member States and the institutions. Each of these remedies should, in principle, be available. However, there seems *in practice* to be limited access to the Court in this context. The majority of cases concerning the environment, including the *Danish Bottles* and *Belgian Waste* cases, were brought by the Commission against Member States under the enforcement action procedure.[64] The Member State enforcement action procedure[65] has, as in other contexts, been little used. Cases have arisen under the preliminary reference procedure,[66] but again these have been infrequent, although it is worth acknowledging that both *Danish Bees*[67] and *PreussenElektra*[68] reached the Court of Justice through this means. However, the Court held in *TWD* that the preliminary ruling procedure would not be available where a party would have had standing to bring a direct action for judicial review.[69] This leads us directly to the question of the availability of judicial review in respect of environmental interests. Judicial review of EU measures is governed by Article 263 TFEU. This raises two issues: the first concerning grounds of review, while the second concerns standing. As noted above, these issues have manifested themselves particularly problematically with regard to environmental protection, but this is evidently bound up with the enjoyment of the right to an effective remedy provided by Article 47 of the Charter.

---

[64] Article 169 EC (now 258 TFEU) Enforcement action for breach of EU law brought against a Member State by the Commission.

[65] Article 170 EC (now 259 TFEU) Enforcement action for breach of EU law brought by one Member State against another.

[66] This is the procedure by which a national court can request a ruling from the Court of Justice on the interpretation or validity of an EU measure; Article 177 EC (now 267 TFEU).

[67] *Ditlev Bluhme* (n 53).

[68] *PreussenElektra* (n 57).

[69] Case C-188/92 *TWD Textilwerke Deggendorf GmbH v Germany* [1994] ECR I-833.

ii. Environmental Protection: A Ground of Review?

Turning first to the question of the grounds of review: given the status of environmental protection as an EU objective, can an EU measure be reviewed for failure to consider environmental interest? The Court has made it clear in *Bettati* that:

> In view of the need to strike a balance between certain of the objectives and principles mentioned in Article 130r [now 191 TFEU] and of the complexity of the implementation of those criteria, review by the Court must necessarily be limited to the question whether the Council, by adopting the Regulation, committed a manifest error of appraisal regarding the conditions for the application of Articles 130r of the Treaty.

This suggests therefore, as observed by Jans and Vedder, that it would only be in a wholly exceptional case that failure to consider environmental objectives would constitute grounds for a measure being declared invalid.[70]

iii. Non-economic Interests and the Test for Standing

Despite having been used by Member States to challenge the basis of EC and EURATOM environmental legislation,[71] the provisions for judicial review under Article 263 TFEU have, like many of the other remedies, had relatively little impact upon EU conduct in relation to substantive environmental law.[72] Although the European Parliament has used it to protect its prerogatives in relation to environmental legislation,[73] it has rarely been used by a natural or legal person. Where such judicial review has been sought, it has failed, due to the failure of the applicants to establish standing, as in the *Greenpeace* case.[74] Many factors affect standing in relation to public interest representation in the EU. As Harlow observed, these are rooted in the Treaty itself.[75]

In 1992 Harlow was justified in concluding that the Court was being increasingly pushed towards adopting a liberal/activist stance, giving effect to the spirit of the law over the written text.[76] The Court was particularly

---

[70] Jan Jans and Hans Vedder, *European Environmental Law: After Lisbon* (4th edn, Groningen, Europa Law Publishing, 2012) 26.

[71] See, inter alia, Case C-62/88 *Greece v Council* [1990] ECR 1527.

[72] It is perhaps significant that the Communication on implementing Community Environmental law relates to Member States', not Community action.

[73] See Joined Cases C-164/97 and C-165/97 *Parliament v Council* [1999] ECR I-1139.

[74] This is discussed below.

[75] C Harlow, 'Towards a Theory of Access for the European Court of Justice' (1992) 12 *Yearbook of European Law* 213; L Kramer, *Focus on Environmental Law* (London, Sweet and Maxwell, 1992) at 229 et seq and 290 et seq; and A Ward, 'The Right to an effective remedy in EC law and environmental protection: A case study of UK Judicial Decisions' (1993) *JEnvL* 221–44.

[76] See below.

activist about the rights of Parliament and eventually the Treaty was amended to reflect the work of the Court in this respect: Parliament was accorded semi-privileged status (standing to protect its prerogatives) in the TEU. [77] There was recognition, however, that this did not go far enough. Full privileged status (standing to challenge any reviewable act of the EU institutions) was subsequently conferred under the Lisbon Treaty (Article 263(2) TFEU). This should facilitate a more effective protection of universal interests, such as human rights or environmental protection by Parliament.

As regards non-privileged applicants, however, the position was, and remains, rather bleaker, diverging even from the Member State norm, where at least established interest groups generally have standing. The standing of natural and legal persons is governed by Article 263(4) TFEU (formerly Article 230(4) EC). Article 230(4) provided that a natural and legal person could challenge a legal act addressed to them or in which they have direct and individual concern. Much has been written about the Court's interpretation of 'direct and individual concern', but it is not intended to rehearse that here. The key issue is that the Court's interpretation of 'individual concern' requires that a person be a member of a closed class of individuals, which is identifiable as being affected by a measure at the time of its adoption.[78] The narrowness of this test has proved controversial in all contexts. It appears particularly inappropriate, however, in respect of measures affecting interests such as environmental protection, which may be deemed to be of universal interest. This was clearly demonstrated by the *Greenpeace* case.[79]

iv. Greenpeace

In the case law examined thus far, environmental protection arose as a consequence of its impact upon the market, in particular its relationship with the requirement of the free movement of goods.[80] Similarly, the interpretation of Article 230(4) EC was undertaken predominantly in respect of instances in which individuals sought to ensure or enforce economic rights or interests. In *Greenpeace*, on the other hand, the Court had the chance to explore the appropriateness of applying criteria which had emerged specifically in respect of economic interests to a situation in which a universal, non-economic interest was engaged.

---

[77] Following Case 294/83 *Parti Ecologiste les Verts v European Parliament* [1986] ECR I-1368.
[78] Case 25/62 *Plaumann & Co v Commission* [1963] ECR 95.
[79] Case C-321/95P *Greenpeace and Others v Commission* [1998] ECR I-1651.
[80] Environmental policy per se emerged as a consequence of the impact of environmental protection upon the market. See ch 2.

Greenpeace concerned a Commission decision to grant funding to the construction of two power stations. This was challenged on the basis that no environmental impact assessment had been carried out and therefore the construction of the power stations breached EC (and national) environmental law. Consequently, it was argued, the Commission decision was unlawful and should be annulled. The CFI held that the action was inadmissible on the grounds that the applicants had no standing.

On appeal, the applicants argued that as environmental interests are intrinsically common and shared, the rights relating to these interests are liable to be held by a potentially large number of individuals, who would never give rise to the kind of closed class necessary to satisfy the criteria arising from the earlier case law. Since the privileged parties (EU institutions, not then including Parliament, and the Member States) were unlikely to challenge such an act, there was an effective legal vacuum.

On the question of standing, as noted above, there were two requirements, both of which had to be satisfied for a natural or legal person to have standing: they were required to have both 'direct' and 'individual' concern. On the question of 'direct' concern, the Court of Justice ruled that it was the construction of the power stations which affected the environmental interests and that the decision to fund the construction did not itself directly affect the environment.[81] Consequently, it held that there was no direct concern in the contested decision. Having reached that conclusion, the Court did not need to address the argument concerning individual concern and universal interests.[82] AG Cosmas had concluded that it would be neither impossible nor inappropriate to ease the requirements of standing in certain circumstances. This was rejected by the Court. However, this argument subsequently found considerable support: both AG Jacobs in *UPA*[83] and the then CFI in *Jégo-Quéré*[84] supported this position, the CFI suggesting that a person should have individual concern in a measure which affects their legal position.[85] (Under this test, the local residents might have had standing, but Greenpeace probably would not.)

In any event, while it is conceivable that such an interpretation could have recognised the individual concern of local residents, as a consequence of the direct impact of the power stations upon them, and may also have

---

[81] *Greenpeace* (n 79) [30]–[31].

[82] See, inter alia, *Plaumann* (n 78).

[83] Case C-50/00 P *Union de Pequenos Agricoltores v Council* [2002] ECR I-6677.

[84] Case T-177/01 *Jégo-Quéré & Cie SA v Commission* [2002] ECR II-2365.

[85] Jacobs proposed that the test of individual concern for an applicant should be whether 'by reason of his particular circumstances, the measure has, or is liable to have, a substantial adverse effect upon his interests' Opinion of Advocate General Jacobs (n 83). De Witte similarly advocated an 'adversely affected' test, framed in such a way as to include associations and public interest groups. B de Witte, 'The Past and Future Role of the European Court of Justice in the Protection of Human Rights' in P Alston (ed), *The EU and Human Rights* (Oxford, New York, Oxford University Press, 1999).

extended to give Greenpeace individual concern by virtue of its particular interest in environmental protection, it would not have addressed the problem of the lack of direct concern in the Commission decision. It is notable that with regard to direct concern in the context of economic interests, the ECJ adopted a rather more pragmatic approach in *Glencore* when it looked behind the contested decision at its subsidiary effects. A similar pragmatic approach could have been adopted in *Greenpeace*, but was not. This difference in approach is the more significant as both cases were decided at the same time.[86]

The approach of the Court in *Greenpeace* and *Danish Bees* will encourage strategic use of Article 267 TFEU[87] to challenge measures affecting non-economic interests. As the Court pointed out in *Greenpeace*,[88] alternative remedies were available to challenge the construction of the power stations and thus protect the environmental interests via national courts.[89] Jacobs argued in *UPA*, however, that the alternative remedies cannot always ensure effective judicial protection.[90] The Court held that it would require treaty amendment to change the test of individual concern.[91] In any case, the Court highlighted that:

> [T]he Treaty has established a complete system of legal remedies and procedures designed to ensure judicial review of the legality of acts of the institutions ... under that system, where natural or legal persons cannot, by reason of conditions of admissibility laid down in the fourth paragraph of Article 173 of the Treaty, directly challenge Community measures of general application, they are able, depending on the case, either directly or indirectly to plead the invalidity of such acts before the Community courts under Article 184 of the Treaty or to do so before the national courts and ask them, since they have no jurisdiction themselves to declare those measures invalid ... to make a reference to the Court of Justice for a preliminary ruling on validity.[92]

However, this position is ultimately unsatisfactory: the test for individual concern is a test of the Court's construction; the Court could have varied the test with regard to universal interests, as suggested by the Advocates-General. Yet, it chose not to: the invitation to revisit the test was firmly rejected by the Court in *UPA*. It may be that this reflected the political

---

[86] Cases C-403 and 404/96 P *Glencore Grain Ltd v Commission*, judgment of 5 May 1998.

[87] Article 267 provides for the preliminary ruling procedure. This provides for a national court to request a ruling from the Court of Justice on the meaning or validity of a measure of EU law in instances in which such clarification is necessary for the national court to make a ruling in the case before it.

[88] *Greenpeace* (n 79) [32]–[34].

[89] Although the Commission decision itself could not be challenged. Following the ruling of the Court in *TWD* (n 69), however, relating to the availability of the preliminary ruling procedure, the applicant has a difficult decision to make as to how to proceed.

[90] *UPA* (n 83) [38]–[49].

[91] *UPA* (n 83). See further ch 2.

[92] *UPA* (n 83) [40].

sensitivity regarding the status to be afforded the protection of rights, including the right to effective judicial protection contained in Article 47 of the Charter, particularly in the light of the fact that the Member States had so recently declared the Charter not to be binding.[93] The pragmatic question is whether, in view of the possibility to bring an alternative action before the national courts, *environmental interests* remain unprotected. In *Greenpeace*, the answer to this question would be no. However, this would not satisfy the dictum of the Court itself in *Les Verts* that 'a direct action [should be] available against all measures adopted by the institutions which are intended to have legal effects'. [94] As noted above, while the focus of this part has been upon environmental interests, the problem regarding the inappropriateness of the traditional test for standing as regards universal interests extends to other universal interests.

v. The Lisbon Treaty Amendment to the Test for Standing of Natural and Legal Persons

The test of standing of natural and legal persons was amended by the Lisbon Treaty, which now provides, in Article 263(4) TFEU, that a natural or legal person may challenge an 'act addressed to that person, or which is of direct and individual concern to them and against a regulatory act which is of direct concern to them and which does not entail implementing measures'. Thus, the test for standing is relaxed in respect of 'regulatory' acts. The key question raised by this amendment was what is a 'regulatory act'? This is not defined by the Treaty. Hartley argued that since the objective of the amendment to the requirements of standing in the Treaty of Lisbon was to remove the lacuna in judicial protection identified in *UPA*, it would be appropriate to adopt a broad definition of 'regulatory acts':

> [U]nder which regulatory acts were any acts of general application—that is, acts laying down general rules rather than deciding particular cases. This more radical suggestion would give non-privileged applicants greater access to the Court, though they would still have to establish direct concern.[95]

a. The Definition of 'Regulatory Act': *Inuit Tapariit Kanatami*
The question of the proper interpretation of 'regulatory acts' came before the General Court in *Inuit Tapariit Kanatami* and was described by the President of the General Court as being 'of some legal complexity'.[96] In this

---

[93] This position has of course changed following the Lisbon Treaty.

[94] *Greenpeace* (n 79).

[95] T Hartley, *Foundations of European Union Law* (7th edn, Oxford, Oxford University Press, 2010) 387.

[96] Case T-18/10 R *Inuit Tapiriit Kanatami v European Parliament and Council*, Order of 30 April 2010 at [46]. *cf* Case T-16/04 *Arcelor v European Parliament and Council*, judgment

case the General Court held that the applicants could not contest the relevant Regulation, since a legislative act such as that in question did not come within the scope of a 'regulatory act'.[97] This was also the view of AG Kokott in her Opinion on the appeal of the General Court's ruling. Recognising that there was substantial support for a broad interpretation of 'regulatory acts' to include legislative acts, Kokott was very clear that this was misplaced. While acknowledging that the objective of the amendment of what was Article 230(4) EC was to increase individual legal protection, she argued that this should be read together with Article 19(1) TEU, which increases legal protection regarding EU law before the national courts.[98] With reference to the *travaux préparatoires* of the draft Constitution and the mandate of the IGC[99] negotiating the Lisbon Treaty, Kokott concluded that a clear distinction is intended between legislative and non-legislative acts, and that the term 'regulatory act' is intended to express this distinction.[100]

Kokott further argued that the very fact that 'individual concern' remains a condition for standing means that the Court's existing jurisprudence, notably *Plaumann*, should be retained.[101] In its ruling, the Grand Chamber of the Court of Justice dismissed the appeal, affirming the ruling of the General Court and the Opinion of AG Kokott.[102] The Court went on to discuss the relationship between Article 47 of the Charter and Article 263(4):

> [T]he conditions of admissibility laid down in the fourth paragraph of Article 263 TFEU must be interpreted in the light of the fundamental right to effective judicial protection, but such an interpretation cannot have the effect of setting aside the conditions expressly laid down in that Treaty.[103]

In so doing, the Court referred once more to *Jégo-Quéré* and *UPA*, and to the fact that it is the responsibility of the Member States to ensure a system of remedies, pursuant to fulfilment of their obligations under Article 19(1) TFEU and Article 47 of the Charter.[104]

Despite the Article 19 EU obligation upon Member States to ensure effective legal protection within the scope of EU law, the lack of availability

---

of 2 March 2010 at [123]. See further A Arnull, 'The Principle of Effective Judicial Protection in EU Law: An Unruly Horse?' (2011) 36(1) *European Law Review* 51; S Balthasar, 'Locus Standi Rules for Challenges to Regulatory Acts by Private Applicants: The New Article 263(4) TFEU' (2010) 35 *European Law Review* 542; R Barents, "The Court of Justice after the Treaty of Lisbon' (2010) 47 *CML Rev* 709, 724–26.

[97] *Inuit Tapiriit Kanatami* (n 96) [46], [56].

[98] Opinion of AG Kokott in Case C-583/11P *Inuit Tapariit Kanatami and Others v Parliament and Council*, Opinion of 17 January 2013 [33]–[35].

[99] Intergovernmental conference.

[100] *Inuit Tapariit Kanatami and Others* (n 98) [40]–[47].

[101] ibid [89].

[102] Case C-583/11P *Inuit Tapariit Kanatami and Others v Parliament and Council*, judgment of 3 October 2013 [58]–[59].

[103] ibid [98].

[104] ibid [99]–[100].

of direct challenge to EU acts adversely affecting universal interests is not ideal and it is by no means certain, therefore, that the limitations for which Article 230(4) EC was criticised have been adequately addressed by the Lisbon amendment contained in Article 263(4) TFEU.[105] This is unsatisfactory in itself, but is all the more so in the light of the EU's obligations under the Aarhus Convention.[106]

B. Access to Justice: The Aarhus Convention

The Aarhus Convention is a UN Convention to which the EU and most of its Member States are signatories and 'represents the most comprehensive and ambitious effort to establish international legal standards in the field of individual environmental rights to date'.[107] The EU has long recognised that it may not satisfy its international obligations in relation to access to justice, which is particularly evident in respect of environmental protection in the light of the Aarhus Convention.[108] A particular criticism concerns the insufficiently broad range of circumstances in which access is provided.[109] Article 9(3) of the Aarhus Convention provides that:

> [E]ach Party shall ensure that, where they meet the criteria, if any, laid down in its national law, members of the public have access to administrative or judicial procedures to challenge acts and omissions by private persons and public authorities which contravene provisions of its national law relating to the environment.

The granting of adequate access, however, has not proved straightforward. Clearly the test in Article 263(4) is central to determining whether individuals will be granted access to the Court. The Court of Justice recently addressed the question of the status and effect of Article 9(3) of the Aarhus Convention under EU law with reference to the rights of standing of environmental organisations, holding that:

> Article 9(3) of the Aarhus Convention does not have direct effect in EU law. It is, however, for the referring court to interpret, to the fullest extent possible, the

---

[105] Particular problems relating to the impact of the narrow interpretation of 'direct and individual concern' in the context of universal interests (such as environmental protection and human rights) will be discussed below.

[106] Convention on Access to Information, Public Participation in Decision Making and Access to Justice on Environmental Matters. The EU ratified the Convention in 2005. See www.unece.org/env/pp/ratification.htm.

[107] M Pallemaerts 'Introduction' in M Pallemaerts (ed), The Aarhus Convention at Ten: Interactions and Tensions between Conventional International Law and EU Environmental Law (Groningen, Europa, 2011) at p 3.

[108] See Proposal for a Directive of the European Parliament and of the Council on access to justice in environmental matters /* COM/2003/0624 final - COD 2003/0246, available at: http://eur-lex.europa.eu/legal-content/EN/TXT/?uri=CELEX:52003PC0624.

[109] ibid. l.

procedural rules relating to the conditions to be met in order to bring administrative or judicial proceedings in accordance with the objectives of Article 9(3) of that convention and the objective of effective judicial protection of the rights conferred by EU law, in order to enable an environmental protection organisation ... to challenge before a court a decision taken following administrative proceedings liable to be contrary to EU environmental law.[110]

Pallemaerts suggests that the reliance of the Court in this ruling upon consistent interpretation, taken together with Article 216(2) TFEU, which provides that international agreements concluded by the EU are 'binding upon the institutions of the Union', could lead to it developing a different test for individual concern regarding environmental interests under Article 263(4); indeed, he argues that under international law, it would be obliged to do so.[111] Yet, as he observes, given the Court's refusal to entertain such a different approach in *Greenpeace* and its consistency of approach thereafter, this seems unlikely. This pessimism appears justified by the position of the General Court and AG Kokott's opinion in *Inuit Tapariit Kanatami*.

The concern expressed by some commentators with regard to the conditions for standing of natural and legal persons was shared by the Aarhus Compliance Committee, which ruled in 2011 that the Court's traditional jurisprudence on individual concern 'is too strict to meet the criteria of the Convention'[112] and, furthermore, 'if [the] jurisprudence of the EU Courts on access to justice were to continue, unless fully compensated for by adequate administrative review procedures, the Party concerned would fail to comply with article 9, paragraph 3, of the Convention'.[113] While the Committee clearly allows for compliance through adequate administrative review, Jans and Vedder have observed that for a Union based upon the rule of law, this is inadequate.[114] It is more encouraging to note that the

---

[110] Case C-240/09 *Lesoochranárske zoskupenie VLK v Ministerstvo životného prostredia Slovenskej republiky* [2011] ECR I-1255.

[111] Marc Pallemaerts, 'Access to Environmental Justice at EU Level: Has the Aarhus Regulation Improved the Situation?' in Marc Pallemaerts (ed) *The Aarhus Convention at Ten: Interactions and Tensions between Conventional International Law and EU Environmental Law* (Groningen, Europa Law Publishing, 2011) 311–12.

[112] UN Economic and Social Council Economic Commission for Europe, Meeting of the Parties to the Convention on Access to Information, Public Participation in Decision-making and Access to Justice in Environmental Matters Compliance Committee, 32nd Meeting, April 2011, Report of the Compliance Committee Findings and recommendations with regard to communication ACCC/C/2008/32 (Part I) concerning compliance by the European Union, adopted 14 April 2011, ECE/MP.PP/C.1/2011/4/Add.1 att para 87, http://www.unece.org/fileadmin/DAM/env/pp/compliance/CC-32/ece.mp.pp.c.1.2011.4.add.1_as_submitted.pdf.

[113] ibid para 88.

[114] Jans and Vedder (n 70) 250. See further David Hart, 'When the EU Implements Aarhus against itself, oh, How Minimally it Does it, UK Human Rights Blog, 3 July 2012. http://ukhumanrightsblog.com/2012/07/03/when-the-eu-implements-aarhus-against-itself-oh-how-minimally-it-does-it. See also Order of General Court of 14 June 2012 Case T-338/08 *Stichting Natuur en Milieu & Pesticide Action Network Europe v Commission nyr*; David Hart, 'What Have the Inuit Got to Do with Keeping EU Law in Check?', UK Human Rights Blog, 20

General Court has recently[115] considered the validity of Article 10(1) of the EC Regulation implementing the Aarhus Convention.[116] This provision provides for a right of NGOs to request internal review of an administrative act of individual scope (although individuals do not have a right to seek review). It was argued by the NGOs and accepted by the Court that the limitation of availability of internal review to administrative acts of individual scope contravenes Article 9(3) of the Aarhus Convention, which it was intended to implement.[117] Crucially, however, this is only relevant to acts adopted by the institutions acting in an administrative capacity. Legislative acts are excluded from Article 9(3). What this ruling does do, however, is ensure that where it is acting in an administrative capacity, an institution will at least have to provide reasons for the act. This is a positive step, albeit a small one.[118]

It should also be recognised as positive that the Court of Justice has consistently proved its willingness to facilitate the pursuit of environmental protection in the context of free movement of goods.[119] This reflects, as in *PreussenElektra*,[120] the development of a growing consensus in relation to the importance of environmental protection as an objective of the EU.[121] Yet, despite the undoubted progress which has been made with regard to the protection of non-economic interests in the EU legal order, there remains a significant lacuna with regard to the extent to which non-economic rights and interests may be enjoyed or enforced, particularly outside the context of the internal market. This reflects a failure of policy by the EU to provide adequate means to guarantee the enforcement and enjoyment of these rights or interests by individuals and relevant interest groups, notwithstanding that the approach of the Court in *Commission v Germany*[122] (moving away from *Viking* and *Laval*[123] to align more closely with its approach in *Schmidberger*)[124] would appear to support the emerging equality of status between the EU's economic and non-economic objectives. This is itself supported by the fact that the Charter of Fundamental Rights now has the same legal status as the Treaties themselves.

June 2012 http://ukhumanrightsblog.com/2012/06/20/what-have-the-inuits-got-to-do-with-keeping-eu-law-in-check/#more-14365.

[115] Case T-338/08 *Stichting Natuur en Milieu and Pesticide Action Network Europe v Commission*, Order of the General Court, 14 June 2012 (nyr).

[116] Regulation (EC) No 1367/2006 of the European Parliament and of the Council of 6 September 2006 on the application of the Aarhus Convention on Access to Environmental Information, Public Participation in Decision-Making and Access to Justice in Environmental Matters to Community Institutions and Bodies [2006] OJ L264/13.

[117] *Stichting Natuur* (n 115) [76].

[118] See further Pallemaerts (n 111).

[119] See *PreussenElektra* (n 57); *Commission v Denmark* (n 52); *Commission v Belgium* (n 56).

[120] *PreussenElektra* (n 57).

[121] See ch 2 for discussion of the emergence and growing significance of environmental protection.

[122] *Commission v Germany* (n 41).

[123] *Viking* and *Laval* (n 34).

[124] *Schmidberger* (n 19).

III. CONCLUSIONS: THE SIGNIFICANCE OF SUSTAINABLE
DEVELOPMENT AND PROPORTIONALITY IN BALANCING
THE EU'S ECONOMIC AND NON-ECONOMIC INTERESTS

A. Balancing Interests: The Need for Proportionality

It is evident from the preceding analysis that the relationship between the
diverse economic and non-economic objectives of the EU is complex and
varies according to the circumstances at issue on each occasion that they
interact. Despite the approach of the Court in *PreussenElektra*, it cannot
be suggested that there is a hierarchy at the summit of which sits environmental protection. Nor do fundamental human rights take priority. Yet
economic interests do not take automatic precedence either. The case law
relating to both human rights and environmental protection in their relation with economic interests is clear: these interests are not absolute and
must be weighed against one another. The application of the proportionality test provides a means by which particular instances of conflict may be
resolved.[125] This is consistent with the approach adopted earlier relating
to the Common Agricultural Policy:[126] in that context too, the Court was
explicit that where a conflict between competing objectives arises, the
institutions must not give effect to one to the exclusion of the pursuit of
the other,[127] although it may give temporary priority to one, where necessary, in light of specific circumstances.[128] Such a balancing approach to
resolving 'conflicting' interests is consistent with the EU's commitment to
'sustainable development'. The problems which can arise where such an
approach is not followed are among those which can be seen in the case
of *PreussenElektra*,[129] thus, for example, that the prioritisation of environmental protection without regard to proportionality unnecessarily permitted the partitioning of the internal market along national boundaries.

B. The Emergence of the Two-Way Application
of the Proportionality Test

It has been seen that it is with respect to the *enjoyment* of non-economic rights
and interests in the EU that the differences in their form and substance become

---

[125] See *Commission v Germany* (n 41).
[126] Cases 80 and 81/77 *Ramel* [1978] ECR 927. The Court held that 'the objectives of free
movement and of the common agricultural policy should not be set against the other nor in
order of precedence, but on the contrary combined'.
[127] Case 197/80 *Ludwigshafener Walzmuhle Erling KG v Community* [1981] ECR 3211
[41].
[128] Case 203/86 *Spain v Council* [1988] ECR 4563 [10]; Case 29/77 *Roquette Freres v
France* [1977] ECR 1835.
[129] *PreussenElektra* (n 57). See Poli (n 60).

significant. It ought to be acknowledged that the nature of economic rights, such as the relatively clear evaluation that is possible of both their value and the impact of any breach, is such that they are perhaps more suited to implementation through law than non-economic interests are.[130] The approach taken to the protection of human rights was relatively straightforward: the Court of Justice played a crucial role in establishing the EU's role in ensuring the observance, within the Member States, of existing fundamental human rights standards. It was seen in chapter two that until the adoption of the Charter, there was no development of an autonomous set of EU (or EC) human rights standards and there was no general objective to develop such standards per se for the EU.[131] Consistent with this, the Court ruled in *Opinion 2/94*[132] that there was no general power for the Community in the field of human rights. Consequently, there could be no question of contradictory Community objectives. The adoption of the Charter complicated this analysis, for it is an autonomous EU 'human rights' document. Although formally it was originally proclaimed to be merely declaratory of existing rights, in fact, as seen above, not all of its rights are indeed derived from other sources. As also noted, however, this position changed under the Lisbon Treaty, following which the Charter has the same legal status as the Treaties. [133]

Originally the human rights questions which arose concerned the occasions on which measures within the scope of EC law may have the subsidiary effect of preventing the enjoyment of human rights, or in which the enjoyment of fundamental human rights encroached upon, and prevented, the enjoyment of EC fundamental rights—for example, the right to protest may interfere with the free movement of goods.[134] Following amendment to the Treaty, particularly that in Lisbon, there is a real possibility of directly conflicting objectives. The question that arises is how such issues have been and should be addressed by the Court. The traditional approach of the Court was to deal with such interference by balancing the free movement of goods with the public policy/public security mandatory requirement rather than in terms of fundamental rights. Where a breach of human rights occurred, but did not engage an issue of Community law per se, the Court was explicit that this was outwith its jurisdiction.[135]

This history and development of approach contrasts sharply with the development of environmental protection, which was much earlier

---

[130] See further discussion in respect of cost-benefit analysis in ch 1.

[131] But note the adoption of the Race and Equal Treatment Directives, and of the Charter of Fundamental Rights, discussed in ch 2.

[132] *Opinion 2/94 Re the Accession of the Community to the European Human Rights Convention* [1996] ECR I-1759.

[133] See ch 2.

[134] See *R v Chief Constable of Sussex ex parte International Traders' Ferry* [1999] 2 AC 418; Case C-263/95 *Commission v France* [1997] ECR I-6959.

[135] Case C-299/95 *Kremzow v Austria* [1997] ECR I-2629.

recognised as an EC objective.[136] That early recognition raised the possibility of environmental protection coming into conflict with the EU's original market objectives and led, as has been seen, to the recognition by the Court that environmental protection could justify a restriction on the enjoyment of free movement of goods. However, such justification was, until *PreussenElektra*,[137] subject to the environmental measure's satisfaction of the proportionality test.

This is the approach which was also eventually adopted in *Schmidberger*[138] when the exercise of human rights caused a restriction on free movement of goods. However, there is one key difference in approach: as has been seen, the Court required that not only that the exercise of human rights but also the enjoyment of the EU fundamental freedom of movement of goods be tested for its proportionality. This two-way balancing process can be characterised as an operationalisation of the commitment to sustainable development. The *Schmidberger* case thus indicated a shift in the status of fundamental rights in terms of their relationship with the EU's economic objectives. Although the Court in *Viking* and *Laval* appeared to move away from the *Schmidberger* two-way balancing approach, it has subsequently reverted to this in *Commission v Germany*.[139]

While *PreussenElektra* appears to clearly prioritise the non-economic interest of environmental protection, the failure to consider the proportionality of the measure led to an unpredictable and unbalanced approach. In contrast, the two-way balancing approach of *Schmidberger* secures consideration of both interests in play and leads to a more predictable result, and one which fully reflects the diverse objectives of the EU. That the *Schmidberger* approach is endorsed in *Commission v Germany* suggests that it is here to remain.

The criticism could be made that the reliance upon proportionality is subjective and unpredictable. However, as discussed above, the 'proportionality' test applied by the Court is one that is generally focused upon the objective elements of appropriateness and necessity, couched in terms of the least restrictive means.

It is therefore argued that having identified and set itself objectives which can come into conflict, the Court of Justice has found a means through which to reconcile these, that is, through the application of the proportionality-based approach. This approach, adopted by the Court in its case law, is consistent with the Treaty provisions developing environmental protection and also in the EU's longer-term strategy documents. Moreover, the failure of the Court to apply the proportionality-based approach in

---

[136] *Procureur de la République* (n 51). See further ch 2.
[137] *PreussenElektra* (n 57).
[138] *Schmidberger* (n 19).
[139] *Commission v Germany* (n 41).

PreussenElektra led to a result which was unnecessarily at odds with the EU's objectives and has unnecessarily left the Court open to criticism.

C. The Two-Way Application of Proportionality as an Operationalisation of Sustainable Development

It has been shown in chapter two that the EU is committed to sustainable development and that the principle of sustainable development requires consideration of the economic, environmental and social (or human rights) impact of development. It is inherent in the principle of sustainable development that none of the three pillars takes absolute or automatic priority over the others. The process of weighing the competing objectives against each other at the heart of the proportionality-based approach can be characterised as an operationalisation of the principle of sustainable development. It is worth noting that this process, while explored in this context in terms of an economic-non-economic tension, could equally be applied to situations in which the non-economic pillars come into tension—for example, if environmental interests suggested that a change in social practice or way of life would be desirable.[140] Thus, in this respect, the commitment to sustainable development is a justiciable commitment.

D. Enforcement of Non-economic Interests Outside the Context of the Internal Market Rules

In sharp contrast to the willingness demonstrated by the Court to give effect to non-economic interests where they come into conflict with the internal market rules, the Court's approach to the question of standing to enforce non-economic rights and interests against acts of the EU institutions is disappointing. There can be little doubt that the lack of capacity to enforce non-economic rights and interests across the EU legal order is not satisfactory. This is underscored by the conclusions with regard to access to justice.

It has been shown in this chapter that the EU has progressively developed the protection offered to non-economic interests, particularly when set in opposition to economic interests in the EU legal order. However, it has also been shown that significant gaps remain as regards the enforceability of these interests as free-standing objectives. This raises questions for the EU with regard to its desire to push this agenda forward at the international level and it is to the EU's external actions that attention now turns

---

[140] Such a tension is manifested in the Kosterhavet National Park case study discussed in ch 2.

4

The EU's Relations with Third States

INTRODUCTION

THE PREVIOUS TWO chapters have considered the emergence and current status of non-economic interests within the EU legal order. To explore how the experience of the EU can shed further light on the balance between the protection of non-economic interests and economic liberalisation in the regulation of international trade, attention now turns to the EU's relations with third states. This is relevant because alongside the internal developments examined above, the EU has actively pursued both human rights and environmental protection in its external relations.

The very fact of the EU having relations with third states merits a pause for consideration: as an organisation which was created as an economic community, its capacity to enter into agreements with states is not to be taken for granted; that the content of such agreements is not limited to economic matters is more striking still; that there should be any question of the EU's approach to such matters having a wider influence is yet more significant. Essentially there are two perspectives regarding the external action of the EU, both of which are relevant to the present study: the first concerns what the EU is empowered to do, from an internal perspective, and the second concerns the potential influence of EU action, the extent to which it may be seen to be either setting an agenda in the international community or contributing to the development of a particular approach to the relationship between economic and non-economic interests. Reflecting these two underlying issues, the first two sections of his chapter will first explore the basis and the exercise of EU external competence. Attention will then turn, in the third section, to examining the EU's competence with regard to its newer objectives, focusing upon human rights and environmental protection. As will be seen, there has been considerable evolution in respect of all these issues since the Treaty of Rome, and the reasons for this will be considered. This will be followed by, in the fourth section, an assessment of the effect of international agreements concluded by the EU.

EU external action is a key element in the picture the EU builds up of itself as an international actor and is also crucial to understanding the culture which the EU might foster internationally with regard to the protection of non-economic interests. The legal basis of EU action is of fundamental significance: if there is a strong basis, this can provide a secure foundation for the development of an influential international stance. However, any instability in the basis of EU external action, or incoherence in its actions, may conceivably weaken the EU's international position. Consistency and coherence of action are also significant for 'good governance', which the EU itself has observed to be relevant to these developments, just as it has been identified as crucial in the internal context with regard to sustainable development.[1] Since the 1990s, the EU has systematically pursued the inclusion of clauses relating to human rights and environmental protection in its agreements with third states. Increasingly, it is also now including reference to sustainable development itself. This raises questions concerning the basis, and even the existence, of its power to do so. In the event that a basis is found, there are questions as to both the scope of that power and how it can be exercised: by the EU acting alone or with the Member States? It is with these questions that the first section of this chapter is concerned.

I. THE BASIS OF EXTERNAL COMPETENCE OF THE EU

The external competence of the EU has long been acknowledged as a complicated issue.[2] It clearly engages the complexity of the inter-relationship between the respective powers of the Member States, the EU acting supranationally (previously in its capacity as the EC) and the EU acting intergovernmentally (the EU as was).

A. Conferral: The Source of EU Powers

The EU's powers are rooted in the Treaty and are limited to those conferred within it.[3] In relation to any specific issue, it must be asked whether the Member States have in fact transferred any power to act to the EU, whether

---

[1] Discussed in ch 2.

[2] See P Eeckhout, *EU External Relations Law* (2nd edn, Oxford, Oxford University Press, 2012); P Koutrakos, *EU International Relations Law* (Oxford, Hart Publishing, 2006); S Dillon, *International Trade and Economic Law and the European Union* (Oxford, Hart Publishing, 2002); A Dashwood and C Hillion (eds), *The General Law of EC External Relations* (London, Sweet & Maxwell, 2000); D O'Keefe, 'Community and Member State Competence in External Relations Agreements of the EU' (1999) 4 *European Foreign Affairs Review* 7; M Cremona, 'External Relations and External Competence: The Emergence of an Integrated Policy' in P Craig and G De Búrca (eds), *The Evolution of EU Law* (Oxford, Oxford University Press, 1999); I Macleod, D Hendry and S Hyett, *The External Relations of the European Communities* (Oxford, Oxford University Press, 1996).

[3] Article 5 EU (ex Article 5 EC).

they have retained any power and, if so, how the respective powers can be exercised. Will it be a matter for joint action or may one party act alone? In addition, it should be asked whether the issue is a matter for inter-governmental cooperation, to be dealt with under the Common Foreign and Security Policy (CFSP), rather than through action by either the Member States and/or the EU acting supranationally (as it had previously through the EC)? The Lisbon Treaty has provided some much-needed clarity on these issues, but questions still remain. The Treaty also, through the principles of subsidiarity and proportionality, imposes limits on the exercise of the competence conferred.[4] The application of these principles indicates a rejection of the 'maximalist' approach to EU competence.[5] The requirement of proportionality in this context means that where the EU is competent to act, its actions must be the least possible to achieve the desired objective.[6] In addition, the achievement of the objective must be balanced against the restrictive effects of the measure on other interests. Where these are excessive, consideration must be given to importance of the aim and whether it merits such effects.[7]

B. The Position under the TEU

i. *The EC: The First Pillar of the EU*

Under the TEU, the EC was the first of the three pillars which together formed the EU. The second pillar was that of the CFSP, and the third pillar concerned Police and Judicial Cooperation on Criminal Matters (formerly Justice and Home Affairs).[8]

Article 281 EC conferred legal personality upon the EC, fully empowering it to enter into legal obligations on behalf of its Member States. Consistent with the doctrine of conferred competence, this power only extended as far as the Member States granted it. As a consequence, any EC action, including in respect of its external relations, had to be based upon a provision of the Treaty, which might either confer express competence to act externally[9] or give rise to 'implied' external competence.[10] Transfer of competence to the EC had to be from the Member States, who would otherwise be the

---

[4] ibid.

[5] See, for example, Case C-376/98 *Germany v Parliament and Council* [2000] ECR I-8419.

[6] See chs 1 and 2 above for further discussion of proportionality.

[7] See T Tridimas, *The General Principles of EU Law*, Oxford, Oxford University Press, 2006.

[8] The third pillar will not be discussed here as it is not of direct relevance.

[9] As in the example of the Common Commercial Policy (Title II TFEU). The EU's external competences will be discussed below.

[10] See below.

competent actors. Tridimas and Eeckhout identified two presumptions concerning the division of competencies between the EC and the Member States: first, that competence to act lies with the Member States and, second, that EC competence is concurrent rather than exclusive.[11] These presumptions meant that where the EC had competence to act internationally, the Member States were not prevented from acting in the same field unless the EC's competence was 'exclusive'.

ii. The CFSP: The Second Pillar of the EU

In contrast to the supranational characteristics of the first pillar (the EC), the second and third pillars of the EU were based upon inter-governmental cooperation. The Amsterdam inter-governmental conference provoked vigorous debate on whether the EU should be given legal personality. Ultimately this did not happen, although the Council was empowered to authorise the Presidency to conclude international agreements where necessary for the implementation of Title V of the Treaty (Provisions on a Common Foreign and Security Policy).[12] Article 2 TEU mandated the EU 'to assert its identity on the international scene, in particular through the implementation of a common foreign and security policy'. Article 3 provided that the consistency of the EU's external relations is to be ensured by the Council *and the Commission*, who 'shall ensure the implementation of these policies, *each in accordance with its respective powers*'. Although Article 18 TEU was explicit that 'the Commission shall be fully associated in [matters coming within the CFSP and the implementation of decisions made under the CFSP]', the distinction between the roles and responsibilities of the EC and the EU was clearly maintained in Articles 24 and 25: these referred to the Commission 'assisting the Council as appropriate' in the conclusion of international agreements in the pursuit of the CFSP, and the Council 'monitoring the implementation of agreed policies *without prejudice to the responsibility of the President and the Commission*'[13] respectively. The existence of the CFSP raised the question for the EU of whether external action should have been undertaken within its inter-governmental framework or by the EC.

---

[11] Until the EC acted in respect of concurrent powers, the Member States could continue to enter into obligations in the relevant field. The existence of concurrent powers did not require the Member States and the EC to act simultaneously—the Member States' competence would only be excluded when the EC had acted in such a manner as to exhaustively occupy the field. See T Tridimas and P Eeckhout, 'The External Competence of the Community and the Case Law of the Court of Justice: Principle versus Pragmatism' (1995) 14 *Yearbook of European Law* 143, 154.

[12] Article 24 TEU.

[13] Emphasis added.

iii. The Distinction between EC and EU Competences

The significance of the identification of whether the EC or the EU had competence, and the related establishment of the appropriate legal base, lay in the resultant procedure by which the competence would be exercised, as the decision-making procedure varied. This variation reflected the intentions of the Member States when they transferred power both as to the extent of transfer they were making and the manner by which action in the pursuit of the objectives could then be undertaken, and by whom.

In the action of the EU 'asserting its identity', it is clear that it was envisaged that the Member States would cooperate and 'uphold the common positions adopted as a result of such cooperation'.[14] Where the Member States chose not to cooperate or did not reach a consensus, the EU had no 'identity' as such to assert, and there would be no common policy to express. This contrasted sharply with the position of the Community, which could, as a legal person, act autonomously, albeit within restricted fields. Thus, although the overlap of responsibilities and relevant institutions (between the EC in respect of its external relations and the EU 'acting' in the pursuit of the CFSP) is readily apparent and recognised, it is unquestionable that each maintained its own sphere of competence. Therefore, the difference between the EC and the EU was not purely semantic. It resulted from, and reflected, the desire of the Member States to restrict the mandate of the EC, and indeed restrict the transfer of their sovereignty, while accepting the need to formalise cooperation in additional fields.[15]

C. The Post-Lisbon Position (2009–)

Under the Treaty of Lisbon, this relatively clear distinction between the EC and the EU has been collapsed; the three-pillar structure has been abolished and the 'Community' as such no longer exists. The Lisbon treaties comprise the TEU and the TFEU. This latter broadly replaces the former EC Treaty. Under Lisbon, the EU itself now has legal personality (Article 47 TEU). Article 5 TEU lays down the limits of EU competence, including that it continues to be governed by the principle of conferral and that the exercise of conferred powers continues to be governed by the principles of subsidiarity and proportionality.

In a new development, Title 1 of the TFEU sets out the categories and areas of EU competence. Article 2 TFEU defines 'exclusive' and 'shared'

---

[14] Article 19. Article 18 also mandated the Presidency to represent the EU and express the position of the EU in international fora.

[15] See further A Dashwood, 'External Relations Provisions of the Amsterdam Treaty' (1998) 35 *CML Rev* 1019.

competence and the substance of the exclusive and shared competences is now explicitly listed in Articles 3 and 4 TFEU respectively. Article 2(1) confirms that with regard to an exclusive competence, 'only the Union may legislate and adopt legally binding acts'. In contrast, under Article 2(2) with regard to shared competence:

> [T]he Union and the Member States may legislate and adopt legally binding acts in that area. The Member States shall exercise their competence to the extent that the Union has not exercised its competence. The Member States shall again exercise their competence to the extent that the Union has decided to cease exercising its competence.

The exclusive competences of the EU include, inter alia, the common commercial policy[16] and:

> [T]he conclusion of an international agreement when its conclusion is provided for in a legislative act of the Union or is necessary to enable the Union to exercise its internal competence, or in so far as its conclusion may affect common rules or alter their scope.[17]

This latter provision recognises the development of implied powers through the case law of the Court of Justice.

Title V TEU concerns general provisions on the EU's external action and specific provisions on the CFSP, thus replacing the old EU Title on CFSP (which was previously, as the second pillar, a matter for inter-governmental cooperation). Article 21(1) TEU states that EU international action is 'guided by the principles which have inspired its own creation, development and enlargement ... democracy, the rule of law, the universality and indivisibility of human rights and fundamental freedoms' and Article 21(2) sets out the objectives of the EU's external action. These include a range of objectives which clearly fall within the overarching objective of sustainable development.[18] It also includes the objective of encouraging 'the integration of all countries into the world economy, including through the progressive abolition of restrictions on international trade'. The objectives in Article 21(1) and 21(2) TEU immediately raise questions regarding the nature of their inter-relationship, demonstrating at a very basic level that the internal question examined in chapters two and three above, concerning the relationship

---

[16]   Article 3(1)(e) TFEU.

[17]   Article 3(2) TFEU.

[18]   Article 21(2): 'The Union shall define and pursue common policies and actions, and shall work for a high degree of cooperation in all fields of international relations, in order to: (a) safeguard its values ... (b) consolidate and support democracy, the rule of law, human rights and the principles of international law; ... (d) foster the sustainable economic, social and environmental development of developing countries, with the primary aim of eradicating poverty; (f) help international measures to preserve and improve the quality of the environment and the sustainable management of global natural resources in order to ensure sustainable development; (h) promote an international system based on stronger multilateral cooperation and good global governance.'

between trade and non-economic interests, extends into the EU's external action and thus into the global context.

II. THE EXERCISE OF EU COMPETENCE

It has been observed above that the doctrine of conferred powers[19] has raised a number of issues over the years. First, fundamentally, every EU act must have an identified legal base within the Treaty. Second, questions arose as to the scope of EC (now EU) competence. Third, questions arose concerning the nature of that competence—for example, was it exclusive? What was the effect of EC competence upon Member State competence? These questions are inevitably inter-related and the answers are illustrative of the tension and sensitivity of the relationship between EU and Member State power, and how this relationship has evolved over the last four decades.

For present purposes, questions arise concerning the nature of EU competency to pursue non-economic objectives in its relations with third states. This is important because a secure basis for such action contributes to the stability of action and policy. That the EU has chosen to pursue non-economic values in its relations with third states reflects two concerns: first, that it does not find itself in breach of its internal and international obligations and, second, its commitment to a holistic view of development, consistent with the principle of sustainable development.

A. Legal Base: Competency to Undertake External Action

As noted above, the doctrine of conferred powers means that it is essential to establish the legal base of any EC/EU Act. This is significant in two respects: first, identification of the legal base of an act confirms the legitimacy of an act in the field and second, the legal base sets out the decision-making process for action in pursuit of the particular policy. This also determines the actors involved. As seen above, post-Lisbon, the TFEU sets out the categories and areas of EU competence, including detailing the nature of that competence.[20] Furthermore, the TFEU also now includes exclusive competence regarding what previously were developed as the 'implied powers' of the EC.[21]

---

[19] That the EC (now EU) may only act in respect of matters for which the Member States have transferred competence to it.
[20] Title I, Articles 2–6 TFEU.
[21] Articles 3(2) TEU and 216 TFEU.

i. Express Powers

The express competences for external EC action were historically fairly limited: Common Commercial Policy;[22] Research and Technological Development;[23] Environmental Protection;[24] and Development Cooperation.[25] In addition, the EC also had the power to participate in international negotiations and enter into agreements relating to Monetary Union.[26] Finally, in what may be termed the 'catch-all' competence, Article 308 EC (now 352 TFEU) gave the EC a general power to take whatever measures were necessary to achieve the objectives of the EC and, under Article 310 EC (now 217 TFEU), the EC was empowered to conclude reciprocal international agreements (with states or international organisations) establishing an association. The competence of the EC with regard to Development Cooperation is worth highlighting. This competency, which was only explicitly provided with a legal base in the Maastricht Treaty,[27] extended to 'the general objective of developing and consolidating democracy and the rule of law, and to that of respecting human rights and fundamental freedoms'.[28] This was significant because this was for a long time the only context in which the EC had any competence to pursue an *objective* relating to human rights. This position has been changed by the Lisbon Treaty: as noted above, Article 21(2) EU imposes an obligation upon the EU to pursue the protection of human rights in its external relations.

ii. Implied Powers

The Court of Justice introduced the 'implied powers' of the EC in *AETR*[29] when it ruled that the EC's internal powers are reflected in its external powers: in parallel to any internal competence, the EC has an implicit competence to act externally in that field. This significantly expanded EC competence in its external relations. The Court held that until the EC acted in a particular field, the external competence was concurrent with the Member States' residual power. However, once the EC legislated in a field, the Member States can no longer act externally in a manner which affected the EC legislation.[30] Thus, when the EC acted internally in a given field, the residual power of the Member States in that field disappeared and

---

[22] Article 113, subsequently Article 133 EC, now Article 3 and Title II TFEU.
[23] Articles 170–81 EC, now Title IX, Article 179 TFEU.
[24] Title XIX, Article 174(1) EC, now Title XX, Article 191(4) TFEU.
[25] Article 181 EC, now Article 211 TFEU.
[26] Article 111 EC.
[27] Article 3 EC (Maastricht).
[28] Article 177(2) EC (Amsterdam).
[29] Case 22/70 *Commission v Council (Re AETR)* [1971] ECR 263.
[30] ibid [17].

the EC's competence was exclusive. In *Opinion 1/75*[31] the Court suggested that external competence did not require the pre-existence of secondary legislation and this was confirmed in *Opinion 1/76*,[32] when the Court ruled that the EC had external competence *without the enactment of internal measures* within the field where 'the participation of the Community in the international agreement is ... necessary for the attainment of one of the objectives of the Community'.[33]

This was entirely consistent with the operation of Article 308 EC (now 352 TFEU), as stated above. This is significant because in its expression of the doctrine of implied powers in *AETR*, the Court referred to fields *in which internal legislation had already been adopted*. Opinions 75 and 76, however, permitted the exercise externally by the EC of the power conferred by the Member States *but not yet acted upon internally*. This was not a contradiction, as the *AETR* statement clearly does not exclude the possibility of EC action without the adoption of internal legislation. The *AETR* judgment did, however, state that following internal legislation the EC's competence externally would be exclusive. *Opinion 1/78* clarified that where competence is shared, negotiation and conclusion of the Agreement must be undertaken jointly.[34] This is consistent with the judgment in *Kramer*.[35]

In *Opinion 2/91* the Court held that ILO Convention 170 fell within the scope of EC action, notwithstanding that in some respects its provisions went beyond existing EC legislation because independent action by the Member States could alter or affect the EC standards.[36] The fundamental question raised concerned the nature of EC competence: was it exclusive? This question was interesting because aside from the nature and state of internal legislation, there were 'external' considerations. First, the ILO Convention covered issues not covered in Association Agreements between the EC and certain of its overseas territories. The international relations of these territories, however, were the responsibility of the Member States and from that perspective, the Member States argued that they had to be involved. In addition, the EC, not being a member of the ILO, was not competent under international law to conclude the agreement. Ultimately, the Court ruled that the conclusion of the Convention was a matter of joint competence. O'Keefe observed that in this Opinion, the consideration of

---

[31] *Opinion 1/75 on the Understanding on a Local Cost Standard* [1975] ECR 1363.

[32] *Opinion 1/76 on the Draft Agreement Establishing a European Laying-up Fund for Inland Waterway Vessels* [1977] ECR 741.

[33] ibid [4].

[34] *Opinion 1/78 Re the Draft International Agreement on Natural Rubber* [1979] ECR 2871 [60].

[35] Joined Cases 3, 4 and 6/76 *Cornelis Kramer and Others* [1976] ECR 1279 [39]–[45].

[36] *Opinion 2/91 Re ILO Convention 170 on Chemicals at Work* [1993] ECR I-1061. In *Opinion 2/00 Re Biosafety Protocol* [2001] ECR I-9713, the Court effectively introduced a 'de minimis' element to this: where the effect would be minimal, there is no need for exclusive EC competence.

EC competence in view of internal legislation suggests that 'the possibility of exclusive Community competence will increase if Community internal legislation is extensive in a given area'.[37] This left open the question of whether the EC could act alone in the absence of internal legislation.

It was subsequently clarified in *Opinion 1/94*[38] that for the EC to acquire *exclusive* competence, prior internal legislation would be required *and* the attainment of the objective and the exercise of the internal power must be inextricably linked to each other, thus emphasising the significance of the requirement of necessity, which was confirmed by *Opinion 2/92*.[39]

Following the Lisbon Treaty, reflecting the conclusions of this case law, Article 216 TFEU now provides that:

> The Union may conclude an agreement with one or more third countries or international organisations where the Treaties so provide or where the conclusion of the Agreement is necessary in order to achieve, within the framework of the Union's policies, one of the objectives referred to in the Treaties, or is provided for in a legally binding Union act or is likely to affect common rules or alter their scope.

Article 3(2) TFEU provides that this power is exclusive. These provisions of the Lisbon Treaty, read together, both recognise the development of implied powers and unambiguously set out the exclusive nature of that power.

iii. The Scope of Conferred Competence: Common Commercial Policy—Opinion 1/94

As noted above, the express powers of the EC concerning external relations were fairly limited, therefore the scope of those powers had a significant impact upon when and how the EC could act. Under Article 133 (ex Article 113) EC, the EC was empowered to develop a Common Commercial Policy (CCP). This power lacked specificity, however, and consequently aroused vigorous debate as to its extent or scope. The scope of the CCP is significant not simply for its own sake, but also in view of its potential to be used as an instrument in the pursuit of the wider EU objectives.

In light of this, questions concerning the scope of the CCP remain significant and have had a significant impact upon subsequent expressions of the policy both in the Nice and Lisbon Treaties. This issue was addressed by

---

[37] O'Keefe (n 2) 15.

[38] *Opinion 1/94 Re the Uruguay Round Treaties* [1995] ECR I-5267; *Opinion 2/92 Re the OECD Third Revised Decision on National Treatment* [1995] ECR I-521.

[39] *Opinion 2/92* (n 38). For detailed discussion of the case law developing the doctrine of implied powers, see A Dashwood, 'Implied External Competence of the EC' in M Koskenniemi (ed), *International Law Aspects of the European Union* (The Hague, London, Kluwer, 1998); A Dashwood, 'The Attribution of External Relations Competence' in Dashwood and Hillion (n 2).

the Court at length in *Opinions 1/94* and *2/92*. The influence of the former upon the development of the CCP can be seen in subsequent amendments to the Treaties.[40] The question of the scope of the CCP also went to the question of whether the EC could act alone in its pursuit. This was one of the central questions before the Court in *Opinion 1/94*. Ultimately the question as to exclusive EC competence could only be answered by determining whether the entire content of the agreement[41] came within the scope of the CCP. The Court's approach was to start with whether the exclusive competence extended to each of the Agreements. This was criticised by Tridimas and Eeckhout, who argued that the question the Court should have answered 'was not whether the Community had exclusive competence on the basis of Article 113 or on the basis of its implied powers ... but whether the entire WTO Agreement comes within the competence of the Community, whether concurrent or exclusive'.[42]

If the entire agreement came within the scope of the EC's competence, then, Tridimas and Eeckhout argued, the EC could act alone. Joint participation would thus be *required* only where the international obligation at issue straddled matters of exclusively Member State and exclusively EC competence.[43] *Opinion 1/94* was further criticised on the grounds that the CCP should include all aspects of economic relations with third countries, including both trade in goods and related services.[44]

The Treaty of Amsterdam provided for the extension of the scope of the CCP regarding services and intellectual property[45] and thus to the areas excluded by the Court in *Opinion 1/94*. Such extension would permit a single approach to the 'framework of global trade', which had been advocated by Pescatore.[46] Under the Treaty of Nice, Article 133(5) EC provided for the 'negotiation and conclusion of agreements in the fields of trade in services and the commercial aspects of intellectual property.' This was, however, limited to some extent by Article 133(6), which maintained a derogation

---

[40] *Opinion 1/94* (n 38); *Opinion 2/92* (n 38).

[41] This includes all the WTO covered agreements—including the GATS, The Agreement on Trade-Related Aspects of Intellectual Property Rights (TRIPS), the Agreement on Technical Barriers to Trade (TBT) and the Agreement on the Application of Sanitary and Phytosanitary Measures (SPS).

[42] Tridimas and Eeckhout (n 11) 173–74.

[43] This question, concerning the exercise of concurrent powers, will be returned to in the context of development cooperation.

[44] N Emiliou 'The Allocation of Competence Between the EC and its Member States in the Sphere of External Relations' in N Emiliou and D O'Keefe (eds), *The European Union and the World Trade Law: after the GATT Uruguay Round* (Chichester, Wiley, 1996) 35. See also P Pescatore, 'Opinion 1/94 on "Conclusion" of the WTO Agreement: Is There an Escape from a Programmed Disaster?' (1999) 36 *CML Rev* 387, 391.

[45] Article 133(5) EC. For recent discussion of this issue, see: P Lamy, S Crossick and N Clegg 'Convention and Trade Policy, Reforming Article 133 to Strengthen the Union' European Policy Centre Dialogue, 6 February 2003.

[46] Pescatore (n 44).

from 133(5), whereby 'cultural and audiovisual services, educational services and social and human health services shall fall within the shared competence of the Community and the Member States'. *Opinion 1/08*[47] considered post-Nice questions of competence and legal basis relating to Article 133 EC. The key issue concerned the fact that while it was beyond doubt that the GATS Schedule of Commitments fell within the scope of the CCP, the agreement covered three different legal bases—Article 133(1), 133(5) and 133(6)—each of which gave rise to a different type of competence. Article 133(1) provided for exclusive EC competence, whereas Article 133(5) and 133(6) provided for two different sorts of shared competence. Thus, each gave rise to a different decision-making procedure. As Cremona observed: 'Arguments as to whether an agreement fell entirely within the CCP (with its competence and voting consequences) became arguments about the proper scope of, and relationship between, the difference paragraphs of Article 133.'[48] However, as noted above, the Lisbon Treaty should resolve this issue since it is now provided unequivocally that the CCP is a matter of exclusive EU competence, and this explicitly encompasses 'trade in services and the commercial aspects of intellectual property'.[49] On the other hand, Article 207(6) TFEU explicitly provides that: 'The exercise of competences conferred by this article in the field of the common commercial policy shall not affect the delimitation of competences between the Union and the Member States.'

iv. Article 2(2) TFEU: Member State Competence Subordinate to EU Competence?

While *Opinion 1/94* highlighted questions concerning the nature of EC competence, the Lisbon Treaty explicitly provides that with regard to shared competence, both the EU and the Member States may legislate in the given area and that:

> The Member States shall exercise their competence to the extent that the Union has not exercised its competence. The Member States shall again exercise their competence to the extent that the Union has decided to cease exercising its competence.[50]

This indicates quite clearly both that the Member States may act to the extent that the EU has not, and that the EU may also act alone. However,

---

[47] *Opinion 1/08 Re Agreements Amending the EC's Schedule of Commitments under the GATS* [2009] ECR I-11129.

[48] M Cremona, 'Balancing Union and Member State Interests: Opinion 1/2008, Choice of Legal Base and the Common Commercial Policy under the Treaty of Lisbon' (2010) 35 *European Law Review* 678.

[49] Article 207(1) TFEU.

[50] Article 2(2) TFEU.

it appears to make the Member States' competence subordinate to the EU competence.

In relation to development cooperation, it was previously explicit in Article 177 EC that EC policy shall be 'complementary to the policies pursued by the Member States'. Similarly post-Lisbon, 'the Union's development cooperation policy and that of the Member States complement and reinforce each other'.[51] This does not suggest a relationship of subordination. Indeed, it is further explicitly provided that:

> [I]n the areas of development cooperation and humanitarian aid, the Union shall have competence to carry out activities and conduct a common policy; however the exercise of that competence shall not result in the Member States being prevented from exercising theirs.[52]

This indicates that Member State competence with regard specifically to development cooperation is not in fact subordinate to EU competence. The fact that this is stated with regard to development cooperation suggests that development cooperation is a special case, reinforcing the different nature of the relationship between EU and Member State competence with regard to other areas of shared competence.

Turning to EU environmental policy, the objectives of this policy include 'promoting measures at international level to deal with regional or worldwide environmental problems, and in particular combating climate change'.[53] Article 191(4) TFEU provides that *'within their respective spheres of competence* the Union and the Member States shall cooperate with third countries and with the competent international organisations'. With regard to environmental policy, therefore, while the EU may cooperate with third states and international organisations, this is again without prejudice to the Member States' competence. Thus, it appears that the Member States have determinedly retained their own competence in these fields, despite the initial impression which might be suggested by Article 2(2) TFEU.

v. Complementary Competence

As observed by Cremona, the primary objectives of complementary policies may vary, but they must be consistent insofar as they may not be contradictory.[54] Complementarity is significant in that it suggests that while the EU is widening its objectives and the Member States are willing to transfer

---

[51] Article 208(1) TFEU.

[52] Article 4(4) TFEU.

[53] Article 191(1) TFEU (ex Article 174 TEC—it is worth noting that the reference to climate change is new).

[54] Cremona (n 2) 172.

the relevant competence to facilitate this, they are not willing to do so at the expense of their own power to take autonomous action. This is of particular importance in relation to development cooperation.[55] Such complementarity is implied in relation to environmental protection through the reference to the respective competences of the EU and the Member States. This again reflects the Member States' individual interests, which were fundamental to the development of environmental protection as an EU objective.[56] It is worth noting that external EU action in pursuit of environmental protection and development cooperation is to be developed pursuant to the ordinary legislative procedure.[57]

A different approach remains with respect to economic and monetary union in this context: the EU may negotiate agreements with third states. Article 219(4) TFEU further provides that: 'Without prejudice to Union competence and Union agreements ... Member States may negotiate in international bodies and conclude international agreements.'[58] This demonstrates a different emphasis from that given to the division of competences in relation to the newer, non-economic objectives. On the one hand, this may be inevitable, given the centrality of monetary union to the EU itself. The EU has been conferred exclusive competence with regard to 'monetary policy for the Member States whose currency is the Euro'.[59] It is unquestionable that the Member States have transferred their competence in this respect. Therefore, any unilateral international action an individual Member State may take in such fields must be consistent with, and therefore subordinate to, EU action and policy.

There is a sharp contrast here with the provisions on development cooperation and environmental protection, which place Member State competence on an equal level with EU competence despite the impression provided by Article 2(2). This may reflect political sensitivity, as well as the original status of these objectives within the EU. Alternatively, it is possible that this simply reflects the fact that environmental protection was initially introduced into the EU as a result of Member State practice and

[55] In light of the history of the Member States and the continuing specific relations which some have with particular developing states (for example, former colonies).
[56] See ch 2.
[57] Articles 92(1) and 209(1) TFEU respectively. Article 192(2) provides for the use of special legislative procedure as a derogation from Article 192(1) for the adoption of: '(a) provisions primarily of a fiscal nature; (b) measures affecting: town and country planning; quantitative management of water resources; land use, with the exception of waste management; (c) measures significantly affecting a Member State's choices between different energy sources and the general structure of its energy supply. The Council, acting unanimously on a proposal from the Commission and after consulting the European Parliament, the Economic and Social Committee and the Committee of the Regions may make the ordinary legislative procedure applicable to the matters referred to in the first subparagraph.'
[58] Article 219(4) TFEU.
[59] Article 3(1)(c) TFEU.

values (providing grounds for an exception to the free movement of goods principles).[60] Consequently, it would be paradoxical if Member State competence in this field could then be limited by EU action.[61]

It is possible that the formulation of the division of competence in the fields of environmental policy and development cooperation influenced the Court to some extent in its approach to external competence in its *Opinions 1/94*[62] and *2/92*.[63] The emphasis placed on joint competence certainly suggests that the Court was retreating from its earlier approach to the division of powers, under which it was very ready to grant exclusive Community competence. This may be in response to the political climate which had developed these new powers in a manner more respectful of the Member States' competence.

In short, the EU has express powers to act in specific fields (where the Member States have transferred their competence). It has been seen that this now includes an express exclusive power for the EU to act internationally where that is necessary for the attainment of one of the objectives of the EU. Where there is no prior internal legislation, the EU's competence (unless provided for as exclusive) is concurrent with that of the Member States, who have not specifically ceded their power.[64] Where the EU has enacted internal legislation in the field, however, these powers may be exclusive, but only to the extent that Member State action would impede the realisation of EU objectives or where the EU has, effectively, occupied the whole field.

III. EU COMPETENCE IN RELATION TO ITS NEWER OBJECTIVES

A. The Significance of Concurrent Powers

Comprehensive occupation of the field is, however, increasingly rare, including in relation to the express powers of the EU. Thus, provision of the EU's newer, non-economic competences emphasises the respective competences of the EU and the Member States. This can be seen, inter alia, in respect of both environmental protection and development cooperation, which encompasses, in turn, human rights competence.[65] This significantly restricts the potential for the development of exclusive EU competence,

---

[60] Case 302/86 *Commission v Denmark* [1988] ECR 4607.

[61] This would also apply to the introduction of human rights as seen in ch 2. This may link into the division of competences in relation to development cooperation, given the human rights element there.

[62] *Opinion 1/94* (n 38).

[63] *Opinion 2/92* (n 38).

[64] Unless the Member States have conferred exclusive competence as in relation to the CCP.

[65] See further ch 2 regarding the development of human rights competence in development cooperation policy.

since even the development of internal legislation cannot encroach upon the competence held by the Member States to act internationally in these fields.

Clearly, EU competence cannot in any field simply 'encroach' upon the competence of the Member States, yet effectively this is what the doctrine of implied powers achieved: as a particular course of action became necessary for the achievement of the EU's objectives, the EU acquired competence. *Opinion 1/94* clarified that this could not be at the expense of the Member States' competence, essentially confirming the terminology of the new EU competences. Yet under the Lisbon Treaty, the concept underlying implied powers has been expressly recognised in Article 216 TFEU, and this is conferred as an exclusive power under Article 3(2). However, it should be acknowledged that a significant limitation upon this power lies in the principles of proportionality and subsidiarity: there is an exclusive power to act, but only to the extent that such action is necessary, and the objective may not be equally achieved through Member State action.

The consequence of explicit provision for complementary competence with regard to environmental protection and development cooperation is that the respective powers of the EU and the Member States are less fluid in these fields than they might otherwise have been held to be: the Member States were clearly protecting their autonomous competence. In light of the *Bangladesh*[66] and *Fourth Lomé Convention*[67] cases, while *Opinion 1/94*[68] protected the competence and role of the Member States as against exclusive EC action, it could not be read as precluding the autonomous exercise of residual competence by Member States. The Court's approach in *Opinion 1/94* did not challenge the retention of national competence and action unless EU action proved necessary. This is reinforced by the inclusion of subsidiarity in the Treaty. Thus, the Member States consciously limited the working of the doctrine of implied powers and this must surely be reflected in the interpretation of Articles 3(2) and 216 TFEU.

If the provisions in relation to environmental protection and development cooperation had not explicitly referred to the respective competences of both the EU and the Member States, it might have been easier to develop wider EU power by subsequently applying the logic of *Opinion 1/94*[69] (as applied to the EU) in reverse: that is, to exclude autonomous Member State action. The fact that these competences are stated to run alongside Member State powers makes it clear that the Member States had no intention to transfer all their power in these fields or even limit themselves to only acting with the EU.

---

[66] Joined Cases C-181 and C-182/91 *Parliament v Council and Commission* [1993] ECR I-3685.
[67] Case C-361/91 *Parliament v Council* [1991] ECR I-625.
[68] *Opinion 1/94* (n 38).
[69] ibid.

B. The EU's External Competence: Environmental Protection

The nature of the EU's external competence with regard to environmental protection has been outlined above. The EU and the Member States have a shared competence with regard to the environment, under which both can negotiate with international bodies and third states and enter into international agreements. The relationship between Articles 174(4), 175(1) (now Articles 191 and 192 TFEU) and Article 133 EC (now 207 TFEU) was considered by the Court in *Opinion 2/00*. The Court applied a centre of gravity approach, holding that the primary purpose of the Agreement was environmental protection, and therefore it ruled out the CCP (Article 133 EC, now 207 TFEU) as a basis.[70] Despite the fact that there was some impact upon trade, and thus some impact upon the EC's exclusive CCP, the Court held that this could not confer exclusive EC competence because harmonisation in the field was minimal. Thus, the Court refined its reasoning in *Opinion 2/91*.[71] The question of how the appropriate legal base of an act should be determined was revisited by the Court in the context of CCP in *Opinion 1/2008*.[72] In this Opinion the Court appeared to recognise the challenges of applying a centre of gravity test with regard to international agreements as these may cover a range of areas. Significantly, different fields confer different types of competences. This in turn gives rise to different roles and interests, which need to be respected, for and of the Member States and the EU.

C. External EU Competence: Human Rights

Attention now turns to the nature of the EU's external competence with regard to human rights. In contrast to the clear position regarding external environmental competence, questions may be raised regarding the historic basis of EC action relating to the pursuit of human rights.

In the context of development cooperation, the position is clear: EC policy, since Maastricht, was directed to 'contribute to the general objective of developing and consolidating democracy and the rule of law, and to that of respecting human rights and fundamental freedoms'.[73] There was considerable uncertainty, however, regarding the proper legal basis and legitimacy of agreements pursuing human rights protection, concluded

---

[70] *Opinion 2/00* (n 36).

[71] *Opinion 2/91* (n 36). The Court subsequently ruled that the substance of the Agreement went beyond what was possible under Article 174(4) and therefore the appropriate basis was Article 175(1), and it was a matter of shared competence

[72] *Opinion 1/08* (n 47).

[73] Article 177(2) EC.

outwith the context of development cooperation, before the entry into force of the Treaty of Amsterdam.

i. The Limits of the Implied External Human Rights Competence

When the ECJ was asked, in *Opinion 2/94*,[74] whether the EC was competent to accede to the ECHR, it appeared to draw a distinction between human rights as a fundamental principle underlying Community action and policies, and competence to develop a specific human rights policy per se. This reflected the fact that human rights were recognised as 'general principles of Community law', but there was no specific power of the EC in relation to human rights.

If the inclusion of respect for human rights as an element of the then EC's international agreements was seen only as an expression of the fundamental principles underpinning EC action, it would certainly not be inappropriate for the EC to respect these fundamental principles in its external as well as its internal actions. If, however, the inclusion of such clauses was seen to demonstrate the development and exercise of a specific policy, then the basis of that policy might be called into question. As Cremona observed, the general principle of respect for fundamental rights did not, of itself, create a human rights competence, even where respect of fundamental rights was a requirement of lawful EC action.[75] Following the Treaty of Amsterdam, the substantiation of the EC's commitment to human rights[76] may have given rise to a parallel power to act in the pursuit of human rights. EC competence with regard to human rights was further extended under the Treaty of Nice, although not into a general competence.[77]

ii. Internal Human Rights: Objective or Transverse Obligation?

In the opinion of the Commission regarding accession to the ECHR, Article 235 EC (now 352 TFEU) could have been used as an appropriate legal basis for adherence. This rested on the establishment of protection of human rights as an *objective* of the EC. Brandtner and Rosas[78] referred to the 'long-standing practice' of using Article 235 EC (now 352 TFEU) as a legal basis for international agreements and referred to the Court's 'validation'

---

[74] Opinion 2/94 *Re the Accession of the Community to the European Convention of Fundamental Rights* [1996] ECR I-1759.

[75] Cremona (n 2) 150, who cites Opinion 2/94 (ibid) at para 34.

[76] See ch 2.

[77] Article 181(a); see ch 2.

[78] B Brandtner and A Rosas, 'Human Rights and the External Relations of the European Community: An analysis of Doctrine and Practice' (1998) 9 *European Journal of International Law* 468.

of this in *AETR*, which concerned road transport, for which the EU had internal competence.[79]

However, as Brandtner and Rosas recognised, the Court denied the existence of an internal power in relation to human rights. The critical element was that human rights protection was not an objective of EC action per se. It was thus not altogether satisfactory to make such a comparison between the ECHR and *AETR* and the potential of Article 235 EC (now 352 TFEU). Brandtner and Rosas focused on the fact that the refusal by the Court to accept Article 235 EC as a possible legal basis for accession 'underlined the institutional implications of adherence to the ECHR and thus does not seem to constitute a refusal to acknowledge an EC human rights competence under Article 235'.[80]

Brandtner and Rosas subsequently argued that human rights, in view of both the preamble and provisions of the TEU, and the Court of Justice's jurisprudence on human rights, were a 'transverse objective' of the EC. However, the Court's case law was founded upon the notion that human rights were to be protected within the EC, and that the EC had an obligation to ensure their observance by the Member States,[81] as they *reflect fundamental principles of the Member States.* Yet in *Opinion 2/94*, as we have seen, the Court was explicit that 'no Treaty provision confers on the Community Institutions any general power to enact rules on human rights or to conclude international conventions in this field'.[82] Brandtner and Rosas themselves observed that there are problems in the assertion of human rights competence, in that 'consensus is still lacking on the precise delimitation of Community competence in the field of human rights'.[83]

Brandtner and Rosas also pointed out that the lack of inclusion of 'environmental protection' as an objective of the EC did not prevent EC environmental action. Until environmental protection was included in the Treaty, however, it could only be pursued to the extent that lack of uniformity was causing competitive distortions, not as an objective in itself. Nevertheless, admittedly this limitation did not prevent the EC from participating in international environmental agreements. It may, however, be asked whether the fact that one area of EC interest was pursued with explicit Member State support,[84] yet without a sound legal basis in the Treaties, legitimates a similar development in another field, without such explicit Member State support.

---

[79] *Re AETR* (n 29) (this case of course established the doctrine of implied powers).
[80] Brandtner and Rosas (n 78) at 472.
[81] Case 5/88 *Wachauf v Germany* [1989] ECR 2609.
[82] *Opinion 2/94* (n 74) [27].
[83] Brandtner and Rosas (n 78) 472.
[84] See ch 2.

Weiler and Fries agreed with Brandtner and Rosas in their acceptance of a EC competence for human rights.[85] However, they appeared to root the EC's competence in the duty, articulated by the Court of Justice, of the institutions to ensure the protection of human rights within the EC, 'within the field' of Community law:

> [S]hould [the institutions] decide to discharge their inherent duty to ensure the observance of fundamental rights in the field of Community law by legislating to do just that, it is hard to see on what ground their overall competences could be challenged.[86]

iii. The Distinction between an Obligation to Respect and a Power to Promote

There could be little argument against the legitimacy of the institutions legislating to discharge their duty to ensure observance of fundamental rights. There is, however, a profound difference between requiring that EU action respects fundamental rights and action which pursues human rights protection as its objective. The former was certainly within the competence of the EC, whereas the position of the latter was far more doubtful, as there remained no discrete objective to protect human rights. To draw an analogy from the internal market, this can be equated with the distinction between requiring that a derogation from EU law must respect fundamental rights, as in *ERT*, and that a derogation may be invoked in pursuit of protection of fundamental rights, as in *Schmidberger*.[87]

Weiler and Fries subsequently questioned the difference between accession to the ECHR and accession to the WTO, which did not require a constitutional amendment despite its dispute settlement mechanism. However, the fact that the CCP has been a keystone of the EC since its foundation is crucial. It would potentially be damaging to the uniformity of the common policy if the EC itself had not been a member of the WTO, given that the Member States were. This contrasts sharply with the position in relation to human rights protection, which had not been the subject of such a common EC policy, so the EC's absence from the Council of Europe would not infringe one of its objectives. Thus, although EU accession to either

---

[85] JHH Weiler and SC Fries, 'A Human Rights Policy for the European Community and Union: The Question of Competences', Harvard Law School, Jean Monnet Chair, Working Papers, 1999.

[86] JHH Weiler and SC Fries, 'A Human Rights Policy for the European Community and Union: The Question of Competences' in P Alston (ed), *The EU and Human Rights* (Oxford, Oxford University Press, 1999) 157.

[87] Case 260/89 *Elliniki Radiophonia Tileorassi AE v Dimotiki Etairia Pliroforissis and Sotirios Kouvelas* [1992] ECR I-2925. Case C-112/00 *Schmidberger v Austria* [2003] ECR I-5659, discussed in ch 3.

organisation raises constitutional questions, the issues do not easily lend themselves to direct comparison.

iv. The Basis of the Human Rights Clause in EU Agreements with Third States

Throughout the 1990s, despite lack of a clearly defined legal basis for it, the EC actively pursued human rights protection in its agreements with third states through the inclusion of a 'human rights and democracy' clause.[88] Yet even though there was no clear basis for external EC action pursuing the objective of human rights protection other than in the context of development cooperation, the EC had a duty to ensure the respect of human rights and democracy in its actions.[89] To discharge that duty through the inclusion of respect of these values as an underlying condition of cooperation with third states was not beyond its competence. Such a condition would permit the EC to suspend cooperation in the event of a violation of these values by its partner state and vice versa. If the EC had failed to include such a clause, it could have found itself in the position of being *unable* to suspend cooperation in the event of a breach of human rights.[90] The effect of this would have been that the EC would have breached its duty to ensure the respect of human rights in its actions. The way to avoid such a situation was to make it clear that the upholding of human rights standards and democracy are essential elements, the breach of which entitles the EU to act under the Vienna Convention.[91]

Thus, on one level, in order to comply with its obligations, the EC was effectively compelled to impose human rights conditionality in its relations with third states. To discharge its duty, however, it was required to do no more than this. Thus, if it went beyond suspension of cooperation or aid and imposed sanctions, that would be a positive act, the *objective* of which would be to ensure human rights standards. Such an act was beyond the competence of the EC, although clearly it would be consistent with the objectives of the CFSP and therefore would be a matter for the Member States acting collectively through the procedures of the CFSP. This clearly highlights the distinction between the obligation, on the one hand, to ensure respect for human rights in its actions and, on the other hand, an EC objective to pursue the protection of human rights. It also shows the limits of the EC's external competence in relation to human rights.

---

[88] See ch 5.
[89] See ch 2.
[90] See ch 3 for direct precedence for this in relations with the African, Caribean and Pacific (ACP) states prior to the negotiation of Lomé IV.
[91] Article 60.

The complexities of the interplay between national law, EU competence and international law are clearly visible in this development, and these were compounded by the limited competence of the EC. These complexities, however, did not of themselves create an EU competence. EC recognition that it must ensure respect of the fundamental principles of the Member States in the operation of its policies did not, of itself, prove the existence of the competence which would legitimise the pursuit of the protection of human rights as an objective of external EC action.

v. *Case C-268/94* Portugal v Council and Commission of the European Community

Even where there is a clear legal basis for the inclusion of a human rights clause, as in the context of a *development cooperation agreement*, the exercise of that power can be contentious. Thus, in *Portugal v Council*,[92] Portugal challenged the use of Articles 113, 130y and 228 EC (now Articles 207, 211 and 218 TFEU) as the bases for a development cooperation agreement[93] on account of the inclusion within the agreement of a human rights and democracy clause. The challenge in this case related to the form of the agreement rather than its substance, which Portugal had no issue with. This case highlighted the necessity that the EC clearly identifies the legal base, and thus the source of its competence to undertake any action.

Article 1 of the contested agreement declares the respect of human rights and democratic principles to be the very basis of cooperation and essential elements of the Agreement.[94] The second paragraph continues that 'the principal objective of the agreement is to enhance and develop, through dialogue and partnership, the various aspects of cooperation between the Contracting Parties'.

Article 130u EC (now amended in Article 208 TFEU)[95] provided that the EC's development cooperation policy 'shall contribute to the general objective of developing and supporting democracy and the rule of law, and to that of respecting human rights and fundamental freedoms'. As seen above,

---

[92] Case C-268/94 *Portugal v Council and Commission of the European Union* [1996] ECR 6177.

[93] Cooperation Agreement between the European Community and the Republic of India on Partnership and Development [1994] OJ L223/23.

[94] This is a standard example of the human rights clause, the development of which was examined in ch 3.

[95] Article 208(1) TFEU provides that: 'Union policy in the field of development cooperation shall be conducted within the framework of the principles and objectives of the Union's external action ... Union development cooperation policy shall have as its primary objective the reduction and, in the long term, the eradication of poverty.' As noted above, these are set out in Article 21(1) TEU.

Article 130y (subsequently Article 181 EC, now Article 211 TFEU) gave the EC competence to conclude agreements with third states in this sphere.

Portugal challenged the use of Article 130y as a legal basis on which to conclude an agreement in which human rights constitutes an essential element, deeming it adequate only for the conclusion of an agreement in which human rights are prescribed as a general objective. Portugal's specific concern was that the consequences of the characterisation of human rights as an essential element were not explicit and that the implication was that the EC would potentially resort to action outwith the scope of the bases chosen. Such action may be appropriate only on the basis of Article 235 (now Article 352 TFEU). In contrast, the Danish Government applied the same logic in reverse by arguing that Article 235 EC would only be appropriate if the main purpose of the Agreement was to safeguard human rights. Conclusion of the agreement under Article 235 would have required unanimous consent. The Council disputed Portugal's 'artificial' distinction between Article 130u (Article 208 TFEU) and 130y (Article 211 TFEU) and 130w (Article 209 TFEU), the result of which it described as paradoxical, since it implied that any action which had the objective of protecting human rights, consistent with Article 130u, would have to be based on Article 235.

The Advocate-General stated that policy in this field required the observance of fundamental rights in order to promote the general objective of respect for such values.[96] Being assured of the relationship between the protection of human rights and the context of development cooperation, he moved on to consider whether the human rights clause in Article 1 might properly form part of an agreement concluded in accordance with Article 130y and found that 'it is designed to allow the Community to exercise the right to terminate the Agreement, in accordance with Article 60 of the Vienna Convention'.[97] Consequently, he concluded that the clause was indeed necessary for the lawful pursuit of development cooperation policy.

The Court itself was similarly clear in its conclusions, ruling that the adaptation of cooperation policy to respect for human rights implies a link between the two, and the subordination of one to the other. Therefore, it might be necessary to impose conditionality with regard to human rights in order to suspend or terminate an agreement in the face of a violation of human rights.[98] The Court went on to observe that 'the question of respect for human rights and democratic principles is not a specific field of cooperation provided for by the Agreement'. Following the approach of the Danish Government, this rules out any question of basing the measure on Article 235 EC (now 352 TFEU) and the Court held that in this respect,

---

[96] Paragraph 26 of the Opinion.
[97] Paragraph 28 of the Opinion.
[98] Paragraphs 26–27 of the judgment.

'the contested decision could be validly based upon Article 130y [Article 211 TFEU]'.

With the exception of a reference to 'cooperation policy' in paragraph 26 (as distinct from development cooperation policy, as seen above), at no time did the Court suggest that EC human rights competence extends beyond development cooperation. Even the reference in paragraph 26 did not suggest the existence of a wider competence, merely considering the relationship between two policies. The Advocate-General's opinion was clear: the essential elements clause was necessary in order to discharge the EC's duty regarding respect for human rights.

In discussing the division of powers between the EC and the Member States, the Court was explicit that although the respective competences were complementary, the EC could act alone where the matters covered within the agreement fell entirely within the EC's competence, be it express or implied.[99] If concurrent powers could be exercised in the same manner as complementary powers, this contrasted with the approach taken by the Court in *Opinion 1/94*.[100] It was, however, consistent with the approach taken to the Member States' exercise of concurrent powers in the *Bangladesh* and *Lomé IV* cases.[101] Where the Agreement also included matters of Member State competence which were not within EC competence (such as intellectual property), their participation was also required and, again, the matter could not be concluded on the basis of Article 181 EC (Article 211 TFEU).[102] This case thus effectively illustrated the division of competences between the Member States and the EC, and the operation of that division in the case of a shared competence, as well as examining the relationship between the different elements of the EC's development cooperation policy.

vi. The Lisbon Treaty Position: Essential Clarification

The Lisbon Treaty provides some much-needed clarity regarding the legal basis of EU external human rights policy. There can be no doubt that under the Lisbon Treaty, the EU has an obligation to pursue the protection of human rights.[103] While this may raise the question as to whether there is a supranational power for the EU to pursue this objective, or whether it should simply be pursued through inter-governmental action, Article 21(3)

---

[99] At paragraph 31 of the judgment. It should be noted that the conclusion of agreements in the field of development cooperation is, as seen above, a matter of complementary competence.

[100] *Opinion 1/94* (n 38).

[101] *Parliament v Council and Commission* (n 66); *Parliament v Council* (n 67).

[102] It is worth recalling at this point that the Lisbon Treaty has broadened the scope of the CCP, so intellectual property is now within it.

[103] Article 21(2)(b) TEU.

provides that this, together with the EU's other objectives, is to be pursued both through action under Title V TEU and in the external action provided for in Title V TFEU, and in the external elements of its other policies. This is a development from the position under the Treaty of Amsterdam, whereby it was the *EU* (as contrasted with the EC) that was charged with the objective 'to develop and consolidate democracy and the rule of law and respect for human rights and fundamental freedoms'.[104] The means for the EU to pursue the objectives of the CFSP were then explicitly inter-governmental.[105]

Prior to the Lisbon Treaty, the Council was empowered to negotiate and conclude agreements with third states or international organisations, where necessary for the implementation of the CFSP, but this required Member State authorisation.[106] The inclusion of a matter within the TEU in no way implied power for independent, relevant or related action by the EC outside the context of development cooperation, in which it was explicitly provided for. The current expression of this provision has no requirement of Member State authorization.[107] Thus, despite the past uncertainty and political sensitivity, there is no doubt that the EU is now, post-Lisbon, competent to pursue human rights protection in its external relations, whatever the context.

IV. THE EFFECT OF INTERNATIONAL AGREEMENTS IN EU LAW

Having examined the nature and extent of EU external human rights and environment competence, it is relevant to consider briefly the effect of international agreements in EU law, as this has a bearing upon the status and enforceability of commitments to non-economic values which are entered into in the context of the EU's external relations. What is their force? Are they reflective of a political commitment or a legal obligation?

In this context it is essential to recall that the effects of international agreements within the EU derive from those characteristics of EU law which make it a unique legal order. Connected to this, the status and effect of EU

---

[104] Article 11. It should be noted, however, that the preamble to the SEA referred to the need for 'Europe' to speak with one voice and refers to the need 'to display the principles of democracy and compliance with the law and with human rights to which they are attached'.

[105] As seen above, the implications of this are by no means trivial: as observed by Lenaerts and de Smijter, the matters encompassed within the second pillar tended to be politically sensitive. The Member States were not inclined to leave such interests to be defended by a supranational institution, See K Lenaerts and E de Smijter, 'The European Union as an Actor under International Law' (1999–2000) 19 *Yearbook of European Law* 95. This demonstrates reluctance to transfer sovereignty in such sensitive fields, which fundamentally affect national interests.

[106] Article 24 EU.

[107] Article 27 EU.

law within and upon the Member States is quite distinct from its effect upon third countries. This distinction is exemplified by the fact that the EU enjoys legal personality within the Member States, which is conferred upon it by Article 47 TEU. Externally, however, such enjoyment is dependent upon recognition by other states, as is clearly demonstrated by *Opinion 2/91*.[108] Such recognition can be sought and given, but not demanded.

Traditionally, the international law of treaties leaves the domestic effect of international treaties to be determined by individual states. The Treaty applies only to the state parties and its internal, domestic effect is determined by national (constitutional) law. The EC Treaties contained no indications as to their effect in the Member States and it could have been assumed that the traditional international law would apply. However, the Court of Justice in *Van Gend en Loos*[109] held that the Treaty created a unique legal system pursuant to which it established the principle of direct effect of EC law.[110] In so doing, the Court imposed a degree of 'monism' upon the EC legal order.[111] The principle of direct effect is significant in this context because it permits an individual to enforce rights arising under a measure, whereas international agreements are traditionally, as a matter of international law, binding upon and enforceable by their signatories (usually states).[112] Even where the *Union* recognises an international agreement, or even certain provisions within such an agreement, as being directly effective, this does not affect the status of the agreement within the partner state. The domestic status of a provision of international law is a matter for national law, as long as the partners fulfil their obligations under the agreement as regards each other.[113] However, the implications of any potential disparity in recognised effect could be interesting, although no more so than the existing disparity between monist and dualist states generally.

---

[108] *Opinion 2/91* (n 36).

[109] Case 49/62 NV *Algemene Transporten Expeditie Onderneming van Gend en Loos v Nederlandse Administratie der Belastingen* [1963] ECR 1.

[110] The Court laid down conditions of direct effect: that the provision must be clear, unconditional and leave no discretion to the Member States. These have been liberally interpreted in subsequent case law: see, inter alia, Case 6/64 *Flaminio Costa v ENEL* [1964] ECR 53; Case 2/74 *Reyners v Belgium* [1974] ECR 631; Case 43/75 *Defrenne v Société anonyme Belge de Navigation Aerienne (SABENA)* [1976] ECR 455.

[111] In that no national incorporation or implementing measure would be necessary to give effect to the provision of EC law meeting the conditions of direct effect.

[112] Of course, national constitutional law may confer such effect upon a provision of international law (eg, under a monist system).

[113] See Cremona (n 2).

A. Direct Effect: A Necessary Condition for Reviewability of the Compatibility of EU Law with an International Agreement

For present purposes, the key question concerns whether, and to what extent, this monistic approach extends to agreements entered into by the EU with third states, which would mean they would be potentially capable of direct effect. If a provision of an international agreement concluded by the EU is capable of direct effect, it may be possible to enforce it before the Court of Justice or national courts. But for the Court of Justice to enforce a provision, it must be established that it has jurisdiction to do so. The Court held in *International Fruit Company*[114] that before it could review the validity of the EU measure, it had to be established that the GATT provision being relied upon could confer rights on individuals. The Court, having considered the spirit, general scheme and the terms of the GATT, concluded that it was not capable of conferring rights on individuals.

The Court subsequently held in *Haegemann*[115] that both Community institutions and the Member States were bound by agreements concluded under the provisions of Article 300 EC (now Article 218 TFEU), since these were concluded by the EC and consequently deemed to be EC Acts, part of EC law, and could even in certain circumstances, have direct effect.[116] Significantly, in its analysis the Court did not distinguish between the elements of the agreement which were of Member State and those of EC competence, although the agreement concerned was a mixed agreement. Thus, as far as these agreements are concerned, the Court appeared, prima facie, to have adopted a monistic approach. As Lenaerts and de Smijter pointed out, however, the Court relied here, inter alia, upon the fact that the Council concluded the agreement through a Decision, which opened the EC up to the agreement concerned.[117] They argued, therefore, that the real test came in relation to the status in the EC legal order of decisions taken by institutions set up by the Agreements to which the EC has been a party.

In *Polydor*[118] the Court was required to consider a provision of the Free Trade Agreement between the EC and Portugal. The Court held that despite the wording of the FTA provision being identical to Article 30 EC (now Article 34 TFEU), it could not be held to have the same meaning, since the aim of the Agreement was not the same as that of the EC. Consequently, it

---

[114] Cases 21–24/72 *International Fruit Company v Produktschaap voor Groenten en Fruit* [1972] ECR 1219.

[115] Case 181/73 *R v Haegemann and Belgian State* [1974] ECR 449 [4]–[6].

[116] This was confirmed in Case 12/86 *Demirel v Stadt Schwäbisch Gmünd* [1987] ECR 3719.

[117] Lenaerts and de Smijter, (n 105).

[118] Case 270/80 *Polydor Ltd and RSO Records Inc v Harlequin Record Shops Ltd and Simons Records Ltd* [1982] ECR 329.

ould not be held to have direct effect. In *Kupferberg*,[119] however, the Court held that a provision of the EEC-Portugal Free Trade Agreement did have direct effect because its application fell within the purpose of the agreement, as well as satisfying the conditions of direct effect. The Court subsequently, in 1989, ruled that a Decision of an Association Council is an integral part of EC law from the date of its entry into force.[120] Thus, the Court once again adopted a monist approach. This case law has been consolidated and this principle now covers decisions taken by organs set up under any form of Agreement to which the EU is a party.[121]

i. Direct Effect? A Two-Prong Test

The Court has developed a two-prong test in order to decide the question of the direct effect of international agreements. First, the 'spirit, general terms and scheme' of the Treaty must be consistent with it having direct effect.[122] Second, the relevant provisions must satisfy the requriements for direct effect (that is, they must be clear and unconditional).[123] These requirements are a clear reference back to the requirements for the direct effect of EU law per se, developed in *Van Gend en Loos* and subsequent case law.[124] In *Pabst*,[125] the Court applied both prongs of the test and found the agreement in question to be directly effective. In *Sevince*,[126] however, the Court demonstrated that both conditions need not be satisfied: finding that although the agreement per se may be too general and conditional, further elucidation of its provisions by an authoritative body may cure that defect and confer direct effect. In contrast, however, a provision complying with the requirements of direct effect may or may not have direct effect according to the objective and nature of the agreement.[127] Thus, it is possible for a specific provision to be directly effective despite being contained within an Agreement which is not generally susceptible to direct effect. Similarly, as provisions must be read in the context of their agreement, two provisions

---

[119] Case 104/81 *Hauptzollamt Mainz v Kupferberg* [1982] ECR 3641.

[120] Case 30/88 *Greece v Commission* [1989] ECR 3711.

[121] Though note Case C-122/95 *Germany v Council* [1998] ECR I-973, in which the ECJ denied direct effect to a provision of an international agreement which conflicted with primary EC law. In contrast, secondary EU law (Case C-286/90 *Anklagemyndigheden v Poulsen and Diva Navigation* [1992] ECR I-6019) and national law (Case 104/81 *Hauptzollamt Mainz v Kupferberg* [1982] ECR 3641) are bound by the EU's international obligations unless they raise issues relating to the fundamental principles (Joined Cases C-402/05P *Kadi v Council and Commission* and C-415/05 P *Al Barakaat International Foundation v The Council and Commission* [2008] ECR I-6351, discussed in ch 2). See further Lenaerts and de Smijter (n 105).

[122] *International Fruit Company* (n 114).

[123] *Kupferberg* (n 121).

[124] *Van Gend en Loos* (n 109).

[125] Case 17/81 *Pabst* [1982] ECR 1331, [1983] 3 CMLR 11.

[126] Case C-192/89 *Sevince* [1990] 1 ECR 3461, [1992] 2 CMLR 57.

[127] *Kupferburg* (n 121).

with virtually identical terms may have different effects.[128] An additional factor to be noted is that where the Court *has* recognised the direct effect of an agreement, the purpose of the agreement under consideration has been similar to that of the EU.

B. Unpacking the Jurisdiction of the Court of Justice to Review the Compatibility of EU Law with the EU's International Obligations

There is no doubt, then, that the Court of Justice has jurisdiction to review the compatibility of EU law with its international obligations. Attention now turns to a more detailed examination of the scope of this jurisdiction, and its applicability to the ECHR, the GATT and the WTO.

i. Questions Concerning the Scope of the Court of Justice's Jurisdiction

In *International Fruit Company* the Court stated that for it to have jurisdiction to review an EU act for compatibility with its international obligations, the particular international obligation in question must have direct effect. It has further been suggested that the Court may only have jurisdiction to review the actions of the EU in relation to an international obligation where that obligation falls within internal EU competence. This is logical, in that a legal basis is required for all acts of the EU, but it raises questions in relation to mixed agreements: to what extent could the Court be competent to review the elements of the agreement falling within Member State competence? Cheyne concluded that as a consequence of the combination of the Member States' right to require compliance with international obligations, and the requirement that the institutions comply with the Treaty, the Court of Justice has the competence to prevent violations of even external legal obligations, and this may not even be a discretionary competence, but may be a requirement.[129]

This question is also discussed by Eeckhout, who concluded that it has not been confirmed by the Court that it has no jurisdiction as regards the provisions of a mixed agreement which fall under national competence, nor that EU law will not determine the status of such provisions.[130] He went on to observe that the Court avoided such statements by interpreting its jurisdiction broadly. Although in *Sevince*[131] the Court viewed decisions of an

---

[128] As seen in *Polydor* (n 118).
[129] Ilona Cheyne, 'International Agreements and the European Community Legal System' [1994] 19 *European Law Review* 581.
[130] P Eeckhout, 'The Domestic Legal Status of the WTO Agreement: Interconnecting Legal Systems' (1997) 34 *CML Rev* 11, 16–17.
[131] *Sevince* (n 126).

Association Council as forming an integral part of EC law, Eeckhout noted that 'the Court has jurisdiction in so far as the agreement is an act adopted by one of the institutions of the Community'. He also noted, however, that this limitation is expressed less strongly in the French version of the judgment. The mere fact that an agreement is concluded as a mixed agreement has no bearing on the competence of the Court of Justice to review or interpret that agreement where the particular provision has some impact upon EU law and if there is no explicit allocation of competences (that is, nothing within the agreement excluding Community competence).[132]

a. Reviewability of EU law for Compatibility with the ECHR

If there are questions concerning the reviewability of a mixed agreement, the ECHR raises still more questions. The EU is not (yet) a party to the ECHR, but, as discussed in chapters two and three, the Court of Justice has found no difficulty in interpreting and ensuring the provisions of the ECHR,[133] notwithstanding that it is not a party to that agreement. The Court traditionally did so, however, on the basis that the Convention reflects the rights, principles and values common to the Member States, which perhaps gave it another ground of jurisdiction: clearly it was required to ensure that the EC acted in accordance with its obligations to the Member States and that they did not breach their international obligations.[134]

b. Reviewability of EU law for Compatibility with the GATT?

In *International Fruit Company*[135] the Court held that there was a direct link between reviewability of the compatibility of Community acts with international law, and the direct effect of the provisions of that international law.[136] The Court is competent to review the compatibility of EU law with the agreements by which the EU is bound. Such agreements prevail over both national law and secondary EU legislation, but can only be relied upon before the domestic courts if they comply with the conditions of direct effect.[137]

---

[132] See Joined Cases C-300 and 392/98 *Parfums Christian Dior v Tuk Consultancy* [2000] ECR I-11307 [35].

[133] See ch 1.

[134] See ch 2 regarding the post-Lisbon role of the Court regarding the ECHR. See also Case C-53/96 *Hermes International v FHT Marketing Choice BV* [1998] ECR I-3603 [22]–[29], which confirms the Court's competence to interpret TRIPS.

[135] *International Fruit Company* (n 114).

[136] This has been widely criticised as it protected the validity of EC acts where the international agreement had no direct effect, as well as confusing the issues of the relationship between the EC legal order and the international agreement, and the national legal orders and the international agreement. See, inter alia, G Zonnekeyn, 'The Status of WTO Law in the Community Legal Order: Some Comments in the Light of the Portugese Textiles Case' (2000) 25(3) *European Law Review* 293.

[137] *International Fruit Company* (n 114).

However, not all agreements or their provisions are held to have direct effect. Perhaps the most significant example of the exceptions is the GATT, which was held not to meet the required conditions of clarity and precision.[138] Under the international law principle *pacta sunt servanda*, the GATT is binding upon its signatories, and the Court recognised in *International Fruit Company* that it was binding upon the EC. It was confirmed in *Germany v Council*,[139] however, that the GATT could not be relied upon by individuals to challenge EC law (in relation to the EC organisation of banana imports). The question had not been raised in relation to the WTO Agreement and renegotiated GATT (of 1994) until *Portugal v Council* in 1999.[140]

c. Reviewability of EU Law for Compatibility
  with the WTO Agreements?

The question of competence to review the legality of Community law for compliance with the WTO Agreements was specifically addressed in *Portugal v Council*,[141] which concerned the 1996 textile agreements between the EC and Pakistan and the EC and India.[142] In this case Portugal sought an annulment of the Council Decision concerning these Memoranda, inter alia on the ground that the decision violated certain provisions of the WTO.[143]

In its judgment the Court held itself not to be competent to review the compatibility of a Council measure with the provisions of the WTO. It based this decision upon the fundamental importance of negotiation in the exercise of the WTO provisions and the possibility for WTO members to reach temporary compromise arrangements to deal with disputes. The Court held that if EC measures were reviewable in the light of the WTO obligations, the EC would lose its ability to negotiate with other WTO members and that this would not be reciprocated, placing the EC at a disadvantage. The Court therefore held that such review would only be possible where 'the Community intended to implement a particular obligation assumed in the context of the WTO, or where the Community measure refers expressly

---

[138] *Portugal v Council* [1996] ECR 6177.

[139] Case C-280/93 *Germany v Council* [1994] ECR I-4973.

[140] Case C-149/96 *Portuguese Republic v Council of the European Union* [1999] ECR I-8395.

[141] ibid. See S Peers 'Fundamental Right or Political Whim' in G de Búrca and J Scott (eds) *The EU and the WTO: Legal and Constitutional Issues* (Oxford, Hart Publishing, 2001); Zonnekeyn (n 136); S Griller, 'Judicial Enforceability of WTO Law in the European Union: Annotation to case C-149/96, Portugal v Council' (2000) 3 *Journal of International Economic Law* 441. It is worth noting that the Portuguese Government sought to separate out the question of reviewability from the existence or not of direct effect, but to little effect.

[142] Memoranda of Understanding between the European Community and the Islamic Republic of Pakistan and the European Community and the Republic of India on arrangements in the area of market access for textile products [1996] OJ L153/47.

[143] Paragraph 24 of the judgment.

to the precise provisions of the WTO agreements'.[144] The Court concluded that this was not at issue in the present case, as the decision was neither intended to implement a particular obligation in the WTO context, nor did it refer to any specific WTO provisions.[145] This ruling was confirmed in *Merck Genericos*.[146] This is particularly striking in view of the amendments made to the GATT in 1994, which reflected a shift to a more rule-based system.[147] This shift might have rendered inapplicable the Court's earlier objections to the direct effect of the GATT. However, the Court emphasised the requirement that the EC maintain its freedom to manoeuvre, negotiate and arrive at temporary arrangements with its WTO trading partners, holding that this denies any possibility of direct effect, which would remove such flexibility.[148] This is, the Court observes, consistent with the final recital to the preamble of Decision 94/800: 'by its nature, the Agreement establishing the World Trade Organisation, including the Annexes thereto, is not susceptible to being directly invoked in Community or Member State courts'.[149] The denial by the Court of direct effect of the post-WTO GATT has subsequently been affirmed in *Cordis*[150] and *T-Port*,[151] in which the CFI rejected attempts to rely upon a panel dispute settlement ruling, and also in *FIAMM* by both the CFI and the Court of Justice.[152]

V. CONCLUDING COMMENTS

In a world of increasing globalisation, and in particular the globalisation of trade, the significance of the development of non-economic interests, concerns and policies within the EU is considerably enhanced if these are coherently carried over into the EU's external relations.

---

[144] Paragraph 49.

[145] Paragraph 51.

[146] Case C-431/05 *Merck Genericos* [2007] ECR I-700. It should be noted that the Advocate-General in this case, AG Colomer, was strongly critical of the Court's reasoning in this area: 'successive developments, far from offering a smooth passage, have constructed a long and winding path, whose complex route demands certain adjustments in order to help its confused users find their way' [33]. He suggested that the Court should have jurisdiction based upon the duty of cooperation and Article 10 EC (now repealed and replaced in substance by Article 4(3) TFEU).

[147] See ch 6 below.

[148] Paragraph 46 of the judgment.

[149] Paragraph 48 of the judgment.

[150] Case T-18/99 *Cordis Obst und Gemuse Grosshandel v Commission* [2001] ECR II-943.

[151] Case T-52/99 *T Port GmbH v Commission* [2001] ECR II-981.

[152] Case T-69/00 *FIAMM v Council* [2005] ECR II-5393; Case C-120/06 P *FIAMM v Council* [2008] ECR I-6513.

A. The Nature of EU External Competence

The extent to which the EU is competent to act externally in these fields depends upon the nature and extent of the EU's external powers. The express external powers of the EC were originally fairly limited, but the Court mitigated this through the development of the doctrine of implied powers, according to which the internal competence was matched by a parallel external competence to conclude whatever acts are necessary to achieve the EC's objective in that field.[153] The initial approach of the Court was to make this a wide power and to tend towards recognising the possibility of exclusive EC competence. Subsequently, however, perhaps in response to the political climate and particularly Member States' uneasiness about a perceived encroachment on their competence, the Court retreated towards recognising EC competence in partnership with the Member States. This is exemplified by the divergent approaches in *Opinion 2/91* and *Opinion 1/94*. Thus, in *Opinion 2/91*[154] the approach of the Court had been to establish first that the ILO Convention fell within the scope of EC competence and then to examine whether that competence was exclusive. In *Opinion 1/94*[155] the Court examined first whether the different sections of the WTO Agreement fell within the scope of the CCP. Having decided that they did not, the ECJ held that Member State participation was required since there was no exclusive Community competence. Had the Court adopted the approach of *Opinion 2/91*, it might have concluded that the EC's competence, although not exclusive, did extend over all sections of the Agreements as concurrent competence.

If concurrent powers operate in the same manner as complementary powers, either holder of the powers may act independently. Thus, there need only be joint action where a matter covers fields of both exclusive EC and Member State competence. In that case, had the Court been of the opinion that the EC was possessed of concurrent powers to conclude the entire WTO Agreements, it could have ruled that the EC was competent to do so without the participation of the Member States.

It is possible that the approach of the Court was influenced by the political attitude of the Member States towards the EC at that point, and it therefore sought a more inclusive solution. The express external competences which were conferred at that time with regard to the EC's (then) new objectives ruled out exclusive EC competence, and were therefore consistent with the impression that the Member States resisted the complete transfer of their power. They expressly provided for independent exercise of their respective competencies by the EC and the Member States, requiring only complementarity between the different acts concluded.

---

[153] *Re AETR* (n 29).
[154] *Opinion 2/91* (n 36).
[155] *Opinion 1/94* (n 38).

Thus, a new era developed in the allocation of powers. This was entirely consistent with the almost contemporaneous development of the principle of subsidiarity, which was certainly a political move. The timing suggests that the factors influencing the development of subsidiarity in the EU also contributed to the Court's approach to *Opinion 1/94*. Underlying all EU action, of course, runs the principle of proportionality. There can be little doubt that the clarification of competences and the nature of those competences in the Lisbon Treaty remain consistent with this trend, despite the potentially misleading expression of the joint competences in Article 2(2) TFEU.[156] These factors together underline the retreat from what may be described as a maximalist approach to the transfer to, and exercise of, the powers of the EU. This is a move away from a requirement of absolute uniformity across the EU, which may only be achieved through imposition from the EU level. Instead, there has been a development of complementary action, respecting the political nuances of different states' policies on different issues and accepting differences insofar as these do not inhibit the achievement of the EU's objectives. Alongside this development in the nature of the EU's external competence is the development of the inter-governmental CFSP, which remains post-Lisbon and demonstrates the reluctance of the Member States to unreservedly transfer power in external relations to the supranational EU.

B. The Nature of EU External Competence in Respect of Human Rights and Environmental Protection

Turning to the specific interests which are the focus of this study, the EU's external environmental competence is unambiguous; it is expressly conferred in Article 191 TFEU. It is significant, however, that it is conferred as a complementary competence; the Member States may also continue to act. This reflects two factors, the first being the Member States' reluctance to lose their competence on an issue which is clearly of national concern. Second, the conferral of an express power concerning environmental protection perhaps indicates recognition of the fact that environmental problems are global and, not respecting national boundaries, may not be effectively addressed by unilateral action even where 'unilateral' refers to the entire EU. The lack of clarity in terms of what is meant by 'environment' may, however, reduce the effectiveness of this provision. This explicit complementarity imposes a caveat upon the interpretation of Article 2(2) TFEU with regard to the exercise of joint competences.

The position in relation to human rights developed rather less straightforwardly. Originally, it was only in the context of development cooperation

---

[156] See text accompanying n 50 above.

that there was any power to actively pursue human rights protection as an objective.[157] However, there was no general express internal power in this field. That notwithstanding, there was a widespread view that there was an underlying EC objective relating to human rights protection. It is argued here, however, that there is a difference between an obligation to uphold and respect certain fundamental principles relating to human rights in the pursuit of the EC's objectives, and an objective to pursue the protection of human rights per se. Without the existence of an internal power, there can be no development of an implied external power. Therefore, outside the scope of development cooperation, the EC did not have any competence to act externally in the pursuit of human rights protection. The limited extension of its human rights competence in the Treaty of Nice is entirely consistent with the development of a deeper policy concerning the protection of human rights generally. Any remaining ambiguity has of course been removed by the Treaty of Lisbon.

C. The Emergence of External Competence as a Mirror of the Development of Internal Competence

The juxtaposition of objectives in the Lisbon Treaty demonstrates the interaction between economic and non-economic objectives. The EU's history with regard to human rights conditionality[158] clearly demonstrates that the observed interaction (and tension) between different interests (now unambiguously objectives) in the internal EU context spills over into the external sphere. The development of external competence in relation to non-economic issues was an indicator that the EU had moved beyond consideration of these purely as incidental to economic issues, to viewing them in their own right. Therefore, in its external relations and competence, there is clear evidence that the EU has transformed itself from being a primarily economic organisation to being an autonomous international actor. In so doing, the EU has ensured that its international presence and concerns reflect its internal evolution.

The emergence of internal environmental competence was on certain levels relatively straightforward and non-contentious; it was clearly established in the Treaty at a relatively early stage. In relation to human rights, EU competence has always been argued to reflect the shared values of the Member States, and a desire not to have these prejudiced in the EU in any context. Thus, the external manifestation of these shared values reflects the internal position. However, regardless of the reasons driving the emergence of these interests as matters for pursuit in the EU's external relations, that very fact of external pursuit carries the potential for significant influence.

---

[157] Article 211 TFEU makes identical provision with regard to development cooperation to that applying to environmental protection.
[158] See ch 5.

D. The Effect of the EU's External Commitments

Union agreements with third states have been recognised as being part of the EU legal order, and consequently binding upon the EU and the Member States. This is now explicit in Article 216(2) TFEU. Union acts are reviewable as to their compliance with international agreements. In addition, provisions of the agreements may have direct effect where such effect would be within the general spirit and objectives of the agreement and they comply with its standard requirements. However, the restrictive approach of the Court with regard to the establishment of direct effect highlights the desire of the EU to ensure that it retains its discretion and flexibility with regard to the implementation of its international commitments. This is particularly important where the EU's partner state does not recognise direct effect: for the EU to do so in such circumstances would give rise to an asymmetry of obligation which could be to its disadvantage. However, even if a provision in an agreement with a third state or states is not 'directly effective', and therefore has limited formal 'enforceability', the very inclusion of non-economic interests in its relations with third states opens the EU up to scrutiny as to the extent to which it is upholding those interests internally. This means that the questions raised in the previous chapter, regarding the limits of the internal protection of non-economic interests, are potentially heightened. The issue of direct effect also raises questions relating to the enforceability of commitments entered into. This has the capacity to be particularly significant where individuals' rights are at issue. Therefore, the inclusion of commitments relating to human rights, and specifically the effect attributed to these, may be particularly controversial. This will be explored in the next chapter.

Thus, when the EU acts externally in a given field, the implications are profound, both for the EU itself and for the Member States, as well as individuals within the Member States. That being the case, the EU requires to be sure that it has an appropriate legal basis for all the elements it seeks to include within its agreements. This is all the more significant because it is open not only to challenge from the Member States if there is a belief that the legal basis specified is inadequate, but also to scrutiny from the third (partner) states as to whether the EU, internally, is complying with its undertakings and also as to whether there is any means to ensure that such commitments are given effect.

In terms of the lessons which can be drawn from the existence of EU external competency with regard to non-economic interests, this can be seen to be clearly tied, first, to ensuring that the EU does not find itself violating its internal obligations through its external relations. Second, more positively, there is an emerging sense that the holistic or integrated approach which the EU applies to 'development' internally is being exported into and through its external relations. The next chapter will explore this in more detail.

5

Human Rights and Environmental Protection in the EU's Relations with Third States

INTRODUCTION

T HE PREVIOUS CHAPTER traced the development of the EU's external competences, focusing in particular upon the extent of competence with regard to human rights and environmental protection. Attention now turns to an examination of the manner in which the EU has included pursuit of human rights and environmental protection in its relations with third states. This is important: the question addressed by this book concerns the manner in which the international community might address contemporary challenges, particularly those in which commitments to different objectives collide, drawing in particular upon the EU experience. Analysis of the practice that the EU has adopted in its relations with third states, and the reception given by third states to that practice, is a crucial element of the exploration of what may be learnt from the EU experience.

The EU has adopted distinct approaches to the external pursuit of human rights and environmental protection, leading to substantial differences in the form, significance and force of commitment to these interests within agreements. These approaches have not always been easy to square with the EU's competence. This chapter aims to address a number of key inter-related issues which arise with regard to the inclusion of human rights and environmental commitments in the EU's relations with third states. From an internal perspective, the extent to which this policy is securely based has been considered in chapter four and it was found that although originally questions could be raised about the basis for this policy in respect of human rights, following the Lisbon Treaty, EU competence for this is unambiguously established. A question which remains, however, concerns the extent to which its external action reflects its internal policy? From a more 'external' perspective, the inclusion of human rights and environmental objectives in the EU's agreements with third states requires the consent of the partner states. If it is indeed the EU that is driving the inclusion of non-economic interests in its agreements with third states, this provides a clear indication of the extent of direct impact of EU policy upon the wider international community. On the other hand, there is a question as to whether 'consent' is freely given if the EU is the 'stronger' party to the agreement.

Related to this, it is relevant to examine the substantive content of the commitments to human rights and the environment in the EU's agreements with third states: what is the nature of the commitment entered into? To what extent does it constitute the imposition of EU standards upon other states? Or is it premised upon wider values and standards, already accepted by the partner state? This in itself has ramifications for the wider applicability of the approach manifested in the EU's relations with third states.

Structure of the Chapter

In addressing these questions, this chapter first presents a brief overview of the various different types of agreements which the EU enters into with its partner states. What clearly emerges from this overview is the extent to which political and strategic objectives bear upon the content and objectives of the EU's relations with its partners. This inevitably impacts upon the nature of human rights and environmental commitment entered into, as will be seen.

Following this overview of the nature and form of EU bilateral and multilateral agreements, an examination is undertaken of the emergence of the human rights and democracy clause, and of the commitment to environmental protection in the EU's agreements with third states. The EU's Generalised System of Preferences (GSP) scheme is then considered. Together, these provide a broad picture of the means by which the EU has integrated economic and non-economic objectives in its relations with third states.

However, any such picture would be incomplete without consideration of both the response of the partner states to the inclusion of non-economic objectives in such agreements and the extent to which these clauses have been enforced or otherwise acted upon. Unsurprisingly, this has been more contentious with regard to the inclusion of human rights commitments than environmental commitments, and when examining the emergence of the human rights clause, attention is also paid both to instances in which the EU has encountered opposition to this and circumstances in which it has subsequently invoked the clause (or not). This contributes to the evaluation of whether the policy of inclusion of reference to non-economic interests in all international agreements contributes to ensuring that these sometimes competing interests are given due weight, and of whether the core value of this policy is essentially legal or political.

I. FORMS AND TYPES OF AGREEMENT BETWEEN
THE EU AND THIRD STATES

As was seen in chapter four, the EU has the competence to conclude agreements with third states (and international organisations) in a variety of fields, eventually including human rights and environmental objectives. The form of agreements concluded has varied according to both the substantive content of the agreements, and the political context and objectives. It is also worth noting that the EU and its Member States' participation in multilateral agreements, such as with the WTO, also substantively impacts upon its other external action.

A. Trade Agreements

Trade agreements based upon Article 207 TFEU deal exclusively with commercial matters, such as imports and exports.[1] Such agreements are negotiated by the EU acting without the Member States, since the common commercial policy (CCP) falls within its exclusive competence. As seen above, notwithstanding the unambiguous nature of the CCP, difficulties arose concerning its scope, particularly as the Member States were understandably resistant to the loss of their own competency through its expansion.[2]

B. Partnership and Cooperation Agreements

The second category of agreements, partnership and cooperation agreements (PCAs), concerns cooperation in trade and varying degrees of cooperation in other fields, including economic, industrial, technical, scientific, transport and/or environmental.[3] PCAs were traditionally based on Articles 113, 235 and 228 EC (subsequently, following the Amsterdam treaty renumbering), Articles 133, 308 and 300 EC). The Nice Treaty added a Title XXI concerning Economic, Financial and Technical Cooperation with

---

[1] For example, Free Trade Agreements such as those signed with the Baltic states in 1994 (Estonia [1994] OJ L373/94; Latvia [1994] OJ L374/94; and Lithuania [1994] OJ L375/94) and including more recently the Free Trade Agreement signed with Korea in 2010. Free Trade Agreement between the European Union, and its Member States, of the one part and the People's Republic of Korea [2011] OJ L127/1.

[2] The relevance of this internal question has subsequently been demonstrated in the context of the conclusion of international agreements and in negotiations with Australia in 1997, discussed below.

[3] For example, 1992 Trade and Commercial and Economic Cooperation Agreements with Estonia, Latvia and Lithuania [1992] OJ L403/92.

third countries: Article 181a(3) EC (now Article 212 TFEU) specifically provides for cooperation with third countries in these areas, agreements concerning which were to be adopted pursuant to Article 300 EC (which has now been replaced by Article 218 TFEU). Therefore, partnership in these areas may now be based upon Articles 207, 212 and 218 TFEU. Such agreements may be reciprocal or non-reciprocal, and originally might be concluded by the EC acting alone or with the Member States. The distribution of competency between the EU and Member States has been discussed in chapter four. If the agreement falls within an area of exclusive competence, only the EU need be involved. The norm post-Lisbon, pursuant to Articles 2 and 3 TFEU, is that the EU may also act alone in areas of shared competence. However, it has been noted above that Article 191(4) TFEU, for example, determinedly retains Member State competence with regard to environmental policy, and questions continue to arise concerning EU exclusivity and mixity, particularly where an agreement spills over from EU environmental objectives to Member State elements.[4]

The framework cooperation agreements tend to be concluded with states which are not of immediate strategic or historic importance, but with which the EU nonetheless desires to achieve a closer relationship, or to pursue slightly wider aims than could be achieved by a pure trade agreement. Typically they aim towards the improvement of conditions of trade and investment, emphasise the protection of the environment and seek to strengthen the political context in which they operate. Thus, relations with Asia and Latin America tend to be concluded on this basis, as are agreements with Russia and Eastern Europe (where these are not envisaged as being a 'stepping stone' on the route to EU accession).

C. Association Agreements

The third category of agreement comprises association agreements. Based upon Articles 207, 217 and 218 TFEU (formerly Articles 113, 228 and 238 EC respectively), association agreements include both trade and political elements, thereby creating strong links between the parties. Such strong links may be a 'stepping stone' to EU membership (as in the case of Europe Agreements, for example that concluded with Hungary in 1991)[5] or have a purely developmental associative purpose (for example development

---

[4] See further ch 4 above and P Eeckhout, *EU External Relations Law* (2nd edn, Oxford, Oxford University Press, 2011) ch 7.
[5] [1993] OJ L347/93.

cooperation agreements, such as, Cotonou).[6] Each of these categories is now generally concluded by the EU acting with the Member States.

i. Development Cooperation Agreements

The EU's current relationship with third states is clearly determined by geographical and historical as well as contemporary political factors. Development cooperation agreements, aimed at less developed countries (LDCs), emerged in the context of relations with the EU's former colonies; the African, Caribbean and Pacific (ACP) states. Complementarity between EU policies and those of the partner states is fundamental to development cooperation, as is coordination of EU, Member State and other international policies. Development cooperation is now governed by Articles 208–11 TFEU (formerly Articles 177–81 EC). The objectives of development cooperation are set out in Articles 21 TEU and Article 208 TFEU.

a. The Development of ACP-EEC Cooperation
ACP-EEC/EU cooperation dates from the very founding of the European Economic Community, when the Treaty of Rome expressed the Member States' solidarity with, and commitment to the prosperity of, their overseas departments and territories. As such, ACP-EEC/EU cooperation provides an excellent example of the emergence and evolution of the EU's development cooperation policy. The Member States initially sought to fulfil their Treaty of Rome commitments through the mechanism of its development funds (EDF). Thus, the Yaoundé Convention, which was in force from 1964 to 1969, committed the EC to providing commercial advantages and financial aid to African former colonies. This cooperation was covered by the 2nd EDF. In 1970 Yaoundé II, (between the Associated African and Malagache countries and the EC) extended the cooperation under the 3rd EDF until 1974. By 1974, however, the EC had changed. The accession of the UK introduced a whole new group with whom development cooperation could be established: the Commonwealth countries. Consequently, the successor to Yaoundé, the Lomé Convention, which ran from 1975 to 1979, included some of these states. The basis of Lomé, which coincided with the 4th EDF, was partnership: the relationship was contractual and comprised a combination of aid, trade and political aspects. The political aspects in particular were matters which were, unquestionably at that time, of Member State rather than EC competence. This notwithstanding, Lomé was signed by the EC acting alone rather than with the Member States. Lomé II (1979–84) introduced no major changes except the introduction of SYSMIN (aid to

---

[6] Article 9 Cotonou Convention, signed 23 June 2000, http://ec.europa.eu/europeaid/where/acp/overview/cotonou-agreement/index_en.htm. The Agreement was to run for 20 years, subject to five-yearly revision.

the mining industry). However, Lomé III[7] (1984–89) shifted the main focus of the convention from the promotion of industrial development to self-reliant, self-sufficient development and food security, and included references to human rights in the preamble and in certain articles.[8]

Lomé IV[9] was signed in 1989 and ran for 10 years. In this convention the emphasis shifted again, with the political focus becoming more pronounced. Thus, the promotion of human rights and democratic principles and good governance were emphasised, alongside strengthening the position of women, environmental protection, decentralised cooperation, diversification of ACP economies, promotion of the private sector and increasing regional cooperation. The mid-term review of Lomé increased the strength of the human rights provisions: states failing to comply with these provisions risked suspension of the agreement. At this point, the EDF was not increased in real terms and the decentralised cooperation, which could be seen in Lomé IV, was broadened to include participatory partnership embracing a variety of actors from civil society.

As development cooperation matured, a steady progression can be seen away from purely financial aid to wider cooperation, moving the focus away from the EC and back to the partner states themselves. Thus, the partnership by the second half of Lomé IV was based on shared objectives and principles as well as on trade and financial benefits.

b. Changing Priorities in the 1990s

Outside the context of development cooperation, two developments during the 1990s meant that by the time of the negotiations for the successor to Lomé, priorities were changing. Internally, the development of the Maastricht Treaty had radically changed the EC, not just in terms of institutional change and the creation of the EU but also in terms of its fields of interest. It has been seen above that the scope of the EC's interest, as distinct from the EU interest, had broadened, and its commitment to more political aims was increased, as is reflected to some extent in the mid-term review of Lomé IV. This development subsequently became even more pronounced in the Treaty of Amsterdam. Alongside internal EC developments, the international context was changing. The contribution of the UN to the nature of international relations, through its conferences on the Environment, Population, Human Rights, Social Development, Women and the World Food Summit, was particularly significant, as it set new standards both for donors and developing nations.

---

[7] (1985) 24 ILM 571.
[8] Articles 4, 119, 122, 125 and 127.
[9] [1991] OJ L229/91.

The principal objectives of the Cotonou Convention,[10] the successor to Lomé IV, were sustainable development and poverty reduction, and to reverse the processes of social, technological and economic marginalisation. These were to be achieved through a combination of political dialogue, development aid and closer economic and trade cooperation. The agreement is based on five inter-dependent pillars: a comprehensive political dimension, participatory approaches, a strengthened focus on poverty reduction, a new framework for economic and trade cooperation, and reform of financial cooperation. It is significant that in the revision of Cotonou in 2010, the EU and ACP states recognised the global significance of, and the challenge posed by, climate change.[11]

ii. The Europe Agreements

The Europe Agreements comprise a significant category of Association Agreements. These developed from 1991,[12] initially with the Central and Eastern European Countries (CEECs)[13] and subsequently the Baltic states (since 1995).[14] The Europe Agreements included five central elements: (i) a commitment aiming to achieve a free trade area over ten years; (ii) limited trade concessions (in agriculture and fisheries); (iii) the liberalisation of services; (iv) the application of competition rules similar to those applying to the EC; and, finally (v) political conditionality. These agreements were developed as a bridge to enlargement and the first of these states joined in 2004.[15]

iii. Other Association Agreements

Certain of the Mediterranean states have or had similar 'associative' status to that formed under the Europe Agreements.[16] However, the main relation with the Mediterranean region was developed at the Barcelona conference and initially aimed to create a free trade area by 2010. This aim was not met: in December 2011, the Council authorised the Commission to open bilateral negotiations 'to establish deep and comprehensive free trade areas'

[10] Above, n 6.

[11] Text agreed 11 March 2010, Decision 2010/648/EU Council Decision of 14 May, 2nd Revision of Cotonou [2010] OJ L287/53. See further: http://ec.europa.eu/europeaid/where/acp/overview/cotonou-agreement/index_en.htm.

[12] Initial links with these states (from 1989) had concerned very limited sectoral cooperation, but since 1989, this had shifted to trade and economic cooperation; see, for example, n 3.

[13] Eg, Hungary (n 5).

[14] Eg, Agreement with Latvia [1998] OJ L26/3.

[15] The Czech Republic, Estonia, Latvia, Lithuania, Hungary, Malta, Poland, Slovakia and Slovenia.

[16] For example, Tunisia [1998] OJ L97/1 and Cyprus [1973] OJ L133/73, the latter of which acceded to the EU in 2004.

with Egypt, Jordan, Morocco and Tunisia, and scoping exercises were launched in March 2012. This has obvious political and strategic significance, as the development of a free trade area should offer some increase in stability in relations which may or may not precede enlargement. Similar strategic interests also arose in relation to the CEECs and the Baltic states following their emergence from Soviet control and the Warsaw Pact, requiring a unique approach. Economic provisions alone, as might have been developed through trade agreements or trade and economic cooperation agreements, would not have been sufficient to develop the economic and political stability, sought by the EC (and subsequently the EU) for each of these areas.

D. European Neighbourhood Policy

Since 2004, relations with both the New Independent States (NIS) and Euro Mediterranean states have been developed under the auspices of the European Neighbourhood Policy (ENP), which, since 2006, has been identified by the Council of Ministers as 'one of the core priorities of the Union's external action'[17] and in 2007 was referred to as a 'core priority of the EU's foreign policy'.[18] As observed by Cremona:

> A policy is driven by the policy-maker. The ENP is clearly and unambiguously an *EU Policy* directed at its neighbours rather than the creation of something new (a space or area) or a shared enterprise (a process or partnership). The word policy also emphasizes the unilateral nature of the ENP.[19]

This is an important observation which underlines the extent to which the EU drives the shape and form of action in this context. The 2014 Joint Communication from the EU High Representative for Foreign Affairs and Security policy recognizes the particular challenges posed to the ENP by recent political developments and challenges across the region. It emphasizes that the policy also:

> anchors countries/societies in transition, and even in crisis situations, to the EU, by proposing a set of values and standards to guide their reform efforts, and generally through the creation of networks linking them to the EU and beyond

---

[17] Council Conclusions on the European Neighbourhood Policy, General Affairs and External Relations Council, 11 December 2006, available at: www.eu-un.europa.eu/articles/en/article_6582_en.htm See further: http://ec.europa.eu/world/enp/policy_en.htm. The ENP is directed towards both the NIS and the Southern Caucasus States. In addition, it extends to the Southern Mediterranean States.

[18] Strengthening the European Neighbourhood Policy, Presidency Progress Report, General Affairs and External Relations Council (GAERC), 18/19 June 2007.

[19] M Cremona, 'The European Neighbourhood Policy: More than a Partnership?' in M Cremona (ed), *Developments in EU External Relations Law* (Oxford, Oxford University Press 2008) 254.

to other partners. It is a framework to work towards, and safeguard, democracy, freedom, prosperity and security for both the EU and its partners.[20]

In so concluding, the Communication also emphasises the role of the EU as a diplomatic actor, in providing security. While the Communication emphasizes partnership, there is a clear sense conveyed, consistent with Cremona's observations, of the leadership role of the EU in securing the objectives of the ENP.

The Treaty of Lisbon provides that relations between the EU and its neighbours should be based upon the EU's values,[21] and these are clearly at the heart of the ENP. However, from the outset, this has been explicitly framed in terms of the international obligations which the EU's neighbours have signed up to, including variously the ECHR, the UN Charter and the UN Declaration on Human Rights, core labour standards, the ILO Conventions and 'a sustainable mode of development'.[22] While this is an EU-driven process based upon the EU's values, the reference to international obligations runs counter to the suggestion that this is the EU paternalistically exporting its standards. Instead, it can be argued that although the EU is promoting its values, it is promoting those to which the partner state is also committed. The political significance of this is considerable: it is an approach which characterises the EU's broader relations with third states.

E. Sectoral Agreements

In addition to the general or framework agreements concluded by the EU with third states, the EU also regularly concludes sectoral agreements, dealing with cooperation in particular fields such as textiles, fisheries, customs, science and technology and transport.

F. Interim Agreements

The final category is that of *interim agreements*, in which the EU acts without the Member States, bringing the commercial elements of Association or Trade and Development Agreements into force ahead of the political or other provisions which concern Member States' competency.[23] In this the EU separates out the matters falling within its exclusive competence and brings

---

[20] Joint Communication from the EU High Representative for Foreign Affairs and Security Policy Neighbourhood at the Crossroads: Implementation of the European Neighbourhood Policy in 2013, Join 2014 12 final; available at: http://eeas.europa.eu/enp/documents/strategy-papers/index_en.htm.
[21] Article 8 TEU.
[22] Commission Communication of 12 May 2004, 'European Neighbourhood Policy: Strategy Paper, COM (2004) 373 final at 12–13.
[23] See, for example, Interim Agreement between the European Community and the United Mexican States, December [1997] OJ C356/10.

them into force ahead of the other provisions. This may be problematic, particularly where commercial cooperation is dependent upon the other areas. Yet it offers tangible benefits to a state to facilitate the achievement of its other commitments, crystallising the cooperation before it can disintegrate, and is standard procedure. Such interim agreements are based upon Articles 207(4) and 218(6) TFEU.[24]

It is clear even from this very brief account of the nature of the EU's relations with third states that the form and focus of the EU's external agreements are intrinsically bound up with the strategic and political interests of the EU in the particular state or area and, in addition, explicitly reflect the political context of the time. The impact of this upon the content of agreements, in particular regarding non-economic commitments and undertakings, will be seen below. One feature of EU cooperation with third states which has been the subject of considerable attention over the years, and is directly relevant to the present study, is the development of human rights conditionality in its external agreements.

II. THE EMERGENCE OF THE HUMAN RIGHTS
AND DEMOCRACY CLAUSE: LOMÉ IV (1990)

The emergence of the 'human rights and democracy clause' has been the subject of considerable comment.[25] However, important questions remain

---

[24] For example, the EU's Interim Agreement (IA) with Bosnia and Herzegovina entered into force on 1 July 2008, following the conclusion of the Stablisiation and Association Agreement in 2006 (which has not yet entered into force).

[25] See, inter alia, L Bartels, *The Application of Human Rights Conditionality in the EU's Bilateral Trade Agreements and Other Trade Arrangements with Third Countries*, European Parliament Report, A6-0200/2008, 29 May 2008 and Legislative resolution, P6_TA(2008) 0252, 5 June 2008; L Bartels, *Human Rights Conditionality in the EU's International Agreements* (Oxford, Oxford University Press 2005); L Bartels, 'Human Rights and Sustainable Development Obligations in EU Free Trade Agreements' (2013) 40 *Legal Issues of Economic Integration* 297; M Cremona, 'Human Rights and Democracy Clauses in the EC's Trade Agreements', in N Emiliou and D O'Keefe (eds), *The European Union and world trade law : after the GATT Uruguay Round* (Chichester, Wiley, 1996); K Smith, 'The Use of Political Conditionality in the EU's Relations with Third Countries: How Effective?' (1998) 3 *European Foreign Affairs Review* 253; P Clestin de Ulimubenshi, 'La Problemmatique de la clause des droits de l'homme dans un accord de cooperation economique: l'example de la Convention de Lomé' (1994) 3 *African Journal of International Comparative Law* 253; JD Saltnes, 'The EU's Human Rights Policy Unpacking the Literature on the EU's Implementation of Aid Conditionality', Arena Centre for European Studies, University of Oslo, Working Paper 2, March 2013. Available at: www.sv.uio.no/arena/english/research/publications/arena-publications/workingpapers/working-papers2013/wp2-13.pdf; M Fouwels, 'The European Union's Common Foreign and Security Policy and Human Rights' (1997) 15(3) *Netherlands Quarterly of Human Rights* 291; E Fierro, 'Legal Basis and Scope of the Human Rights Clauses in EC Bilateral Agreements: Any Room for Positive Interpretation?' (2001) 7(1) *European Law Journal* 41; PJ de Kuyper, 'Trade Sanctions, Security and Human Rights and Commercial Policy' in M Maresceau (ed), *The European Community's Commercial Policy after 1992: the Legal Dimension* (Dordrecht, London, M Nijhoff, 1993); A Paasch, 'Human

to be addressed. The 'human rights' clause (not, at that time, also referring to democracy) first appeared in the context of development cooperation in Article 5 of the Fourth Lomé Convention:

1. Cooperation shall thus be conceived in accordance with the positive approach, where respect for human rights is recognized as a basic factor of real development and where cooperation is conceived as a contribution to the promotion of these rights.

   In this context development policy and cooperation are closely linked with the respect for and enjoyment of fundamental human rights …

2. Hence the Parties reiterate their deep attachment to human dignity and human rights … the rights in question are all human rights, the various categories thereof being indivisible and interrelated, each having its own legitimacy: non-discriminatory treatment; fundamental human rights; civil and political rights; economic, social and cultural rights …

   ACP-EEC cooperation shall help abolish the obstacles preventing individuals and peoples from actually enjoying to the full their economic, social and cultural rights.

The Community had sought to introduce such a clause in Lomé III (1985), but this had been blocked by the partner states, who were suspicious of both what they perceived as political intervention[26] and the crucial question of how 'human rights' would be interpreted. In particular, the EC's approach to human rights focused on the individual, whereas the ACP states were concerned with the protection of collective rights, including the right to development.[27]

Article 5 listed the type of human rights intended by the parties and provided for the allocation of financial resources to schemes promoting human rights. The Commission, in answer to a parliamentary question in 1991, stated that the response made to requests for funding would 'depend on the intrinsic value of the operations proposed and … the competence of the bodies with which these operations would be mounted'.[28]

[26] De Ulimubenshi (n 25).

[27] See de Kuyper (n 25); Pollet (n 25).

[28] Answer given by Mr Marin on behalf of the Commission (in response to parliamentary written question No. 2698/90 by Mr Ernest Glinne, 4 December 1990) on 14 January 1991 [1991] OJ C107/53. The EC subsequently concluded an agreement with Argentina with a more strongly worded clause: Article 1 states that: 'Cooperation ties between the Community and Argentina and this agreement in its entirety are based upon respect for the democratic principles and human rights which inspire the domestic and external policies of both the Community and Argentina.'

A. Article 366a: Introducing Human Rights Conditionality to Lomé (1995)

The revised Lomé IV introduced a suspension provision in Article 366a, under which, if a party believed there had been a violation of Article 5 Lomé, it could invite the other party to consultations to assess the situation and seek a remedy. Article 366a set out the procedure to be followed, including timetables for the consultations. If the deadline specified in the timetable expired without resolution of the problem, the party which invoked the consultations could take appropriate steps to address the situation. Such steps included, where necessary, the partial or full suspension of application of the Convention to the party in breach. Any measures adopted would be communicated to the party in breach and revoked as soon as the reasons for their adoption had been resolved. Crucially, Article 366a thus introduced the element of conditionality to Lomé—that the agreement and its continued operation are dependent upon the parties adhering to these conditions.

In 1996 the Commission proposed a Council Decision laying down the procedure for implementing Article 366a,[29] which was subsequently enacted in 1999.[30] This provided the framework to be followed by the Council when opening consultations at the initiative of the Commission or a Member State. It was invoked on several occasions, the first being in relation to Togo.[31] Article 366a did not, however, result in suspension of cooperation beyond a moratorium on additional financial aid.

B. The Cotonou Agreement (2000)

Under the Cotonou Agreement,[32] respect for human rights, democratic principles and the rule of law remain essential elements of the partnership,

---

[29] COM (96) 0069 [1996] OJ C119/7; see also Parliamentary Resolution on the Proposal for a Council Decision on a framework procedure for implementing Article 366a of the Fourth Lomé Convention [1997] OJ C200/256.

[30] Council Decision 99/214/EC of 11 March 1999 on the procedure for implementing Article 366a of the Fourth ACP-EC Convention [1999] OJ L75/32.

[31] Consultations with Togo took place on 30/07/98 (Europe 01/08/98) See also COM (99)204 Communication from the Commission to the Council on the opening of consultations with Niger pursuant to Article 366a of the Lomé Convention; COM (99) 295 concerning the opening of consultations with the Comoros; COM (99) 361 on the opening of negotiations with Guinea-Bissau (and COM (99) 491 on the *conclusion* of negotiations with Guinea-Bissau); COM (99) 695 Proposal for a Council Decision *concluding* consultations with the Comoros; COM (99) 899 on the opening of consultations with the Cote d'Ivoire; COM (2000) 460 final on the opening of consultations with Fiji; COM (2000) 486 final on the opening of consultations with Haiti.

[32] The successor to the Lomé Convention, the Cotonou Agreement, signed 23 June 2000, at: http://ec.europa.eu/europeaid/where/acp/overview/cotonou-agreement/index_en.htm.

and indeed are required to underpin the domestic and international policies of the parties.[33] In addition, 'good governance'[34] is also a fundamental element of the agreement, and 'serious' cases of corruption will constitute a violation of the agreement.

There is a new procedure to deal with violations of the essential elements: Article 96 sets down the framework for consultations in the event that one party considers the other[35] has failed to fulfil its obligations regarding the essential elements: it can invite the other party to participate in consultations with a view to remedying the situation. In the case of 'special urgency', the party may take 'appropriate measures', which must be proportionate and conform to international law. Thus, action may be taken *before proceeding to consultations*. Suspension *may* be invoked *as a last resort*.[36] The development whereby parties may take 'appropriate measures' prior to opening consultations is a significant one, as it permits an urgent response to a situation in which political negotiation and consultation may be impractical.

The inclusion of 'good governance' as an essential element is also significant and reflects the EU's own focus upon developing governance in different contexts. Together with the possibility of pre-emptive action, this permits a more holistic view to be taken of a situation, without waiting for a total collapse in governance before acting. It reflects the development in the Treaty of Nice whereby the Council may act if it believes there is a 'clear risk' that an EU Member State will seriously violate human rights.[37] As it permits pre-emptive action, Cotonou can be said to provide a potentially more effective instrument for the protection of fundamental rights. However, it could also give rise to an increased risk of allegations of coercion of ACP states by the EC.

The first revision to Cotonou (in 2005) introduced Annex VII, which sets out the procedure for political dialogue on human rights, under Articles 8 and 9(4), to precede consultations under Article 96. It also provides additional rules on consultation under Article 96.

---

[33] Article 9(2). Article 9 provides: 'Cooperation shall be directed towards sustainable development centred on the human person, who is the main protagonist and beneficiary of development; this entails respect for and promotion of all human rights ... Respect for all human rights and fundamental freedoms, including respect for fundamental social rights, democracy based on the rule of law and transparent and accountable governance are an integral part of sustainable development.'

[34] Article 9(2) defines good governance as transparent and accountable management of human, natural, economic and financial resources for the purposes of equitable and sustainable development.

[35] The parties are: the EC and its Member States; and the ACP states.

[36] See House of Commons, European Scrutiny Committee, Nineteenth Report, www.publications.parliament.uk/pa/cm199900/cmselect/cmeuleg/23-xix/2321.htm. Within the EC, partial suspension requires a decision by qualified majority of the Council, whereas full suspension would require unanimity.

[37] Article 7 TEU, which is discussed in ch 2.

Following its second revision (2010), the Cotonou Agreement provides in respect of political dialogue that:

> The dialogue shall focus, inter alia, on specific political issues of mutual concern or of general significance for the attainment of the objectives of this Agreement, such as the arms trade, excessive military expenditure, drugs, organised crime <u>or child labour, or discrimination of any kind, such as race, colour, sex, language, religion, political or other opinion, national or social origin, property, birth or other status</u>. The dialogue shall also encompass a regular assessment of the developments concerning the respect for human rights, democratic principles, the rule of law and good governance.[38]

The addition of the focus upon 'discrimination of any kind' is in line with internal developments within the EU, for example, secondary legislation prohibiting discrimination.[39] However such issues touch on deep sensitivities. Clearly the focus in both revisions of Cotonou has been upon the development of dialogue and a desire to make cooperation work to achieve the objectives, rather than pushing for penalties for failure to achieve the objectives. This is consistent with the underlying ethos of GSP+.[40] It is also worth noting that the second revision of Cotonou includes an amendment to Article 9 whereby: 'The principles underlying the essential and fundamental elements as defined in this Article shall apply equally to the ACP States on the one hand, and to the European Union and its Member States, on the other hand.'[41] Thus, an element of reciprocal commitment is introduced.

C. The Human Rights and Democracy Clause in Agreements with Central and Eastern European States

i. Ex Ante Human Rights Consideration

Despite the initial appearance of the human rights clause in the context of development cooperation, it was in the context of agreements with states of Central and Eastern Europe that human rights 'conditionality' first appeared, that is, that respect for human rights became a condition of cooperation.

---

[38] The underlined section was added in the Second Revision.
[39] See ch 2.
[40] GSP and GSP+ are discussed below; see text accompanying n 58.
[41] See Agreement amending for the second time the Partnership Agreement between the members of the African, Caribbean and Pacific Group of States, of the one part, and the European Community and its Member States, of the other part, signed in Cotonou on 23 June 2000, as first amended in Luxembourg on 25 June 2005 [2010] OJ L287/4, Article 6(b), see Consolidated text, http://ec.europa.eu/europeaid/where/acp/overview/documents/cotonou-consolidated-fin-ap-2012_en.pdf.

In its relations with Eastern Europe, the EC initially afforded special treatment to those countries which made the greatest progress on political reforms (Hungary and Poland) and withheld any prospect of any agreement with those countries which blatantly violated human rights (Bulgaria and Romania). Despite this political approach, there was no reference to human rights in the agreements then concluded.[42] An element of conditionality was applied *before* the substantive stage was reached. The dangers of this approach are evident. Either party may enter into an agreement on the basis of certain political conditions and circumstances, yet a change in those circumstances does not give rise to a right to suspend the agreement. This had occurred in the EC's earlier relations with the ACP states and had indeed prompted the inclusion of the human rights clause in Lomé IV.[43]

ii. Human Rights Conditionality within Agreements with European States

Human rights conditionality within agreements emerged in 1992 and 1993, when the EC concluded trade and cooperation agreements with Albania, the Baltic states and Slovenia, as well as Uruguay.[44] Subsequent Europe agreements also contain the clause, as do the trade and cooperation agreements with the remaining former Soviet republics.

The evolution of this clause in the European context is easily explained. First, on a practical level, the sheer number of agreements being formed between the EC and this part of the world increased the likelihood of developments occurring there. Second, on a strategic level, the political interest that the EC had in realising and maintaining stability in this part of Europe, particularly in view of events occurring at that time, is clearly instrumental. Third, given that the Europe Agreements were a precursor to accession, and that the recognition and protection of human rights were (and remain) conditions of membership of the EU, the protection of human rights had to be ensured prior to accession. Evidently these three factors are themselves related.

iii. The Substance of the Clause in Agreements with European States

Two levels may be observed in human rights conditionality. The first level was the essential elements clause itself. Pursuant to this, adherence to certain standards of human rights and democracy were essential elements of

---

[42] Eg, Agreement with Hungary [1993] OJ L347/1.

[43] See de Ulimubenshi (n 25) and de Kuyper (n 25) 408–10.

[44] Agreements with Estonia, Latvia and Lithuania (n 3); Albania [1992] OJ L343/2; Slovenia [1993] OJ L189/2; Uruguay [1992] OJ L94/2.

cooperation and agreement between the EC and its partner states. Second, the human rights clause was subsequently backed up by a non-compliance clause. Two formulations of the non-compliance clause have been seen: first, that of explicit suspension (the Baltic clause)[45] and, second, that of general non-execution (the Bulgarian clause).[46] The more extreme Baltic clause was used only in agreements with the Baltic states, Albania and Slovenia.[47]

In these clauses there is no equivalent of Article 7 TEU or of the possibility to act pre-emptively in relation to human rights violations, which occurs as a result of the inclusion of 'good governance' as an essential element in Cotonou.[48] Having been used initially as a condition of the conclusion of an agreement and subsequently as an element of the continued operation of an agreement, it should be noted that adherence to human rights and democratic standards is now a requirement for accession to the EU,[49] following which Article 7 TEU will apply.

D. Universal Inclusion of the Human Rights Clause

By 1993, it had been decided that a human rights and democracy clause would be included in every agreement concluded by the EC with third states.[50] In 1993 Commissioner Marin stated that: 'Very explicit clauses on human rights and basic freedoms are now an integral part of all agreements concluded by the Community with non-member countries.'[51]

The implementation of this policy has not always been easy. In 1995 the Commission observed that 'although Commission guidelines [on the

---

[45] '[T]he Parties reserve the right to suspend this agreement, in whole or in part with immediate effect if a serious breach of its essential elements occurs.'

[46] '[I]f either Party considers that the other Party has failed to fulfil an obligation under this Agreement, it may take appropriate measures. Before doing so, except in cases of special urgency, it shall supply the Association Council with all relevant information required for a thorough examination of the situation with a view to seeking a solution acceptable to the Parties. In the selection of measures, priority must be given to those which least disturb the functioning this Agreement. These measures shall be notified immediately to the Association Council and shall be the subject of consultations within the Association Council if the other Party so requests.' The Bulgarian clause is generally accompanied by a provision that 'cases of special urgency' include the breach of essential elements of the Agreement. See eg, Agreement with the Ukraine (Partnership and Cooperation Agreement between the European Communities and their Member States, and the Ukraine [1998] OJ L49/3), where this was provided for in a Special Declaration regarding Art 102.

[47] See, for example, Agreement with Slovenia (n 44).

[48] Above, n 6.

[49] Article 49 TEU.

[50] Commission Decision of 26/1/93, MIN 93 1137 pt XIV.

[51] 'Commission Communication on the Inclusion of Respect for Democratic Principles and Human Rights in Agreements between the European Community and Third Countries' COM (95) 216 final.

inclusion of these clauses] have been respected, the objectives of a systematic approach have not yet been achieved'. It concluded that 'there is a need ... to improve the consistency, transparency and visibility of the Community approach and make greater allowance for the sensitivity of third countries'.[52] The commitment to human rights and democracy is evident not only in the appearance of the clauses themselves, but also in the development since 1996 of a specific title within agreements of 'Cooperation on Matters relating to Human Rights and Democracy' providing for cooperation:

> [O]n all questions relevant to the establishment or reinforcement of democratic institutions, including those required in order to strengthen the rule of law, and the protection of human rights and fundamental freedoms according to International law and OSCE principles.

This appears in the 1996 Partnership and Cooperation Agreements with Uzbekistan and Azerbaijan, but not in the earlier (1995) Europe Agreement with Lithuania.[53]

i. A Universal Policy with Varying Reference Points and Content

The form and strength of commitment expressed varies not only chronologically but also according to geography. The (earlier) 1994 partnership and cooperation agreement with Ukraine, for example, includes reference to human rights and democracy in Title II (Political dialogue).[54] In the Agreements with Uzbekistan, Georgia and Azerbaijan,[55] it goes even further:

> [T]he Parties shall endeavour to cooperate on matters pertaining to the observance of the principles of democracy and the respect, protection and promotion of Human Rights, particularly those of persons belonging to minorities and shall hold consultation if necessary on relevant matters.[56]

The EC had earlier refrained from the inclusion of provisions concerning minority rights in its Europe Agreements, notwithstanding that minority rights were undoubtedly a crucial issue in this context. This is in turn significant, since in general economic, political and legal terms, the PCAs

---

[52] ibid.

[53] Partnership and Cooperation Agreement with Azerbaijan [1999] OJ L246/3, Title VII, Article 71; Partnership and Cooperation Agreement with Uzbekistan [1999] OJ L229/1; Europe Agreement with Lithuania [1998] OJ L51/3.

[54] [1998] OJ L49/3.

[55] Partnership and Cooperation Agreements with Azerbaijan and Uzbekistan (n 53); Partnership and Cooperation Agreement with Georgia [1999] OJ L205/1.

[56] See also COM (95) 219 final, where it is stated that the protection of minorities is of paramount importance to the establishment of the partnership.

have been deemed to be 'looser' than the Europe Agreements.[57] Certainly, the PCAs, being based on Article 113 and 235 EC (now Articles 207 and 352 and 353 TFEU), do not create the associative status of the Europe Agreements, which were also based on Article 238 EC (now 217 TFEU). The different objectives create a different level of link. However, the Association Agreement with Tunisia concluded in 1995 refers to 'coordination on international issues of common interest', but does not specify human rights and democracy, again creating a less explicit obligation within what might have been described as a 'closer' relationship.

The difference in form and strength of commitment partly reflects the difference in purpose of each type of agreement: partnership and cooperation as contrasted with association (although this does not explain the varying approaches within specific types of agreements). It also reflects the particular importance that the EC placed upon human rights and democracy issues on its doorstep. There was an urgent need to consolidate progress made on these fronts in these states following the break-up of the Soviet Union, particularly in the light of the risk to the EU in the event of a failure to do so.

E. Human Rights Conditionality and the EU GSP

One very significant context in which the EU has sought to bring together trade and human rights, and impose stringent conditionality, is its GSP. The GSP is an autonomous trade instrument, the objective of which is to 'assist developing countries in their efforts to reduce poverty and promote good governance and sustainable development'.[58] Under the GSP, the EU offers developing states preferential access to the EU market, subject to certain conditions. In addition to the core GSP tariff preferences, the EU also operates a system of positive conditionality: GSP+. Under GSP+, eligible states which commit themselves to key, universal obligations relating to human rights, labour rights, the environment and good governance may apply for additional preferences. Under a third tier of the scheme, 'everything but arms', least developed states (defined by the UN) can benefit from free market access for all products relating to the arms trade.

i. Positive Conditionality under the GSP

The GSP has existed since 1971 and operates as part of the EU's common commercial policy. A new regulatory framework took effect from January

---

[57] Christophe Hillion, 'Partnership and Cooperation Agreements between the EU and NIS' (1998) 3 *European Foreign Affairs Review* 399.
[58] Regulation (EU) No 978/2012 of the European Parliament and of the Council of 25 October 2012 applying a scheme of generalised tariff preferences and repealing Council Regulation (EC) No 732/2008 [2012] OJ L303/1, Preamble, para 5.

2014,[59] replacing the previous system, which had run from 2009.[60] The EU had introduced positive conditionality to the GSP in 1991, when a small group of states were granted additional trade benefits.[61] The objective of this original additional scheme was to combat the production of drugs by encouraging the planting of crops other than narcotics. In 1992 and 1995 a number of additional states joined the scheme.[62] However, at this stage, the purported focus shifted from addressing production of drugs to combating trafficking (although how this was realised by the scheme was far from clear). In 2001 Pakistan also joined the scheme, a development which proved the catalyst for a challenge: India complained to the WTO that the drugs arrangements breached the WTO requirement of non-discrimination. This led to the scheme being ruled to be inconsistent with the WTO.

A further version of positive conditionality had been introduced in 1994 as a separate scheme, alongside the drugs scheme. Under this scheme, GSP beneficiaries could apply for additional preferences if they had ratified and implemented certain labour and/or tropical timber conventions. Beneficiaries of this scheme included Sri Lanka and Moldova for compliance with labour standards. In addition, China applied for additional preferences on the basis of compliance with tropical timber conventions.

Following the 2004 WTO ruling regarding the drugs arrangements, the EU revised both schemes, creating GSP+. Questions have emerged concerning the decision making pursuant to which states are granted GSP+; in particular, there was criticism of a lack of transparency.[63] There were also questions concerning the review of implementation of the relevant Convention requirements for the granting of GSP+ benefits. These issues, among others, are addressed under the revised GSP.

ii. Negative Conditionality

Clearly there is an element of negative conditionality operating under the GSP in that GSP+ may be withdrawn from states which fail to comply with their obligations under the relevant conventions. In addition to this, the regular GSP benefits may be withdrawn in the face of failure to comply with the specific, stipulated non-trade norms.

---

[59] Regulation (EU) No 978/2012 of the European Parliament and of the Council of 25 October 2012 applying a scheme of generalised tariff preferences and repealing Council Regulation (EC) No 732/2008 [2012] OJ L303/1.

[60] Council Regulation (EC) No 732/2008 of 22 July 2008 applying a scheme of generalised tariff preferences for the period from 1 January 2009 to 31 December 2011 [2008] OJ L211/1 ('the GSP Regulation') as extended (to 31 December 2013) by Regulation 512/2011 OJ L145/28–29.

[61] Bolivia, Colombia, Ecuador and Peru.

[62] Costa Rica, El Salvador, Guatemala, Honduras, Nicaragua, Panama (1992) and Venezuela (1995).

[63] See Bartels, *The Application of Human Rights Conditionality* (n 25) 8.

iii. Reform of the GSP

As indicated above, there was some criticism of a lack of transparency in the previous regulatory framework. This applied both with regard to eligibility for GSP+ and regarding the reasons for withdrawal of preferences generally. The EU has explicitly sought to address this in the new regulation.[64] In the preamble to the proposed regulation, it is stated that:

> [T]he special incentive arrangement for sustainable development and good governance is based on the integral concept of sustainable development ... consequently, the additional tariff preferences ... should be granted to those developing countries which are vulnerable due to a lack of diversification and insufficient integration within the international trading system, in order to help them assume the special burdens and responsibilities resulting from the ratification of core international conventions on human and labour rights, environmental protection and good governance.[65]

While the same three categories of the scheme continue, the number of GSP beneficiaries has been reduced from 177 to 90, consistent with the intention to focus the GSP upon the states which have greatest need. While the GSP+ scheme has been expanded under the new regulation, its monitoring system for compliance is more rigorous and transparent, including both regular reporting by the Commission and also the involvement of the European Parliament. Under Article 10, states wishing to benefit from GSP+ must submit a request in writing, detailing their compliance with the relevant conventions.[66] Under Article 15, the burden of proof of compliance with the Conventions lies with the GSP+ beneficiary state. There are now stronger incentives in place for GSP+, which is consistent with the EU's internal focus upon sustainable development and good governance, but there is also enhanced monitoring. Failure to comply with the obligations resulting from these conventions 'shall' result in temporary withdrawal of the GSP+ (the procedure for which is also set out in Article 15).

The general arrangements may also be temporarily withdrawn for, among other factors, 'serious and systematic violation' of the principles contained in the Annex VIII conventions.[67] Once again, the procedure for withdrawal is set out in the Regulation. There is no definition of 'serious and systematic violation', although the Preamble states that:

> [T]he reasons for withdrawal of the three arrangements should include serious and systematic violations of the principles laid down in certain international

---

[64] Regulation (EU) No 978/2012 of the European Parliament and of the Council of 25 October 2012 applying a scheme of generalised tariff preferences and repealing Council Regulation (EC) No 732/2008 [2012] OJ L303/1.
[65] ibid, Preamble, para 11.
[66] These are set out in Annex VIII.
[67] Article 19.

conventions concerning core human rights and labour rights, so as to promote the objectives of those agreements.

Article 2 of the Regulation defines 'effective implementation' as 'the integral implementation of all undertakings and obligations undertaken under the relevant conventions, thus ensuring fulfilment of all the principles, objectives and rights guaranteed therein'.

iv. Temporary Withdrawal of GSP Benefits

It is not common for benefits to be withdrawn under GSP+. Where they are withdrawn, this is explicitly temporary, reflecting the intention that GSP conditionality should be used as an incentive to make progress on sustainable development and good governance. However, benefits under GSP+ were withdrawn in respect of Sri Lanka following an exhaustive Commission investigation between October 2008 and 2009.[68] The investigation drew from UN reports and statements, and additionally the findings of established human rights NGOs. Particular problems were identified relating to Sri Lanka's implementation of the International Covenant on Civil and Political Rights (ICCPR), the Convention against Torture (CAT) and the Convention on the Rights of the Child (CRC).[69] The decision to temporarily withdraw benefits was made in February 2010, to take effect six months later. In June 2010 the EU offered to delay the entry into force of the withdrawal by six months in exchange for 'tangible and sustainable progress on a number of outstanding issues'.[70] However, the Sri Lankan Government failed to respond to this offer and the withdrawal of benefits took effect in August 2010. It is clear from this experience that the EU was more interested in progress on the human rights issues than the sanction of withdrawal of benefits.

In addition to the measures taken against Sri Lanka, the Commission also initiated investigations into El Salvador in 2008 concerning the incorporation and effective implementation of ILO Convention No 87.[71] This investigation

---

[68] Implementing Regulation (EU) No 143/2010 of the Council of 15 February 2010 temporarily withdrawing the special incentive arrangement for sustainable development and good governance provided for under Regulation (EC) No 732/2008 with respect to the Democratic Socialist Republic of Sri Lanka [2010] OJ L045, 20 February 2010, 0001—0002.

[69] See further Brussels, 17 May 2011, COM (2011) 271 final, Report from the Commission to the European Parliament and the Council: Report on the status of ratification and recommendations by monitoring bodies concerning conventions listed in Annex III to Council Regulation (EC) No 732/2008 applying a scheme of generalised tariff preferences pursuant to Article 8(3) of this Regulation GSP+ [SEC(2011) 578 final].

[70] 'EU Regrets Silence of Sri Lanka Regarding Preferential Import Regime', Commission press release, 5 July 2010, http://trade.ec.europa.eu/doclib/cfm/doclib_section.cfm?sec=160 &langId=en.

[71] Commission Decision 2008/316/EC of 31 March 2008 providing for the initiation of an investigation pursuant to Article 18(2) of Council Regulation (EC) No 980/2005 with respect

was terminated when the Commission decided that its findings did not justify the temporary withdrawal of the GSP. More recently still, the Commission initiated an investigation into Bolivia concerning the effective implementation of the United Nations Single Convention on Narcotic Drugs.[72] Bolivia had withdrawn from the Convention as of 1 January 2012. The Commission investigation, however, found that Bolivia continued to give effect to the Convention and on 10 January 2013, Bolivia's request to re-accede was accepted. The Commission investigation was terminated as of March 2013.[73]

The range of sources and actors drawn upon by the Commission in its investigation into Sri Lanka is reflected in the new Regulation, in which it is provided that 'the Commission shall seek all information it considers necessary, inter alia, the conclusions and recommendations of the relevant monitoring bodies. In drawing its conclusions, the Commission shall assess all relevant information'.[74] Although the European Parliament had earlier called for its own right to initiate an investigation,[75] that right remains with the Commission under the new Regulation. However, another of the Parliament's recommendations, that the Commission undertake a regular review of implementation of the relevant Conventions for GSP+, has been incorporated. It is provided in respect of this review that:

> In drawing its conclusions concerning effective implementation of the conventions referred to in Annex VIII, the Commission shall assess the conclusions and recommendations of the relevant monitoring bodies, as well as, without prejudice to other sources, information submitted by third parties, including civil society, social partners, the European Parliament and the Council.[76]

Thus, there is the potential for a wide range of actors and voices to participate in the review process.

There can be no doubt that the EU's use of withdrawal as a sanction has been sparing. This is consistent with the above-mentioned objective of the GSP+; it is intended to encourage 'good behaviour', so it is used as a carrot rather than a stick. Notwithstanding the rarity of its invocation, questions

---

to the protection of the freedom of association and the right to organise in El Salvador [2008] OJ L 108, 18 April, 29.

[72] 2012/161/EU: Commission Implementing Decision of 19 March 2012 providing for the initiation of an investigation pursuant to Article 17(2) of Council Regulation (EC) No 732/2008 with respect to the effective implementation of the United Nations Single Convention on Narcotic Drugs in Bolivia.

[73] Commission Implementing Decision of 15 March 2013 terminating the investigation initiated by Implementing Decision 2012/161/EU (2013/136/EU).

[74] Article 15(6).

[75] European Parliament, Report on the proposal for a Council regulation applying a scheme of generalized tariff preferences for the period from 1 January 2009 to 31 December 2011, Committee on International Trade, Rapporteur Helmuth Markov, A6-0200/2008 and Legislative Resolution, P6_TA (2008) 0252, 5 June 2008, Amendment 24.

[76] Article 14.

have arisen regarding the legality of human rights conditionality in the context of GSP[77] and, in particular, there are ongoing concerns relating to GSP+. These concerns have arisen in particular from the perspective of compliance with WTO law. There are also significant questions which arise regarding the consequence of the EU incentivising support for particular industries or practices which may not be sustainable.[78]

F. Sectoral Agreements

One striking feature of the EU commitment to include the human rights and democracy clause in every agreement concluded with third states is that this commitment does not extend to sectoral agreements. Bartels highlighted this in his 2008 Report for the European Parliament and it was similarly identified by the International Federation for Human Rights (FIDH) in 2010.[79] FIDH specifically engaged with this in its recommendation that the policy of inclusion of human rights clauses in agreements with third states should be continued, including in sectoral agreements.

The problematic nature of this lacuna is evident in the example highlighted by Bartels, whereby the EC concluded a fisheries partnership agreement with Mauritania in July 2008. Three weeks later, there was a coup in Mauritania. The Community suspended cooperation under the Cotonou Agreement (pursuant to Article 96). However, the initial Commission response concerning the fisheries partnership agreement was to verify whether the conditions for its implementation continued to be met. The conclusion appears to have been that they did continue to be met, as the Community subsequently made payments to Mauritania under the Agreement in exchange for fishing opportunities.[80] Clearly the fact that fisheries' cooperation was not premised on respect for human rights and democracy meant that the fisheries agreement was not brought into question by events in Mauritania. As Bartels concluded, 'from an economic perspective, this might be justifiable, but from the perspective of human rights and democratic principles this is clearly insupportable'.[81]

The lack of inclusion of human rights conditionality in sectoral agreements is clearly problematic from the perspective of human rights protection. There can be no doubt that it undermines the idea of a universal

---

[77] WTO Appellate Body Report, *EC-Tariff Preferences*, WT/DS/246/AB/R, adopted 20 April 2004, para 167.

[78] These questions are beyond the scope of this present study.

[79] FIDH, 'Contribution to the Informal COHOM Dedicated to the Strategic Review of the EU Human Rights Policy' October 2010, available at: www.fidh.org/FIDH-Contribution-to-the-Informal.

[80] See Bartels, *The Application of Human Rights Conditionality* (n 25) 4.

[81] ibid.

policy applied to every agreement concluded by the EU. Setting aside this notable exception, Bartels observed broad success regarding the policy to include human rights conditionality in every agreement signed with third states. However, questions arise if the negotiating history with regard to the clause is examined, particularly in the light of different outcomes in instances in which the inclusion of the clause has been resisted by partner states.

G. External Opposition to Inclusion of the Human Rights Clause: Mexico and Australia

By 1997, the policy of inclusion of the human rights and democracy clause in all agreements concluded with third states had encountered isolated yet significant problems. Negotiations on economic cooperation agreements with both Mexico and Australia faltered over the proposed inclusion of the human rights and democracy clause. The Commission expressed the inclusion of the clause in such an agreement 'not as imposing a condition, but in the spirit of a joint undertaking to promote universal values'.[82] This indicated a political agenda. The observation that the clause represents the promotion of universal values is significant: it suggests not only a holistic view of economic liberalisation and development, but also a desire to avoid a suggestion of paternalism in the policy. These are both certainly consistent with the EU's subsequent focus on good governance and sustainable development.

Yet the EC's stance raised questions regarding the basis of its competence for pursuit of human rights and democracy, particularly as the internal duty to ensure that these interests are respected in the operation of its policies did not give rise to a parallel external competence. The practical distinction between a condition to uphold human rights, and the fulfilment of a joint undertaking to promote universal values, is ambiguous.

i. Mexico

The negotiating difficulties with Mexico were ultimately resolved. Both the Interim Agreement and Framework Agreement, signed in December 1997,[83] included the protection of human rights and democracy as an essential element. It should be noted, however, that in April 1999, the then

---

[82] 'The European Union and the External Dimension of Human Rights Policy' COM (95) 567 final.
[83] [1997] OJ C356 and C350.

International Confederation of Free Trade Unions (ICFTU)[84] called for a delay in the ratification of the EU-Mexico Agreement. The complaint was that the agreement was 'without adequate provisions on social, environmental and human rights issues'.[85] The ICFTU was particularly concerned by the fact that the EU-Mexico Agreement was 'a pioneering agreement because of its scope and depth and the first of several between the EU and the first of several between the EU and Latin American countries'.

With respect to human rights, the Agreement provides in Article 1 that:

> [F]undamental rights and democratic principles as contained in the Universal Declaration of Human Rights (UDHR) are essential elements of the agreement, underpinning both the domestic and external policies of the parties.

There is nothing, specifically, concerning social rights: however, the UDHR provides that: 'Everyone ... is entitled to realization ... of the economic, social and cultural rights indispensable for his dignity and the free development of his personality.'[86] More specifically, Article 23 UDHR refers to the right to work, choice of employment and just and favourable conditions of employment,[87] including equal pay for equal work,[88] and remuneration ensuring an existence worthy of human dignity and supplemented, if necessary, by other means of social protection.[89] Article 24 concerns the right to limited working hours and paid holidays. Article 25 guarantees an adequate standard of living in terms of health and well-being, and Article 26 provides for the right to education. Thus, although the agreement with Mexico does not per se explicitly guarantee specific social rights, they are included through the reference to the UDHR. The doubts expressed by the ICFTU demonstrate, however, the reality of the questions surrounding the interpretation of 'human rights' which the ACP states baulked at in the 1980s. On the other hand, that the commitment to human rights is premised in terms of the UDHR supports the suggestion that this policy is concerned with the promotion of universal values rather than an imposition of EU values.

ii. Australia

The EC's failure to conclude an 'Agreement' with Australia demonstrates the problematic consequences of lack of certainty regarding the definition of 'human rights' in this context. The Commission's statement that the human rights clause would reflect a joint undertaking to promote universal values rather than the imposition of a condition belies the fact that the

---

[84] The International Confederation of Free Trade Unions (ICTFU) was the predecessor of the International Trades Union Confederation.
[85] ICFTU Online 082/270499/DD (press release, 27 April 1999).
[86] Article 22.
[87] Paragraph (1).
[88] Paragraph (2).
[89] Paragraph (3).

protection of human rights in Australia is controversial, particularly with regard to the Aboriginal people. This is particularly striking given that the protection of indigenous peoples was at the relevant time being strengthened at an international level.[90]

Ultimately, the human rights clause proved a fundamental sticking point: the EC and Australia failed to conclude a framework agreement and instead the parties issued a 'Joint Declaration'. This declaration is not binding and contains no equivalent of human rights conditionality, although the political declaration includes some references to the protection of human rights and democracy. However, it sets a framework for cooperation which is in practical terms the equivalent of a framework agreement and it has indeed been followed by a 'Mutual Recognition Agreement'.[91] The sectoral agreements subsequently concluded with Australia obviously do not contain reference to human rights.[92]

By concluding a 'joint declaration' as the basis of cooperation, the EC technically avoided breaching its own policy regarding the inclusion of the human rights clause in every agreement concluded with third states. There is no indication, however, that trade relations or the development of closer commercial ties were in any way hampered by the failure to conclude a 'Framework Agreement'. The situation with regard to Australia posed some questions for the future universality of the EC's policy. Yet, had the clause been included, it might have provided a catalyst for the raising of serious issues concerning the enforcement of the clause.[93]

H. Questions Regarding the Definition and Perception of Human Rights at Issue: A Truly Universal Policy?

It is clear from the statements surrounding the negotiation procedure that the EC did not consider the protection of human rights to be an issue in Australia. Yet there are, and were at the time, very real questions concerning

---

[90] GA Resolution 47/53 1992 UN Declaration on the Rights of Persons belonging to National or Ethnic, Religious and Linguistic Minorities; UN GA Res 48/163, of 21/03/93 declared 1995–2004 Decade of Indigenous Peoples; Resolution 1995/32—UN Commission on Human Rights Established working group on Draft Declaration on the rights of indigenous peoples. See UN Factsheet No 9 Rights of Indigenous Peoples; R Higgins, 'Minority Rights: Discrepancies and Divergences between the International Covenant and the Council of Europe System' in R Lawson and M de Blois (eds), *The Dynamics of the Protection of Human Rights in Europe: Essays in Honour of Henry G. Schermers*, (Dordrecht, London, Nijhoff, 1994).

[91] Agreement on Mutual Recognition in relation to conformity assessment certificates and markings between the EC and Australia [1998] OJ L229/3.

[92] Sectoral agreements do not include the clause. See text accompanying n 79, above.

[93] Or, as observed by Ward, questions concerning the competence of the EC to include human rights requirements in trade and economic cooperation agreements; see Ward (n 25) 518–20.

the rights of Australian Aborigines. These concern, in particular, the treatment of minorities and the right to collective ownership of property. The EC, by its action and statements, clearly did not intend to address such issues through its use of this clause in this particular context. However, the terms in which the standard essential elements clause is framed refer to the UDHR, which does provide for the protection of these rights.[94]

Moreover, the rights of people belonging to minority groups have been afforded particular protection in the partnership and cooperation agreements concluded with Uzbekistan, Georgia and Armenia.[95] If the EC had succeeded in concluding an agreement with Australia, the evidence from the negotiation procedure and its surrounding publicity suggests that allegations of breach of human rights conditionality would have emerged from both Aboriginal groups within Australia and the international community.

Subsequent developments with respect to Chile support this speculation. The Community concluded an Association Agreement with Chile in 2002. This agreement included the human rights clause. A European parliamentary question was soon raised by Miquel Mayol i Raynal regarding the fact that Chile did not recognise indigenous peoples, had refused to ratify the ILO Convention on indigenous and tribal people, and that there were allegations of violation of the rights of indigenous peoples by the Chilean state.[96] In answer, the Commission replied confirming its awareness of 'the situation of the Mapuche people', highlighting a number of EU-led and other measures to support the Mapuche people, including Chilean state measures, and affirming its belief that 'the Chilean Government's policy for indigenous peoples is a step in the right direction'.[97] In this instance the Commission's view was that the essential element was fulfilled even if the protection offered was incomplete. It is worth noting that the commitment to the environment tends to be couched in such aspirational, non-absolute terms.

I. Continuing Resistance to Human Rights Conditionality

It is worth noting at this juncture that resistance to the human rights clause in trade agreements has not diminished: in 2010, India's opposition to the clause contributed to deadlock in the negotiation of a new EU-India

---

[94] Articles 2 and 17.

[95] Agreement with Uzbekistan (n 53); Agreement with Georgia (n 55); Partnership and Cooperation Agreement with Armenia [1999] OJ L239/1.

[96] Parliamentary Written Question E-3634/02 by Miquel Mayol i Raynal (Verts/ALE) to the Commission on the Association Agreement between the EU and Chile and respect for the rights of the Mapuche people, 17 December 2002 [2003] OJ C137 E, 12 June 2003, at 233.

[97] Answer to parliamentary written question [2003] OJ C137 E, 12 June 2003, at 234.

cooperation agreement.[98] The negotiation of the EU-Japan Strategic and Economic Partnership Agreements is also under pressure due to the EU's call to include human rights conditionality. While the human rights clause continues to be included in the EU's agreements with third states, its form and strength varies, including with regard to its implementing measures.[99]

J. Factors Influencing the Form and Strength of the Human Rights Clause

There can be no doubt that it is possible to identify factors which have influenced the type and strength of human rights clauses included by the EC in its various relations with third states. These originally included the type of agreement concluded, but that appears to be less significant now. The strategic importance of certain states, both politically and geographically, has been seen to be a significant factor: notably in the emergence of 'conditionality' in the context of Eastern Europe.

The outcome of negotiations with Mexico and Australia, each of which initially opposed the clause, demonstrates that the bargaining power of the partner state is a significant factor. There are, however, questions hanging over Australia's bargaining 'strength' which suggest that a Western perception of democracy and fundamental rights within a state is also significant. Australia was perceived to be a democracy sharing the values of the EC, so human rights were not perceived to be a significant issue. At the same time, Australia had significant strategic economic impact as a gateway to the Asian markets.

The varying content of the clauses in different contexts suggests that the determining factor regarding the inclusion or form of the clause reflects a combination of two underlying considerations. The first of these is the relative strength of the parties. Second, there is an apparent reluctance on the part of the EU to risk compromising either cooperation itself or risk the loss of a particular benefit for a specific interest (such as the protection of minority rights). This may also suggest a related EU sensitivity to its own long-term weaknesses with regard to the protection of minority rights.[100] Ultimately, however, it can be concluded that the EU's policy is determined by political and economic considerations operating on varying levels.

---

[98] Although at the time of writing (2014) negotiations have resumed, there is as yet no new EU-India cooperation agreement.

[99] See, further, J Wouters, I Goddeeris, B Natens and F Ciortuz, 'Some Critical Issues in EU-India Free Trade Agreement Negotiations', Leuven Centre for Global Governance Studies, Working Paper No 102, February 2013, updated August 2013. See also Paasch (n 25).

[100] See now Article 19 TFEU (Ex Art 13 EC) and Article 21 Charter of Fundamental Rights.

III. EU ENFORCEMENT OF THE HUMAN RIGHTS CLAUSE

If the EC had succeeded in concluding an agreement with Australia which included the human rights clause, we can only speculate as to how it might have reacted to allegations that Australia was in breach of its human rights obligations. The EU has demonstrated its willingness to invoke the clause on several occasions,[101] indicating that the human rights clause is not merely symbolic. However, it has been seriously criticised for inconsistency in its action; in particular, its relative willingness to invoke the clause in respect of ACP states has been contrasted with its reluctance to invoke the clause in other contexts.[102] However, Dohlie Saltnes has criticised the selection bias evident in the evidence provided in support of contentions that the EU prioritises its own interests in deciding whether to implement the human rights clause.[103]

Regardless of the consistency or not of the implementation of human rights conditionality, much of the significance and efficacy of the clause may come in the awareness that it raises among states, and the pressure which it imposes upon partner states, or potential partner states, at a diplomatic level. This is consistent with the approach to human rights conditionality in the context of GSP+. If the existence of the clause can persuade states to maintain or impose, in the interests of cooperation, standards they would not otherwise achieve, that is more successful than suspension of an agreement for violation of these rights. If the dialogue which increasingly surrounds the clause can in fact minimise violations, then the absence of formal enforcement in the face of a breach is not determinative of the failure of the policy.

Where the situation may break down is in the application of this theory and in any failure by the EU to apply this pressure consistently and transparently, although not necessarily uniformly. The use of the term 'democratic principles' in Lomé IV, rather than a requirement of functioning democracy per se, suggested that the EC did not require its partner states to already be fully fledged democracies. This was supported by the commitment of the EC to:

[G]uarantee the consistency of Community measures to promote human rights and democratic principles ... ensuring that action is better attuned to the needs of partners and better coordinated with Member State' initiatives.[104]

Simultaneously, the EC vigorously guarded its ability to exercise discretion in its consideration of the partner states' 'social, economic and cultural

---

[101] Above, n 31.
[102] See Paasch (n 25).
[103] Saltnes (n 25).
[104] COM (97) 357 final at 6.

circumstances'. Similarly, it recognised that 'democratic principles' refer to a gradual, ongoing 'dynamic process leading to democracy which must take account of a country's socio-economic and cultural context'.[105] This makes sense. Experience, however, may give rise to questions concerning the extent to which the EU may be seen to exercise its discretion to the best effect, and intentions, of the clause.

A. Meaningful Conditionality? The Partnership and Cooperation Agreement with Russia

The difficulties which the EU may encounter have been seen to varying degrees in relation to Australia, Mexico, Chile and Mauritania. They are clearly demonstrated, however, by circumstances surrounding the conclusion and coming into force of the partnership agreement signed with the Russian Federation in June 1994. This agreement was followed by conclusion of a standard interim agreement signed in December 1994, which in turn was swiftly followed by the outbreak of the 'Chechen crisis'. As a response to this, in January 1995, the European Parliament passed a resolution on the subject of the human rights clause, endorsing the Commission's decision to suspend ratification of the agreement.[106] The Council and the Commission were requested not to ratify the agreements until both the military attacks by Russia on Chechnya *and* the human rights violations had ceased.[107]

In March, the EU made ratification of the interim agreements dependent on the permanent presence of the Organization for Security and Cooperation in Europe (OSCE) in Chechnya, entry of humanitarian aid into the country, a ceasefire and a serious search for political solutions to the conflict. By the end of March, the OSCE reported the continuation of serious breaches of humanitarian law. This notwithstanding, in early April the EU indicated it would be satisfied by Russia 'undertaking to honour its obligations soon'. (This is consistent with the principle that states need not have achieved the goals sought, but should demonstrate a willingness to do so.) Russia demonstrated its 'willingness' to 'honour its obligations' by continued breach of its international obligations, OSCE principles, and principles within the agreements at issue (observed by the European Parliament to be ongoing

---

[105] ibid at 5.

[106] Resolution on the situation in Chechnya [1995] OJ C43/04.

[107] See E Riedel and M Will, 'Human Rights Clauses in External Agreements' in P Alston with M Bustelo and J Heenan (ed), *The EU and Human Rights* (Oxford, Oxford University Press, 1999) at 741–42 for an account which views this as an example of the anticipatory effect of the human rights clause. This is a dubious reading of the events, which appeared more like EC capitulation to a strategically important state.

in mid-June).[108] These continued breaches notwithstanding, the European Council had decided at the end of June that, satisfied with progress over Chechnya, it would sign the interim agreement, which subsequently came into force in February 1996. The cooperation treaty itself entered into force in December 1997,[109] following parliamentary consent which had been given in November 1995[110] in view of the continuing ceasefire.

Reaching this decision despite documented ongoing serious breaches must bring into question the operation, and universal credibility, of the EU's policy. The EU may argue that it could reasonably bring the agreements into force because Russia had made real progress. Hillion describes the move as an 'exercise in Realpolitik aiming at reducing the causes of such crisis, in order to prepare for long-term change'.[111] It has been acknowledged that the decision was ultimately based upon the strategic importance of Russia to the EU and was 'justifiable' by the fact that Russia's treatment of Chechnya was seen as a short-term issue.[112]

These facts together, however, must have made it more difficult for the EU to react with any power to the subsequent attack of Chechnya by Russia. If the strength of the clauses is to come from their persuasive, political or 'anticipatory' effect, then these must be rigorously exercised and pursued, failing which the policy loses credibility.[113]

B. Discretion and Consistency in Relation to the Human Rights Clause

Part of the confusion and difficulty concerning the policy of inclusion of the human rights clause arises from the fact that the EU has chosen what appears on the one hand to be an 'absolute' stance on human rights in terms of making their protection a legally binding condition of cooperation. Yet the EU desires to maintain the political discretion that it would be free to exercise by pursuing this policy on a purely political level.

Whether the EC would have been inclined to act in relation to Australia, a state which is of crucial economic importance to the EC due to its links with Asia, and which does not, prima facie, fit the general perception of a state committing human rights abuses, is another question. Many states, however, expressed their concern as to Australia's human rights record regarding

---

[108] [1995] OJ C166/4.

[109] [1997] OJ L327/1.

[110] [1995] OJ 339/45.

[111] Hillion (n 57) 417.

[112] ibid 418; see also Declaration of the EU's Presidency on the situation in Chechnya, IP 4215/95, 17 January 1995.

[113] Such issues are being thrown into sharp relief once more by Russia's recent intervention in Ukraine.

its treatment of the Aboriginal people during the negotiating period.[114] If the EC had concluded an agreement and not acted, it is unlikely that that would have gone unnoticed. The credibility of the EC's policy would consequently have been damaged, regardless of its intentions in this respect.

This may be dismissed as mere speculation. The rights of indigenous peoples are, however, the focus of not inconsiderable international attention, particularly within the UN.[115] A case such as this could not have been sidelined by the EC if the universality of its policy, on which much of its political strength depends, is to be genuinely upheld.

The contemporary Australian situation with regard to the Aboriginal people could offer little comfort to the EU. While the EU has pursued the development of its commercial links with Australia without reference to human rights standards, within Australia itself, controversy concerning land rights continued long after the conclusion of its negotiations with the EC. Indeed, the controversy surrounding the treatment of the Aborigines continued to grow with the reaction to mandatory sentencing, a penal policy which has a disproportionate impact upon Aboriginal people.[116] This also did not fail to attract international attention.[117] Questions may be raised as to why the EU, a significant trading partner of Australia, could not have exerted some of its economic power to compel Australia to have accepted the clause.

C. The Subsequent Challenge: Standing to Enforce the Clause?

There is a further question regarding the inclusion of human rights conditionality in every agreement concluded with a third state. In the event of a

---

[114] See, eg, comments of the South African delegation to Canberra, *Sydney Morning Herald*, 21 November 1997.

[115] Australia has a lengthy history of criticism on this issue from the UN. See Record of the 1059th Meeting of the Committee on the Elimination of Racial Discrimination, 12 August 1994, CERD/C/SR.1059, Consideration of 9th Periodic Report on Australia (CERD/C/223/Add.1). See nn 116 and 117 below detailing more recent criticism regarding specific policy.

[116] In 2008 the UN Committee against Torture recommended the abolition of mandatory sentencing due to its 'disproportionate and discriminatory impact upon the indigenous population': CAT/C/AUS/CO.3, 22 May 2008, Article 11; previously, Amnesty International had noted that: 'In 2000 the Aboriginal people comprise 2.1% of the Australian population, but 18.8% of the prison population, the figures in relation to juvenile detention, on which mandatory sentencing is having a particular impact are no less disturbing.' See Amnesty International press releases: ASA 12/003/2000 of 14 March 2000 and ASA 12/006/2000 of 5 July 2000.

[117] The UN Human Rights Committee in July 2000 reached disturbing conclusions re Australia's record of civil and political rights, particularly concerning human rights issues arising today as a result of the 'stolen children' policy of the 1950s, mandatory sentencing and mandatory immigration detention. The response of the Australian Government a month later was to announce that it would be pulling out of certain UN human rights obligations. Amnesty International Press release ASA 12/010/2000 of 5 September 2000. See also UNHCHR report, December 1999.

dispute, which court has jurisdiction to rule on it? If a Court can be identified, those who would have standing to enforce the clause are the contracting parties, that is, the EC (now the EU) and the Member States (assuming the agreement has been concluded as a mixed agreement) and the third state, for example, Australia.[118] If the provisions of the agreement meet the requirements of direct effect, there is a question as to whether a natural or legal person would have standing. In an instance in which the EU and the Member States did not view human rights as an issue, would anyone be able to enforce the clause?

i. Mugraby v Council and Commission

Such hypothetical questions were tested before the Court of Justice in the case of *Mugraby v Council and Commission*.[119] Mr Mugraby was a human rights lawyer resident in Lebanon. His criticism of the Lebanese judicial system has led to the authorities preventing him from working in Lebanon since 2003. Furthermore, he had suffered harassment by the authorities and certain of his fundamental rights had been violated. The Association Agreement between the EC and Lebanon includes a human rights clause (Article 2) and Article 86 provides that:

(1) The Parties shall take any general or specific measures required to fulfil their obligations under this Agreement. They shall see to it that the objectives set out in this Agreement are attained ...

(2) If either Party considers that the other Party has failed to fulfil an obligation under this Agreement, it may take appropriate measures.

The third paragraph provides that any such measures should be proportionate.

In 2009, Mr Mugraby wrote a letter requesting that: the Commission suspend its economic aid programmes, in view of the violation of Article 2 of the Agreement. He further requested that the Commission recommend to the Council that it take measures concerning its economic aid programmes, including freezing economic aid. In the same letter he requested that the Council invite the Commission to take measures regarding economic aid pending resolution of issues relating to Lebanon's breach of its obligations under Article 2. No such action was undertaken and the applicant brought an action before the General Court. In his action, Mr Mugraby claimed that the Commission and the Council failed to act in the face of Lebanon's violation of fundamental rights and that they had incurred non-contractual liability for harm he suffered as a consequence of their failure to enforce the human rights clause in the Association Agreement. It was argued by the

---

[118] See below for discussion on the direct effect of international agreements and the possible implications re EC nationals.

[119] Case T-292/09 *Mugraby v Council and Commission* [2011] ECR II-255.

Commission that the applicant did not have standing to bring the action concerning failure to act as he was not directly and individually concerned by it.[120]

The Court found that failure to act can only be invoked where there is an obligation to act and that this did not apply regarding suspension or a recommendation of suspension of aid, since both the Commission and the Council retain discretion to act. Having so determined, the Court did not consider the question of standing. With regard to the human rights clause itself, the Court held that it 'is not intended to permit or indeed to impose the recourse to and adoption of measures if the parties to that agreement fail to comply with the clause relating to fundamental rights in that article'.

Turning to the claim of non-contractual liability, the Court found that the conditions of liability (that the institution's conduct must be unlawful, actual damage must be suffered and there must be a causal link between the unlawful conduct and the damage suffered) were not satisfied in this case.[121] In particular, the Court noted once again the discretion conferred upon the parties by Article 86 of the Association Agreement regarding measures to be adopted. Further, it held that even if the conditions of liability were satisfied, Article 86 does not give rights to individuals.[122] In particular, it held that it does not satisfy the conditions of direct effect.[123]

This ruling[124] confirms the view that the human rights clause in that particular form may not be enforced by individuals, and in so doing highlights the distinction between legal strength and political force. The lack of potential for individuals to legally enforce the human rights clause does not, alone, suggest that it is worthless.

D. Reliance on the Exercise of Political Discretion in the Enforcement of the Human Rights Clause

Ultimately, a breach may have no direct legal remedy, but instead may be reliant upon a political decision and action. Where a political decision is made by the EU, that action will not be taken against the abuse of certain human rights, that decision itself will not be subject to challenge in the interests of those rights.

However the EU cannot be completely objective in its judgments in this respect. This is itself demonstrated by the compromise to the universality of

---

[120] ibid [28].
[121] ibid [54].
[122] ibid [61].
[123] ibid [65]–[69]. See ch 3 for discussion of the criteria for direct effect. It is worth noting that this was the subject of an appeal to the ECJ: C-581/11 P *Mugraby v Council and Commission* order of 12 July 2012 (nyr).
[124] Which was upheld by the Court of Justice on appeal: ibid.

its policy which the EU was willing to accept in relation to Australia, where a strong economic interest was at stake, as well as in its response to the Chechen situation. Such lacunae may well leave the human rights interest unprotected in much the same manner, as seen with respect to the internal protection provided for the environment by the EU.[125] There are clear reasons to limit the right of action and, indeed, there is no reason to suppose that the EU and the Member States are not *competent* to judge a situation, or to respond to lobbying, and proceed on the basis of third parties' complaints. Such judgments, however, remain subject to political compromise and discretion, and therefore ultimately may be inconsistent.

With regard to the negotiations with Australia, there were issues which the EC did not view as being relevant to the conclusion of an agreement, yet which parts of the international community viewed with concern in relation to the protection of human rights. This concern was shared by groups within Australia itself. The ongoing situation in Australia suggests that had the EC and Australia concluded an agreement (including the standard clause), pressure would undoubtedly have been brought to bear upon the then EC to take action flowing from the human rights clause. There would be no means, however, by which any non-contracting party could compel the EC to even consider the matter. Yet such a scenario, again, would clearly damage the credibility of the EU and its policy. The EU faces a real problem in that the standard clause itself is framed in such a way that it includes minority or aboriginal rights. In certain cases the clause includes specific reference to such rights.

It is impossible to overstate the political sensitivity of this whole area and the EU clearly defends its ability to exercise its discretion. It would be possible for the EU to narrow the terms of the clause to clarify what rights it intends to protect according to the circumstances. However, this exposes a tension between the desired universality of the clause, the pursuit of which perhaps unnecessarily leaves the EU open to criticism, and the counter-criticism which would follow were the EU to explicitly pursue different rights, seeking to apply different standards, in different contexts.

It may be significant that in 1998 the EU, acting under the 'second pillar' that is, in the context of the CFSP, adopted a Common Position concerning human rights, democratic principles, the rule of law and good governance in Africa.[126] The preamble to this states that 'human rights are universal, indivisible, interdependent and intrinsically linked'. Article 1 describes the objective of the EU as being 'to work in partnership with African countries

---

[125] See the discussion of Case C-321/95P *Greenpeace v Commission* [1998] ECR I-1651 and access to justice on environmental issues in ch 2.

[126] 98/350/CFSP: Common Position of 25 May 1998 defined by the Council on the basis of Article J.2 of the Treaty on European Union, concerning human rights, democratic principles, the rule of law and good governance in Africa [1998] OJ L158/1.

to promote respect for human rights, democratic principles and good governance' and states that 'this approach shall serve as a framework for the actions of the Member States'. Article 2 continues by recognising 'the right of sovereign states to establish their own constitutional arrangements and to institute their own administrative structures according to their history, culture, tradition and social and ethnic composition'. Article 2 continues by setting out the principles underlying the EU's approach. These include protection of human rights, including civil and political, social, economic and cultural; respect of basic democratic principles; the rule of law and good governance.

The common position explicitly provides for the exercise of discretion by the EU in deciding policy towards individual countries on the basis of their starting point and the general direction and pace of change within these countries, thus reiterating the position of the Commission in COM (97) 357 final.[127] This is significant as it suggests that the EU has a wide vision of the human rights that it seeks to support, although taking account of the particular situations of individual countries.

IV. THE PROTECTION OF THE ENVIRONMENT IN THE EU'S RELATIONS WITH THIRD STATES

The commitment to the protection of the environment in the EC's external relations developed initially, like human rights, in the context of development cooperation. However, this evolved more quickly into a general EC competence to conclude international environmental agreements, which was, and remains, complementary to the competence of the Member States.[128] The degree of development of environmental protection in the EC's external relations has contrasted sharply with that of human rights, and not altogether as might be expected. Over the years, the EU has developed its commitment to sustainable development, which reinforces its commitment to environmental protection. Recently, the emergent focus within this has been upon climate change. Thus, the internal focus, manifested in the 2020 Strategy, is carried through into the EU's external relations.

A. Development Cooperation Agreements

The original Lomé Convention referred to the need for social development, but made no reference to the environment or human rights per se. Lomé II,

---

[127] 'Proposal for a Council Regulation on the Development and Consolidation of Democracy and the Rule of Law and Respect for Human Rights and Fundamental Freedoms' COM (97) 357 final, 24 July 1997.
[128] Article 174 (now Article 191 TFEU). See ch 4 above.

however, referred to environmental protection in Article 76, in the context of cooperation on energy and in relation to 'Agricultural Cooperation'.[129] Protection of the environment appeared again, more significantly, in Article 93, with reference to financial and technical cooperation, and Article 112, which stated that in the context of 'project and programme appraisal', 'particular attention shall be paid to the effects of the programme on the environment'.

This is significant in that environmental protection was already, at this relatively early stage, being integrated into other policy areas in the EC's external relations. In contrast, the EC had sought at this stage to include a commitment to human rights and democracy, but this had been blocked by the partner states. Environmental protection was clearly not so sensitive an issue with the partner states as the highly political, and contentious, protection of human rights.

By Lomé IV, not only was the protection of human rights accepted as an essential element, as seen above, but the commitment to environmental concerns was also strengthened, albeit not to the same degree. Article 6 provided that 'priority must be given to environmental protection and the conservation of natural resources which are essential conditions for sustainable and balanced development both from the economic and human viewpoints'. More significantly, environmental protection had its own title (I) in Part II (Areas of Cooperation), in which Article 33 made a comprehensive commitment to all aspects of environmental protection.[130]

It is striking, however, that the agreement committed only the ACP states to this development, albeit with EC support. There was no corresponding undertaking by the EC. The protection of the environment within the EC was, at this point, governed by the provisions of the Single European Act (SEA), which, as well as committing the EC to environmental protection internally, provided for complementary EC and Member State competence to conclude international environmental agreements.[131] This, however, does not explain the lack of reciprocal undertaking with respect to environmental protection by the EC or its Member States. Arguably, such an undertaking was unnecessary, due to equivalent commitments of the Member States in other contexts, including the EC. As an explanation, however, that is problematic. In particular, it gives rise to difficulties in relation to a hypothetical failure within the EC to effectively protect the environment, in contrast to the obligation upon the ACP states. The EC could have challenged a breach

---

[129] Title VI, Articles 83–84.

[130] 'The protection and the enhancement of the environment and natural resources, the halting of the deterioration of land and forests, the restoration of ecological balances, the preservation of natural resources and their rational exploitation are basic objectives that the ACP States concerned shall strive to achieve with Community support with a view to bringing an immediate improvement in the living conditions of their populations and to safeguarding those of future generations.'

[131] Article 130r (5), ECT (Single European Act) [1987] OJ L169 at 11. See ch 2 above.

within the ACP states, but these same states would have been powerless in the face of such an equivalent failure within the EC.

This is clearly not a problem which would have concerned the EC unduly, but it is an omission for which it may legitimately be criticised: it indicated a paternalistic approach to EC aid and cooperation. However, in the context of a development cooperation agreement, that may not be inappropriate. The EC was not unreasonable in imposing conditions upon its provision of aid. On this basis, however, the EC and its Member States should be certain that they already provide the level of protection (or at least commitment to environmental protection) required of the partner states. Yet, as has been seen in chapter three, the protection offered to the environment within the EC was by no means guaranteed, even 11 years after Lomé, despite the commitment in the Treaties.[132]

This was not a legal problem per se; there is no doubt that within the EC, there were undertakings to meet at least these environmental standards. Thus, there was arguably no *need* for Lomé to impose obligations upon the EC. However, assuming that these standards were already met, it would have been a merely symbolic gesture to include a mutual obligation. The lack of reciprocal obligation could, however, have created credibility problems, particularly in view of the fact that the EU, internally, still does not meet its international obligations relating to 'Access to Justice on Environmental issues'.[133] Thus, the early days of the development of environmental protection in the EC's international agreements raised their own questions.

i. The Cotonou Agreement

The Cotonou Agreement focuses strongly on the need for sustainable development and emphasises environmental protection as well as human rights protection. Article 20 describes the approach of the Agreement, which is to pursue integrated strategies, incorporating economic, social, cultural, environmental and institutional elements, reflecting the internal EC approach towards the environment. As regards the environment, ACP-EC cooperation strategies are to aim at 'promoting environmental sustainability, regeneration and best practices, and the preservation of natural resource base'.[134]

---

[132] See ch 3.

[133] See ch 3. It is worth noting at this juncture that following the 2nd Revision of Cotonou, Article 9 provides that 'the principles underlying the essential and fundamental elements as defined in this article shall apply equally to the ACP States on the one hand, and to the EU and its Member States on the other hand'. While the essential elements are human rights-based, this indicates recognition of the significance of reciprocity and perhaps a shift in balance in the EU's relations with the ACP states.

[134] Article 20(e) Cotonou (n 6).

This is to a degree tautological as the preservation of the natural resource base is itself an inherent element of sustainability. Environmental issues are also included in the 'thematic or cross-cutting themes' to be taken into account in all areas of cooperation.[135] As a result, the environment is also to be supported through, for example, regional cooperation.[136]

Since Lomé, the inclusion of clauses relating to environmental protection has become standard practice in trade and economic cooperation agreements as well as in development cooperation, although the commitment has never had the same strength as that generally given to human rights and democracy. Notably, environmental requirements tend to be aspirational, for example to 'give priority to', 'strive' or 'take into account' rather than creating absolute requirements which must be achieved. This notwithstanding, cooperation is dependent upon the partner states complying with their undertakings and demonstrating that they do so. The second revision to Cotonou is striking for its recognition, among other developments, of the 'global challenge of climate change as a major subject for their partnership'.[137]

ii. Environmental Protection in the Europe Agreements

Environmental protection was a significant issue in the Europe Agreements for two reasons: first, in view of the scale of environmental degradation and pollution in these states, and the pre-accession requirement that the states reach EU standards; and, second, environmental problems in these states were local to the EU and had a tangible impact upon it, so the interest of the EU in having them cleaned up is both profound and immediate. Environmental protection standards were initially a stumbling block to accession for most applicant states. However, ultimately, sufficient progress was made on the incorporation of the environmental acquis.[138] This issue did, however, prove particularly difficult in the northern states.[139]

A fairly typical example of the commitment to environmental protection in the Europe Agreements may be taken from the 1994 agreement with Slovakia.[140] Under Title VI (Economic Cooperation), Article 72 provided that sustainable development was to be a 'guiding principle' of economic

---

[135] Article 20(2). This is expanded upon in respect of the environment in Article 32.

[136] Article 30.

[137] http://ec.europa.eu/europeaid/where/acp/overview/cotonou-agreement/index_en.htm. See further K Kulovesi, E Morgera and M Munoz, 'Environmental Integration and Multi-faceted International Dimensions of EU Law: Unpacking the EU's 2009 Climate and Energy Package' (2011) 48(3) *CML Rev* 829, 844.

[138] See ch 2. For a report on the candidate countries' compliance, see http://europa.eu.int/comm/enlargement/report2002/index/htm.

[139] Opinion of the Committee of the Regions on the 'Communication from the Commission on a northern dimension for the policies of the Union [1999] OJ C374/01.

[140] [1994] OJ L359/1.

and social development, and that this should guarantee the integration of environmental protection.

Article 81 concerned the environment and committed all parties to the development, and strengthening, of cooperation on both environment and human health. The second paragraph listed the areas of cooperation and the third how this cooperation would be achieved. The areas of cooperation were fairly comprehensive, as were the means, which included exchange of information and experts, training programmes, joint research activities, approximation of laws (Community standards), cooperation at the regional level and development of strategies, particularly with regard to global and climatic issues.

Clearly the fact that such agreements were a stepping stone to accession, which would not be possible without progress on the environmental acquis, was a significant factor with regard to both the substantive content of the environmental commitment in this context and the extent to which that commitment was fulfilled.

The Committee of the Regions described cooperation in the Baltic Sea region as 'an outstanding example of regional cooperation in Europe, encompassing nearly all areas of politics, society and the economy'.[141] The extreme climatic conditions make this a complex area to manage environmentally, particularly in relation to the sustainable management of natural energy resources. The challenges this poses are exacerbated by the serious pollution, which has been caused in part by the manner of the exploitation of these natural resources.[142] These problems have been addressed by the Arctic Council since 1990. The Committee of the Regions has observed that particular attention must be paid to both environmental considerations and the rights of the indigenous people. This clearly reflects recognition of the pragmatic link between human welfare and environmental protection.[143]

Finland's extensive shared border with Russia has a significant effect on the external dynamics of the EU and upon the challenges facing the EU internally in relation to environmental protection. Environmental impact pays no heed to state borders, which of course increased the strategic EU interest in cooperation with the Baltic states to improve environmental conditions.[144]

---

[141] Above, n 139.

[142] For further discussion of these problems, see ibid.

[143] ibid at para 11.24.

[144] Opinion of the Committee of the regions on the 'Communication from the Commission, to the Council, the European Parliament, the Economic and Social Committee, the Committee of the regions and the candidate countries in central and eastern Europe on accession strategies for environment: meeting the challenge of enlargement with the candidate countries in central and eastern Europe' at para 1.2. It should be noted that the Baltic states acceded to the EU in 2004.

B. Partnership and Cooperation Agreements

As seen above, relations with those states which have not yet acceded fall either into the category of Europe Agreements or PCAs, for example, with Ukraine.[145] The preamble to the Ukraine agreement refers to the wish to achieve 'close cooperation in the area of environmental protection, taking into account the interdependence existing between the Parties in this field'. The approximation of Ukraine's laws to those of the EU, to facilitate economic links, extends, inter alia, to environmental protection.[146] It is not surprising, therefore, to see 'environment' appear in Title VII (Economic cooperation), where once again policies are to fully incorporate environmental considerations and be guided by principles of sustainability.[147] Both industrial and energy cooperation again make specific reference to the requirement to consider environmental implications.[148] However, it is in Article 63, 'Environment', that the specific provisions relating to the environment are laid down. In this context the environment is linked explicitly to human health and the provisions are fairly typically wide-ranging.

Since 2007, Europe's relations with Ukraine have fallen under the ambit of the Black Sea Synergy. On its establishment, it was anticipated that 'Specific Black Sea Synergy sector partnerships will address transport, energy and the environment'; the Black Sea Environmental Partnership was launched in March 2010.[149] Environmental issues continue to comprise a significant focus for this cooperative strategy. The Black Sea Synergy comprises in turn one of the regional cooperation initiatives under the ENP discussed above.[150]

The EU's relations with the southern Mediterranean states have latterly been subject to the Euro-Mediterranean Partnership, focusing more recently upon the Barcelona Process which was relaunched in 2008 as the Union for

---

[145] Above, n 54.
[146] Article 51.
[147] Article 52.
[148] Articles 53 and 61 respectively.
[149] See www.eeas.europa.eu/blacksea/index_en.htm and http://ec.europa.eu/environment/enlarg/danubeblacksea_en.htm.
[150] See above, n 17. The first Action Plan under the ENP was indeed agreed with Ukraine in 2005, providing a mandate for the development of the first European Neighbourhood Agreement with Ukraine. The key principles of the ENP are that 'ENP is a strategy based on partnership and joint ownership to promote modernisation and reform; ENP is a single, inclusive, balanced and coherent policy framework; Performance-driven differentiation and tailor-made assistance remain essential for EU relations with the neighbouring countries; ENP remains distinct from the question of EU membership and does not prejudge any possible future developments of partner countries' relationship with the EU'. See Council Conclusions on Strengthening the European Neighbourhood Policy, General Affairs and External Relations Council (GAERC) 2007 available at: http://register.consilium.europa.eu/doc/srv?l=EN&f=ST%2011016%202007%20INIT.

the Mediterranean. Once again, environment and energy are squarely built into the agenda for action in this context.

C. Cooperation Agreements

In the wider context, the EU's Cooperation Agreements are again interesting. The 1988 Cooperation Agreement with the Gulf Cooperation Council[151] included the environment as one of the areas of cooperation.[152] Elaboration of this commitment is, however, even more general and unspecific than in the development cooperation context, providing only for exchange of information and cooperation on environmental protection and wildlife development and protection.[153]

Limited as this commitment is, being effectively little more than a declaration of intent and interest, it is perhaps significant that it is included at all. This agreement contains no reference to human rights and democracy. That in itself is not surprising as it was concluded before the human rights clause had been introduced even into the context of development cooperation. The fact that environmental protection was included suggests that the explicit treaty basis of competence was of real significance: this existed in relation to the environment, following the SEA, but not in relation to human rights and democracy. It also potentially reflects, once again, the political sensitivity surrounding fundamental rights, which was not felt in relation to the environment.

The disparity between the obligation on the part of the ACP states, limited as it is, and the loose commitment of the Gulf states, dating initially from about the same period, is readily explained by the different context. The scope and objectives of development cooperation are quite different from those of 'economic' cooperation. Related to this, the EU's commitment to financial assistance in the development cooperation agreement permitted it to impose conditions and standards which would be inappropriate in a narrower commercial agreement.

---

[151] Cooperation Agreement between the European Economic Community, of the one part, and the countries parties to the Charter of the Cooperation Council for the Arab States of the Gulf (the State of the United Arab Emirates, the State of Bahrain, the Kingdom of Saudi Arabia, the Sultanate of Oman, the State of Quatar and the State of Kuwait) of the other part—Joint Declarations—Declaration by the European Economic Community—Exchange of Letters [1989] OJ L54/3.
[152] Article 1.
[153] Article 9.

D. Trade Agreements

In the early trade, commercial and economic cooperation agreements with Central and Eastern Europe, the protection of the environment per se was not an objective of cooperation. In the Agreement with Lithuania, for example, the objectives of economic cooperation include no reference to the environment.[154] The areas of economic cooperation to be particularly promoted for the achievement of the objectives do, however, include environmental protection. Article 34, 'Cooperation on environment and natural resources', provides for comprehensive consideration and protection of the environment in all areas, including cooperation measures, the development of environmental legislation and protection. It also provides a basis for the conclusion of a sectoral environmental agreement.

Such sectoral environmental agreements have been concluded: for example, the 1989 Cooperation Agreement between the European Economic Community and the Republic of Finland on research and development in the field of protection of the environment.[155] This agreement provided for Finnish participation in the EC multi-annual environmental research and development programme.[156]

E. The Agreement with Mexico

The 1997 Agreement with Mexico, in which the inclusion of the human rights clause proved highly controversial,[157] also provided for the possibility of a separate environmental cooperation agreement. In addition, Article 34 of the Economic Partnership Agreement commits the parties to consideration of: 'The need to preserve the environmental and ecological balances ... in all cooperation measures undertaken by the Parties under this Agreement.' Furthermore:

> [T]he Parties undertake to develop cooperation to prevent degradation of the environment; to promote the conservation and sustainable management of natural resources; to develop, spread and exchange information and experience on environmental legislation, to stimulate the use of economic incentives to promote

---

[154] [1992] OJ L403/20, Article 15.

[155] Cooperation Agreement between the European Community and the Republic of Finland on Research and development in the field of the protection of the environment [1989] OJ L304/9 (Note that Finland has since acceded to the EU).

[156] Adopted by Council Decision of 10 June 1986, Multiannual research and development programmes in the field of the environment (1986–90), including, inter alia, a programme on protection of the environment. Again, it is worth noting that Finland is now, since 1995, a Member State of the EU.

[157] Framework Cooperation Agreement between the European Community, the Member States and Mexico 1997.

compliance; to strengthen environmental management at all levels of government; to promote the training of human resources, education in environmental topics and the execution of joint research projects; to develop channels for social participation.[158]

Bilateral EC-Mexico high-level policy dialogue on environment and climate change was launched in 2008, with the fourth dialogue taking place in 2013.[159] This is now established as an annual dialogue facilitating cooperation, however no separate agreement has been concluded.[160]

F. Australia

The other nation with whom the human rights clause provoked much argument and controversy should not technically enter into the discussion here, as the negotiations ultimately resulted in a joint declaration rather than a binding framework agreement. It is, however, interesting to briefly consider the declaration, which has, after all, formed the basis of cooperation. The *preamble* refers to the parties' shared commitment to the respect and promotion of human rights, and also refers to their common interest in sustainable development. Similarly, the *common goals* refer to the need to 'pursue policies aimed at achieving a sound world economy marked by ... sustained economic growth with low inflation, a high level of employment, *environmental protection*, equitable social conditions and a stable international financial system'.

Thus, the less economic objectives (essential constituents of sustainable development) are couched squarely amongst the more economic. Specifically, in relation to the environment, the parties 'confirm that we will continue to strengthen our cooperation on environmental matters, both bilaterally and through international agreements and conventions'. This is itself perhaps surprising, given the Australian position that human rights had no place in a commercial agreement. It would not be illogical to assume that that position applied equally to other non-economic interests and a joint declaration on trade. The major difference between the commitment in the joint undertaking and what was originally proposed lies in the fact that these common goals are non-binding.

However, if the objection to the inclusion of human rights in a trade agreement concerned the principle that consideration of such interests has

---

[158] Economic Partnership, Political Coordination and Cooperation Agreement between the European Community and its Member States, of the one part, and the United Mexican States, of the other part [2000] OJ L276/45.

[159] http://ec.europa.eu/environment/international_issues/relations_mexico_en.htm.

[160] See EC/Mexico Cooperation 2007–2013 Country Strategy Paper Mid-Term Review, at: www.eeas.europa.eu/mexico/docs/2010_midterm_mexico_annex_en.pdf. See also http://strategicpartnerships.eu/pays/eu-mexico/

no place in a trade context, it could be asked where this principle ended. The different approaches perhaps reflect the fact that environmental issues have been more comfortably received in economic contexts than human rights issues. As will be seen below, this is the case in the context of the WTO. This reflects in turn the fact that they are less politically sensitive. Ultimately, in this case the statement regarding the environment is comparable to that made in the other cooperation agreements examined, and indeed is rather similar to that given in relation to human rights in that Declaration.

G. The Emergence of an Integrative Approach: Sustainable Development in the EU's Agreements with Third States

Since the 1993 Europe Agreement with Hungary, which required that 'Policies designed to bring about the economic and social development of Hungary ... should be guided by the principle of sustainable development', sustainable development has become an increasingly regular and stronger feature of the EU's agreements with third states.[161] It is included as one of the core objectives of the Cotonou Agreement.[162] To this end, the approach is explicitly integrative, so Article 20(2) requires the mainstreaming of specified cross-cutting themes. Since the second revision, these include: '*human rights*, gender issues, *democracy, good governance, environmental sustainability, climate change, communicable and noncommunicable diseases* and institutional development and capacity building'.[163] In that context, sustainable development was explicitly focused upon improving standards of living and poverty eradication.[164] This integrative approach is wholly consistent with the EU's internal commitment to sustainable development and with the EC's earlier position relating to the integration of the environmental dimension into the development process.[165] The EU-Central America Agreement commits the parties to 'achieving sustainable development', referencing certain multilateral environment agreements and the

---

[161] Article 68(2) Europe Agreement establishing an Association Agreement between the European Communities and their Member States of the one part and the Republic of Hungary of the other part [1993] OJ L347/2.

[162] Article 19 Cotonou lists the core objectives: 'poverty reduction and ultimately its eradication; sustainable development; and progressive integration of the ACP countries into the world economy'.

[163] Those in italics were added in the second revision.

[164] Articles 2 and 4.3.

[165] See also European Parliament and Council Decision 2179/98/EC of 24 September 1998 on the review of the European Community Programme of Policy and Action in relation to the environment and sustainable development 'Towards Sustainability' [1998] OJ L275/5, which proposed a stronger role for the EC in international cooperation in environment and sustainable development.

fundamental ILO Conventions. Sustainable development is now recognised as an 'overarching objective' of cooperation in the EU's recent free trade agreements, for example, the 2011 Free Trade Agreement (FTA) with South Korea.[166] The preamble to the Framework Agreement with Korea recognises the parties' desire to promote sustainable development in its economic, social and environmental dimensions. The Framework Agreement includes the 'standard' human rights 'essential elements' clause, but the FTA only refers to human rights in the preamble. However, it is explicit in Article 43(3) of the Framework Agreement that any specific cooperation agreements concluded by the parties within the scope of the Framework Agreement are governed by the Framework Agreement. Thus, this must include the 'essential element' of respect for human rights.

In 2000, the Community's Comprehensive Strategy Communication had noted the need for more in-depth discussions on integrating the environment into sectoral cooperation policies and stressed the need for coherence in EC policies, particularly in the formulation of economic and structural adjustment policies, 'in order to achieve structural growth without environmental degradation'.[167] This was rapidly followed up with communications on the integration of the environment into the common agricultural policy and future directions of Europe's environment.[168] It is also, of course, fully consistent with the objectives and approach adopted under the GSP and GSP+, which include a number of environmental treaties among those for which compliance will be rewarded with additional benefits for eligible states.[169] The Commission concluded, however, that overall responsibility lies with the developing countries themselves and that there are three crucial elements to integration in the development process: political will, formal inclusion in the organisational structure, and institutional priority

---

[166] Article 1.1.(g) Free Trade Agreement between the European Union and its Member States, of the one part, and the Republic of Korea of the other part [2011] OJ L127/1.

[167] COM (2000) 264 final at 4.1.

[168] Communication from the Commission to the Council and the European Parliament—Indicators for the integration of environmental concerns into the common agricultural policy COM (2000) 20 final; Opinion of the Economic and Social Committee on the 'Communication from the Commission—Europe's Environment: What Directions for the Future? The Global Assessment of the European Community Programme of Policy and Action in relation to the environment and sustainable development' [2000] OJ C204/14.

[169] Convention on International Trade in Endangered Species of Wild Fauna and Flora (1973); Montreal Protocol on Substances that Deplete the Ozone Layer (1987); Basel Convention on the Control of Transboundary Movements of Hazardous Wastes and Their Disposal (1989); Convention on Biological Diversity (1992); United Nations Framework Convention on Climate Change (1992); Cartagena Protocol on Biosafety (2000); Stockholm Convention on Persistent Organic Pollutants (2001); Kyoto Protocol to the United Nations Framework Convention on Climate Change (1998). See Annex VIII, Regulation (EU) No 978/2012 of the European Parliament and of the Council of 25 October 2012 applying a scheme of generalised tariff preferences and repealing Council Regulation (EC) No 732/2008 [2012] OJ L303/1.

and sound management of the integration process.[170] Both the GSP and GSP+ and the Cotonou Agreement, particularly following its subsequent revisions, are clearly in keeping with this conclusion.

i. The Integration of the Environmental Dimension in Development

The amended *proposal for integration of the environmental dimension in the development process of developing countries* noted again the international commitments of the EC in this field and the need for coherence between the internal and external aspects of the EC's environment policy. It linked the strategy underlying EC environmental policy to these international commitments[171] and recalled that the Parliament and Council *Decision on the review of the fifth action programme*[172] called for a stronger role for the EC in international cooperation in terms of the environment and sustainable development.

A key element of this included the full integration of environmental policy in other policies, notably including, again, development policy. The Decision provided for both direct and indirect support for a wide range of environmental purposes. Significantly, sustainable development in this context is defined as being 'the improvement of the standard of living and welfare of the relevant populations within the limits of the capacity of the eco-systems by maintaining natural assets and their biological diversity for the benefit of present and future generations'.[173] The key elements of the Brundtland definition are present, yet although 'welfare' also suggests consideration of social issues, the emphasis is on environmental elements. This is not surprising in a measure whose purpose is the integration of environment into other policies. In that light, it is worth noting that Article 4.3 provided that particular attention should be paid to activities which contribute to, inter alia, poverty eradication. This demonstrates, once again, that the EC took a broad view of the inter-dependence of environmental, social and economic objectives.

The Comprehensive Strategy Communication observed that: 'While other EC Development Cooperation policies are also highly relevant to the sustainable development of developing countries, the extent to which environmental considerations can be integrated varies.' It noted that, particularly in policies with *indirect* environmental links, there could be more

---

[170] Above, n 167.

[171] Such as the OECD's 'Shaping the 21st Century Strategy, the Convention on Biological Diversity, The Framework Convention on Climate Change'.

[172] European Parliament and Council Decision 2179/98/EC of 24 September 1998 on the review of the European Community Programme of Policy and Action in relation to the environment and sustainable development 'Towards Sustainability' [1998] OJ L275/5.

[173] ibid Article 2.

systematic analysis of environmental considerations.[174] In view of this, it proposed the initiation of more in-depth discussions on integrating environment into sectoral cooperation policies and stressed the need for coherence in Community policies, particularly in the formulation of economic and structural adjustment policies, 'in order to achieve structural growth without environmental degradation'.[175] Such consideration has been forthcoming. In addition, environmental standards are included together with human rights among those interests for which the EU operates its generalised system of preferences.

V. CONCLUSIONS

The EU has sought to establish a consistent external policy, requiring the protection of non-economic interests in its agreements with third states. In this it has achieved varying degrees of success.

A. On Human Rights Conditionality

In relation to human rights, one of the first questions is whether the EU has competence to pursue this policy at all. What competence it originally had was narrow and, other than in the context of development cooperation, the EC competence did not, until Nice, extend beyond ensuring that its own actions did not support violations of human rights. However, one consequence of that limited obligation was that the requirement of conditionality was essential for the EU to remain within the bounds of its competence.

Accepting that the inclusion of a human rights clause now has a proper legal basis, the next question concerns enforcement. On an inter-state level, the EU has left itself open to criticism by adopting the approach of universality and conditionality, while retaining political discretion as to when to act. This problem could be avoided by adjusting the terms of the clause to reflect different circumstances and, notably, to exclude issues in which the EU does not intend to get involved. That could, however, damage the strength the policy gains from its purported universality, notwithstanding that the human rights instruments referred to already vary according to geography.

On the other hand, the EU is clearly moving in that direction by increasing the emphasis on the requirement as being not to *achieve* particular standards, but to demonstrate some progress towards the achievement of

---

[174] This contrasts with the position of the Court in Case C-321/95P *Greenpeace and Others v Commission* [1998] ECR I-1651, discussed in ch 3.
[175] COM (2000) 264 final at 4.1.

standards. Cooperation on such a basis may facilitate the realisation of the desired standards. The EU should, however, address the problem that the exercise of its policy has been inconsistent, generally where a significant EU interest has been at stake and it has been unable to reach a consensus with the partner state.

B. On Environmental Protection

In relation to the environment, conditionality manifests itself in the context of the GSP and GSP+ as well as the ENP (increasingly ex ante), and is also applied with regard to accession. Outside the GSP, there is no equivalent to the essential elements and suspension clauses which apply to breaches of human rights. The broad scope of environmental protection, and how it may be defined, is relevant to this. This may equally be said of human rights, however, and indeed the EU has run into difficulties in this respect. That difficulty notwithstanding, the commitment to human rights has been enforced and has led on occasion to the suspension of elements of the agreements.

It is surprising that the internal commitment to the environment was not carried through into the EU's external relations more forcefully at a time when concerted action was being taken to promote another non-economic interest in the same relations. Yet this is less surprising when viewed from the perspective that human rights conditionality was required as a consequence of the EU's duty not to breach human rights. Thus, the particular pressures which shaped the emergence of fundamental rights protection within the EU legal order have also been crucial to the shape of external action in this field. There was a clear element of conditionality in the environmental obligations in relation to the Europe Agreements. If a partner state failed to comply with its undertakings, it would not be permitted to accede to the EC. In that context, the lack of conditionality *within* the agreement became an irrelevance; it operated at a different level and the partner state would have to continue to endeavour to improve its standards or it would never accede. This 'ex ante' environmental conditionality continues to be seen in the context of the ENP.

This is similar to the early approach taken to human rights, where conditionality effectively operated before the conclusion of the agreement. Thus, while in that case the incentive was cooperation itself, in the enlargement context, the incentive was accession, and in the ENP context, the incentive is cooperation. The problem encountered before the introduction of human rights conditionality in agreements—that partner states failed to continue to apply human rights standards following the conclusion of cooperation agreements—should not occur where the state has acceded to the EC. It is conceivable, however, that such issues may arise in the ENP context. In contrast, straightforward environmental conditionality can be seen in the GSP+.

C. The Significance of Relativity in the Pursuit of Non-economic Interests in the EU's External Relations

There is no doubt that whatever the motivation, the strategic importance of a partner state, be it geographical or economic, is crucial to the form and force of the non-economic interest clauses, just as it is to the form of agreement per se. The particular human rights issues specified in different contexts also demonstrate the importance of a common view as to what standards are to be applied. This is demonstrated rather less positively in relation to the negotiation experience with Australia. However, regardless of its primary motivation, the EU has sought to integrate these non-economic interests into its agreements with third states and has shown itself to be willing to act upon that.

i. Mitigating the Charge of Imperialism

The EU has been subject to the criticism that by imposing human rights or environmental conditionality in its agreements with third states, it is exporting its values in a paternalistic, or even imperialistic, fashion. Clearly, recognition by the EU of the significance of non-economic interests and the pursuit of these within its own rules is quite a different thing, in terms of legitimacy, from the imposition of its values on other states through economic means such as development cooperation. However, the consistent reference to universal or regionally specific international instruments (such as the UDHR, or ECHR in the European context) helps to protect it from this particular charge. Further protection is garnered from the shift to reciprocity or mutuality of obligation, including in the context of development cooperation: that the EU now also declares itself to be bound by these standards sends an important message in this regard. A further implication of this is that by tying the commitment to international rather than EU standards, the EU is cultivating a more universal culture or context for this development, which potentially has the capacity to extend beyond EU bilateral and multilateral agreements.

ii. The Creation of Regulatory Space for the Protection of Non-economic Values

However, there is a further reason why the use of international legal instruments, rather than EU standards, as the reference point for human rights and environmental values is important. In addition to insulating against the charge of imperialism in the EU's relations with third states, the use of international instruments as reference points serves an internal function. For the EU, it secures regulatory space inside the international legal architecture in which the EU can ensure the protection of values and rights for its own citizens. Thus, it supports EU internal regulation and action to protect its own citizens' human rights or environmental interests within, for example, the WTO framework. Arguably, this is effectively what the Court of Justice has done in *Kadi*[176] (albeit that the overarching framework of rules in that instance was of UN rather than WTO origin). Thus, the EU's interaction with international bodies of law is not only an exercise in external legitimation, but is also internal. Put simply, the Court of Justice was on stronger ground in *Kadi* because it referenced and sought to uphold fundamental rights recognised and protected through a non-EU international instrument rather than by purely domestic standards.

While the Australian, Indian and, to a lesser extent, Mexican negotiating experience reinforces the significance of consent of the partner state, it also highlights questions which may be asked about the nature of consent if one partner (frequently in this context the EU) is stronger than the other. Again, in obtaining agreement, the use of international instruments as reference points is crucial. However, the more recent development whereby these commitments are entered into reciprocally, committing the EU as well as the partner state(s), is also significant in this regard. The EU may legitimately be criticised for inconsistencies in the application or enforcement of its 'universal' policy. However, there can be little doubt that it is, in putting non-economic interests on the agenda as it enters into cooperative agreements with third states, contributing to the development of a wider culture in which non-economic interests are considered alongside economic objectives. As noted above, in so doing, it is also creating for itself, and more widely, the regulatory space in which such interests may be insulated against challenge from other international regimes. In this respect, the contribution of the EU to the approach taken to the relationship between economic and non-economic interests can be seen to manifest itself directly and indirectly, and as such it is a significant contribution.

D. EU External Policy as a Reflection of its Internal Policy

It is significant that the Cotonou Agreement emphasised sustainable development and the linking of environmental considerations and human rights.

---

[176] Joined Cases C-402/05 P *Kadi v Council and Commission* and C-415/05 P *Al Barakaat International Foundation v Council and Commission* [2008] ECR I-6351, discussed in ch 2.

That these two concerns should be tied together externally and increasingly internally (as in the development of the Charter and the focus upon sustainable development under the Europe 2020 Strategy) merits closer comparison of them in the international context as well. As seen above, sustainable development has now been explicitly recognised as an 'overarching objective' of cooperation in recent EU FTAs.[177] The evolving terms of the EU's inclusion of human rights and environmental protection in its agreements with third states thus clearly mirror the evolution in its internal policy. The developing focus upon sustainable development, integrated approaches and good governance is fully consistent with, for example, the 2020 Strategy.

E. Lessons Which May Be Drawn from the EU's Experience in Reconciling the Pursuit of Economic and Non-economic Interests

At this point, before moving on to examine the question of the relationship between economic and non-economic interests in the international context, it is worth briefly recapping some of the conclusions regarding the EU experience.

The analysis in the first section has demonstrated that the EU internally has grappled with the issue of reconciling the pursuit and protection of economic and non-economic interests since the early 1970s and, for a variety of reasons, including that this is necessary in order to ensure that the EU does not breach its own internal obligations, its concern for non-economic interests has subsequently been exported into its relations with third states. It has also been seen, however, that certain conditions were in play internally in the emergence of human rights in particular, which simply do not apply in the international context: the particular characteristics of the EU legal order, the role of the Court of Justice, the significance of the principles of supremacy and direct effect, and the existence of a body of rights to which the Member States were independently and collectively committed. The significance of these characteristics is such that it cannot be expected that such an evolution will be easily replicated in the international context, even if it were deemed desirable.

More recently, however, the internal experience is one in which a growing focus upon issues of good governance, democratic accountability and transparency of decision making has had a tangible impact upon policy development. Alongside this, we have seen the emergence of an integrated approach to pursuit of human rights, environmental and economic objectives—a pragmatic recognition of the fact that these may not be effectively or sustainably pursued individually. This is well understood within the

---

[177] Free Trade Agreement with Korea (n 166), Article 1.1(g).

overarching concept of 'sustainable development' which is now explicitly recognised as such in the EU's new generation of FTAs, including that with Korea.

Having recognised the significance of sustainable development as an overarching conceptual framework for the management of the relationship between economic and non-economic objectives, the question which arises is whether this has any practical effect. Regarding this particular issue, it was seen in chapter three that the EU has indeed given effect to the principle of sustainable development through the approach taken to determining the legitimacy (or not) of restrictions to trade on the grounds of environmental protection or human rights. As was seen, the application of the principle of proportionality is crucial to this process.

The Court of Justice has therefore found an instrumentalist approach to the determination of the appropriate balance between economic and non-economic interests where they collide in the internal market. Alongside this development, however, the EU has also sought to manage the relationship between economic and non-economic interests through more general policy development. This process has been characterised by the emergence of 'new governance', including public and stakeholder participation.[178] As attention turns to the international context, the question of what can be drawn from the EU experience has several dimensions, not least the extent or limits of the transferability of the EU approaches and whether it is possible to adopt, in the international context, an instrumentalist approach such as that of the Court of Justice.

In addition to the internal development of EU environment and human rights policy, it has been seen that since the 1980s, the EU has systematically pursued the inclusion of human rights and environmental commitments in its agreements with third states. Having succeeded in including reference to human rights as an 'essential element' in Lomé IV, the EU has broadened this out into the development of a universal policy of human rights conditionality and has similarly sought to develop commitment to environmental policy in its external agreements.

The nature and scope of EU external competency has a complex history. In that context, the systematic pursuit of inclusion of non-economic interests reflects a very deliberate policy choice. While there were initial doubts as to the competency of the then EC to pursue this policy, it can be seen to have been initially explicable as a necessary means by which to ensure that the EU did not breach its internal obligations. Since the Lisbon Treaty, any doubts regarding competency have been removed. In pursuing non-economic interests in its relations with third states, there can be little

---

[178] When contemplating stakeholder engagement, it is of course relevant to note the distinction between engagement to determine policy objectives as contrasted with stakeholder engagement to deliver policy objectives.

doubt that the EU has contributed to shaping the international context in which the relationship between economic and non-economic interests will be resolved. In that light, it is significant that the approach adopted by the EU in its external relations reflects its emergent internal approach. In other words, the pursuit of human rights, environmental protection and economic development are progressively seen as linked or mutually-dependent objectives: EU policy is premised upon an integrated conceptualisation of development, that is, sustainable development, which requires progress on all three objectives. This conceptualisation has been seen to have been operationalised in the internal context and it has been exported into the EU's relations with third states, explicitly in its more recent framework and free trade agreements. The question is whether this has any contribution to make to the wider international approach to reconciliation of pursuit of these sometimes competing objectives.

Part II

Balancing Economic and Non-economic Interests in the International Legal Order

6

The International Context: The WTO Legal Order

INTRODUCTION

THE FIRST PART of this book examined the EU experience with regard to the inter-relationship between economic interests (specifically the pursuit of trade liberalisation) and non-economic interests (including, specifically, human rights and environmental protection). The very clear lesson which emerges from that EU experience is that these interests are inherently inter-related, even mutually dependent, and that they should be pursued together.[1] These interests are tied together by the principle of sustainable development and their pursuit should be shaped by that overarching principle. It has been demonstrated that the EU has achieved an operationalisation of this in the context of the application of the internal market rules,[2] notwithstanding that its capacity for the enforcement of non-economic interests as free-standing objectives is rather weaker. It has also been seen that the recognised inter-relationship between these interests carries over into the EU's external policy, where it is manifested by the inclusion of human rights and environmental commitments in the EU's agreements with third states,[3] notwithstanding that it was by no means clear that there was competence for this prior to the Lisbon Treaty.[4] If contemporary global challenges pose new questions of the international legal order, inviting (or requiring) integrated approaches, it is relevant to assess the extent to which that EU experience may inform the response of the international community.

The second part of this book therefore turns to the international context. The tension between economic and non-economic interests has been particularly evident in questions concerning the relationship between free trade and non-economic interests including in particular environmental protection and human rights. These questions have been particularly acute

---

[1] See ch 2.
[2] See ch 3.
[3] See ch 5.
[4] See ch 4.

because the international framework for trade liberalisation, the WTO legal order, includes binding dispute settlement. One consequence of this is a strong possibility of spillover, with the effects of dispute settlement decisions reaching beyond the immediate context of trade regulation.[5]

The present chapter sets out the international context within which the relationship between trade liberalisation and the non-economic interests is addressed. The first section of the chapter is therefore concerned with the purpose and rules of the WTO that provide the core framework for international trade. The second section of the chapter unpacks the relationship between WTO rules and other international law.

I. THE FRAMEWORK FOR INTERNATIONAL TRADE: THE WTO

The core framework governing international trade is that of the WTO.[6] The original agreement, the GATT, governs any measures impinging on trade in goods, whatever their objective. In addition to the GATT, the covered agreements of the WTO include those relating to, inter alia, sanitary and phytosanitary measures (SPS), technical barriers to trade (TBT), trade in services (GATS), and intellectual property (TRIPS).[7] The WTO regulates both its members' trade measures and regional trading arrangements, such as the EU itself. The ultimate regulation of any trade measures is therefore carried out through the WTO.[8]

It is worth noting in this context that, as Doaa Abdel Motaal observed, 'the WTO's principal mandate is to work towards an open, equitable, non-discriminatory trading system. It only addresses environmental issues in so far as environmental policies have trade related aspects'.[9] This applies equally to the pursuit of any non-economic interest. The WTO therefore only impinges upon the trade related elements of the EU's policies. Yet the EU experience demonstrates that the maintenance of a sharp division in this respect is not possible in practice, particularly as the commitment to sustainable development deepens. The GATT Secretariat stated in its 1992 *Report on Trade and the Environment* that international trade and sustainable development are not inherently linked, but that trade is a 'magnifier', enabling countries with adequate sustainable policies to pursue these better.

---

[5] See chs 7 and 8.

[6] See below for discussion of the development of the GATT and WTO.

[7] These agreements are contained in Annex 1A of the WTO Agreement.

[8] For the consequent discrepancies in the application of WTO rules, see M Cremona, 'Neutrality or Discrimination? The WTO, the EU and External Trade' in G de Búrca and J Scott (eds), *The EU and the WTO: Legal and Constitutional Issues* (Oxford, Hart Publishing, 2001).

[9] DA Motaal, 'Trade and Environment in the WTO: Dispelling Misconceptions' (1999) 8(3) *Review of European Community and International Environmental Law* 330–35 at 330.

However, as discussed in chapter two, in the EU context, sustainable development is included in Article 11 TFEU, which also contains the duty of environmental integration. Furthermore, in confirming that economic growth and social cohesion may not be separated from environmental protection, the Commission's strategy on sustainable development recognises the lessons learnt from the EU's experience. Notwithstanding the GATT Secretariat's 1992 conclusions, the Preamble to the Agreement Establishing the WTO refers to sustainable development and environmental protection among its objectives. Yet the WTO has, inevitably, a fundamentally different approach from that of the EU regarding the relationship between trade and non-economic interests—'inevitably' in the light of the narrower focus of the WTO. The objective of the WTO rules is trade liberalisation, in contrast with the EU's broader developing polity.

Following an outline of the background to the WTO, this chapter will continue by considering its purpose, which should shape the interpretation of the rules. The key principles and rules relevant to the present inquiry are then set out, including relating to dispute settlement. This provides the backdrop for not only an analysis of the relationship between WTO law and general international law, in the second section of this chapter, but also the subsequent two chapters, which examine the relationship between WTO rules and environmental protection and WTO rules and human rights.

A. Background to the WTO

Like the original European Economic Community, the GATT arose as a response to the devastation of the Second World War. The original vision behind it was that an 'International Trade Organization' (ITO) be formed within Bretton Woods, alongside the International Monetary Fund (IMF) and the International Bank for Reconstruction and Development. The GATT came into provisional force in 1948 by virtue of a Protocol of Provisional Application and was to be attached to the ITO on its creation. The US Congress, however, failed to ratify the Havana Charter, which would have created the ITO (it proved politically unacceptable for it to rescind its sovereignty in relation to international trade). As a result, the Havana Charter was abandoned in 1951 and the GATT itself became the focus of the contracting parties in resolving trade disputes. The Havana Charter had included detailed provisions concerning the governance of the proposed ITO and also included provision on labour rights.[10] Although these were not included in the General Agreement, it did comprise sufficient

---

[10] In Article 7.

general provisions for a workable governance structure to be established among the contracting parties.[11] The GATT existed in this form for almost 50 years and functioned, during that period, through the 1948 'Interim Commission for the ITO', which became a de facto GATT Secretariat. There was an unsuccessful attempt in 1955 to create a mini-organization (the Organization for Trade Cooperation) through which to solve institutional problems, but the US Congress again refused to ratify it. Various revisions of the GATT culminated in the Uruguay Round of negotiations which created, finally, the long-sought WTO, the agreement of which incorporates the GATT.

There were two aspirations among the negotiators of the GATT, both of which were consistent with traditional economic theory: first, that more liberal trade and a reduction in the use of trade restrictions would facilitate better relations between nations, promoting world peace; and, second, that more liberal trade would promote economic well-being.[12] The then European Economic Community and the GATT thus shared the objective of international cooperation with a view to maintaining peace and security, although the EC sought, and the EU has developed, a far greater degree of mutual inter-dependence and integration.

B. Liberal Trade: A Means to an End?

Adam Smith's eighteenth-century vision of liberal trade saw its pursuit as being for the promotion of economic development and welfare gain.[13] These benefits were, and still are, viewed as being fundamental guarantors of peaceful cooperation and restraint from conflict.[14] Smith himself recognised that the pursuit of non-economic objectives could justify, or even require, a departure from the pure liberal trade or comparative advantage model.[15] A nation could therefore diverge from the objective of wealth maximisation. Jackson recognises that there is little in international trade

---

[11] For discussion of the development of the GATT, ch 1; M Trebilcock and R Howse, *The Regulation of International Trade* (London, Routledge, 2012); S Lester, B Mercurio and A Davies, *World Trade Law: Text, Materials and Commentary*, 2nd edn (Oxford, Hart Publishing, 2012) JH Jackson, *The World Trade Organization, Constitution and Jurisprudence* (Chatham House Papers, Royal Institute of International Affairs, 1998) chs 1–2; or JH Jackson, *The World Trading System Law and Policy of International Economic Relations* (Cambridge, MA, MIT Press, 1989) chs 1–2.

[12] See J Jackson, *The World Trading System Law and Policy of International Economic Relations* (Cambridge, MA, MIT Press, 1989) ch 1.

[13] Adam Smith, *The Wealth of Nations* (1776) Book IV, ch 2. There has been both historical and contemporary recognition of this, which is discussed in ch 9.

[14] An example of the successful operation of this principle can be seen in the creation and experience of the EC, including its subsequent enlargements and proposed accessions.

[15] Smith (n 13) Book IV, ch 2.

law which could deny the right to make that choice; however, he argues that a nation making such a choice should pay the whole cost of that policy and should not pass it on to other states through any form of regulation.[16] This could arguably work the other way: should a nation be compelled to incur GATT compliant regulatory costs in the pursuit of a particular policy, where a cheaper national solution would perhaps be to impose a ban? The answer under WTO rules is yes: a nation would be compelled to adopt a more costly regulatory system rather than a ban if it wishes to benefit from the advantages of liberal international trade.[17]

In both the EU and the WTO it is significant that liberal trade is, or was originally, seen as a tool towards the enhancement of both international relations and (primarily economic) welfare gains. In neither vision is it seen as an end in itself. In the WTO context this was highlighted by the then Director-General, Pascal Lamy:

> [T]he WTO does not advocate open trade for its own sake, but as a means for 'raising standards of living, ensuring full employment and a large and steadily growing volume of real income and effective demand.'[18]

This is significant regarding the issues facing each organisation today in the resolution of potential conflict between trade liberalisation and non-economic interests. Essentially, if trade liberalisation was originally developed as a 'tool' to promote welfare gain, the status it has achieved in that role should not mean that it is now pursued as an end in itself. Where the priorities of the international community are changing, trade policy should evolve to reflect this. If one major objective of free trade is welfare gain (even primarily economic), then free trade should not be pursued to the exclusion of consideration of other welfare issues: that is, trade liberalisation should not be pursued as an end in itself.[19] The risk, however, is that the dominance of the neoliberal agenda in the WTO excludes this wider context.[20] The significance of sustainable development to the global community cannot, in this context, be ignored; the relationship between economic and non-economic interests lies at the heart of sustainable development.

The EU's commitment to sustainable development is substantial.[21] The question before us is whether anything can be learnt from the EU approach to assist the WTO in addressing this issue. In order to answer this, it is necessary first to establish how the WTO handles the question of

---

[16] Jackson (n 12) 19.

[17] *Thailand-Restrictions of Importation of and Internal Taxes on Cigarettes*, Report of the Panel Adopted on 7 November 1990 (DS10/R–37S) (BISD 37S/200).

[18] P Lamy, speech at the opening of the academic year of the Geneva Graduate Institute, 3 October 2012.

[19] Discussed further in ch 9.

[20] See further ch 9.

[21] See ch 2.

the relationship between economic and non-economic issues. The central approach of the WTO rules can be seen in the GATT.

C. Fundamental Principles and Rules of the GATT

Before examining the provisions concerning non-economic interests in the GATT, it is useful to briefly note the core provisions of the GATT for the pursuit and protection of liberal trade.[22] The primary focus of the GATT was restriction of tariffs. Article I provides for the negotiation of reciprocal concessions which must subsequently be applied in a non-discriminatory fashion, irrespective of the origin of the goods. Thus, any concessions concerning goods which are negotiated between two Contracting Parties (now Members) must be applied equally to all 'like products' originating in, or destined for, any other Contracting Parties to the GATT: the Most Favoured Nation (MFN) principle. The essence of this requirement is non-discrimination among Contracting Parties. Article XXIV provides for the exemption of various regional blocs from the principle of MFN, subject to certain conditions.[23] It is this provision that permits the existence of not only the EU, but also other regional trade blocs, including the North American Free Trade Agreement (NAFTA) and Mercosur. Without this exception, they would, through breach of the principle of MFN, be unlawful. Related to this, the GATT also grants specific waivers for certain preferential agreements, such as the EC-ACP agreement.[24]

Article III requires that imported products be treated no less favourably than domestically produced 'like products'[25] (the 'national treatment' rule) and Article XI prohibits quantitative restrictions and other measures applied on the importation of products.[26] There are certain exceptions to the principle of non-discrimination, notably that concessions in existence before the negotiation of the GATT are exempt.[27] Certain of the non-tariff barrier codes adopted during the Tokyo round are also exceptions, only the countries which have signed up to these specific codes are subject to their rights and obligations).[28] In addition, Article XX provides an exhaustive list of general exceptions to the GATT rules.

---

[22] The focus at this point is upon the GATT rules, as the applicable core principles can be seen in these.

[23] Article XXIV.

[24] www.europa.eu.int/comm/development/cotonou/agreement_en.htm. Waiver confirmed, Doha Ministerial Declaration, 2001.

[25] The definition of 'like products' has proved controversial; see ch 7.

[26] With certain exceptions, such as for border tax adjustment.

[27] Article 1.

[28] For example, the Code on Government Procurement.

These rules form, essentially, a framework of negative integration, which can be contrasted with the EU model of positive integration.[29] Thus, the WTO creates a liberal trade area, whereas the EU has created a single market. What this means is that, in principle, any restriction will be permissible under the GATT unless it discriminates between imported and domestic like products or constitutes an import ban.[30] The GATT clearly contains many more rules and exceptions relating to both tariff reduction and the elimination of non-tariff barriers; however, it is these fundamental principles and rules that most closely concern the balance between the protection of economic and non-economic interests.

D. Provision for the Protection of Non-economic Interests within the WTO Legal Order

The key provision concerning non-economic interests in the GATT is Article XX, which provides for general (public policy-related) exceptions from the GATT rules: these include measures: necessary to protect public morals (XX(a)); necessary to protect human, animal or plant life or health (XX(b)); necessary to secure compliance with laws or regulations that are not inconsistent with this Agreement (XX(d)); concerning the products of prison labour (XX(e)); and *relating to* the conservation of exhaustible natural resources (XX(g)). The Article XX exceptions are subject to an additional requirement, the 'chapeau', that excepted measures do not constitute 'a means of arbitrary or unjustifiable discrimination between countries where the same conditions prevail, or a disguised restriction on international trade'. Similar provision exists in the GATS, while the question of the applicability of Article XX GATT to the Agreements on Technical Barriers to Trade and Sanitary and Phytosanitary Measures has prompted much debate. In Article XX it is clearly recognised that trade liberalisation may need to be constrained in the light of regulation in pursuit of other values or key objectives of public interest. The objectives of environmental protection and sustainable development are both referred to in the Preamble to the WTO, yet neither is mentioned in the GATT itself, nor are there any specific WTO agreements relating to them.[31] The following two chapters explore the relationship between trade and environment and trade and human rights respectively in the WTO legal order. One key feature

---

[29] Which includes the possibility of the harmonisation of standards.

[30] See JHH Weiler, 'The Constitution of the Market Place: Text and Context in the Evolution of the Free Movement of Goods' in P Craig and G de Búrca (eds), *The Evolution of EU Law* (Oxford, Oxford University Press, 2011); P Holmes, 'The WTO and the EU: Some Constitutional Comparisons' in de Búrca and Scott (n 8).

[31] Environmental protection is, however, specifically referred to in the other agreements such as the SPS and the TBT.

of the WTO legal order is that it has its own dispute settlement process which can be invoked in the event that Members find that the behaviour of another state means that they are not enjoying the benefits of membership.

E. The Dispute Settlement System

It is profoundly significant that the WTO has its own Dispute Settlement Understanding (DSU) and binding dispute settlement process, which are intended to secure application of and compliance with the rules. Under the DSU, disputes between Members are heard by a panel. Panel rulings may be appealed to the Appellate Body. The jurisdiction and procedure of the panels and the Appellate Body are set out in the DSU;[32] this essentially encompasses disputes between parties to the WTO concerning the 'covered agreements' of the WTO.[33] Complaints may be brought to the dispute settlement body by Members. When a panel is requested, there is a tight timeframe for its creation, proceedings and report. A report may be appealed on a point of law to the Appellate Body. If a measure is found to breach the obligations of the GATT, the offending state will be required to bring its measures into conformity. Failure to do so may give rise to compensation or to a temporary suspension of concessions. The 'temporary suspension of concessions' is a tool with variable strength, dependent on the complaining state's economic development. Panel and Appellate Body rulings are binding upon the parties to the dispute. Prior to the establishment of the WTO, there had been a system for dispute settlement under the GATT. A significant weakness of the original GATT system was that the adoption of GATT panel reports could be vetoed by the defending state. The WTO DSU removes this possibility: the adoption of a report can now only be prevented by unanimity or by lodging an appeal.

The DSU provides a unified dispute settlement system for all the agreements under the WTO,[34] but it has proved controversial, not least as a consequence of the encroachment on national sovereignty which binding settlement entails.[35] The impact that dispute settlement may have on national policy choices in fields such as environmental protection and human rights is potentially significant, particularly if there is no mechanism by which to balance such issues. This is of course particularly relevant to the present inquiry. This impact of binding dispute settlement raises questions in turn as to whether the WTO is an appropriate body to be carrying out such a balancing act and whether it should be considering such issues

---

[32] Articles 3, 11, 13 and 19 DSU.
[33] The covered agreements include the GATT, GATS and TRIPS. A full list is contained in Appendix 1 to the GATT DSU.
[34] Article 1 DSU (although certain of the Agreements specify particular procedures).
[35] See Jackson *The World Trade Organization* (n 11) ch 4.

at all. It is worth emphasising that under WTO dispute settlement, the substantive law at issue is WTO law. This raises various questions, notably how the panel and the Appellate Body should respond where other international law is also concerned, and it is to this issue that attention now turns.

II. THE RELATIONSHIP BETWEEN WTO LAW AND INTERNATIONAL LAW

The relationship between WTO law and other forms of international law is clearly of key importance to the present inquiry, concerning as it does the relationship between economic and non-economic interests. Clearly the WTO rules pursue trade liberalisation rather than non-economic interests, so the dispute settlement system means that the manner in which the trade liberalisation rules are interpreted can have a substantial impact upon the enjoyment of other interests which are protected through their own distinct legal frameworks; that the dispute settlement system is binding increases this effect. The manner in which the panels and the Appellate Body interpret the relationship between WTO rules and other international law thus has the capacity to affect the effectiveness of those other legal regimes. This second section of the chapter is therefore concerned with unpacking the relationship between WTO law and other international law. The principles established in this general relationship are also of fundamental importance when attention turns to the specific questions of the relationship between WTO law and environmental law and human rights law.

A. WTO Law: No Clinical Isolation from International Law

WTO law has been characterised as a 'self-contained regime'.[36] Significantly, while the jurisdiction of the regime is limited to the interpretation and administration of the obligations of the regime, it does not preclude the application of other rules of international law within the system.[37] Yet, as Trachtman observes, 'there is no mechanism for integrating diverse legal rules, that is, for determining which law takes precedence when diverse laws conflict'.[38] To what extent therefore should other international law be taken account of or applied in the context of WTO dispute settlement?

---

[36] B Simma and D Pulkowski, 'Of Planets and the Universe: Self-contained Regimes in International Law' (2006) 17 *European Journal of International Law* 483.

[37] See further J Harrison, *The Human Rights Impact of the WTO* (Oxford, Hart Publishing, 2007).

[38] J Trachtman, 'The Domain of WTO Dispute Resolution' (1999) 40 *Harvard International Law Journal* 333, 338. See also G Marceau, 'WTO Dispute Settlement and Human Rights' (2002) 13 *European Journal of International Law* 753, 761.

Within the WTO Agreements, Article 3.2 DSU provides that 'the Dispute Settlement system ... serves to clarify the existing provisions of [the covered agreements] *in accordance with customary rules of interpretation of public international law*'.[39] In its first report, *US Gasoline*, the Appellate Body seminally attributed this to 'a measure of recognition that the *General Agreement* is not to be read in clinical isolation from public international law'.[40] The customary rules of interpretation of international law are codified in Article 31 of the Vienna Convention,[41] which therefore, pursuant to Article 3.2 DSU, clearly applies. Article 31(3)(c) is of particular relevance for the present purposes: 'There shall be taken into account, together with the context: ... (c) any relevant rules of international law applicable in the relations between the parties.' It should be emphasised that while Article 31(3)(c) refers to the applicability of rules of customary international law, this applicability is to the *interpretation* of international treaties. Similarly, Article 3.2 DSU stipulates only that such international law rules are relevant to the *interpretation* of the WTO Agreements. Thus, these provisions do not suggest the substantive applicability of international law within WTO law. This is reinforced by the fact that the panels and the Appellate Body cannot 'add to or diminish the rights and obligations' of the agreements;[42] they have no jurisdiction to enforce or interpret other rules of international law. Article 31(3)(c) raises two questions. The first is what are 'relevant rules of international law'? The second concerns the interpretation of 'applicable ... between the parties'. Provisions meeting these criteria are relevant to the interpretation of the WTO agreements, raising a further question: what does the obligation to take these rules into account require?[43]

---

[39] Emphasis added.

[40] Appellate Body Report, *United States—Standards for Reformulated and Conventional Gasoline (US-Gasoline)*, WT/DS2/AB/R adopted 20 May 1996 DSR 1996:I, 29, 17.

[41] Vienna Convention on the Law of Treaties 1969. Article 31(1) provides for a 'good faith' interpretation 'in accordance with the ordinary meaning to be given to the terms of the treaty in their context and in the light of its object and purpose' ('the basic rule'). Article 31(2) provides that the context includes 'in addition to the text, including its preamble and annexes: (a) any agreement relating to the treaty which was made between all the parties in connexion with the conclusion of the treaty; (b) any instrument made by one or more parties in connexion with the conclusion of the treaty and accepted by the other parties as an instrument related to the treaty'. See further A Aust, *Modern Treaty Law and Practice* (2nd edn, (Cambridge, Cambridge University Press, 2007) 230.

[42] Article 3.2 DSU. On the political significance of these provisions, see J Klabbers, 'On Rationalism in Politics: Interpretation of Treaties and the World Trade Organization' (2005) 74 *Nordic Journal of International Law* 405, 411.

[43] A question made all the more pertinent by the case made by Klabbers that 'often enough the rules are paid tribute to but ignored, distorted or manipulated in actual use, either by design or out of ignorance': ibid 416. This, however, does not detract from the intention that WTO rules be interpreted consistently with rules of customary international law.

B. Relevant Rules of International Law

The principal sources of international law relevant to this research and considered below are customary international law and treaty law.

i. Customary International Law

It is relatively straightforward to establish the relevance of customary international law insofar as it is universal and therefore applicable between the parties.[44] In its ruling in *Korea-Government Procurement*, the panel noted its *obligation* to apply customary rules of *interpretation* of international law, but added that customary international law has a wider effect upon WTO law than this interpretative obligation:

> [T]o the extent that there is no conflict or inconsistency, or an expression in a covered WTO Agreement that implies differently ... the customary rules of international law apply to the WTO treaties and to the process of treaty formation under the WTO.[45]

The panel also explicitly ruled out the 'implication that rules of international law other than rules of interpretation do not apply'.[46] Pauwelyn argues that the panel should have referred to general principles of international law in addition to customary international law.[47] The relevance of these has indeed been recognised by panels and the Appellate Body.[48] Being universal, the general principles are applicable between the parties and are therefore relevant in the WTO context if they constitute 'rules of international law'. In *EC-Biotech* the panel questioned whether it is 'self-evident that [general principles] can be considered as rules of international law within the meaning of Art. 31(3)(c)', but accepted the Appellate Body ruling (in *US-Shrimp*) that general principles of international law are to be taken into account in the interpretation of WTO provisions.[49] While this finding is not itself

---

[44] Unless contracted out of, on which see further J Pauwelyn, *Conflict of Norms in Public International Law: How WTO Law Relates to other Rules of International Law* (Cambridge, Cambridge University Press, 2009) 212.

[45] Panel Report, *Korea-Measures Affecting Government Procurement*, WT/DS163/R, adopted 19 June 2000, DSR 2000: VIII 3541, para 7.96, emphasis added.

[46] ibid, note 753.

[47] Pauwelyn (n 44) 211.

[48] See, inter alia, Report of the Panel, *European Communities-Measures Affecting the Approval and Marketing of Biotech Products*, WT/DS291/R, WT/DS292/R, WT/DS293/R, Add.1 to Add.9, and Corr. 1, adopted 21 November 2006, DSR 2006: III-VIII; Report of the Appellate Body, *European Communities—Measures Affecting Meat and Meat Products (Hormones)*, WT/DS48 and WT/DS26, 13 February 1998, DSR 1998:I, 135: see further Marceau (n 38).

[49] Report of the Panel (n 48) para 1.67, referring to the Appellate Body Report, *US-Import Prohibition of Certain Shrimp and Shrimp Products*, WT/DS58/AB/R, adopted 6 November 1998, DSR 1998:VII, 2755, para 158 and note 157. See further Pauwelyn (n 44) 268.

problematic, *EC-Hormones* demonstrated the difficulty which can arise in establishing *when* a principle becomes a general principle of international law. The Appellate Body ruled in that dispute that 'whether [the precautionary principle] has been widely accepted by Members as a principle of general or customary international law appears less than clear'.[50]

ii. The Impact of Provisions of International Treaties

A further question concerns the extent to which provisions of *international treaties*, unquestionably 'rules of international law', may or may not be applicable. The answer hinges on the interpretation of the phrase 'applicable between the parties'. Are only treaty provisions which apply between *all* parties to the WTO to be taken into account in the interpretation of the WTO Agreements? Or are provisions of treaties applicable between all the parties to a specific WTO dispute intended? What of treaties applicable only between some of the parties to a specific dispute? The answer to this question hinges upon the answer to a further question: what is the nature of WTO obligations—do they comprise a series of bilateral obligations or are they collective obligations, applying *erga omnes* to all WTO Members?[51] If they are the former, provisions of international treaties to which particular states are party will be applicable in disputes between those parties. If the latter, the provisions of such bilateral treaties will not be applicable.

In *US-Shrimp* the Appellate Body applied an evolutionary principle of interpretation requiring that 'exhaustible natural resources' (in Article XX(g) GATT) be read 'in the light of contemporary concerns of the community of nations about the protection and conservation of the environment [not as it was understood in 1947]'.[52] The Appellate Body identified the appropriate interpretation with reference to contemporary international treaties, noting 'that modern international conventions and declarations make frequent references to natural resources as embracing both living and non-living resources'.[53] Significantly, in determining the appropriate contemporary meaning, the Appellate Body referred to treaties which were not applicable to all the disputing parties. As observed by the panel in *EC-Biotech*, 'the mere fact that one or more disputing parties are not parties to a convention does not necessarily mean that a convention cannot shed light on the

---

[50] Report of the Appellate Body (n 48) (discussed below), which concluded that it was 'unnecessary and probably imprudent' to take a position on this question in view of the facts of the dispute.

[51] See J Pauwelyn, 'A Typology of Multilateral Treaty Obligations: Are WTO Obligations Bilateral or Collective in Nature?' (2003) 14 *European Journal of International Law* 907. See further below.

[52] Appellate Body Report (n 49) paras 128–32.

[53] ibid para 130 (referring, inter alia, to the UNCLOS and the Convention on Biological Diversity).

meaning and scope of a treaty term to be interpreted'.[54] However, the panel further noted that *US-Shrimp* could be distinguished from *EC-Biotech*, since in *US-Shrimp* it was *necessary* to interpret 'exhaustible natural resources', and to that end the international conventions were informative.[55]

There is a crucial distinction here, indicated above, between the role that a provision of international law might play in *informing the interpretation* of a provision of the WTO Agreement and the *applicability* of an international treaty provision within WTO law. The *EC-Biotech* panel stated that 'it makes sense to interpret Art. 31(3)(c) as *requiring* consideration of those rules of international law which are applicable in the relations *between all parties to the treaty which is being interpreted*', observing that such an approach would contribute to the consistency of international law and the avoidance of conflict.[56] The panel therefore concluded that a rule of international law which is not applicable to all the parties to a particular dispute 'is not applicable in the relations between all WTO members' and therefore that it was not required to take that rule into account.[57] The panel explicitly noted that as it was not faced with a situation in which:

> [T]he relevant rules of international law are applicable in the relations between all parties to the dispute, but not between all WTO members ... we need not, and do not, take a position on whether in such a situation we would be *entitled* to take the relevant rules of international law into account.[58]

It is striking that the panel raised this question as to whether there is any entitlement to take such rules into consideration, rather than simply observing that it was not *required* to do so. In questioning even the possibility of entitlement to take such provisions into consideration, the panel reinforced the second arm of Article 3.2 DSU: 'Recommendations and rulings of the DSB cannot add to or diminish the rights and obligations provided in the covered agreements.'[59] To take into consideration, in a particular dispute, rules applying between the parties to that dispute, but which do not apply to all the parties to the WTO, would potentially give rise to differing effects of the covered agreements, depending on the parties to a particular dispute. Pauwelyn has argued that since WTO obligations are essentially bilateral in

---

[54] Report of the Panel (n 48) para 1.94.
[55] On the issue of evolutionary interpretation (and in particular sustainable development), see Gabcikovo-Nagymaros (Hungary/Slovakia) Judgment, ICJ Reports 1997, 7 at 78, para 140: 'new norms have to be taken into consideration, and ... new standards given proper weight, not only when States contemplate new activities but also when continuing activities begun in the past'. This was subsequently applied in the *Arbitration Regarding the Iron-Rhine, Railway (Belgium v The Netherlands)*, Permanent Court of Arbitration—Award of the Arbitral Tribunal, 24 May 2005, paras 58–59, www.pca-cpa.org/upload/files/BE-NL%20 Award%20240505.pdf.
[56] Above n 49, para 1.70 (emphasis added).
[57] Report of the Panel (n 48) para. 1.71.
[58] ibid para 1.72 (emphasis added).
[59] This is reiterated at Article 19.2 DSU.

nature, there is no reason why rules applying between the parties to a particular dispute, even if not to all WTO members, should not be applied.[60] If in contrast WTO obligations were *erga omnes*, such an approach would not be possible.

Petersmann criticised the Panel's approach, arguing that:

> [P]romoting the legal coherence of WTO rules by such legal formalism risks to entail unnecessary inconsistencies with the international legal system, even if the Panel mitigated its rigid interpretation by noting that 'other treaties' could always be taken into account as factual evidence for the 'ordinary meaning' of the terms used in WTO provisions.[61]

That said, to allow other rules of international law to be taken into consideration in individual cases could lead to inconsistencies *within the WTO legal order*, while reducing rather than eradicating the possibility of 'inconsistencies' or conflict with the international legal order. Pauwelyn recognises that this 'may complicate the matrix of rights and obligations between members', but characterises this as inevitable in the absence of a single international law legislature.[62] To permit the WTO to recognise and give effect to other rules of international law where those other rules apply to all the parties to a particular dispute is attractive. Doing so would neither add to nor diminish the rights or obligations which apply in the total relations between particular parties to a WTO dispute, who are also parties to another international treaty. It seems appropriate: those parties are bound by all their international commitments. Yet arguably the very act of giving effect to that other treaty could impact upon (add to or diminish) the rights and obligations under the covered agreements per se by varying their effects. Marceau strongly opposed such an approach, which would lead to the panel or Appellate Body being put in the problematic position of interpreting human rights rules.[63]

To remove all inconsistencies in the relationship between WTO law and the international legal order in different cases, it would be necessary to apply uniform interpretations and accommodate the same rules of international law in all cases. Yet such an approach would not reflect the diversity of international obligations of WTO Members.

So what can be extrapolated from the rulings of the AB regarding the relationship between WTO law and other international law? The above

---

[60] J Pauwelyn, 'The Role of Public International Law in the WTO: How Far Can We Go?' (2001) 95 *American Journal of International Law* 535.

[61] EU Petersmann, 'Defragmentation of International Economic Law through Constitutional Interpretation and Adjudication with Due Respect for Disagreement' (2008) 6 *Loyola University Chicago International Law Review* 209, 241.

[62] Pauwelyn (n 60) 567.

[63] Marceau (n 38) 777–78; see also JP Trachtman, 'The Domain of WTO Dispute Resolution' (1999) 40 *Harvard Journal of International Law* 333, 342–43.

analysis demonstrates that the rules of customary international law apply to the covered agreements and bind WTO Members, dispute settlement panels and the Appellate Body. However, the panels and the Appellate Body have no jurisdiction or legitimacy to enforce these. Provisions of international law that are binding on all the parties to the WTO (including general principles and treaty provisions) should be used to assist in the interpretation of WTO rules, but are not substantively applicable by the panel or Appellate Body as such. There are strong arguments in support of this. If a state violates an international treaty obligation which it has signed up to, this cannot be a matter for the WTO, unless action would be consistent with WTO rules. The panel or Appellate Body would rightly face questions over its legitimacy should it authorise a violation of WTO rules in such circumstances. On the other hand, it can refer to the treaty to inform its interpretation of WTO rules.

While highlighting the distinction between the interpretative significance of other rules of international law and the (lack of) applicability or enforcement of other international law by the panels and the Appellate Body, it must be recalled that WTO Members are bound by all their obligations under international law.[64] The question remains outstanding as to whether international treaty rules which are binding on all parties to a particular dispute, but not all WTO Members, may be taken into account, other than to the extent that they shed light on the ordinary meaning of WTO provisions.

Having set out in the present chapter the general context within which the relationship between the non-economic interests in question and trade liberalisation is determined, chapters seven and eight turn to explore the specific questions of the relationship between trade and the environment and trade and human rights respectively.

---

[64] This is consistent with the Report of the Appellate Body in *Measures Affecting the Importation of Certain Poultry Products (EC-Poultry)* WT/DS69/AB/R, adopted on 23 July 1998, para 79.

7

Trade and Environment in the WTO Legal Order

INTRODUCTION

T HE GENERAL RELATIONSHIP between WTO law and other international law was examined in chapter six. Building on this analysis, attention now turns to the specific question of the relationship between WTO law and environmental protection measures. The first section of the chapter sets out the background against which the relationship between environmental protection and WTO law is now determined. The second section of the chapter specifically examines first the pre-WTO, GATT case law arising from environmental regulatory measures, before turning to analyse the approach adopted towards trade environment matters under the WTO covered agreements. The third section of the chapter raises questions arising from emerging environmental issues: notably the desire of states to develop and promote renewable energy production and use, and the question of whether a particular regime should be developed with regard to trade in 'green goods'. Throughout the analysis of the GATT and WTO case law, attention is paid to how the approach adopted by the panels and the Appellate Body compares to the approach of the Court of Justice to similar cases; this comparative analysis is continued into an examination, in the fourth section of the chapter, of the tests applied by the panel and the Appellate Body, which are compared with the Court of Justice approach. The findings of this chapter reinforce the view that trade and environment issues are inherently inter-related and raise concerns regarding the potential impact of decisions made by trade experts under the WTO legal order.

I. BACKGROUND TO THE TRADE-ENVIRONMENT NEXUS UNDER THE GATT/WTO

At the time of the negotiation of the GATT in the post-war context of the mid-twentieth century, the environment was not an issue of global concern. Given that context, it is unsurprising that Article XX does not explicitly refer to 'environmental protection'.[1] The grounds of exception allowed are, however, capable of encompassing measures of environmental protection, and the Appellate Body has explicitly acknowledged that the interpretation of Article XX(g) (concerning conservation of natural resources) should be informed by contemporary understanding, recognising its applicability to environmental conservation.[2]

As a result, Article XX has been central to the environment-related disputes that have come before the dispute settlement procedure, both under the GATT and the WTO. This provides direct comparison with the original EC Treaty, in which the exceptions to the prohibition on restrictions to free movement of goods provisions were modelled upon the GATT provisions and include 'the protection of health and life of humans, animals or plants'.[3] Because Article XX(b) also ties together human, animal and plant life and health, the analysis in this section will also take account of developments relating to health-related measures, as this is equally relevant to the underlying question concerning the balance to be drawn between economic and environmental interests.

In 1971 the GATT Secretariat was asked to make a contribution to the preparation for the UN Conference on the Human Environment (Stockholm, 1972). The report which was duly produced was presented to the Contracting Parties in 1971 and the Director-General encouraged the Contracting Parties to further consider the implications of environmental measures on trade. Subsequently, the GATT set up the 'Environmental Measures and International Trade' group. This group was to meet at the request of GATT members. Twenty years passed, however, before the first request to meet was made (by the EFTA members) in the run-up to the Rio Conference (1992). During this period, environmental protection had a growing impact upon international trade and was increasingly regularly considered in the context of the GATT. The question of environmental protection and trade barriers was also considered in the Tokyo Round in the development of the Agreement on Technical Barriers to Trade (the TBT Agreement). In 1982, questions were raised at GATT ministerial level as to the environmental and health implications of the export of domestically prohibited goods. This led ultimately, in 1989, to the creation of the Working Group on the Export of Domestically Prohibited Goods and other Hazardous Substances.[4]

---

[1] GATT Article XX is introduced and discussed in ch 6.

[2] As evidenced by the Appellate Body report in *United States-Import Prohibition of Certain Shrimp and Shrimp Products*, AB-1998-4 WT/DS58/R (98-0000), 12 October 1998, (1998) 38 ILM 121.

[3] Article 36 TFEU (ex Article 36 EEC). This is unsurprising since Article 36 was modelled upon Article XX GATT.

[4] See further www.wto.org/english/tratop_e/envir_e/hist1_e.htm.

The TBT and Sanitary and Phytosanitary (SPS) agreements do contain explicit recognition of environmental objectives.[5] Similarly, in relation to agriculture, environmental programmes are exempt from cuts in subsidies. In relation to subsidies and countervailing duties, the agreement permits subsidies of up to 20 per cent of firms' costs in adapting to new environmental laws. The GATS and TRIPS agreements also provide exemptions relating to the protection of human, animal or plant life.[6]

A. The Committee on Trade and Environment

In 1994 the WTO set up a Committee on Trade and Environment (CTE). This is essentially a consultative and policy developing body which has no executive or legislative powers. Its mandate is twofold: to identify the relationship between environmental measures and trade, and to make recommendations on any necessary changes to the WTO agreements. These must, notably, be compatible with the principle of non-discrimination. The CTE operates within certain parameters: that the WTO is a trade rather than an environmental organisation; that the GATT permits the pursuit of non-discriminatory environmental policies; that environmental policies require coordination within as well as among states; and that market access is fundamental. The success of the CTE in fulfilling its role is dependent on the interpretation of these parameters: for example, satisfaction of the requirement that national policies are non-discriminatory depends upon the interpretation given to 'like' products. Quick draws attention to the radical nature of the CTE's first report in 1996.[7] This report highlighted a general consensus among Members that environmental interests outside a particular state should not be pursued through that state adopting unilateral environmental measures. Furthermore, there appeared to be general agreement that disputes concerning trade-related measures contained within multilateral environmental agreements (MEAs) should be dealt with through the MEA. It also contained discussion of process and production measures, in particular whether these are covered by the TBT Agreement. However, as Quick notes, despite discussing these issues in some detail, the report did not draw substantive conclusions and the CTE's subsequent reports were rather less significant.

---

[5] Discussed below.
[6] See Article XIV GATS and Article 27 TRIPS.
[7] R Quick, 'Do We Need Trade and Environment Negotiations or Has the Appellate Body Done the Job?' (2013) 47 *Journal of World Trade* 957, 958–59.

B. The GATT Status of Trade-Related Measures in MEAs

The question of the GATT status of MEAs was raised in the *US-Shrimp* dispute. There are a significant number of MEAs (the WTO website currently refers to 20) which include trade-related measures.[8] As noted above, the 1996 first report of the CTE indicated that such measures should be dealt with through the MEA rather than the GATT. Following considerable speculation, the ruling in *US-Shrimp* suggests that such measures will be looked upon favourably. This is supported by Article 31 of the Vienna Convention, as seen above in relation to questions of extra-territorial effect. This, while reassuring to environmentalists, leaves a rather wide lacuna: Article 31 recognises the importance of rules of international law which apply between the parties. As noted above, the position concerning a measure from an MEA where one party to a dispute is not a party to the MEA continues to be uncertain.

It is worth recalling that such questions are a consequence of the fragmented nature of international law, whereby various bodies of law exist in parallel. MEAs are distinct from the WTO Agreements and are separately administered. From the WTO perspective, the question of the relationship between a provision of an MEA and WTO law will only arise if a dispute comes before the panel or the Appellate Body in which the two normally separate systems of law coincide. As seen in chapter six, provisions of an MEA may inform the panel or the Appellate Body with regard to the interpretation of particular WTO rules, but they are not substantively applicable by the panel or the Appellate Body. It should be recognised that when considering environmental measures, the dispute settlement panel inevitably approaches the question from the perspective of its expertise and mandate: the trade rules. Thus, it is essential that there be scrutiny and assessment of the legitimacy of the interpretative processes used by the WTO panels.[9]

The cases which lead to difficulty are those in which there is no explicit conflict, or even no clearly defined conflict, but an ambiguity as to how the relevant provisions on the different interests should be interpreted. This requires a judgment to be made by the panel or the Appellate Body as to the appropriate line to be drawn between the economic and non-economic interests. The Appellate Body has referred to the need to 'weigh and balance' the competing interests.[10] This suggests a degree of subjectivity in the

---

[8] www.wto.org/english/tratop_e/envir_e/envir_neg_mea_e.htm. The WTO Matrix of MEAs containing trade measures can be found at, the WTO: https://docs.wto.org/dol2fe/Pages/FE_Search/FE_S_S006.aspx?Query=%28@Symbol:%20wt/cte/w/160/rev*%29&Language=ENGLISH&Context=FomerScriptedSearch&languageUIChanged=true#.

[9] See below.

[10] WTO, *Korea-Measures Affecting Imports of Fresh, Chilled and Frozen Beef* (11 December 2000), WTO Docs WT/DS161/AB/R and WT/DS169/AB/R (Appellate Body Report), discussed below.

decision making of the panel and the Appellate Body, which must therefore be subject to careful scrutiny. In particular, one question which arises is whether there are any objective mechanisms which may be applied by the panel or the Appellate Body to avoid the super-imposition of its subjective judgment over that of the national regulatory authority.

The question of the relationship between multilateral environmental agreements and WTO rules is, as noted above, one which has recurred and to which responses have evolved. In the 1990s there was a view that resolution of this issue would likely require an amendment or addition to WTO rules. Thus, for example, Schoenbaum proposed an amendment to Article XX to provide an exception for measures adopted to implement provisions of MEAs.[11] Dependent upon how such an amendment was expressed, this might remove the need for the dispute settlement balancing act, but achieving consensus on the necessary exception would be difficult. In the run-up to Doha, a number of options were recognised as being available to resolve the question of the relationship between the WTO Agreements and MEAs.[12] Although maintenance of the status quo was among these, there was a real sense that amendment (or addition) to the rules would be necessary in order to satisfactorily resolve the relationship between WTO rules and MEAs. However, it proved impossible to find a means to carry this forward either in the Special Session or since. While, as Quick observes, this is consistent with the more general experience in the Doha negotiations, he also discerns a change in tack—that 'members began to realize that rule changes were not necessary'.[13] Instead, there was growing recognition that the issue could be addressed through 'principles of "no-hierarchy between WTO and MEAs", "mutual supportiveness between WTO and MEAs" and "deference"'. Quick attributes this change in tack to both the limited mandate of the discussions and the rulings which had emerged from the

---

[11] See, inter alia, T Schoenbaum, 'International Trade and Protection of the Environment: The Continuing Search for Reconciliation' (1997) 91 *American Journal of International Law* 268. On the question of the status of MEAs, see further J Schultz, 'Environmental Reform of the GATT/WTO International Trading System' (1994) 18 *World Competition* 77, 104; F Francioni, 'Environment, Human Rights and the Limits of Free Trade' in F Francioni (ed), *Environment, Human Rights and International Trade* (Oxford, Hart Publishing, 2001); Quick (n 7).

[12] Maintaining the Status Quo; Amending GATT Article XX; Granting Multi-Year Waivers and Developing Non-Binding Guidelines; Setting 'Differentiated WTO Disciplines' for Trade Measures Pursuant to MEAs; Designing a Coherence Clause; Developing a Principles and Criteria Approach; Reversing the Burden of Proof under GATT Article XX & Developing a Code of Good Conduct; Developing Non-Binding Interpretative Guidelines; Developing an Understanding (to apply across the entire WTO Agreement, on differentiated treatment for trade measures applied pursuant to MEAs); Creating a Voluntary Consultative Mechanism (VCM); Promoting Mutual Supportiveness and Deference. Committee on Trade and Environment, Special Session, *Multilateral Environmental Agreements (MEAs) and WTO Rules; Proposals made in the Committee on Trade and Environment (CTE) from 1995–2002*, TN/TE/S/1, 23 May 2002.

[13] Quick (n 7) 961.

Appellate Body, in particular *US-Shrimp*.[14] This is also consistent with the approaches to managing the relationship between different bodies of law, as discussed above.

More recently, the emphasis has shifted, reflecting both recognition that the WTO does not exist in 'clinical isolation' and the general shift away from pursuit of rule changes. The WTO has recognised the need for cooperation with other organisations and bodies of law, including MEAs. The development of links and mutual support has been intensified. Recognition of the interaction between distinct organisations and bodies of law is consistent with the integrated 'sustainable development'-based approach adopted in the EU.[15]

II. ENVIRONMENTAL REGULATORY MEASURES AND DISPUTE SETTLEMENT

In the treatment of the environment in the GATT, a parallel may once again be seen between the GATT and the then European Economic Community in that there was a lack of central action, but there were developments outside the core of the GATT.[16] During the pre-WTO period, several environment-related disputes came before a GATT panel. Unlike the European Court of Justice, however, the GATT panel did not take a leading role in environmental protection. The framework nature of the EC Treaty and the interpretative role of the (then) ECJ are significant here. These are not characteristics shared by the GATT and the Dispute Settlement Body (DSB). This is inevitable given the different principles underlying these organisations: the EC pursuing positive integration and the GATT seeking primarily national treatment. Once again, we return to the fundamental difference, even in the early stages, of what each organisation seeks to achieve. This impacts directly upon the extent of the ability of each organisation to accommodate non-economic interests. It is particularly significant in this regard that the GATT had (and WTO has) no autonomous law-making power, therefore it is not possible for it to develop policy as the EC (and latterly the EU) has done. Notwithstanding this constraint, the objective of sustainable development was consistently pursued by Director-General Lamy, both within and outside the context of the Doha negotiations.[17]

---

[14] ibid 962; *US-Shrimp* (n 2).
[15] See ch 3.
[16] See ch 1.
[17] Discussed below.

A. Trade/Environment Disputes before the GATT Panel

i. Tuna and Tuna Products

The first 'environmental' dispute to come before the GATT panel was brought by Canada against the US, following a US import prohibition on tuna and tuna products.[18] It is worth examining the facts of this dispute in some detail as they highlight the sensitivity of the issues at stake. Canada had seized 19 US fishing vessels and arrested a number of fishermen because the vessels were fishing, without authorisation, in waters they considered to be under its fisheries jurisdiction. However, the US did not recognise Canada's jurisdiction over these waters and therefore introduced a retaliatory import prohibition.[19] Canada argued that this measure was discriminatory and therefore breached Articles I and VIII.[20] It also argued that in negotiations under Article XXIII:1, the US delegation had not disputed that the measure breached the GATT and had been ready to negotiate compensation.[21]

The US response was that the measure was justified by Article XX(g) GATT[22] was not discriminatory, as 'similar measures had been taken for similar reasons against imports from other countries (e.g. Costa Rica and Peru)', and was not motivated by trade considerations.[23] The US justification for the measure (Article XX(g)) was based upon a number of factors, the first being that tuna was an exhaustible resource; this was accepted by Canada. Second, the measure allegedly met the requirements of non-discrimination as it was taken in conjunction with domestic measures concerning the consumption and production of tuna, although not specifically Albacore tuna, which was the subject of the ban in question. Third, it concerned the international management of tuna conservation. Finally, the US argued that the measure was not a disguised restriction on trade, as the effect on trade was 'at most nominal'.[24] The reason for the measure was, however, retaliation for Canada's action. The US argued that this

---

[18] *US-Prohibition of Imports of Tuna and Tuna Products from Canada*, BISD 29S/91, Panel Report adopted 22 February 1982.

[19] Section 205 of the Fishery Conservation and Management Act 1976 provides that 'if the Secretary of State determined that any fishing vessel of the United States, while fishing in waters beyond any foreign nation's territorial sea, to the extent that such sea was recognized by the United States, being seized by any foreign nation as a consequence of a claim of jurisdiction which was not recognized by the United States, the Secretary of Treasury should immediately take such action as may be necessary and appropriate to prevent the importation of fish and fish products from the foreign fishery involved' (Panel Report, *Tuna and Tuna Products* ibid, para 2.2).

[20] ibid para 3.1.

[21] ibid para 3.3.

[22] Which provides an exception for measures relating to the conservation of natural resources.

[23] Panel Report, *Tuna and Tuna Products* (n 18) Paragraph 3.5.

[24] Paragraph 3.9.

action 'significantly impaired' the international management approach and, being unilateral, was unsuitable for the management of a highly migratory species. No international measures had been adopted, however, regarding Albacore tuna. The US also argued that its measure was to encourage other states to cooperate in the international conservation of tuna. Canada, in response, referred to the fact that it was apparent that the protection of US commercial fishing interests, not conservation, was the primary objective of the US measure.[25] This interpretation was supported by the fact that the US lifted its embargo following the grant of access to Canadian waters to within 12 miles to US fishermen.

The question raised by these facts concerns the required relationship between the measure in question and the objective of conservation of natural resources, that is, the meaning of 'relating to' in Article XX(g). The US, inevitably, argued that this did not require that conservation of natural resources be the primary intention of the measure, but that the measure must 'relate to' conservation.

a. Findings of the Panel

The panel found that the US prohibition on the import of tuna and tuna products from Canada did indeed constitute a prohibition under Article XI (concerning the prohibition of quantitative restrictions) and therefore examined whether it fell under one of the exceptions listed in Article XI:2. It found that even if import restriction had been necessary to conserve certain species of tuna, a total ban was outwith the scope of Article XI:2, first, as it covered species which had not been the subject of domestic regulation and, second, because it was maintained when catch restrictions had been lifted. In addition, the panel held that in any case, the language of Article XI:2(c) could not justify an import prohibition.[26]

This raised the question of whether Article XX(g) could justify the measures taken. The panel held that, in the light of measures adopted against Costa Rica, Mexico and Peru, the measure against Canada was not necessarily arbitrary or unjustifiable. Nor was it a 'disguised' restriction on trade, as it had been announced as a trade measure. This seems paradoxical—had the measure been announced as an environmental measure but been demonstrated to be a trade measure, it would have been seen as a disguised restriction on trade and would have failed on that basis. However, the question considered by the panel was whether the measure, a blatant restriction on trade, could be justified on environmental grounds. The panel held that the measure failed the requirement that it be taken in conjunction with restrictions on domestic production or consumption, as no restriction had been applied to various individual species of tuna, including Albacore tuna,

[25] Paragraph 3.13.
[26] Paragraph 4.6.

nor was any evidence provided that consumption of tuna or tuna products had been restricted in the US.[27] Finally, the panel briefly addressed what might be thought to be a matter of crucial significance—that the measure was retaliatory. It stated only that it 'could not find that this particular action would in itself constitute a measure of a type listed in Article XX'.[28] The panel did not explicitly address the question of how the requirement that the measure 'relate to' conservation should be interpreted. Thus, it failed to address what Article XX(g) means.

This dispute demonstrates one of the central difficulties facing the WTO/GATT: how to distinguish legitimate environmental measures from unlawful protectionist measures. The measure adopted by the US was proclaimed as a trade measure whose alleged motivation was concern for conservation, yet it was a direct retaliation for a Canadian measure which was itself inspired by concern for the same resources.

ii. The Herring and Salmon *Dispute*

The subsequent *Herring and Salmon* dispute[29] dealt once more with a fisheries dispute between the US and Canada. In this case the dispute concerned a Canadian requirement that herring and salmon caught within Canadian waters must be processed in Canada. Canada argued that this requirement was necessary in order to maintain accurate catch control, which was argued to be necessary in order to balance conservation objectives with the goal of sustaining a viable domestic processing industry. The US complained that this measure was neither 'necessary nor particularly useful' as it regularly provided the relevant data to Canada and that it objected to the interpretation of 'conservation measures' which seemed to include balancing conservation with socio-economic concerns (namely the protection of a domestic industry).[30]

a. Findings of the Panel
In this case the panel did address the question which had been raised by the US in the *Tuna* dispute concerning the interpretation to be placed upon the requirement under Article XX(g) that the measure 'relate to' conservation. In its report the panel was unambiguous that 'relating to' meant that the measure must be 'primarily aimed at' conservation, which it held to be less than the Article XX(b) requirement of 'necessity' of the measure to achieve

---

[27] Paragraph 4.8–4.12.

[28] Paragraph 4.13.

[29] *Canada-Measures Affecting Exports of Unprocessed Herring and Salmon* BISD 35 S (1988) 98.

[30] There is a question as to whether this objective would be legitimate if an exception were permitted on the basis of 'sustainable development', which is now referred to in the WTO preamble.

the desired objective. Significantly, in order to ascertain the 'primary intent' of the measure, the panel considered the 'least restrictive means' available to the restricting state rather than the legislative history of the measure. This contrasts sharply with the approach of the panel to the issue of 'disguised restriction on trade' in the *Tuna* dispute.[31]

In terms of reasoning, this case can be compared with EU case of *Commission v UK*,[32] in which the UK sought to impose a ban on the importation of UHT milk on the grounds of public health. The Court of Justice, having considered the ban and its objective, concluded that the ban breached Article 30 EEC (now Article 34 TFEU) and could not be justified by Article 36 (now Article 36 TFEU), as there were less restrictive means by which the public health objective could be achieved. Consequently, the ban was held not to be 'necessary'. This is interesting because the panel in the *Herring and Salmon* dispute held that the requirement that the measure 'relate' to conservation was not as strong as the requirement of 'necessity', yet, in finding that the measure 'related to' conservation, the panel applied what in the EU would be a 'necessity' test.

In each of these disputes, an impartial observer could argue that there was an apparently economic protectionist motive for the measure rather than a genuine and primary concern for the environment. Thus, the findings of the panels (that the measures breached the GATT) appear relatively uncontroversial.

iii. Thai Cigarettes

The 'least restrictive means' test applied by the panel in the *Herring and Salmon* dispute was followed in the *Thai Cigarettes* panel report.[33] This dispute concerned a complaint by the US against Thai provisions that prohibited the import of cigarettes and other tobacco products, while permitting the sale of domestic cigarettes, on which excise, business and municipal taxes were imposed. The US argued that these provisions were inconsistent with Article XI:1 GATT and, as they concerned products which were not agricultural or fisheries-related, could not be justified under Article XI:2(c). Nor could they be justified by Article XX(b), as they were not necessary to protect human health. In addition, the US maintained that the internal taxes breached Article III:2 since they permitted higher taxation on imported than domestically produced cigarettes.

Thailand requested that the panel find the restriction on imports consistent with Article XI, as tobacco was an agricultural product and Thailand

---

[31] *Tuna and Tuna Products* (n 18).

[32] Case 124/81 *Commission v UK* [1983] ECR 203.

[33] *Thailand-Restrictions of Importation of and Internal Taxes on Cigarettes, Report of the Panel Adopted on 7 November 1990 (DS10/R—37S)* (BISD 37S/200).

had taken action to reduce both the area within which tobacco could be grown domestically and the production of cigarettes. In relation to Article XX(b), it argued that measures to control smoking had been adopted by the Government and that these would only be effective if imports were prohibited because chemicals and other additives contained in US cigarettes might make them more harmful than Thai cigarettes.[34] In relation to the excise, business and municipal taxes, it asserted that these were not higher for imported cigarettes than for like domestic products, and therefore were not in breach of GATT Article III.

a. Findings of the Panel

The panel held that the Thai restriction on imports did breach Article XI because no imports had been permitted during the last ten years, which constituted a total restriction. In considering whether this measure could be justified, the panel held that it could not because Article XI:2(c)(i), which refers to agricultural products, has been defined as referring to 'fresh' products and that the domestic product affected had to be that produced by farmers.[35] Accordingly, the only domestic restrictions relevant to Article XI:2(i)(c) were those that Thailand had imposed on the production of leaf tobacco, and that therefore the only imported products which could be similarly restricted were 'like' products: leaf tobacco and such products as met the requirements of the note on Article XI:2(c). Thus, cigarettes could not be included as eligible for exception.

Regarding Article XX(b), the panel held that smoking does constitute a serious risk to human health and therefore measures to reduce smoking could be within the scope of Article XX(b). However, the panel stuck at the requirement of 'necessity'. It followed an earlier report which had considered a potential exception under Article XX(d):

> [A] contracting party cannot justify a measure inconsistent with other GATT provisions as 'necessary' in terms of Article XX(d) if an alternative measure which it could reasonably be expected to employ and which is not inconsistent with other GATT provisions is available to it.[36]

In the light of this, the panel examined whether alternative measures were available to the Thai Government that could satisfy its concerns. Concerning quality, the panel concluded that measures such as labelling

---

[34] ibid para 28.

[35] See note ad Article XI:2(c), Annex 1, GATT 1947, which under Article XXXIVGATT 1947 is an integral part of the General Agreement. This definition (of Agricultural products in Article XI: 2(c)) was confirmed in Report of the Panel on *Canada-Import Restrictions on Ice Cream and Yoghurt* L/6568, para 66, adopted 4 December 1989 and Report of the Panel *on Japan-Restrictions on the Import of Certain Agricultural Products* BISD 35S/163, para 5.3.12, adopted on 22 March 1989.

[36] Report of the Panel on *United States-Section 337 of the Tariff Act 1930* L/6439, para 5.26, adopted on 7 November 1989.

and ingredient disclosure requirements would be appropriate. Regarding the objective of reducing consumption, the panel held that this could potentially be achieved by advertising bans. Therefore, the contested measure failed the necessity test. In reaching this conclusion, the panel ignored evidence demonstrating that such alternative measures as had been identified were routinely circumvented. Such evidence might have led the panel to question the reasonable availability of alternatives.[37] With reference to the taxes, the panel found that the current Thai regulations which removed the discrimination were compliant with the GATT.

Thus, in this case the 'least restrictive means' test was again used to establish necessity. This dispute highlights a significant problem facing the panels in the interpretation of the exceptions under Article XX. In invoking the necessity test,[38] the panel did not consider the *practicalities* for the Thai Government of adopting such other measures: it ignored the regulatory or compliance costs which might be incurred. Significantly, it did not explore whether the alternatives would meet the desired level of protection. This in itself raises a question regarding the panel's *judgment* of the 'availability' of alternative measures and, particularly, whether the restricting state may 'reasonably be expected to apply' such alternatives. This specific issue arose in *Korea-Beef*, in which both the panel and the Appellate Body held that WTO law 'could well entail higher enforcement costs for the national budget'.[39] While the necessity of a measure had up to that point been interpreted as requiring that there is no reasonably available alternative, in *Korea-Beef* the Appellate Body refined this test, indicating that:

> Determination of whether a measure, which is not 'indispensable' may nevertheless be necessary, involves in every case a process of *weighing and balancing* a series of factors which prominently include the contribution made by the compliance measure to the enforcement of the law or regulation at issue, the importance of the common interests or values protected by that law or regulation, and the accompanying impact of the law or regulation on imports or exports ...

> In our view, the *weighing and balancing process* we have outlined is comprehended in the determination of whether a WTO-consistent alternative measure which the Member concerned could 'reasonably be expected to employ' is available, or whether a less WTO-inconsistent measure is 'reasonably available'.[40]

It is worth noting that the question of whether the Appellate Body did in fact engage in 'weighing and balancing' has been regularly raised.[41]

---

[37] *Thai Cigarettes* (n 33) para 55.
[38] ibid.
[39] Panel Report, *Korea-Measures Affecting Imports of Fresh, Chilled and Frozen Beef, (Korea-Various Measures on Beef)* WT/DS/161/R, adopted 10 January 2001, para 673; and Appellate Body Report, *Korea-Various Measures on Beef*, WT/DS161/AB/R, adopted 10 January 2001, para 181.
[40] Appellate Body Report (n 39) paras 164 and 166 (emphasis added).
[41] Discussed below.

b. Comparison with the European Court of Justice Approach

Once again, this provides for an interesting comparison with the Court of Justice approach. Discriminatory measures are difficult to justify on the grounds of public health as they either fail the proportionality test or constitute arbitrary discrimination or a disguised restriction on trade. Thus, it seems likely that the Court of Justice would also have condemned the Thai import ban. However, there is some uncertainty in this, arising from *Commission v Ireland*.[42] In that case, the Court permitted an import licence requirement, although less restrictive means would have been available on the grounds of the particular health standards of Irish poultry. The Court held that it was necessary to balance the inconvenience of the administrative and financial burden as against the danger to animal health. While the Court balanced the burden of the restriction against its outcome, it took account of the particular circumstances in Ireland and permitted a scheme the equivalent of which had been found not to be justifiable in the UK.[43] This suggests that the Court does take account of circumstances in the particular state and would therefore consider the practical availability of alternative, less restrictive measures. This would certainly extend to human health. On the other hand, the complexity of introducing a less restrictive measure was rejected by the Court as a justification for the more restrictive measure in *Regenerated Oil*.[44] That case concerned a scheme whereby, for ecological reasons, regenerated Italian oil was taxed at a lower rate than ordinary oil. Imported regenerated oil did not benefit from the same tax advantage and therefore the scheme was held to breach EC law. In *PreussenElektra*, however, the Court shifted its position again, not even considering the possible application of less restrictive measures. Both *Regenerated Oil* and *PreussenElektra* concerned environmental/ecological measures. It is certain, however, that it would not be possible to justify a discriminatory import *ban* in this manner in the EU, whereas a restriction may be viewed more sympathetically. Issues which impinge upon the practical availability of a less trade-restrictive approach are more pressing in developing countries than developed countries and are perhaps less likely to occur in the relatively homogenised EU than globally.

iv. Superfund

Returning to the GATT, the *Superfund* dispute concerned a new issue for the panel. *Superfund* concerned discriminatory taxation of imports of petroleum and chemical products by the US. The only justification offered by the US in relation to the tax on imported petroleum products

---

[42] Case 74/82 *Commission v Ireland (Protection of Animal Health)* [1984] ECR 317.
[43] Case 40/82 *Commission v UK* [1982] ECR 2793.
[44] Case 21/79 *Commission v Italy* [1980] ECR 1.

was that there was no breach of GATT because the effect of the measures was minimal. The panel responded that there was a prima facie breach of Article III. In relation to the tax on imported chemical products, however, the US offered the justification that the tax was no greater than that levied on US producers to make the same chemicals. Therefore, the US claimed that it complied with the Article II:2(a) conditions for exemption from the obligation of national treatment, as it was 'equivalent to an internal tax … in respect of an article from which the imported product has been manufactured in whole or in part'.

The US internal tax was a response to the environmental harm caused by the use of the constituent products. The complainants argued that this tax, in relation to imported products, was on environmental harm occurring outside the US. The US products which were exported were tax-exempt and therefore did not have to pay for the environmental damage caused by their manufacture. In contrast, imported products would, on their import to the US, be subject to border tax adjustment. In some cases the producers would have already paid for the environmental damage caused by their manufacture in their state of origin under the 'polluter pays' principle. Therefore, assuming they overcome the disincentive to import to the US, imported products will potentially have paid the equivalent taxes twice and thus may be placed at a competitive disadvantage in the US. In contrast, the export tax-exemption for US products could give US exports a competitive advantage over competing products in the state of destination.

a. Findings of the Panel

The panel held that the 'polluter pays' principle had not been adopted by the GATT and therefore could not be considered.[45] In addition, it held that border-tax-adjustment provisions 'do not distinguish between taxes for different policy measures'.[46] Therefore, the objective of the taxes could not be considered as a factor in the determination of eligibility or otherwise of border-tax adjustment. Thus, although the issue of measures relating to environmental damage outside the restricting state was raised in this case, the panel did not find it necessary to consider it in its report. The consequence of this decision appears to be that although imported product Y does not itself cause environmental damage in the US, the US can impose a similar tax upon it to that imposed on manufacture of 'Y' in the US to counteract the environmental damage caused by (use of X in) 'Y's' production. Consequently, the border tax looks like a tax imposed on production outside the US.

---

[45] Panel Report, *US-Taxes on Petroleum and Certain Imported Substances* BISD 34th Supp (1988) 136, 17 June 1987 (L/1675—34S/136), paras 3.2.8–3.2.9.
[46] ibid para 5.2.4.

b. Comparison with European Court of Justice Jurisprudence

The decision in *Superfund* contrasts with the decision of the Court of Justice in *Commission v Italy*.[47] Similarly, in *Hansen*[48] it was held that a German tax relief for fruit spirits made by small businesses and collective farms must be equally applicable to spirits imported from other EU Member States satisfying these requirements. The distinction between the Court's approach and that of the GATT may, once again, be explained by the different levels of integration being sought by the two organisations and the fact that the GATT prohibits discrimination, whereas the EU also considers indirect distortions of competition.

To apply border eco-taxes consistently, *tax adjustment* should be permitted where use of the product in the territory will cause harm, and *tax-exemption* on this basis for exported products. It should not be permissible to tax on import merely because this is allegedly 'equivalent' to tax on domestic production where the domestic tax is applied on the basis of harm caused during the production process rather than by use of the product itself. In that sense, in view of the purpose of the tax, the products are not 'like'—the one product causes harm to the US, whereas the other (manufactured in, for example, the EU) does not. This does not appear to be genuine 'national treatment'. If a state chooses to exempt products destined for export, this would be a policy choice which that state is free to make, as the damage and costs affect or do not affect its own territory.

The central difficulty in this respect lies in the refusal of the panel to examine the objective of the border tax and the tax being adjusted for. Consistency with the treatment of any other trade barriers or restrictions would require an examination of the purpose and application of the measures, not least to establish whether or not the measure is protectionist. The second difficulty arises from a lack of universal treatment of environmental costs. If all states used the same mechanism as the US, there would be no competitive advantage. Equally, if all states used the 'polluter pays' principle, there would be no competitive disadvantage.

v. US Restrictions on Imports of Tuna *(1991)* (Tuna-Dolphin)

In the *Tuna-Dolphin* dispute[49] the GATT panel was called upon to consider the environmental objective underlying the US Marine Mammal Protection Act, 1972 (MMPA). This measure concerned the method by which tuna are

---

[47] *Commission v Italy* (n 44).

[48] Case 148/77 *Hansen v Hauptzollamt Flensburg* [1978] ECR 1787.

[49] *United States-Restrictions on Imports of Tuna*, BISD 40S/155 (DS21/R), not adopted. The facts and issues of the case are outlined at www.wto.org/english/tratop_e/envir_e/edis04_e.htm. The Panel Report has been reproduced in (1991) 30 ILM 1594. See also M Trebilcock, R Howse and A Eliason, *The Regulation of International Trade*, 4th edn (New York, Routledge, 2012) ch 17; B Kingsbury, 'The Tuna Dolphin Controversy, the World

caught in the Eastern Pacific and it applied both to the US fleet and to any other boats operating in that part of the Pacific. The measure set out 'dolphin protection standards' in the form of commercial fishing methods and imposed a prohibition on the importation into the US of yellow-fin tuna and any of its derivatives, unless the US had established that the harvesting state had a similar programme to that of the US *and* that the average rate of take of 'incidental' marine mammals was comparable to that of US vessels.

Mexico claimed that this measure breached Articles XI (prohibition of quantitative restrictions), XIII (non-discriminatory administration of quantitative restrictions) and III (requirement of national treatment) GATT. In response, the US argued that as the measure also applied to domestic tuna, it concerned only Article III, with which it was consistent, but not Article XI (the US argued that the measure was not a quantitative restriction).[50] Furthermore, it argued that, if found not to be consistent with Article III, the measure was justified under the public policy exceptions of Article XX(b) and (g).

a. Findings of the Panel

The panel controversially held that Article III, the requirement of national treatment, concerns internal regulatory measures relating to products, not production methods. Because the measure in question concerned the manner in which tuna was produced or taken, the panel therefore rejected the US argument that the measure concerned only Article III (not Article XI). In the light of this conclusion, the panel considered the measure to be a quantitative restriction breaching Article XI. The question for the panel was whether the measure could be justified by Article XX. On this point, its approach was simple: it held that Article XX could not apply to protect animal life outside the state adopting the measure. Thus, since the US measure was extra-territorial in its approach, Article XX(b) could not be applied. Having imposed this restriction on the application of Article XX, the panel went further by stating that the requirement of 'necessity' in Article XX(b) meant that in any case, the US would have to demonstrate that all possible avenues of resolution of the problem had been exhausted before resorting to an import restriction. In relation to Article XX(g), the panel held that it could only be invoked to protect the restricting state's own environment.

Trade Organization and the Liberal Project to Reconceptualize International Law' (1994) 5(1) *Yearbook of International Environmental Law* 1.

[50] This argument of the US was based upon the Annex 1 GATT note ad Article III, which stipulates that: 'Any internal tax or other internal charge, or any law, regulation or requirement of the kind referred to in paragraph 1 which applies to an imported product and to the like domestic product and is collected or enforced in the case of the imported product at the time or point of importation, is nevertheless to be regarded as an internal tax or other internal charge, or a law, regulation or requirement of the kind referred to in paragraph 1, and is accordingly subject to the provisions of Article III.'

Although not adopted, this report is indicative of the stance and approach of the panel.

b. Implications

The environmental implications of this report were startling. National boundaries do not apply to the environment: air and water pollution spread; species migrate. In holding that a state cannot pursue the protection of the environment outside its jurisdiction, the panel imposed a highly artificial condition. The product-process distinction also proved highly controversial. Essentially, a state may not regulate the import of a product on the basis of its production method, but only upon the basis of the effects of that product in its territory. Yet despite the problematic implications of the reasoning employed in this ruling, there can be little doubt that on the facts, the correct result was arrived at.

vi. US-Restrictions on Imports of Tuna *(1994)* (Tuna-Dolphin II)

In *Tuna-Dolphin II*[51] the EC and the Netherlands brought a complaint relating to the embargo within the US MMPA against tuna from 'intermediary-countries' which have handled the tuna en route from the specific exporting country (ie, Mexico) to the US. The EC and the Netherlands argued that the 'intermediary-country' embargo was also in breach of Articles III and XI:1 and could not be saved by an Article XX exception. The panel found that this was the case, but again the report was not adopted.

In this instance, in contrast to the ruling in *Tuna Dolphin I*, the panel 'could see no valid reason supporting the conclusion that the provisions of Article XX(g) apply only to ... the conservation of natural resources located within the territory of the contracting party invoking the provision'. However, the panel qualified this with the restriction that governments could only enforce the measure extra-territorially against their own nationals and vessels.[52]

a. Comparison with European Court of Justice Jurisprudence

In one respect these cases can be compared to the Court of Justice *Red Grouse* case.[53] The *Red Grouse* case concerned the legality of a Dutch ban on the import of red grouse which had been lawfully killed in the UK. EC law permitted states to introduce stricter protection than was provided for in the EC Wild Birds Directive. However, the Court held that import controls could not be imposed by a state in respect of a species which did not

---

[51] Panel Report, *US-Restrictions on Imports of Tuna* (1994) GATT Doc. DS29/R. Report circulated 16 June 1994, not adopted, reproduced at (1994) 33 ILM 839.
[52] ibid at para 5.20.
[53] Case C-169/89 *Gourmetterie van den Burg* [1990] ECR 2143.

inhabit its territory and which could lawfully be hunted under the Directive. In each of these cases the success of the environmental measure (in terms of realising its objective) would be dependent upon a change of practice in another state, so the link between the measure and the achievement of its objective is tenuous. Consequently, the measure in *Red Grouse* failed the proportionality test.[54] It was not an appropriate measure with which to pursue the environmental objective. Although arriving at the same result as the GATT cases and on similar grounds, the reasoning in *Red Grouse* is inherently less problematic, as it addresses the specific facts rather than setting up restrictive precedent for future cases.

Cheyne has observed that in *Tuna-Dolphin*, the panel drew a distinction between extra-territorial and extra-jurisdictional application of Article XX.[55] The panel's recognition of extra-territorial jurisdiction is based upon the concept of 'active personality jurisdiction', according to which a state may regulate its citizens' actions. This is supported by Article 31 of the Vienna Convention,[56] which requires that, in the interpretation of treaties, both the context of the treaty and 'any relevant rules of international law applicable between the parties' must be considered. This clearly includes relevant jurisdictional rules and, as Schoenbaum recalls, 'it is well established as a matter of international law that states have an obligation to prevent damage to both the environment of other states and areas beyond the limits of national jurisdiction'.[57] The *Tuna-Dolphin* decisions became, in Schoenbaum's words, a 'cause célèbre', despite the consensus that there are better ways than unilateralism to protect the environment[58] (although Schoenbaum recognised the place of 'creative unilateralism' where it operates within the bounds of public international law).[59]

A further dispute in which the panel's report was not adopted concerned US (environmental) car taxes.[60] The US imposed a 'luxury' tax on cars sold for more than $30,000 and a 'gas-guzzler' tax on the sale of cars which could not average more than 22.5 miles per gallon. It was held that each of these measures was consistent with Article III:2 GATT. The accompanying 'Corporate Average Fuel Economy' regulation required average fuel economy of cars sold in the US to reach a minimum of 27.5 mpg. This regulation imposed a separate fleet accounting system for imported and domestic cars, and a fleet averaging system which was calculated on the basis of factors which did not relate to the products themselves, but to control or ownership

---

[54] ibid, Opinion of AG Van Gerven.

[55] Ilona Cheyne, 'Environmental Unilateralism and the WTO/GATT System' (1995) 24 *Georgia Journal of International and Comparative Law* 433, 453–54.

[56] Vienna Convention on the Law of Treaties, 1155 UNTS 331.

[57] Schoenbaum (n 11).

[58] ibid, 312.

[59] ibid.

[60] Panel Report, *US-Taxes on Automobiles*, DS31/R, reproduced at (1994) 33 ILM 1399.

of manufacturers or importers. The panel held the separate fleet accounting system to be inconsistent with Article III:4 (because it discriminated against imported cars) and unjustifiable under Article XX(g). The panel did not consider the fleet averaging system itself in relation to Article XX(g), but found that the Regulation itself could not be justified under Article XX(d).

vii. Trade and Environment under the GATT: Comment

In each of the above disputes, the panels interpreted the provisions of the GATT according to the fundamental objective: trade liberalisation. Yet in the majority of these cases, it appears that environmental protection was indeed being used opportunistically to justify trade protectionism. Thus, although it may be argued that the panels were not impartial in considering the balance to be drawn between free trade and environmental protection, this is not surprising given the panels' mandate. Since the panels were set up to enforce the GATT, it would also be of questionable legitimacy if they prioritised anything other than free trade.

Furthermore, there appears to be a lack of consistency surrounding the measures being implemented or the commitment of the parties to environmental protection. However, when the panel was faced with the situation in which it was forced to address the competing values of liberal trade and environmental protection (the *Tuna-Dolphin* disputes), the system of legitimisation arguably broke down. The panel's response was to apply its standard approach, interpreting the GATT to achieve a trade liberalisation result. In order to do so, the panel characterised the matter as being one of domestic sovereignty. Because the GATT permits exceptions on the grounds of domestic environmental policy, it must also respect the decisions of sovereign states as regards the pursuit of their domestic policy. Therefore, the US could not be permitted to impose its environmental policy upon Mexico. Although this approach appears to be reasonable and rational, it is significant that the US was not in fact seeking to impose its policy upon Mexico within Mexico, but to enforce it upon those wishing to trade with the US as regards their actions in international waters, with the objective of protection of the 'global environmental commons'. Thus, the sovereignty argument is not altogether straightforward in this instance: the US was not seeking to unilaterally compel any other state to adopt its regulatory measures with regard to their action in international waters other than with regard to products destined for its jurisdiction.

The panel's approach had the effect of blocking a potentially crucial field of application of Article XX, and it is by no means certain that this was intended by the contracting parties when they formulated the exceptions. Thus, the following question arose: how could this sweeping approach by the panel be legitimised? In the event, the fact that the report was not adopted prevented this issue from being addressed. The number of unadopted reports from this period in fact demonstrates one of the central weaknesses inherent in the GATT dispute settlement system: that the state complained against, if found to be in breach of its GATT obligations, could veto the adoption of a report. Yet, as observed by Howse, this 'weakness' saved the dispute settlement system from closer scrutiny and a legitimacy crisis.[61] Subsequently, however, as Howse observed, the introduction of the WTO system removed this 'safety valve'. As a result, the panels have been required to at least appear objective in considering the balance to be adopted. The reasoning and implications, if not the results, have changed.

B. Trade/Environment Disputes under the WTO Dispute Settlement System

i. US-Gasoline

The *US-Gasoline*[62] dispute appears initially to be more notable for being the first dispute to go before the Appellate Body than for its substance per se. The dispute centred upon US rules on the chemical standards for imported gasoline, which were stricter than those applied to domestically produced gasoline. Venezuela and Brazil complained that this violated the principle of national treatment, did not fall under the Article XX exceptions and breached Article 2 of the Agreement on Technical Barriers to Trade. The US responded that it did not contravene Article III, but came within the Article XX exception under paragraphs (b), (d) and (g). The panel held that the measure did breach Article III and was outside the Article XX exceptions.

The US appealed this decision unsuccessfully, arguing that the measure was consistent with Article XX(g). Venezuela argued that a measure 'can only be "relating to" or "primarily aimed at" conservation if it was both primarily intended to achieve a conservation goal and had a positive conservation effect'.[63] Both Venezuela and Brazil further argued that even if the Appellate Body overruled the panel on this point, the measure (being applied in an arbitrary or discriminatory manner) did not satisfy the Article XX 'chapeau'. The Appellate Body accepted this.

---

[61] R Howse, 'The Early Years of WTO Jurisprudence' in JHH Weiler (ed), *The EU, the WTO and the NAFTA: Towards a Common Law of International Trade* (Oxford, Oxford University Press, 2001) 39.

[62] Panel Report, *United States-Standards for Reformulated and Conventional Gasoline*, WT/DS2/R.

[63] Appellate Body Report, *United States-Standards for Reformulated and Conventional Gasoline*, AB-1996-1, Report of the Appellate Body WT/DS2/AB/R, at B.

a. Findings of the Appellate Body

The Appellate Body criticised the panel for having considered whether the 'less favourable treatment' afforded to imports by the gasoline rule was primarily aimed at the conservation of natural resources. It held that the Article XX chapeau is clear: the *measure itself* should be primarily aimed at this objective. It further criticised the panel for having applied the same necessity test to Article XX(g) as it had applied to Article XX(b), despite the different expressions of the requirements of these different exceptions. Thus, whereas (b) refers to measures 'necessary', (g) requires that the measure 'relate to' the conservation of natural resources. The Appellate Body qualified what could have been a significant broadening of the scope of the exception contained in Article XX(g), stipulating that it must be read in the context of the whole GATT and therefore that it should not be applied in such a manner as would nullify Article III(4). Similarly, it held that Article III should not be applied so as to render Article XX inapplicable.

The significance of the Appellate Body exploring the different expressions and requirements of the exceptions contained in Article XX should not be underestimated. On one level, this potentially widened the application of the Article XX exceptions, but simultaneously restricted the possibility of their abuse. This reasoning was subsequently relied upon by the Appellate Body in the context of the *US-Shrimp* dispute, although not by the panel.[64]

ii. United States-Import Prohibition of Certain Shrimp and Shrimp Products (US-Shrimp)

The seminal *US-Shrimp* dispute concerned a US measure to protect certain species of sea-turtle from incidental capture in shrimp-fishing. In 1987, the US enacted a regulation requiring US shrimp trawlers to use 'turtle excluder devices' when fishing in areas where sea-turtles were likely to be. In 1989, a provision was introduced prohibiting the import of shrimp or shrimp products harvested with technology which may adversely affect sea-turtles,[65] unless the harvesting nation certified annually to the US that it had a regulatory programme (and incidental take rate) similar to that of the US. Consequently, any country wishing to export shrimp or shrimp products to the US, with a natural population of sea-turtles within its waters, had to impose US style requirements on their shrimp fishermen—effectively requiring turtle excluder devices.

It is significant that in introducing this provision, the US did not treat all exporting states in the same manner. The provision originally applied to

---

[64] Panel Report, *United States-Import Prohibition of Certain Shrimp and Shrimp Products*, WT/DS58/R (98-1710), 15 May 1998; Appellate Body Report AB-1998-4 WT/DS58/R (98-0000), 12 October 1998, (1998) 38 ILM 121.
[65] Section 609 US Public Law 101–02, WTO.

states of the Caribbean and Western Atlantic, but from 1996, all imports from all states had to be accompanied by a declaration that the shrimp had been harvested in a manner that did not adversely affect sea-turtles or originated in a 'certified' country. Almost immediately this changed again: only shrimp originating in 'certified' states could be imported into the US. Thus, the US moved from a restriction based on the process of catching the specific shrimp to a restriction based on its country of origin.

a. The Findings of the GATT Panel

The panel held that this measure constituted a 'prohibition or restriction' on import and therefore a breach of Article XI, and that the provision had breached the 'national treatment' requirement of Article III. Prima facie, the measure complied with that requirement: imported shrimp must satisfy the requirements applied to US-produced shrimp. But the question of what constitutes a 'like' product arose.

The GATT panels have consistently held the requirement of 'like' to refer to the product and its specifications itself, and not to its process of production or extraction. The US requirement concerned the *process* of extraction or production rather than the product itself, and indeed differentiated on the basis of *assumptions* about processes used in its state of origin. Thus, it breached the national treatment rule under Article III, as it affords different treatment to potentially similar shrimp dependent on how and where it is produced, rather than on the basis of the qualities of that shrimp. As Scott observes, the effect of this is that 'while de jure the principle of national treatment is preserved, de facto it has been undermined in the case of product standards'.[66]

b. The Ruling of the Appellate Body

In contrast with the findings of the panel, the Appellate Body ruled that the measure fell within the scope of Article XX(g), notwithstanding that it constituted the application of US standards on activities taking place outside the US and although it sought to distinguish on grounds of method of production. The Appellate Body reached this conclusion on the grounds that the species were migratory and therefore could be viewed as being a shared 'natural resource'.[67] Consequently, it found that there was a 'sufficient nexus between the migratory and endangered marine populations involved and the United States for the purposes of Article XX(g)'.[68] Thus, the US, because of its share, could be deemed to have an interest in the conservation of this resource. However, the Appellate Body held that the

---

[66] Joanne Scott, 'Trade and Environment in the EU and WTO' in Weiler (n 61).

[67] As noted above, the Appellate Body looked to other bodies of international law in order to reach this conclusion concerning the interpretation of Article XX(g).

[68] Appellate Body Report (n 64) at para 133. This approach contrasts sharply with the approach taken in the *Tuna-Dolphin* dispute (n 49).

provision failed to comply with the requirements of the chapeau. Notably, the US had negotiated with some states and not others, so there was construed to be arbitrary discrimination in the application of the restriction. The Appellate Body expressed a clear preference for multilateral measures in such contexts, but, significantly, stated that unilateral measures would not always be prohibited.

c. The Significance of this Report

This ruling is of great significance: although the provision itself was ultimately judged not to comply with the requirements of Article XX, this failure was a result of the manner of application of the provision rather than its purpose or substance. In its ruling, the Appellate Body recognised a potential right of a state unilaterally to require the application of its standards by other states for the purposes of gaining access to its markets. This is an enormous leap from the ruling in the *Tuna-Dolphin*[69] dispute. As Bianchi observed, 'the Appellate Body reversed the trade-centred approach that the prior GATT-WTO jurisprudence had seemed to adopt by acknowledging the importance of environmental measures and recommending multi-lateral ones'.[70] Bianchi viewed the Appellate Body's approach as introducing an 'element of reasonableness' to the test for compatibility of an environmental measure, which he compares to the Court of Justice's approach in *Danish Bottles*.[71]

Sands emphasised that this development, albeit a departure from existing jurisprudence, did not occur 'out of the blue'.[72] He attributed it to a combination of 'globalisation', 'technological innovation', 'democratisation' and 'privatisation', which he views as part of a general shift in the development of international law. This shift is observed in the change in international actors, the increasing numbers of systems of international law and the development of international courts, particularly in view of the discretion available to 'judicial' bodies where any ambiguity has been left in the rules or law being applied, as in the *US-Shrimp* dispute.[73]

It is worth recalling that it was in *US-Shrimp* that the Appellate Body applied an evolutionary approach to the interpretation of Article XX(g), recognising the informative significance of contemporary multilateral treaties in shedding light on the appropriate interpretation of 'conservation of natural resources'.[74] However, while opening the door to the possibility of recognising the legitimacy of environmental measures reflecting interna-

---

[69] *Tuna-Dolphin* dispute (n 49).
[70] Andrea Bianchi, 'The Impact of International Trade Law on Environmental Law and Process' in Francioni (ed) (n 11) 120.
[71] Case C302/86 *Commission v Denmark* [1998] ECR 4607, discussed in ch 2.
[72] Philippe Sands, 'Turtles and Torturers: The Transformation of International Law' 33 (2000) *New York University Journal of International Law and Politics* 527, 536 et seq.
[73] *US-Shrimp* (n 2).
[74] Discussed above.

tionally agreed standards and as arising from multilateral environmental agreements, the Appellate Body has not given any indication of a similar relaxation with respect to measures reflecting unilateral standards.

It is significant that in *US-Shrimp*, the Appellate Body indicated that it would look to the process behind a measure, rather than its substance, to determine its legitimacy. This is an approach which was consolidated in the *EC-Hormones* report[75] and which is supported by the Appellate Body's reading of the chapeau to Article XX as being a two-prong test: of proportionality and of freedom from arbitrary discrimination. In contrast, the Court of Justice tends to roll these tests into one. The Appellate Body has made it clear that a measure which is within the Article XX exceptions, and is even proportionate, will breach the chapeau if due process is not observed in its adoption, constituting arbitrary discrimination. As Cremona observes, in this respect the Appellate Body sees the right to invoke an Article XX exception as being in direct competition with the rights of other WTO members to benefit from its provisions.[76]

In this sense the WTO does not have a vision of shared interest in the protection of the Article XX public policy interests, again confirming a lack of common global interest or polity in the WTO. Yet the requirement of due process and fair consideration of alternative standards and measures is consistent with the approach of the ECJ to indirect discrimination.[77] However, the emphasis placed upon the unilateral action of the US clearly is not reflected in EU law, where exceptions are inherently unilateral.[78]

US-Shrimp is also significant in that it concerned what was undoubtedly a process-related measure, which would traditionally have been excluded from consideration for application of the general exceptions. Yet the Appellate Body was willing to contemplate the application of an exception for a process and production-based measure. The measure only failed on account of its arbitrariness.

iii. EC-Asbestos

The *EC-Asbestos* dispute[79] concerned a French ban on the manufacture, processing, import or sale of all varieties of asbestos and asbestos fibres.

---

[75] *EC-Measures Concerning Meat and Meat Products*, Report of the Panel, 18 August 1997, WT/DS26/R; Report of the Appellate Body, 16 January 1998 WT/DS26,48/AB/R.

[76] M Cremona, 'Neutrality or Discrimination? The WTO, the EU and External Trade' in G De Búrca and J Scott (eds), *The EU and the WTO: Legal and Constitutional Issues* (Oxford, Hart Publishing, 2001) 56, referring to *US-Shrimps* Appellate Body Report (n 2) para 159.

[77] It is also consistent with the approach of AG Van Gerven in *Red Grouse*. See J Scott, 'Trade and Environment in the EU and WTO' in Weiler (n 61).

[78] See Cremona (n 76) 156–58.

[79] Panel Report, *European Communities-Measures Affecting Asbestos and Asbestos Containing Products* WT/DS/135/R, 18 September 2000; Appellate Body Report WT/DS/135/AB/R,

Canada challenged this ban on the grounds that as it gave less favourable treatment to Canadian asbestos than 'like products', it violated national treatment. The fundamental question was what constitutes a 'like product'. Canada alleged that asbestos and its substitutes were 'like products' on the basis of their shared product characteristics, end uses and tariff classification. The EC responded that the products' characteristics and properties were different, so they were not 'like'. Strictly, this dispute concerned human health rather than environmental protection; however, it is clearly of relevance to the present study as it concerns the interpretation of Article XX(b). The panel rejected the argument that health risk should be taken into consideration in determining likeness, arguing that this was an issue to be considered under Article XX(b). However, the Appellate Body held that like products must be in some kind of competitive relationship and that health considerations may be a relevant factor in determining or excluding likeness. It also emphasised that consumer preferences can have a bearing upon likeness and that including health concerns in the determination of likeness did not render Article XX irrelevant.

This finding is important: if consumer preferences can render an otherwise similar product 'unlike', it may be possible to determine that there has been no breach of national treatment and therefore no need to have recourse to the Article XX exceptions. As will be seen below, this is potentially of great significance in relation to human rights considerations, which are not included in the Article XX general exceptions.[80]

iv. Testing the Legitimacy of Members' Regulatory Measures: 'Weighing and Balancing'?

In *EC-Asbestos*[81] the Appellate Body had emphasised that it is for Members to determine their chosen level of protection. As seen above, in *Korea-Beef* the Appellate Body introduced the requirement of a 'weighing and balancing' process to be applied both to the analysis of the necessity of the measure and to the availability of reasonable alternatives.[82] However, the chosen level of protection is not itself to be put in the balance. Therefore, there is in fact no balancing of the merits of the particular objective pursued and its trade restrictiveness; instead, the 'necessity' review requires consideration of the trade restrictive effects of the measure.

---

12 March 2001. See R Howse and E Tuerk, 'The WTO Impact on Internal Regulations: A Case Study of the Canada-EC Asbestos Dispute' in De Burca and Scott (n 76).

[80] See ch 5.
[81] Appellate Body Report (n 79).
[82] Above, n 39; see also text accompanying n 40 above.

The Appellate Body revisited this in *Brazil-Retreaded Tyres*.[83] Once again, it highlighted the right of Members to set their desired level of protection and, once again, the Appellate Body stated that the contribution of the measure has to be weighed against its trade-restrictive effect.[84] Yet, on the facts, it was sufficient that an undefined contribution to health was presumed for the measure to be ruled to be legitimate. Therefore, once more, there was no weighing and balancing of the measure and its effects. There was indeed no evaluation of the effects of the measure. The Appellate Body emphasised that a measure that is prima facie justifiable on one of the grounds of Article XX may be held to breach the chapeau if it is applied in an arbitrarily or unjustifiably discriminatory manner '"between countries where the same conditions prevail", and when the reasons given for this discrimination bear no rational connection to the objective falling within the purview of Article XX'.[85]

Therefore, notwithstanding the language of 'weighing and balancing', the Appellate Body has avoided substituting its evaluation of the balance to be struck between the particular objective pursued and the restrictive impact upon trade of the measure in question. By focusing upon the restrictive effects of the measure and the availability of alternatives, the Appellate Body can base its ruling upon objective criteria rather than substituting subjective evaluation. There is no doubt that engaging in subjective analysis would increase the legitimacy questions which might be posed concerning the Appellate Body's substitution of its judgment for that of the national regulator.

Each of the cases considered above concerned the GATT itself, some pre-dating the establishment of the WTO. The SPS and TBT Agreements have also, however, had an impact on this debate, notably in relation to the approach taken to public health exceptions.

C. The Agreement on Sanitary and Phytosanitary Measures (SPS Agreement)

The SPS Agreement, having been established to 'define the manner in which member governments should create measures which reflect national policy regarding plant and animal health, as well as human health which depend-

---

[83] *Brazil-Measures Affecting imports of Retreaded Tyres*, WT/DS332/AB/R, 3 December 2007.

[84] ibid para 210

[85] ibid para 227.

supon these standards',[86] invites trade/environment/health disputes.[87] The agreement focuses upon preventing discrimination: permitting national standards as long as they do not constitute unjustifiable discrimination.[88] Yet the line to be drawn between legitimate domestic regulation and unlawful restriction on trade has proved controversial. This is particularly a consequence of the differing views and tolerance of risk by different societies. Unlike the GATT, the SPS Agreement encourages harmonisation of standards through the adoption of international measures.[89] Significantly, however, it recognised that Members make different choices regarding their desired level of protection on SPS matters, and Article 3 permits this. The adoption of higher standards must be premised upon scientific evidence of risk or follow a risk assessment.[90] Where there is insufficient scientific evidence, a state can adopt an interim measure, on the basis of available information; however, this must be periodically reviewed. In adopting measures, Members are bound to consider the objective of reducing trade-restrictive effects. Article 5.6 requires that measures must not be 'more trade-restrictive than required to achieve their appropriate level of sanitary or phyto-sanitary protection'. Significantly, a note to Article 5.6 SPS clarifies that 'a measure is not more trade-restrictive than required unless there is another measure, reasonably available taking into account technical and economic feasibility, that achieves the appropriate level of sanitary and phyto-sanitary protection'. Article 4 SPS also provides for the application of mutual recognition (that a product which is lawfully marketed in one Member should be able to access the market in other Members, so any restriction on this must be justified).[91]

i. The Nature of Review: EC-Hormones

The application of these rules has proved highly complex and controversial, with particular questions arising concerning the standard and the nature of review of national measures carried out by the panels and the Appellate Body. The question of the nature of review arose in the *EC-Hormones* case.[92] The Appellate Body held that the standard of review 'must reflect the balance established in [the SPS Agreement] between the jurisdictional

---

[86] S Dillon, *International Trade and Economic Law and the European Union* (Oxford, Hart Publishing, 2002) at 128.

[87] See J Scott, *The WTO Agreement on Sanitary and Phyto-Sanitary Measures: A Commentary* (Oxford, Oxford University Press, 2007).

[88] Preamble to the SPS Agreement.

[89] Article 3.

[90] Article 5. See further Scott (n 87).

[91] The implications of mutual recognition are discussed in ch 3 above.

[92] *EC-Measures Concerning Meat and Meat Products (EC-Hormones)*, Report of the Appellate Body WT/DS26/AB/R, WT/DS248/AB/R, adopted 13 February 1998, DSR 1998:1, 135 at para 181.

competences concluded by the Members of the WTO and the jurisdictional competences retained by the Members for themselves'.[93] The dispute concerned an EC ban on imports of beef from hormone-treated cattle.[94] The US challenged the ban on the grounds that it breached Articles I and III GATT, as well as the SPS Agreement. The EC sought to rely upon the precautionary principle in this case, but this did not comply with the SPS rules on risk and scientific evidence. This indicates the problems arising as a consequence of different principles and law in different jurisdictions. The panel found that relevant international standards existed for most of the relevant hormones and that the EC measure was not based upon these standards. The EC had argued that these international standards were not relevant as they were maximum residual standards rather than standards for ongoing use. Consequently, the next question was whether the EC standards could be justified by scientific evidence or a scientific risk assessment. The panel found that there had been a risk assessment, but that the measures were not based on this. Subsequently, it found that there was no scientific evidence capable of justifying the EC measures. Accordingly, it held that the measure was an unacceptable restriction on trade.

On appeal, the Appellate Body considered the issue of the relationship between risk assessment and the measure more deeply, concluding that for a measure to be legitimate, there must be a 'rational' relationship between the two. It went on to rule that in this case there was no rational relationship between the two. One question which arises from this concerns the relationship between a 'rational justification' and proportionality. Apparently, if the threshold of risk is satisfied, the Appellate Body will not consider balancing the objective of the measure with its costs.[95] In its report on the subsequent *Continued Suspension* dispute, the Appellate Body drew a distinction between review of the substance of a decision based on risk assessment (which it held was not within its power) and review (for objectivity and coherence) of the reasoning on which a decision is based, which the Appellate Body held is within the power of the panel.[96] In ruling that it was not within its power to review the substance of the decision, the Appellate Body demonstrated some deference towards the regulatory choices of the Member. However, questions remained concerning the nature of review of the reasoning. Despite such questions, this approach, distinguishing

[93] ibid para 115.

[94] *EC-Hormones* (n 92). See Howse (n 61); Dillon (n 86).

[95] See *Japan-Measures Affecting Agricultural Products (Japan Varietals)*, 19 March 1999, WT/DS76/AB/R at paras 82–84 for confirmation of need for 'real support' of risk assessment. That notwithstanding, it will explore whether there is a less restrictive alternative.

[96] *US-Continued Suspension of Obligations in the EC-Hormones Dispute*, Report of the Appellate Body, WT/DS320/AB/R, adopted 14 November 2008, DSR 2008:X 3507; *Canada-Continued Suspension of Obligations in the EC-Hormones Dispute*, Report of the Appellate Body, WT/DS320/AB/R, adopted 14 November 2008.

between review of the substance and review of the reasoning, was recalled and affirmed by the Appellate Body in its *Australia-Apples* report.[97]

The disputes referred to above hinge upon the line to be drawn between the recognised right of Members to determine their own standards where issues of environmental or health risk are at issue and the objective of removing protectionist trade restriction. In this context, scientific evaluation, as manifested in the risk assessment, has been grasped as an objective means by which to distinguish between legitimate regulation and protectionism. However, as the present author and others have recognised elsewhere, this does not itself take account of the reality whereby what is presented as 'science' itself is not invariably objective.[98] This is an issue which raises key questions concerning accountability for decision making and democracy.[99]

D. The Agreement on Technical Barriers to Trade

This agreement is based on the same premise as the SPS Agreement, which is that national technical regulations may be justifiable, but should not constitute unnecessary restrictions on trade. This Agreement covers all products except those falling under the SPS and government purchases. Like the SPS, the starting point is that international standards should be used, but that where that is inappropriate, for example, due to climatic reasons, other standards may be adopted. Both the SPS and the TBT govern the processes which are followed in the development of national regulation rather than pursuing specific substantive outcomes. In principle, if the process-related requirements are complied with, it should be possible to ensure the legitimacy of national regulatory measures. The emphasis has been upon the right of members to determine the standard of protection they want.[100] The key provisions of the TBT for present purposes are Articles 2.1 and 2.2. Article 2.1 imposes a requirement of national treatment; Article 2.2 provides that technical regulations 'shall not be more trade-restrictive than necessary to fulfil a legitimate objective'. What is significant is that Article 2.2 clearly imposes a restriction on Members' regulatory autonomy.

---

[97] *Australia-Measures Affecting the Importation of Apples from New Zealand*, Report of the Appellate Body, WT/DS367/AB/R, 29 November 2010.

[98] See further MJ Angelo, 'Harnessing the Power of Science in Environmental Law: Why We Should, Why We Don't and How We Can' (2008) 86 *Texas Law Review* 1527 et seq; O Perez, 'Anomalies of the Precautionary Principle: Reflections on the GMO Panel's Decision' (2007) 6 *World Trade Review* 265 et seq; E Reid, 'Risk Assessment, Science and Deliberation: Managing Regulatory Diversity under the SPS Agreement' (2012) 4 *European Journal of Risk Regulation* 535.

[99] Discussed below.

[100] See, for example, *EC-Trade Description of Sardines*, Panel Report WT/DS231/R, 29 May 2002, para 7.120.

Even a non-discriminatory measure will breach Article 2.2 if it is more restrictive than 'necessary'. The test for exceptions is necessity, taking into account the risks of non-fulfilment of the objective. A rebuttable presumption applies that a national measure based on international standards will not be unnecessarily restrictive,[101] indicating a preference for multilateral rather than unilateral standard setting, notwithstanding the Members' right to determine their own level of protection. Two recent disputes have shed light on the interpretation of these provisions.

i. US-Clove Cigarettes

The *US-Clove Cigarettes* dispute[102] concerned a US measure which banned the sale, in the US, of cigarettes containing certain additives, including clove. Crucially the measure continued to allow the production and sale in the US of cigarettes containing menthol. Whereas clove cigarettes are largely imported into the US (principally from Indonesia), the US produces menthol cigarettes. Thus, the measure permitted a US product, but banned an imported product. The question was whether these were like products, in which case the measure breached the requirement of national treatment (required under Article 2.1 TBT as well as under Article III.4 GATT). The panel found that the products were like and that the measure, in distinguishing between them, breached Article 2.1 TBT. That being the case, the panel held that there was no need to consider the applicability or not of Article III.4 GATT or of Article XX GATT, which the US had invoked in respect of Indonesia's claim under Article III.4 GATT. However, it did not uphold Indonesia's argument (under Article 2.2 TBT) that the ban was unnecessary: it found that Indonesia had failed to demonstrate that the measure was more trade-restrictive than necessary to pursue a legitimate objective (the ban was intended to reduce smoking among young people).

The Appellate Body upheld the panel's finding that the measure breached Article 2.1 TBT. However, whereas the panel had reached this conclusion with reference to the regulatory purpose of the measure,[103] the Appellate Body explicitly rejected this approach.[104] It further highlighted that:

> Determining likeness on the basis of the regulatory objectives of the measure, rather than on the products' competitive relationship, would require the identification of all the relevant objectives of a measure, as well as an assessment of which objectives among others are relevant or should prevail in determining

---

[101] Article 2.5 TBT.
[102] *United States-Measures Affecting the Production and Sale of Clove Cigarettes*, Panel Report WT/DS406/R, 2 September 2011; Appellate Body Report WT/DS406/AB/R, 4 April 2012.
[103] Panel Report (n 102) para 7.119.
[104] Appellate Body Report (n 102) para 112.

whether the products are like. It seems to us that it would not always be possible for a complainant or a panel to identify all the objectives of a measure and/or be in a position to determine which among multiple objectives are relevant to the determination of whether two products are like, or not.[105]

The Appellate Body observed that a purpose-based approach to 'likeness' would not necessarily afford Members greater regulatory autonomy, as panels would be required to determine which of the various purposes a measure may pursue is the more important, and which should take priority in the event of conflicting objectives.[106] Drawing from earlier analysis of likeness under Article III.4 GATT,[107] the Appellate Body here states that:

> [T]he regulatory concerns underlying a measure, such as the health risks associated with a given product, may be relevant to an analysis of the 'likeness' criteria under Article III:4 of the GATT 1994, as well as under Article 2.1 of the *TBT Agreement*, to the extent they have an impact on the competitive relationship between and among the products concerned.[108]

Likeness, therefore, is once again determined by reference to the competitive relationship between the affected products rather than the purpose of the measure.

With regard to the application of Article 2.2, the panel applied a two-stage test: first, the measure must pursue a legitimate objective; and, second, it must not be more trade-restrictive than 'necessary'. The panel was clear that the burden of proof for determining that the measure was unnecessary lies with the complainant, in this instance Indonesia.[109] The panel was also explicit that the finding as to likeness under Article 2.1 is quite distinct from the question of necessity under Article 2.2.[110]

ii. US-Measures Concerning the Importation, Marketing and Sale
   of Tuna and Tuna Products (US-Tuna II) (Mexico)

The *US-Tuna II(Mexico)* dispute[111] concerned a US labelling requirement applied to tuna to be sold in the US. Crucially the regulation required that tuna caught by setting on dolphin in the Eastern Tropical Pacific (ETP) could only be labelled 'dolphin friendly' if it had an international observer certification that no dolphin had been killed or seriously injured in the set,

---

[105] ibid para 113, referring to *Japan-Taxes on Alcoholic Beverages*, WT/DS8/ABR, WT/DS10/ABR, WT/DS11/ABR, 4 October 1996.
[106] Appellate Body Report, *US-Clove Cigarettes* (n 102) para 115.
[107] Appellate Body Report, *EC-Asbestos* (n 79).
[108] Appellate Body Report, *US-Clove Cigarettes* (n 102) para 119.
[109] Panel Report, *US-Clove Cigarettes* (n 102) para 7.331.
[110] ibid para 7.332. This approach was subsequently followed in *US-Measures Concerning the Importation, Marketing and Sale of Tuna and Tuna Products (US-Tuna II (Mexico))* WT/DS381/AB/R.
[111] ibid.

and provided that the relevant US authority found no evidence of 'adverse impact on any depleted dolphin stock in the ETP'.[112]

This measure was challenged by Mexico on the grounds that it violated the Article 2.1 national treatment requirement and did not comply with the Article 2.2 requirement of 'necessity'. The panel found that since it would be possible that the Mexican fleet could comply with the US ETP requirements or fish outside the ETP, there was no violation of the national treatment requirement. However, the Appellate Body reversed this finding, holding that the US labelling provisions adversely affected 'the conditions for competition in the US market' to the detriment of Mexican products. It is worth noting that in doing so, the Appellate Body noted that the US applied more lenient labelling rules for tuna caught outside the ETP, despite the harm to dolphins caused by fishing techniques in those other areas. Therefore, the measure was not 'even-handed'.[113] The Appellate Body approach is consistent with that it applied in *US-Shrimp*; the measure failed because of its arbitrariness rather than its substantive content. If the arbitrariness was removed (if the same requirements were universally applied), the measure could be TBT-compliant. The reliance of the Appellate Body upon the arbitrariness of the measure is in this instance drawn from the preamble to the TBT Agreement, in the absence of any such reference in Article 2.2.

With regard to evaluating the 'necessity' of the measure, the Appellate Body held that the appropriate test is to 'weigh and balance' '(i) the degree of contribution made by the measure to the legitimate objective; (ii) the trade-restrictiveness of the measure; and (iii) the nature of the risks at issue and the gravity of the consequences that would arise from non-fulfillment of the objective(s)'.[114] Once again, however, the Appellate Body did not in fact engage in any such weighing and balancing, but focused instead upon whether the Mexican proposed alternative measure would meet US objectives. While the panel had indicated that use of AIDCP[115] standards would be appropriate, the Appellate Body rejected this conclusion on the basis that the US standard was stricter and offered greater protection for dolphins. Schaffer points out that the narrow definition of the respondent's objectives makes it difficult to establish that a measure is 'unnecessary' (that is, it is difficult to establish that an alternative will meet the specific objective). Therefore, as in *US-Clove Cigarettes*, the US failed to comply with

---

[112] Setting on dolphins refers to the tuna fishing practice which exploits the natural tendency of tuna to swim in schools below schools of dolphin: mile-long purse seine nets are set around the dolphins to catch the tuna. However, this practice also catches and kills dolphins.
[113] *(US-Tuna II Mexico)* (n 110) para 297.
[114] ibid paras 321–22.
[115] Agreement on International Dolphin Conservation Programme.

non-discrimination obligation (Article 2.1), but there was no breach of the necessity requirement, so there was no violation of Article 2.2.

For the Appellate Body to rule that a measure is in breach due to violation of the national treatment obligation is less controversial than for it to rule that it is 'unnecessary', since the former may be determined on the basis of an objective assessment of the facts, while the latter involves an inevitably subjective superimposition of the Appellate Body's view over that of the national regulator.[116] The focus of the TBT Agreement, like the SPS Agreement, reflects a desire to leave the choice of applicable standards to the Members, while seeking to ensure that this respect for Members' legitimate regulatory autonomy is not exploited through the imposition of overly restrictive, protectionist measures.

III. EMERGING ENVIRONMENTAL MEASURES POSING PARTICULAR CHALLENGES FOR THE WTO

A. Energy

One area currently pressing upon the WTO, which epitomises the challenge involved in reconciling pursuit of economic and non-economic objectives, concerns developments in the energy sector. Traditionally energy has been perceived to be outside the WTO, yet there appears to be little basis for this in the rules.[117] While originally the major oil and gas-exporting states were outside the WTO, many of these have now joined or are in the process of doing so. Marhold[118] argues that although, de facto, energy has traditionally been treated as being outside the scope of WTO law, de jure it is very much within its scope.

Pauwelyn notes that the lack of WTO consideration of energy issues reflects the traditional WTO focus upon the removal of import restrictions. One consequence of the relative lack of energy exporters, and the widespread need to import energy, is that import restriction has not really been a problem in the energy sector. The key reason for its recent emergence as an issue of controversy concerns the inter-relationship between energy and climate change, and in particular the emergence of renewable sources of energy and policies supporting their development. Meyer has observed

---

[116] See further G Schaffer, 'The WTO Tuna-Dolphin II Case (US-Measures Concerning the Importation, Marketing and Sale of Tuna and Tuna Products', University of Minnesota Law School Legal Studies Research Paper Series Research Paper No 12-62 available at: http://ssrn.com/abstract=2176863; E Reid, 'National Regulatory Autonomy in the EU and WTO: Defining and Defending its Limits' (2010) *Journal of World Trade* 44, (4), 877–901.

[117] A Marhold, 'The World Trade Organization and Energy: Fuel for Debate', *ESIL Reflections*, 30 September 2013, available at: www.esil-sedi.eu/node/417.

[118] ibid.

the problematic phenomenon whereby measures supporting renewables are being subject to scrutiny which has never been applied to fossil fuels.[119] As he goes on to observe, this is despite the fact that: 'Global renewable energy subsidies totalled only $88 billion in 2011—roughly one sixth of fossil fuel subsidies.'

The key complaint against renewables programmes is that they tend to offer incentives for use of domestic production, which falls foul of the WTO's non-discrimination rules. The leading examples of this concern the *Canada-Renewable Energy* dispute.[120] There were two issues raised by the renewable energy and feed-in-tariffs disputes. The first concerned a domestic content requirement and the second was the argument that the 'feed-in-tariff' was a prohibited subsidy under the Subsidies and Countervailing Measures (SCM) Agreement. On this second point, the Appellate Body held that the panel had erred in holding that the relevant market was a single market for electricity, regardless of source. The Appellate Body held that the relevant market was rather 'shaped by the government's definition of an energy supply mix' and that the key issue should have been 'competitive prices for wind power and solar [photovoltaic] generation'. That said, the Appellate Body held that it had insufficient evidence to make a determination as to whether there was a breach.

In substantive terms, as noted above, these disputes and others pending[121] concern the WTO's non-discrimination and subsidies rules. Underpinning this, however, there are two greater issues: the global imperative to undertake measures to combat climate change and the desire of Members to achieve energy security. Pursuit of both of these has tended to involve state subsidy to boost nascent green energy production industry, which does not sit easily with current understandings of WTO rules. The real question facing the WTO is how it can, or will, engage with these issues which are in turn being tackled in their own regulatory contexts. In particular, how should the WTO accommodate the product of those regulatory contexts?[122] The challenge of climate change is one in which the crucial inter-relationship between trade, environment and social interests is manifest. The response of the WTO to this particular challenge may well determine its broader future relevance.

---

[119] T Meyer, 'Energy Subsidies and the World Trade Organization', *ASIL Insights*, 17(22), 10 September 2013, available at: www.asil.org/insights.cfm.
[120] *Canada-Certain Measures Affecting the Renewable Energy Generation Sector, Canada-Measures Relating to the Feed-in Tariff Program*, WT/DS412/AB/R, WT/DS426/AB/R, 6 May 2013; Request for Consultations by the United States, *India-Certain Measures Relating to Solar Cells and Solar Modules*, WT/DS456/1.
[121] *India-Solar Cells* (n 120).
[122] This is discussed further below.

B. Trade in Environmental Goods

The emerging questions regarding energy and the WTO have also increased the international focus upon trade in 'environmental goods'. While the Doha Declaration mandates Members to negotiate on 'the reduction or, as appropriate, elimination of tariff and non-tariff barriers on environmental goods and services',[123] little progress has been made on this. This is an issue in which the divergence between developing and developed states is highlighted: developing states have been reluctant to support liberalisation of trade in environmental goods in view of the impact it would have upon the development of their own nascent green industries. The very early stage of development of developing states' green industries has also meant that they have not had significant exports of these goods, and therefore liberalisation implies loss of tariff revenue, without bringing the benefits of access to other markets. A 2012 UNEP, ICTSD[124] and ITC[125] joint policy brief on trade in environmental goods highlights that real gains for least developed countries (LDCs) and developing states through tariff liberalisation would be realised only in respect of liberalisation between developing states. Removal of non-tariff barriers would potentially bring more benefits in terms of market access. One of the real challenges in this context derives from the fact that many environmental goods are the product of industry which has high technological barriers to entry.

These difficulties notwithstanding, renewed political interest in trade in environmental goods was demonstrated in President Obama's Second Term Climate Plan.[126] A fundamental challenge for the development of a specific regime for 'trade in environmental goods' concerns how to define 'environmental goods'. In 2011 the APEC states agreed to reduce tariffs to five per centor less on a list of 54 'environmental goods'. Obama's climate action plan identifies this list as the one which will provide the basis for a 'global agreement in the WTO' and that such agreement should initially be formed among those willing—a voluntary agreement to which others may sign up in due course. However, the UNEP-ICTSD policy briefing notes that although there is some consistency regarding the identification of the goods which should benefit from such a specialised regime, the cumulative total when different agreed lists of environmental goods are put together sits at 514 products. It also notes that developing states are generally reluctant to participate in negotiations on environmental goods and that the goods

---

[123] Paragraph 31(3). See www.wto.org/english/tratop_e/envir_e/envir_neg_serv_e.htm.
[124] International Centre for Trade and Sustainable Development.
[125] International Trade Centre.
[126] 'The U.S. will work with trading partners to launch negotiations at the World Trade Organization towards global free trade in environmental goods, including clean energy technologies such as solar, wind, hydro and geothermal.'

generally listed are not of export interest to developing states. Quick also discusses the limitations of basing any agreement upon the APEC list, in particular the lack of consideration of commodities (simply reflecting the cooperative context in which the list had been drawn up).[127]

Howse observes a further challenge, however, that the APEC declaration relates to normal tariffs, but does not apply to tariffs imposed through 'trade remedies' that is anti-dumping duties or countervailing duties.[128] That this is a significant concern is demonstrated in Lester and Watson's observation of a substantial increase in the use of trade remedies against green products since 2011.[129] Whether this is deemed to be problematic reflects a policy decision relating to the extent to which the (often nascent) industry producing these should be supported. Howse suggests that 'a WTO pact on environmental trade could require a prior period of negotiations, or that all alternatives be exhausted, before states resort to punitive unilateralism'. Fourteen WTO members[130] have indeed launched negotiations for an agreement on trade in green goods. The negotiations, announced at Davos in January 2014, will take the APEC list as their starting point, notwithstanding the limitations identified by UNEP-ICTSD;[131] however, it is anticipated that this list will not be exhaustive.

IV. APPLICATION OF THE DIFFERENT TESTS IN THE DETERMINATION AS TO WHETHER A MEASURE MAY JUSTIFY A TRADE RESTRICTION

In the exploration of how the objectives of free trade and non-economic interests may be balanced, and any inherent conflict treated, it is evident

---

[127] Quick (n 7) 963–66.

[128] R Howse, 'Obama's Free-Trade Green Plan Has a Chance of Breaking WTO Inertia', *Globe and Mail* (27 June 2013) www.theglobeandmail.com/report-on-business/economy/economy-lab/obamas-free-trade-green-plan-has-a-chance-of-breaking-wto-inertia/article12870243.

[129] S Lester and KW Watson, 'Free Trade in Environmental Goods: The Trade Remedy Problem', Herbert A Steifel Center for Trade Policy Studies, Free Trade Bulletin No 54, 19 Aguust 2013.

[130] The 14 members involved are: Australia, Canada, China, Costa Rica, Chinese Taipei, the EU, Hong Kong (China), Japan, Korea, New Zealand, Norway, Switzerland, Singapore and the US. These members collectively account for around 90 per cent of trade in green goods. See further European Commission Press Release, European Commission–IP/14/71 24/01/2014, at: http://europa.eu/rapid/press-release_IP-14-71_en.htm; and Joint Statement regarding trade in environmental goods, available at: http://trade.ec.europa.eu/doclib/docs/2014/january/tradoc_152095.pdf.

[131] UNEP, ITC and ICTSD; (2012); Trade and Environment Briefings: Trade in Environmental Goods; ICTSD Programme on Global Economic Policy and Institutions; Policy Brief No. 6; International Centre for Trade and Sustainable Development, Geneva, Switzerland, www.ictsd.org available at: http://www.unep.org/greeneconomy/Portals/88/documents/research_products/PolicyBriefs/environmental-goods.pdf.

that the test applied in different contexts to the interface between these interests is of crucial importance. It is therefore surprising how little clarity there has been on this matter.

A. The Necessity Test

As seen above, the GATT applied a 'necessity' test in the *Thai-Cigarettes* ruling[132] requiring both a causal link between the measure and the objective pursued under Article XX, and that no reasonably available less restrictive, alternative measure existed. The extent to which the panel is competent to judge upon the 'reasonable availability' of alternatives is, however, questionable. Subsequently, in the *Tuna-Dolphin* dispute,[133] the necessity test required that 'no alternative' to the measure existed. The requirement of 'reasonable availability' of alternatives resurfaced, however, in *US-Gasoline*.[134] It has been explicitly recognised that reasonably available alternatives may incur compliance costs.[135]

More recently, with regard to Article 2.2 TBT, the Appellate Body has identified a two-part test for the evaluation of 'necessity'—that the measure contribute to the achievement of its (legitimate) objective and that there is no less trade-restrictive means by which to achieve the desired objective.[136] It appears from the 'least-restrictive means' test that the fundamental aim is to remove trade restrictions, or at least to minimise their effect. Trebilcock and Howse[137] have argued that a 'least-restrictive means' test avoids the concerns, which may apply to a proportionality test (dependent upon the definition of that test), about the legitimacy of a trade panel carrying out cost-benefit analyses or 'second-guessing' the objectives of a state in implementing a trade-restricting provision. Moreover, it has the advantage of potentially reconciling the objective of prevention of disguised protectionism with that of deferring to domestic choices about environmental aims. This is based on the premise that trade liberalisation should not necessarily take precedence over environmental objectives.[138]

The requirement in Article XX(g) GATT that a measure 'relate to' the stated objective has been interpreted as requiring that it is 'primarily aimed

---

[132] *Thai Cigarettes* (n 33).
[133] *Tuna-Dolphin* (n 49).
[134] *US-Gasoline* (n 62).
[135] *Thai Cigarettes* (n 33).
[136] *US-Clove Cigarettes* (n 102) and *US-Tuna II (Mexico)* (n 110) .
[137] Trebilcock and Howse, *Legal Regulation of International Trade*, 3rd edn (Oxford, Routledge, 2005).
[138] Compare to the Court of Justice's approach, where proportionality includes consideration of whether there is a less restrictive means; see below and T Tridimas, *General Principles of EU Law* 2nd edn, (Oxford, Oxford University Press, 2006) 133–36.

at' the objective, and thus that it is a less stringent test than the necessity test required under Article XX(b). However, this distinction has been undermined by the examination by the Appellate Body of the availability of less restrictive 'alternatives', as well as whether the restriction was 'disproportionate' in terms of the costs imposed, when applying the chapeau in the context of Article XX(g).[139] A requirement of 'necessity' has therefore effectively been imposed through the application of the chapeau.

B. The Relationship between GATT/TBT 'Necessity' and EU Proportionality

The 'necessity' test has been consistently interpreted as concerning: (i) the appropriateness of the measure in terms of its contribution to the objective; and (ii) that there are no less restrictive alternatives. This test is therefore drawn in substantially the same ambit as that which in the EU is expressed as the 'proportionality' test.[140] However, it is interesting to consider the *Danish Bottles* case, in which the Court of Justice provided its fairly standard expression of the test of proportionality: that is, whether the measure implemented constituted the 'least restrictive' possible measure.[141] Yet, in its application of the test in *Danish Bottles*, the Court appeared to go beyond 'least restrictive' and weigh up the trade restriction as against the environmental benefit.[142] This is significant because the Court has rarely engaged in such weighing up, which could be said to introduce an element of 'proportionality stricto sensu'.[143] This resonates with the question explored by the Appellate Body in *US-Gasoline*, concerning whether the restriction was 'disproportionate' in terms of the costs imposed. The Court in *Danish Bottles* concluded that the national measure in question was indeed legitimate,[144] which to some extent neutralised what might otherwise have raised concerns about the Court substituting its judgment for the democratically accountable choices of the national decision maker.

This disparity between the expressed definition of proportionality (which includes the third arm, 'proportionality stricto sensu') and its routine application has given rise to some inconsistency of application of the test by the Court of Justice.[145] There is, however, some indication in the case

---

[139] Appellate Body Report, *US-Gasoline*.
[140] See chs 1 and 3.
[141] Discussed above.
[142] *Commission v Denmark* (n 71).
[143] N Notaro, 'The New Generation Case Law on Trade and Environment' (2000) 25 *European Law Review* 467.
[144] *Commission v Denmark* (n 71).
[145] See, inter alia, ibid; Case C-67/97 *Criminal Proceedings Against Ditlev Bluhme (Danish Bees)* [1999] 1 CMLR 612.

law that the Court will attempt to weigh up the objective and its restrictive effect[146] where such an analysis has supported the legitimacy of the contested national measure, as in *Danish Bottles*. Van Gerven AG in *Red Grouse*[147] defined 'necessity' as requiring both a causal link between the objective and the measure and that there is no less restrictive measure available. He defined 'proportionality' as concerning the relationship between the obstacle introduced and the objective pursued.

The critical element of either the proportionality test as it is usually applied by the Court of Justice and the 'necessity' test as expressed by the Appellate Body in *US-Clove*, among others, is that both move the decision away from being one based purely, or predominantly, upon trade-restricting (or liberalising) considerations. It also encompasses the question of whether there is a less trade-restrictive alternative.

C. The Appellate Body: 'Weighing and Balancing' Competing Interests?

Since the conclusion of the WTO Agreement, the dispute settlement panels have in their reasoning given greater consideration to the competing interests and objectives at stake, while continuing to consistently reach results which give precedence to trade liberalisation. As noted above, the Appellate Body has explicitly expressed the tests for both the necessity of the measure and the availability of reasonable alternatives in terms of 'weighing and balancing'.[148] In *US -Shrimp* the Appellate Body made explicit reference to the chapeau as a balancing requirement 'between the right of a Member to invoke one or another of the exceptions of Article XX ... on the one hand, and the substantive rights of the other Members under the GATT 1994, on the other hand'.[149]

Yet, despite this expression, as observed above, there is little evidence that the Appellate Body has indeed engaged in 'weighing up' the extent of the contribution of the measure to its stated objective, as balanced against the restrictive effects of the measure. This is reminiscent of the ECJ's traditional reluctance, when undertaking its review of the proportionality of a measure, to engage in a review of the proportionality of the measure *stricto sensu*.

---

[146] *Danish Bees* (n 145), although see Case C-379/98 *PreussenElektra AG v Schleswag AG* [2001] ECR I-2099, in which the ECJ did not even consider this issue.
[147] Case C-169/89 *Gourmetterie van den Burg* [1990] ECR 2143.
[148] WTO, *Korea-Measures Affecting Imports of Fresh, Chilled and Frozen Beef* (11 December 2000) WTO Docs WT/DS161/AB/R and WT/DS169/AB/R (Appellate Body Report); *Brazil-Tyres* (n 83). See also *US-Clove Cigarettes* (n 102).
[149] Appellate Body Report, *US-Shrimp* (n 2) para 156.

D. The Application of the Court of Justice and Appellate Body Tests Compared

When the tests applied are unpacked, it appears that there is more common ground between the Court of Justice and the Appellate Body than might appear from the rhetoric. In light of this, it is interesting to compare what might have been the outcome before the WTO of two significant (and each in their own way controversial) Court of Justice cases: *Ditlev Bluhme*[150] and *PreussenElektra*.[151]

i. Ditlev Bluhme

Ditlev Bluhme concerned a Danish prohibition on keeping a certain species of bee within a particular territory, for the purpose of protecting the indigenous species of bee, which would otherwise die out. The Court of Justice found that this was a measure equivalent to a quantitative restriction of imports, as it satisfied the seminal *Dassonville* definition that it be 'actually or potentially, directly or indirectly capable of hindering trade between Member States'.[152] The Court held that:

> [M]easures to preserve an indigenous animal population with distinct characteristics contribute to the maintenance of biodiversity by ensuring the survival of the population concerned. By so doing, they are aimed at protecting the life of those animals and are capable of being justified under Article 36 of the Treaty.

On the question of justification, the Court dealt with the matter under Article 36 of the Treaty rather than exploring the applicability of a mandatory requirement, pursuant to *Cassis de Dijon*.[153] In assessing the 'necessity and proportionality' of the measure, the Court referred to Article 8a of the Rio Convention, which recognises the legitimacy of pursuing the protection of biodiversity through the designation of areas in which a species enjoys special protection. The Court finally found that the threat to the Laeso bees was genuine (on account of their recessive gene) and therefore held that the measure was justified.[154]

If this measure were challenged in the WTO, how would it be treated? Were this measure to be dealt with under the GATT, the first issue concerns whether it constitutes an import restriction, prima facie a breach of Article XI. In this instance, the import restriction is a border manifestation of internal national regulation. Pursuant to the GATT Annex I note Ad

[150] *Ditlev Bluhme* (n 145), discussed in ch 3 above.
[151] *PreussenElektra* (n 146), discussed in ch 3.
[152] Judgment of the Court, *Ditlev Bluhme* (n 145) [19].
[153] See ch 3 above.
[154] Judgment of the Court, *Ditlev Bluhme* (n 145), [36–38].

Article III,[155] the measure therefore falls to be considered as an internal regulatory measure under Article III (the requirement of national treatment). However, is this a discriminatory measure? The answer must be no, because it affects Danish as well as other bee keepers who wish to sell to that particular territory, so it does not breach Article III. In this respect it may be distinguished from the *Tuna and Tuna Products* ruling, in which a total import ban was rejected because there was no internal regulation. Because the measure is not discriminatory, it does not breach Article III, so there is no need to explore the possibility of justification under Article XX GATT, although it has been established that Article XX(g) can in principle be invoked in pursuit of the protection of endangered species;[156] therefore, the measure would come within its scope. Following this through, the question would thus be whether the measure were 'primarily aimed at' conservation, which appears to be the case. This in turn raises the question of 'necessity' in the application of the chapeau. Ultimately it appears that were this measure to be challenged before the WTO, it would stand if the substantive law at issue were the GATT.

However, this measure, a ban on keeping any bees other than a specific species in order to ensure that the protected species does not become extinct, is arguably a measure in the pursuit of the life or health of animals. In this case the matter potentially falls within the scope of the SPS Agreement. The position regarding national measures to regulate against invasive animal species is not entirely certain. However, a Standards and Trade Development Facility Seminar held at the WTO in July 2012 concluded that some clarification on the application of SPS rules in this area would be helpful.[157] In particular, the principal focus of the OIE's[158] work has been dealing with preventing the spread of animal disease rather than biodiversity per se. The Convention on Bio-Diversity concerns risk to indigenous population; however, there are some gaps between its work and that of the OIE. Both also overlap with the SPS, but again there are gaps.[159] The sixth Conference of the Parties to the CBD urged that combatting invasive alien species should be a priority.[160] The SPS permits states to adopt measures for the protection of animal health against pests. That being the case, if the prohibited bees were a 'pest', the measure would surely fall

---

[155] Discussed above at n 50.

[156] *US-Shrimp* (n 2).

[157] Standards and Trade Development Facility (STDF), *International Trade and Invasive Alien Species*, available at: www.standardsfacility.org/Files/IAS/STDF_IAS_EN.pdf.

[158] The World Organisation for Animal Health.

[159] While the SPS recognises the work of the OIE in the adoption of standards, as noted above, this work primarily relates to the prevention of disease rather than risk to biodiversity itself. This is one of the gaps identified by the STDF Seminar.

[160] COP 6 Decision VI/23, text of the Decision available at: www.cbd.int/decision/cop/?id=7197.

within the scope of the SPS.[161] In this event, while such a measure would be permissible, it must be based upon scientific evidence. This highlights a disjuncture between GATT rules and the SPS—whereas under the GATT, a non-discriminatory internal regulatory measure would be allowed, under the SPS, the measure must be based upon scientific evidence to be allowed to stand, even if it is non-discriminatory. This reflects the degree of susceptibility of health regulation to protectionist abuse. Thus, were the measure to be challenged and ruled to fall within the SPS Agreement, Denmark would have to produce scientific evidence to support the ban.

ii. PreussenElektra

The Court of Justice's judgment in *PreussenElektra*[162] was controversial, not least because it did not test the German measure for proportionality;[163] rather, it held that the environmental objective justified the German measure, which therefore did not breach Article 34 TFEU. In the WTO, the outcome would have been different. This was a scheme which would breach Article III, since it concerned a matter of internal regulation, but was directly discriminatory, thus breaching the national treatment requirement. This raises the question of whether it comes within the Article XX exceptions. It was a measure primarily aimed at the conservation of natural resources, so could come within paragraph (g). Thus, it must be primarily aimed at the conservation of natural resources. However, the application of the Article XX chapeau would raise the question of necessity or the availability of a less restrictive alternative. There is no doubt that a less restrictive means was available: Germany could simply have required certification of origin to identify energy which should be subsidised. The scheme would fail the less restrictive means test. In the interests of liberalisation of markets, there is no doubt that this would have been the correct outcome.[164] It avoids the problems of the Court of Justice's approach whereby it appears that any measure pursuing environmental protection will not breach Article 34 TFEU, which invites segregation of the market.[165]

What the above comparisons demonstrate is the significance of the difference in objectives of the WTO and EU: while the WTO seeks liberalisation of markets and to remove obstacles to trade, the EU has moved beyond that. The limitation of environmental protection outlined in chapter three—that it is seen predominantly in terms of its relationship with free movement—is

---

[161] It could be argued that it would require a broad definition of 'pest' to catch a species that out-competes another species rather than systematically attacks it in some way.

[162] *PreussenElektra* (n 146).

[163] Discussed in ch 2 above.

[164] It is also the outcome which would be consistent with earlier Court of Justice jurisprudence.

[165] See discussion in ch 3 above.

being eroded. *PreussenElektra* perhaps indicates that its 'integration' has moved environment to a new level; it is now an element of a discernable polity. The EU's system of governance is developing: it is clearly distinguishable from the WTO perspective, and indeed from its own original position.

V. CONCLUSIONS

It is ultimately the states themselves that have the responsibility to ensure that WTO rules are compatible with other obligations, as they are bound to ensure that they comply with all their obligations under international law. The WTO DSB responsibility is to enforce the rules of the covered agreements. However, the panel and the Appellate Body should endeavour where possible to provide interpretations of its provisions which are consistent with its obligations under wider international law. Where the WTO cannot do so, the responsibility returns to the Members to bring the WTO rules into line with those binding obligations of international law. This may not be possible, however, as it is difficult to achieve a consensus on the amendment of the GATT for any purposes.

That there is a core of environmental agreements which contain trade measures is in sharp contrast to the lack of trade agreements containing environmental provisions.[166] One possible reason for this, offered by Schoenbaum,[167] is that it is rarely necessary to regulate the environment to protect trade, but it is frequently necessary to regulate trade in order to protect the environment.[168]

Regulation of trade to protect the environment would equate, in practice, to regulation of how commercial entities may exploit the environment (to protect the long-term interests of both trade and the environment). Regulation of the environment may be viewed as being positive protection, whereas regulation of commercial entities could be viewed entirely negatively, as a restriction. Either way, however, it appears to be impossible to separate them, suggesting that there is no inherent conflict between protecting each of these interests, but, rather, a long-term mutual dependency. This is not to deny the existence of short-term conflict of interest, the effects of which should not be underestimated. Ultimately, the problem of regulation is political: as regulation may cause short-term pain, governments, which are dependent upon electoral support, may be reluctant to undertake the necessary regulation to ensure the long-term benefit.

---

[166] Although EC agreements tend to now make reference to environment, they do not, as seen above, provide for specific measures to protect the environment.

[167] Schoenbaum (n 11) 282.

[168] Arguably this is a short-term view: long-term trading interests require sustainability, which in turn requires the conservation of necessary natural resources.

This highlights once again the underlying question of why pursuit of trade liberalisation is prioritised. What are its objectives? If the objectives include even economic *development*, this implies a longer-term interest, which in turn requires some consideration of sustainability, and should not be primarily concerned with the protection of current economic interests. If, however, governments prove reluctant to bite the bullet on this issue, it seems all the more unfortunate, if inevitable, that decisions on how the environment may be protected should be left to a body of trade experts, the WTO panels and the DSB.

The current position is that if a measure satisfies the conditions and chapeau of Article XX, it will not be held to breach the GATT. To satisfy Article XX requires not only that the measure be necessary (including that it is the least restrictive means by which to achieve its objective), but also that it be imposed with respect to due process. Similar approaches are applied in respect of the other WTO Agreements (including the GATS, SPS and TBT Agreements). Despite recognition of the potential legitimacy of a unilateral measure, the DSB has expressed a clear preference for multilateral measures. However, these too must satisfy the given exceptions (eg, Article XX GATT) and be applied in a manner which is not arbitrary or discriminatory.[169]

It is evident that the recognition by the Appellate Body that WTO law is located within, and interacts with, the broader body of international law has been crucial to both its accommodation of members' environmental measures and also its continued relevance. If the WTO rules had been unable to accommodate environmental measures without amendment, which would have been impossible to achieve, the WTO would have found itself increasingly marginalised in the face of emerging global concern.

Clearly, many of the questions which have arisen in the context of the environment and free trade also arise in relation to the protection of human rights and their relationship to free trade. There are, however, further difficulties in this context, not least that there is no reference to human rights in the WTO Agreement, nor an exception which prima facie lends itself to the protection of human rights issues. A deeper, underlying difficulty surrounds the very definition of 'human rights'.[170] It is these questions which will be explored in the next chapter.

---

[169] See in particular *US-Shrimp* (n 2).
[170] See ch 1 above.

8

Human Rights Protection and WTO Law

INTRODUCTION

THE GENERAL RELATIONSHIP between international law and WTO law was examined in chapter six. It was seen that while the rules of customary international law bind the WTO, its members and its institutions, there is no jurisdiction for a WTO panel or the Appellate Body to enforce these rules. Similarly, while provisions of international treaties may shed light upon the interpretation of WTO rules, they are not substantively applicable by the panel or the Appellate Body. Building upon the analysis of the relationship between WTO law and other international law presented above, this chapter focuses specifically upon the relationship between WTO rules and human rights. The way in which 'trade and human rights' has been addressed in different international contexts differs significantly from the approach to environmental protection and trade. As was seen in chapter two in the analysis of the EU experience, the inter-relationship between human rights and economic matters has not always been recognised.[1] However, it has also been seen above that it is sometimes necessary to regulate trade to protect human rights, just as there are times when it is necessary to regulate trade to protect the environment. Whereas this latter necessity has been recognised in the international context, as evidenced by the inclusion of trade regulatory measures in certain multilateral environmental agreements,[2] there are no examples of trade regulatory measures in human rights agreements.

Despite the separate legal regimes which exist in respect of human rights and trade, it has been seen in the European context that these interests can and do collide. That being the case, this chapter identifies and explores the primary points of interaction between human rights rules and WTO rules, with particular focus upon the rules of the GATT. As indicated in chapter six, attempts to define the relationship between human rights, however understood, and trade give rise to a tendency to seek to 'shoe-horn' human

---

[1] See ch 2.
[2] See ch 7.

rights into the WTO legal framework. This carries some risks, not least that it subordinates human rights to trade law. Any analysis of the relationship between human rights and trade must therefore be alert to this risk; addressing it asks questions of our understanding of the purpose of WTO law.[3]

One difficulty which very quickly emerges with regard to the relationship between 'human rights and trade' is that to talk simply of 'human rights' is fundamentally problematic: different rights carry different weight and recognition of specific rights varies (both among people and also over time).[4] Thus, to refer to 'WTO law and human rights' as a single issue is misleading and ultimately unhelpful. It belies the complexity that flows from the diversity of weight, standing and substance of rights. The question of definition of particular human rights at issue therefore emerges as crucial in determining the relationship with WTO rules.

The first section of this chapter briefly outlines the background concerning the relationship between international human rights law and trade law, including the use of trade measures to pursue human rights objectives. The second section then locates the main points of interaction between WTO law and human rights. The third section examines the relationship between labour rights and WTO law. This case study of labour rights exposes the difficulties with regard to definition of human rights, as well as their uneasy relationship with the WTO rules. It also tests the principal points of interaction between WTO rules and human rights which have been identified in abstract in the second section. Subsequently, recognising the difficulties identified in the relationship between WTO law and human rights, and the lack of WTO human rights-based disputes from which to draw, the fourth section compares the likely outcome before the WTO dispute settlement panel of seminal Court of Justice case law. This exercise demonstrates that despite the problematic relationship perceived between WTO law and human rights, the rules may in fact be able to deal with this issue. This, however, is premised upon a 'discrimination-based' approach.[5]

I. BACKGROUND: INTERNATIONAL HUMAN RIGHTS LAW AND THE WTO

A. No Coherent Relationship

In practical terms, the difficulty arising from the lack of a coherent relationship between international trade law and international law is that the

---

[3] This will be addressed in ch 9.
[4] This temporal dimension was seen in ch 2 in the context of the EU.
[5] Discussed below.

WTO dispute settlement system makes no provision for the application or enforcement of rules of international law: the jurisdiction of the panel extends only to 'applicable WTO law'. Applicable WTO law includes the rules laid down in the WTO covered agreements.[6] Consequently, although the WTO (as an international legal person) is bound by rules of international law, there is no provision by which, in the event of a breach of international human rights law, the WTO can act to enforce that law. This is prima facie entirely appropriate: the WTO has narrowly defined objectives and a developed set of rules through which to achieve its objectives. It also has a binding dispute settlement system to ensure that its members adhere to its rules. It would be abusing its competence to seek to use that system of rules to enforce values and rights which go beyond the scope of its mandate.

Yet to turn this around raises some questions: if, for example, a state acts to restrict imports on the basis that the exporting state is utilising forced labour, then (unless this can be brought under one of the general exceptions to the GATT) the exporting state could hypothetically bring a complaint against the importing state for breach of its obligations under the GATT. Recognising the human rights problem at issue, the WTO dispute settlement panel would be obliged to interpret the WTO rules consistently with human rights law insofar as was possible. In the event of a conflict between the human rights rule and the WTO rules, the dispute settlement panel would not be able to rule other than that the import restriction was a breach of the GATT rules. Notwithstanding that the WTO and its Member States are bound by the rules of international law, the WTO has no jurisdiction (or responsibility) to ensure non-WTO rules.[7] As Marceau observes: 'A distinction exists between the binding obligations of states (WTO members)—for which states are at all times responsible —and the "applicable WTO law".'[8] It is the responsibility of the Member States to act to ensure that the GATT could not be used in this manner. Essentially, therefore, it is for the members of the WTO to act to amend the GATT to permit an exception to uphold some other rules of international law. The difficulty with this would be in achieving the necessary consensus to make this amendment, and in defining the terms of the amendment. The members, however, remain bound by their international legal obligations, including those of international human rights law, and remain liable, under the rules of state responsibility,

---

[6] For a discussion of the extent of WTO applicable law, see G Marceau ,'WTO Dispute Settlement and Human Rights' (2002) 13 *European Journal of International Law* 753.

[7] The exception to this would concern the situation in which the human rights obligation breached was a *jus cogens* obligation, in which case the Member States of the WTO would not have been able to contract out of its application and the WTO obligation which inadvertently conflicted with the *jus cogens* obligation would be set aside. However, this raises its own difficulties, not least who would determine the conflict between the *jus cogens* obligation and the WTO obligation, and who could set the WTO obligation aside.

[8] Marceau (n 6) 756.

for any breach of their international legal obligations. As a consequence, it is possible that an act may breach a human rights treaty, but be compliant with WTO law, or, as in the forced labour example, breach WTO law while seeking to enforce a human rights obligation. Thus, there may be a prima facie conflict of obligations. It should, however, be possible to act in compliance with both sets of rules at once. Thus, there should not be any necessity for a WTO-inspired measure to breach a human rights obligation. This notwithstanding, the relationship between international human rights law and the WTO is undoubtedly complex. The difficulties derive from the parallel systems of international law in operation, both human rights and international trade being 'subsets' of the broad body of international legal rules. States are bound by both systems simultaneously. Yet, although the WTO, its institutions and Members are bound by international law and the DSU includes the obligation that WTO rules are interpreted in conformity with rules of international law,[9] there is no mechanism by which, when the two systems impact upon one another, the relevant interests may be balanced against each other.

Notwithstanding the relative lack of reference to human rights in trade agreements, the use of trade measures to protect various human rights is not a new phenomenon, not least because international law, despite its recognition of state sovereignty and prohibition of intervention in the internal affairs of a sovereign state, does not prohibit non-forcible, economic measures to promote human rights. As Cleveland has observed, 'even if human rights measures do violate the non-intervention norm ... they may constitute an acceptable use of non-forcible countermeasures to retaliate against violations of international human rights'.[10] It was established by the International Court of Justice (ICJ) in the *Nicaragua* case that while the principle of non-intervention applied to (and therefore prohibited) US *military* support for the Nicaraguan contras, this principle did not extend to prohibit the US's *economic* coercion in pursuit of the same goal.[11] This confirmed the judgment of the Court in *Barcelona Traction*[12] that all states have an interest in the protection of human rights.

On the other hand, the limits imposed upon state intervention in the pursuit of human rights are not so clear, nor is how states may seek to 'enforce' an *erga omnes* obligation. Article 42 of the Draft Rules on State Responsibility[13] indicates that all states would have sufficient interest to

---

[9] Article 3(2) Dispute Settlement Understanding.

[10] S Cleveland, 'Human Rights Sanctions and the WTO' in F Francioni (ed), *Environment, Human Rights and International Trade* (Oxford, Hart Publishing, 2001) 298.

[11] *Military and Para-military Activities (Nicaragua v US)* [1986] ICJ 14.

[12] *The Case Concerning Barcelona Traction, Light and Power Company Ltd (Belgium v Spain)* [1970] ICJ 3.

[13] International Law Commission, *Draft Rules on State Liability*, Report of the International Law Commission on the work of its Fifty-third session, Official Records of the General Assembly, Fifty-sixth session, Supplement No 10 (A/56/10), ch IV.E.

enforce the responsibility of the state violating *erga omnes* norms; however, this only authorises a state to use a recognised dispute settlement mechanism to do so. It is far from clear that the rules would allow a state which is not directly affected to use counter-measures against a state violating human rights law.[14] Yet it has been explicitly recognised by the UN Human Rights Committee that provisions of the ICCPR, as a human rights covenant for the benefit of individuals, may not be the subject of reservations.[15]

This serves to reinforce the significance of establishing which human rights are protected as *jus cogens* obligations and customary international law. Any state may claim an interest in the breach of an *erga omnes* obligation, and that interest may be in events which would otherwise be 'extra-jurisdictional'. It is unclear, however, what action may be taken as a consequence of that interest. Extreme violations of human rights have been held to constitute a risk to international peace and security, triggering the possibility of action under Chapter VII of the UN Charter 'to maintain or restore international peace and security'. It has been suggested that serious violations may now automatically constitute such a threat, triggering action even without Security Council authorisation. Although speculative, Marceau has suggested that 'if such unilateral force can be used against massive violations of human rights, the WTO may be interpreted in parallel so as to allow trade measures to react against some such violations'.[16]

Thus, despite the lack of reference to human rights in the WTO rules, there can be little doubt that just as human rights have developed special status and rules under international law, their relationship to international trade rules cannot be considered in isolation from broader consideration of international law.[17] Having recognised the de facto relationship between WTO rules and human rights, it is necessary to explore that relationship in detail.

II. UNPACKING THE INTERACTION BETWEEN HUMAN RIGHTS AND WTO RULES

The starting point in the exploration of the relationship between WTO law and human rights is to identify the points of interaction between WTO rules

---

[14] See Marceau (n 6).

[15] UN Human Rights Committee, General Comment 24 (52) General Comment on issues relating to reservations made upon ratification or accession to the Covenant or the Optional Protocols thereto, or in relation to Declarations made under the Covenant, UN Doc CCPR/C/21/Rev.1/Add.6.

[16] Marceau (n 6) 812.

[17] It is acknowledged here that both the definition and the selection of rights under consideration impact upon the ensuing recommendations. However, what is ultimately proposed is a procedural approach which would allow for relativity. While the present analysis does not focus upon IP rights, for example, the approach could be applied to measures seeking to protect IP rights. Similarly, public morals are not subject to detailed consideration, but as public morality would come within the social pillar of sustainable development, it would be able to be accommodated within the approach ultimately proposed.

and human rights, and how that inter-relationship may be understood and treated. There is a risk that analysis of this question can be interpreted as suggesting primacy of WTO law, that it is a concession that human rights be considered or accommodated within the framework of trade law. As highlighted by Lang, the prevailing approach to the 'trade and ....' linkage discourse can reinforce this impression.[18] Such a characterisation may be interpreted as suggesting the subordination of human rights to a primary purpose—trade liberalisation. Such an interpretation is vigorously rejected here. Yet there is no escaping the practical implications of the developed trade law regime: pragmatically, it is essential to explore the inter-relationship between trade and human rights in terms of locating human rights within the trade law regime. This is done, however, with the express caveat that it does not accept any inherent primacy of trade law; rather, it reflects a practical concern regarding how to manage the coincidence of diverse legal systems, one of which is substantially more deeply developed than the others.

The relationship between human rights and international trade rules raises some new questions as well as revisiting some of the familiar issues from the trade and environment debate. Questions relating to the balance between the protection of economic interests and the environment have arisen primarily in the context of how an existing exception may (or should) be interpreted, and how two interests which are acknowledged to interact should be treated and balanced. Two distinct issues arise with regard to the relationship between WTO rules and human rights: first, the identification of which, if any, human rights may justify, or require, an exception to WTO rules; and, second, the identification of any provision within the WTO rules which recognises the inter-relationship between WTO rules and human rights.[19]

A. Locating Human Rights in the WTO Legal Order

The WTO regime is concerned with regulation of trade between states, and the GATT in particular is concerned with the liberalisation of trade in goods.[20] As indicated in chapter six, the key provisions of the GATT (for

[18] See ATF Lang, 'Reflecting on Linkage: Cognitive and Institutional Change in the International Trading System' (2007) 70(4) *MLR* 523–549; A Lang, *World Trade Law after Neoliberalism: Reimagining the Global Economic Order* (Oxford, Oxford University Press, 2011); see also JL Dunoff, '"Trade and": Recent Developments in Trade Policy and Scholarship—and Their Surprising Political Implications' (1996–97) 17 *Northwestern Journal of International Law and Business* 759; Alvarez et al, *Symposium—The Boundaries of the WTO* (2002) 96 *AJIL* 1; S Dillon, 'A Farewell to Linkage: International Trade law and Global Sustainability Indicators' (2002–03) 51 *Rutgers Law Review* 87; S Cho, 'Linkage of Free Trade and Social Regulation: Moving Beyond the Entropic Dilemma' (2005) 5 *Chicago Journal of International Law* 625.

[19] The focus of the present analysis rests upon the rules of the GATT.

[20] Although the primary focus here is upon the GATT regime, reference will also be made to other agreements as appropriate.

present purposes) are Articles I and III.[21] In addition, Article XX provides an exhaustive list of 'general exceptions' to the rules, which are subject to the requirement that they 'are not applied in a manner which would constitute a means of arbitrary or unjustifiable discrimination between countries where the same conditions prevail, or a disguised restriction on international trade'.[22] Thus, the fundamental rules of the GATT are such that there appear to be three principal means by which human rights could be recognised and protected within it: first, as rules of international law, this includes rules binding upon the WTO as an international legal person (and thus binding upon its institutions, including the DSB)[23] and also those rules of international law to be taken into account in the clarification (or potentially application) of WTO law.[24] Second, since Article III GATT requires no less favourable treatment of imported goods than domestically produced 'like' products, the key issue is that of likeness: if products are not deemed to be 'like', there is no obligation of national treatment. This raises the question whether products may be distinguished on the basis of human rights factors, thus accommodating human rights concerns.[25] Third, human rights could be protected within the GATT framework if human rights fall within the scope of the Article XX exceptions.[26] An examination of these three routes will reveal considerable complexity and a common issue: if human rights are to be recognised and protected within the WTO legal order, there must first be a consensus on that and, second, there must also be a consensus as to the content of the rights to be protected.

i. International Law and the WTO

The first point of interaction between WTO rules and human rights derives directly from the relationship between general international law and WTO law. It has been seen above that in the clarification of WTO law, the panels and the Appellate Body should take into account any relevant rules

---

[21] As a reminder, Article I requires the application of the 'most favoured nation' principle (that concessions extended to one member should be extended to all other members). Article III requires 'national treatment' (that imported goods should be treated no less favourably than domestically produced like products).

[22] The exceptions provided for which may be of particular relevance in this context are measures: (a) necessary to protect public morals; and (b) necessary to protect human, animal or plant life or health. This is discussed further below.

[23] For example, rules of customary international law.

[24] Including rules arising from treaties binding upon (some) Members of the WTO but not on the WTO itself. See section II, above.

[25] See Cho (n 18) 653–55; RL Howse and DH Regan, 'The Product/Process Distinction: An Illusory Basis for Disciplining "Unilateralism" in Trade Policy' (2000) 11 *European Journal of International Law* 249; JH Jackson, 'Comments on *Shrimp-Turtle* and the Product/Process Distinction' (2000) 11 *European Journal of International Law* 303.

[26] Cho (n 18) adds a fourth means by which the DSB might address such issues, judicial restraint; however, this does not strictly involve the accommodation of human rights within WTO rules.

applicable between the parties.[27] In *Korea-Government Procurement*[28] it was held that customary international law applies to the WTO treaties (not just in relation to their interpretation). In *US-Shrimp*[29] it was held that general principles of international law are to be taken into account in the interpretation of WTO law, but *EC-Hormones*[30] subsequently demonstrated that to establish that a principle has become a general principle of international law is not always straightforward.

Rules of international law applicable between the parties are to be taken into consideration and, as seen above, it was established in *US-Shrimp* that provisions of international treaties can inform the interpretation of WTO law. In *EC-Biotech*[31] the panel held that a rule which is not applicable between all the parties to a dispute is not required to be taken into account, but explicitly refrained from taking a position on the situation where a treaty provision is applicable to all the parties to a particular dispute, but not to all WTO members.

Drawing from this, the international law position concerning the applicability of human rights rules with regard to the WTO legal order may be summed up as follows. First, rules of customary international law are binding upon the WTO (including its institutions and members) and should be taken into account in the interpretation and application of WTO law. This is subject to the limitation that if there is a fundamental conflict between the human rights rule and a WTO rule, the WTO panel and the Appellate Body have no jurisdiction to enforce the human rights rule. Thus, while the WTO panel or the Appellate Body may be entitled, or even obliged, to take a human rights rule into account, it never has an obligation to enforce a human rights rule. Second, international treaty provisions relating to human rights can inform the panel and the Appellate Body in the *interpretation* of WTO rules. Third, extrapolating from *EC-Biotech*, international human rights treaty provisions are not applicable and do not need to be taken into account in a dispute involving a party which is not also a party to that treaty. Uncertainty remains as to whether a human rights treaty may be taken into account in relation to a dispute concerning only WTO Members which are also parties to that human rights treaty. There would be two consequences if this were possible: first, that a lack of uniformity could

---

[27] See ch 6 above.

[28] Panel Report, *Korea-Measures Affecting Government Procurement*, WT/DS163/R, adopted 19 June 2000, DSR 2000: VIII 3541, para 7.96.

[29] Appellate Body Report, *US-Import Prohibition of Certain Shrimp and Shrimp Products*, WT/DS58/AB/R adopted 6 November 1998, DSR 1998: VII, 2755.

[30] Report of the Appellate Body, *European Communities-Measures Affecting Meat and Meat Products (Hormones)* (WT/DS48 and WT/DS26) 13 February 1998, DSR 1998:I, 135.

[31] Report of the Panel, *European Communities-Measures Affecting the Approval and Marketing of Biotech Products*, WT/DS291/R, WT/DS292/R, WT/DS293/R, Add 1 to Add 9, and Corr 1, adopted 21 November 2006, DSR 2006: III–VIII.

emerge in the application of WTO rules; and, second, that the panel or the Appellate Body would find itself in the position of interpreting human rights instruments which it has neither expertise in nor a mandate for, as opposed to using it as an aid to interpretation of WTO rules.[32]

However, as has also been touched upon above, those human rights which have developed into *jus cogens* or *erga omnes* obligations bind the WTO, its institutions and its members. As such, they may provide legitimate justification for or even require a restriction of trade. The central question is one of definition and classification: which rights constitute *jus cogens* obligations and which human rights, if any, constitute customary international law? The differential impact of different types of international law rules highlights the significance of accurately identifying and determining the nature of the particular human rights rule at issue. This is also relevant to addressing the criticism that the possible invocation of human rights standards within the WTO context may be exploited for protectionist ends.[33] This concern, particularly among developing states, is similar to that which also arose in relation to the early attempts of the (then) European Economic Community to include the human rights clause in its development cooperation agreement with the ACP states.[34] In that context, the failure by the EU to consistently define the human rights it seeks to protect and promote in its relations with third states has been a weakness.[35] Clarity in the definition of the human rights at issue is crucial to establishing both the legitimacy of their pursuit in this context and also their force.

ii. *The Relevance of Human Rights Considerations in the Determination of 'Likeness' under Article III GATT*

Turning to consideration of the application of Article III GATT (the national treatment rule), as a point of entry for human rights into WTO law, the key question is whether human rights considerations may form the basis of a decision that products are not 'like'. It is accepted that factors such as consumer preference are relevant to the determination of likeness, notwithstanding their cultural relativism and potential susceptibility to protectionism. Such factors may be particularly relevant in relation to human rights—for example, is a carpet produced by child labour 'like' a product produced by adult labour? Consumers may well have views upon

---

[32] Pragmatically, such circumstances would arise only if a party to a human rights treaty complained that its WTO rights were being infringed by a restricting measure imposed by another party to the human rights treaty as a consequence of the first state's violation of its human rights obligations. Politically, it may be rare that a state which is failing to fulfil its human rights obligations will want to publicise that failure in this way.

[33] See discussion below regarding labour standards/rights.

[34] See ch 5.

[35] ibid.

this. It is worth noting that traditionally under the GATT, products could only be distinguished on the basis of the inherent characteristics of the products themselves rather than their processes of production:[36] this would preclude consideration of human rights issues arising in the manufacture of products. The product/process distinction, which was difficult to maintain in relation to environmental protection,[37] becomes even more problematic when extended into the wider non-economic context, as will be seen below with regard to labour rights. It was seen in chapter seven, however, that in more recent case law, notably *US-Shrimp*, the Appellate Body has effectively accepted the potential legitimacy of a production process-related measure. The crucial weakness of the measure in question in that instance was its arbitrary application rather than that it concerned a production or process measure. Thus, it may be possible to distinguish products under Article III on the basis of human rights considerations, depending on the definition of human rights in question.

iii. Invocation of an Exception under Article XX GATT

The first question with regard to the invocation of Article XX is whether human rights indeed come within its scope, since they are not explicitly included within its exhaustive list of exceptions. Is it, however, possible to interpret any of the listed exceptions to include human rights? The appropriateness of an evolutionary approach to interpretation was established with regard to environmental protection.[38] In that context, Article XX(b) concerning measures for the protection of human, animal or plant life or health and Article XX(g) regarding conservation of natural resources have been interpreted to allow measures pursuing environmental protection. There has been some argument that Article XX(a), the exception on grounds of public morality, could encompass the protection of human rights.[39] 'Public morality' is itself inherently a relative issue and is highly susceptible to protectionism. Yet the panel in *China-Publications* recognised that 'the protection of public morals ranks among the most important values or interests pursued by Members as a matter of public policy'.[40] Beyond Article XX(a), the definition and content of the particular

---

[36] There is inevitably considerable concern as to the potential for protectionism in respect of the invocation of process-based considerations. On the product-process distinction, see, inter alia, Howse and Regan (n 25); Jackson (n 25).

[37] See ch 7 above.

[38] Appellate Body Report, *US-Shrimp* (n 29); ch 7.

[39] See further S Charnovitz, 'The Moral Exception in Trade Policy' (1998) 38 *Virginia Journal of International Law* 689; see also NF Diebold, 'The Morals and Order Exceptions in WTO Law: Balancing the Toothless Tiger and the Undermining Mole' (2008) 11 *Journal of International Economic Law* 43.

[40] Panel Report, *China-Measures Affecting Trading Rights and Distribution Services for Certain Publications and Audiovisual Entertainment Products*, WT/DS/363/R 12 August

human right at issue is clearly crucial. Thus, for example, Article XX(b), concerning the protection of human health, could be relevant in relation to particular human rights (whether directly health-related, relating to the availability of health care, or indirectly, as might be the case in relation to health and safety or working hours). The contentious nature of interpreting Article XX(b) in such a way would be compounded where a restricting measure were introduced to protect the human rights of people in another state—that is, outwardly directed protection of human rights—since that would involve the imposition of the regulating state's values upon the other state. Therefore, it may be possible to invoke the Article XX exceptions in some instances depending on the particular right at issue and the location of the interest to be protected.

In order to fully understand the potential and, indeed, limits of these points of entry for human rights into the WTO regime, it is helpful to move the analysis away from the abstract. For a variety of reasons, the relationship between labour rights or standards and WTO law has been a particular focus for debate,[41] making it an ideal case study in the present context. In the course of this case study, we will explore the background relationship between labour rights and the GATT, questions concerning the definition of labour rights, and will subsequently apply labour rights and the GATT to scrutiny in terms of the identified interactions between the GATT and human rights.

B. Case Study: Labour Rights

Uncertainty and questions concerning the relationship between labour standards and trade rules have a long history. A requirement to 'uphold fair labour standards' was included within the Havana Charter[42] and since the 1950s, there have been assertions that Article XXIII GATT gave a ground of action against states which did not eradicate 'unfair labour standards', and that a specific provision on labour standards should be included within the GATT to reflect that contained in the Havana Charter. It has also been argued that as Article XXIX GATT incorporated the provisions of the Charter, these, including Article 7 relating to labour standards, must

---

2009, para 7.817. *China-Periodicals* was the first dispute in which the panel had ruled upon the meaning of 'public morality' in the GATT, and it accepted the definition set out by the panel in respect of Article XIV GATS in the 2004 Panel Report in *United States-Measures Affecting the Cross-Border Supply of Gambling and Betting Services* (*US-Gambling*) WT/DS/285/R 10 November 2004.

[41] HA Cullen, *The Role of International Law in the Elimination of Child Labour* (The Hague, Martinus Nijhoff, 2007) ch 7.
[42] Article 7.

also be upheld under the GATT. In 1978, the ICFTU[43] proposed a GATT social clause 'linking participation in the multilateral trading system to the observance of minimum labour standards'.[44] Each of these proposals raises the question of which standards might or should be protected under such a provision.

It is worth recalling at this point that there is a set of treaty-based 'core' or 'fundamental' labour rights which have international recognition; however, the existence of this body of rights serves to highlight the difficulty in identifying when a right becomes a norm, part of customary international law or a general principle of international law. There are therefore questions regarding the status of these rights which are relevant to their weight within the WTO legal order. The potential for protectionist abuse in the invocation of labour standards is also evident.

i. The Singapore Ministerial Declaration

By 1996, the debate had shifted from *whether* labour standards should be considered to *where* the appropriate forum is for their consideration. It was concluded by the Ministerial Conference in Singapore that despite 'commitment to the observance of internationally recognised core labour standards', the WTO was not the appropriate forum for the protection of these interests.[45] There was a concern, particularly among developing states, that the introduction of these rights into the trade regime could be exploited for protectionist ends. It was agreed that the ILO was the appropriate forum and that the Members of the WTO 'support its work in promoting them'.[46] The approach of the developing states was—and ultimately the current position of the WTO is—that the WTO is not the appropriate forum for the definition and establishment of labour standards. In an equally significant development, there appears to have been a shift in the approach to the issue of 'labour standards', with the focus now on the issue of 'labour (or workers') rights'.

However, this was not the end of the matter: the Chairman of the Conference, Mr Yeo Cheow Tong, stated in his concluding remarks to the Conference that there was nothing in the text to suggest that the WTO could acquire the competence to develop the relationship between labour standards and trade. However, the US Acting Trade Representative,

---

[43] International Confederation of Free Trade Unions.
[44] See F Weiss, 'Internationally Recognized Labour Standards and Trade' (1996) 1 *Issues of European Integration* 162, 169–70.
[45] World Trade Organization, Singapore Ministerial Declaration, WT/MIN(96)/DEC/W, 13 December 1996, para 4.
[46] ibid; progress on this issue in the ILO will be considered below.

Charlene Barshevsky, dismissed this as simply being Yeo Cheow Tong's interpretation of the text and indicated that the declaration does not preclude further consideration of this issue.[47] More generally, questions continued regarding the impact of this statement upon the future of the debate between trade and human rights.

The fundamental issue concerns the extent to which trade liberalisation (the central objective of the WTO) may (or should) be restricted to promote (or enforce) the protection of labour standards. The WTO Members in 1996 'renew[ed] our commitment to the observance of internationally recognized core labour standards' and 'affirmed' their support for the ILO's work in promoting them. This raises the following question: what are the 'internationally recognised core labour standards' and, if they are identifiable, what is their status—can they constitute universal fundamental rights? This raises two further issues: what is the nature of the 'commitment to the observance' of core labour standards and what is the nature of the 'support' for the ILO's work? Taking these points in reverse order, first, with regard to the nature of the support for the ILO's work, the members subsequently clarified that they:

> [R]eject the use of labour standards for protectionist purposes, and agree that the comparative advantage of countries, particularly low-wage developing countries, must in no way be put into question. In this regard, we note that the WTO and ILO Secretariats will continue their existing collaboration.[48]

'In this regard' may thus suggest that WTO/ILO collaboration would continue only for this purpose (combating protectionism). For the rest, will the WTO support the ILO's work, but not collaborate with it? What practical implication could there be of such a distinction? Indeed, what is intended by 'support'? In 'supporting the ILO's work', were the WTO Members indicating that they adhere to the ILO standards? Are they now bound by these standards? If not, what is the value of the Ministerial declaration? Some of these questions were answered by the then Director-General (Ruggiero), who declared shortly afterwards that the language of the declaration only permits the exchange of information between the WTO and the ILO on matters such as the compatibility of ILO conventions with international trade rules.[49] This would suggest that there is relatively little legal value in the declaration and the support described is weak.

---

[47] See V Leary, 'The WTO and the Social Clause: Post Singapore' (997) 1 *European Journal of International Law* 118.

[48] World Trade Organization (n 45). The Singapore Ministerial Declaration was reiterated in the Doha Ministerial Declaration in 2001.

[49] 'Ruggiero Says Declaration Only Allows Information Swaps with ILO', www.askSam. cam, cited in S Charnowitz, 'Trade, Employment and Labour Standards: The OECD Study and Recent Developments in the Trade and Labour Standards Debate' (1997) 11 *Temple International and Comparative Law Journal* 131.

Second, concerning the WTO's commitment to the 'observance of internationally recognized core labour standards', it is unclear whether or not this indicates that the WTO and its members are bound by internationally recognised labour standards, nor is it clear which 'core standards' are intended here. At the very least, if the WTO is committed to the observance of the standards, it would be inconsistent to read the GATT to restrict compliance with, or observance of, these standards, and therefore it may be argued that internationally recognised labour rights may constitute fundamental principles underlying WTO rules. In light of this, it is timely to explore which core standards the WTO is 'committed to the observance of', with a view to considering the effect the Declaration might have.

ii. Defining Labour Rights

Notwithstanding the ambiguity surrounding the Declaration, it does recognise the existence of a set of 'core' labour standards. It is therefore pertinent to explore what these 'core standards' are, the nature of their relationship with labour rights, and whether any of these could be deemed to be customary international law. Notably, the Ministerial Declaration predates both the ILO 'core standards' and the OECD standards.

iii. Unpacking the Core Standards

Under the auspices of the ILO, there has been a proliferation of 'labour standards' carrying varying weights and demanding different degrees of priority. Some of these are referred to as 'standards' and others as 'rights'. This distinction has been the subject of not insignificant academic comment[50] and is also reflected in the ILO's own work.[51] It is worth examining this distinction, not least in the light of the persuasive force of rights.

iv. 'Labour Standards' to 'Labour Rights': Merely a Rhetorical Shift?

Whether labour issues are badged as rights or standards, the critical issue is one of substance. Are there any rights or standards which represent customary international law, obligations *erga omnes* or (specifically) *jus cogens* obligations and, if so, can these bind the WTO and its Members without any need for specific exception within the WTO Agreements? Alternatively,

---

[50] See, inter alia, A Blackett, 'Whither Social Clause? Human Rights, Trade Theory and Treaty Interpretation' (1999) 31 *Columbia Human Rights Law Review* 1; and B Langille, 'Eight Ways to Think About International Labour Standards' (1997) 4 *Journal of World Trade* 27.
[51] See below.

do any fall within the scope of the Article XX exceptions? To answer this question, it is of course necessary to establish what it is that is being considered. Leary observes that 'discussions concerning a social clause are often confused and the terminology employed is often unclear'.[52] Such lack of clarity is manifested in the shift between 'standards' and 'rights'. Leary herself goes on to use the terms 'social clauses', 'internationally recognized workers' rights' and 'minimum labour standards' interchangeably, stating that 'these terms concern basically the same issues'.[53] In a later section, it is the definition of 'internationally recognized labour standards' which Leary explores. To distinguish between these terms with greater precision may permit some clarification as to what is at issue and even contribute to the realisation of the desired protection in relation to certain categories, perhaps utilising the ILO development of 'fundamental' rights.[54]

v. Labour Rights as Human Rights?

In order to refine our understanding of which 'standards' or 'rights' are being sought to be protected at different levels and how these may be distinguished, it is useful to look first at the different ways in which labour standards have been viewed. It is notable that generally there is (and traditionally has been) very little consideration of *labour rights* by human rights activists or writers; Amnesty International has been the only 'human rights' organisation to consistently attend the ILO conference. This reflects and reinforces the assumption that 'labour standards' are, essentially, not a human or fundamental rights issue.[55] On the other hand, certain basic labour rights are expressed in the Universal Declaration of Human Rights as well as in the International Convention on Civil and Political Rights (ICCPR)[56] and the International Convention on Economic, Social and Civil Rights (ICESCR).[57]

Why is there so little crossover between labour rights and human rights? One practical consideration concerns resources: setting aside the unique

---

[52] V Leary, 'Workers' Rights and International Trade: The Social Clause (GATT, ILO NAFTA, US Laws)' in J Bhagwati and R Hudec (eds), *Fair Trade and Harmonization Volume 2, Legal Analysis* (Cambridge, MA, MIT Press, 1996) 178.

[53] ibid 179.

[54] Declaration on Fundamental Principles and Rights at Work, June 1998, www.ilo.org.

[55] See V Leary, 'The Paradox of Workers' Rights as Human Rights' in LA Compa and SF Diamond (eds), *Human rights, Labor Rights, and International Trade* (Philadelphia, PA, University of Pennsylvania Press, 1996). This approach is not inconsistent with the EU approach to human rights in its trade agreements. As has been seen above (ch 5), there is a similar (and equally problematic) lack of definition in that context, although it appears to be the rights relating to physical integrity, 'fundamental' human rights, which the EU seeks to protect universally in its external relations, rather than social and economic rights, which receive much more patchy consideration.

[56] ICCPR Arts 8 and 22.

[57] ECESCR Arts 6–8.

contribution of the ILO and the international trade union movement, human rights organisations tend to focus on the states with the most 'serious' human rights violations; labour standards tend to be pursued by trade unions operating in more 'localised' contexts. One compelling pragmatic reason for the lack of crossover is the understandable concentration in organisations of limited resources on eliminating violations of a physical nature, such as torture and genocide. Eradicating the most extreme human rights violations is recognised as a necessary pre-requisite to the protection of social and economic rights. However, practical constraints such as these do not affect states working together as an international community to the same extent. Yet, even for states, an enduring restraint arises from the lack of certainty concerning the extent to which international law will permit the international community to pursue 'social and economic rights' in other states. There is a lack of certainty regarding the extent to which the protection of such rights is an exception to the principle of non-intervention in a sovereign state. There is thus a degree of circularity in the questions to be addressed in the developing protection of different 'classes' of rights. Once again, it is also evident that in order to pursue the protection of these interests with any degree of binding force, international consensus as to their status is required.

It is relevant to consider whether there is or might be any logic in the different terminology used to label labour standards and rights which might be informative regarding their status. Clarification of the terminology used requires identification and recognition of different classes of rights, including those which have universal acceptance. Any such universally accepted rights may be distinguished from other labour issues. However, such rights, once identified as such, would potentially be binding. According to Blackett, human 'rights' suggests adherence to specific set of principles, whereas 'standards' appear too dictatorial. Thus:

> [T]he language of human rights enables proposals to be crafted in terms of the convergence between the principles identified in general international human rights norms and the more detailed and arguably more authoritative expressions of those rights in the selected ILO Conventions.[58]

On the other hand, Blackwell describes 'worker rights' as 'deontological and normatively more compelling than labour standards'.[59] Labour rights, if they are universally accepted, *may* be capable of defeating free trade. The indications at present, however, are that labour standards, such as minimum

---

[58] Blackett (n 50) 27–28.
[59] Blackwell, R, contribution to *Session One: Globalization, Development and Human Rights: Clarifying the Terms of the Debate*, in Business and Human Rights: An Interdisciplinary Discussion Held at Harvard Law School in December 1997. Published (1999) by the Harvard Law School Human Rights Program. Available online at http://hrp.law.harvard.edu/wp-content/uploads/2013/08/BusinessandHumanRights.pdf at 15.

wages, will not be able to defeat liberal trade.[60] Fields rejected the ILO rights because they are not respected, but suggested that the prohibition on slave labour, the prohibition on unsafe working conditions (without full information!), the prohibition on children working long hours (where family circumstances permit) and the right to freedom of association may be capable of defeating trade.[61] This is indeed a minimalist approach which offers little in the way of absolute protection: it is on the basis of this very limitation that Fields suggests it may be acceptable. Yet it would be of relatively little value, and the danger is that if such an approach were adopted it could, in providing a floor, reduce the possibility of acceptance of more protective rights in the future.

It may be possible to discern some practical implications of the distinction between 'rights' and 'standards' if the EU's experience in relation to human rights and environmental protection is recalled. While there is strict conditionality in relation to human rights protection in the EU's agreements with third states, there is no such conditionality in relation to environmental protection.[62] As has been seen, provision in relation to the environment tends to extend towards a commitment to seek to achieve specific *standards*. This is an aspirational rather than an absolute commitment. This may imply that whereas rights are more concrete, even if not absolute, standards are more malleable. Yet this is too simplistic. The distinction in terms of the form of commitment likely reflects only the nature of the subject matter: it is the substance which gives rise to classification as a 'right' or 'standard', and which has a consequent effect upon universality or enforceability. Merely re-designating a particular 'standard' as a 'right' does not create any inherent obligation to uphold that 'right', unless there has been a shift in global perceptions to reflect the shift in designation. Blackwell is very clear in his assessment of 'rights':

> [W]orker rights are human rights norms that govern the way in which labour is treated internationally, regardless of a country's level of development. They include individual rights like freedom of opinion and freedom of expression, as well as collective rights like freedom of association, and freedom to organize. Poverty is no excuse for slavery...

Thus, it is the *substance* of the right that determines its status rather than any suggestion that *classification* as a 'right' brings an obligation. However, if such substantive distinction could be carried over into the terminology, that could be the basis for a practical distinction regarding the status of labour rights and labour standards. A practical distinction such as this

---

[60] See also Langille (n 50).

[61] GS Fields, 'International Labour Standards and Economic Interdependence' (1996) 49 *Industrial and Labor Relations Review* 571, 572. Cited in Blackett (n 50) 32.

[62] See ch 5 above.

could facilitate the identification of which if any such interests should constitute exceptions to the WTO rules.

Blackwell's very straightforward approach[63] is generally accepted by the 'labour movement'.[64] The difficulty is in carrying this use of terminology outside that context, into the wider human rights and corporate context, and endowing it with legal effect. One attraction of the approach is that it feeds readily into the distinction subsequently established within the ILO context by the adoption of the ILO fundamental rights. It is of course upon the ILO that the WTO has helpfully endowed all responsibility in this field. There is thus a workable distinction which has been drawn between such labour rights and other labour standards. This distinction is not merely semantic, but has tangible implications in the way in which a balance may be sought between the protection of these rights and the interests of free trade, as compared with the balance that may be held between the enforcement of labour standards and free trade. As Blackwell further observes, once the 'workers' rights' are in place, the workers have some strength (as a body) with which to pursue, for themselves, labour standards which may be appropriate to their economic context. Such standards are not appropriate for uniform international determination. It seems eminently sensible that compliance with specific labour standards should not be a matter to provide a general exception to WTO rules: it would be inappropriate to attempt, for example, to impose a specific minimum wage universally.

Thus, it has been seen that before it is possible to evaluate the balance to be drawn between protection of labour rights and operation of the WTO rules, it is first necessary to establish what substantive rights are in issue. There has been a great deal of inconsistency in the terminology in this field and there is no doubt that the discourse of rights has greater persuasive force than that of standards. Yet it has also been shown that it is possible to draw a workable distinction between labour standards and labour rights, which adds clarity and can assist in the identification of how the balance should be drawn between the interest at stake and the WTO rules.

vi. Testing the Interaction between Human Rights and the WTO Rules with Reference to Labour Rights

Regardless of the semantics or terminology applied, the key issue to which attention now turns concerns the interaction between identified labour rights (or standards) and WTO rules. In the first section of this chapter,

---

[63] Blackwell (n 59).

[64] It is also accepted by the OECD and the ILO (as agreed at the World Social Summit in Copenhagen, March 1995) and is consistent with broader human rights instruments, including the UN Charter, the UDHR and the Covenants; see Langille (n 50). On the OECD study, see Charnovitz (n 49).

272 *Human Rights Protection and WTO Law*

three points of interaction between human rights and WTO law were identified: it is time now to examine the status of labour rights in respect of each of these. Thus, do any labour rights or standards constitute binding obligations of international law? Can they constitute a reason by which to distinguish products? Or is it possible to bring any of these rights (or standards) under the Article XX exceptions.

a. Labour Rights as Customary International Law?

If any labour rights constitute binding obligations of international law, the WTO and its Members are bound by those and they would have to be taken into account in the interpretation and application of WTO law (although they would not be enforceable by the panel or the Appellate Body). The ILO Declaration of Fundamental Principles and Rights at Work provides a list of 'core' labour rights, reflecting those agreed at the World Social Summit in Copenhagen in 1995.[65] This identifies four core fundamental rights: freedom of association and the effective recognition of the right to collective bargaining; the elimination of all forms of forced or compulsory labour; the effective abolition of child labour; and the elimination of discrimination in respect of employment and occupation.[66] These generally focus upon the 'political' labour rights rather than an individual's economic rights (which might include, for example, a minimum wage).[67] Significantly, they comprise a core of very basic, potentially universal human rights, which arguably could be defended in any country, with any state of development, and the denial of which could ask serious questions of any state at any stage of development.[68] However, even this development has had its universality questioned and has been described as 'a reasonable and essential set of rights from a Western point of view [although] the existence of some consensus does not mean complete consensus nor the ability and willingness to comply'.[69] The declaration of these rights as core by the ILO

---

[65] 86th Session, Geneva, June 1998, www.ilo.org/public/english/standards/decl/declaration/text/tindex.htm.

[66] Article 2 Declaration of Fundamental Principles and Rights at Work.

[67] The ILO Governing Body has identified eight ILO Conventions as 'fundamental to the rights of human beings at work, irrespective of levels of development of individual member states'. These fall into four categories—freedom of association—Freedom of Association and Protection of the Right to Organize Convention, 1948 (No 87), Right to Organize and Collective Bargaining Convention, 1949 (No 98); abolition of forced labour—Forced Labour Convention, 1930 (No 29), Abolition of Forced Labour Convention, 1957 (No 105); equality—Discrimination (Employment and Occupation) Convention, 1958 (No 111), Equal Remuneration Convention, 1951 (No. 100); Elimination of Child Labour—Minimum Age Convention, 1973 (No 138), Worst Forms of Child Labour Convention, 1999 (No 182). See www.ilo.org.

[68] Compliance with these Conventions forms part of the basis for grant of additional trade preferences under the EU's GSP+ scheme [2008] OJ L334/90. See further W Zhou and L Cuyvers, 'Linking International Trade and Labor Standards: The Effectiveness of Sanctions under the European Union's GSP' (2011) 45 *Journal of World Trade* 63.

[69] E Cappuyns, 'Linking Labour Standards and Trade Sanctions: An Analysis of Their Current Relationship' (1998) 36 *Columbia Journal of Transnational Law* 659, 664.

may, however, indicate their more universal rather than purely Western acceptance, given that they are now accepted and recognised as core by over 170 ILO Member States. The ILO has also been identified by the WTO as the competent body. Yet, one major hurdle remains: the ILO has neither any means of enforcement of these rights by its members, nor any sanction that may be applied in the face of their breach.

Despite the potential universality of the rights contained within them, the ILO core conventions do not comprise customary international law: it is stated in the annex to the Declaration that it is 'of a purely promotional nature'.[70] Alston has therefore observed that despite the 'intentional ambiguity' concerning the status of these rights and notwithstanding that certain parties and ILO officials would be happy if these rights were to become customary international law (CIL), this has not yet occurred.[71] While states that have ratified the Conventions are bound by them, as noted above, the ILO has no means by which to enforce compliance. The most that can be said is perhaps that the Conventions constitute soft law; therefore, they are not per se binding upon the WTO or its institutions. On the other hand, those rights which are contained within the UDHR, the ICCPR and the ICESCR may, as customary international law, be binding upon the WTO and its institutions. As treaty law, it might be possible to refer to any of these rights (including those contained in the ILO Conventions) to inform the interpretation to be applied to the WTO covered agreements, including perhaps Article XX.[72] But, consistent with the discussion above, any move by the panel or the Appellate Body to interpret these rights would be controversial due to its lack of relevant expertise, as well as the absence of a mandate to do so. Faced with a fundamental conflict between WTO rules and labour rights, the panel and the Appellate Body are limited to application of the rules contained within the covered agreements and therefore would not be able to compel any states to enforce the fundamental rights, or to take action against the breach of fundamental rights, unless they were drawn from customary international law. Given the limited extent of labour rights which might form the basis of such action, this is not a route that could have great substantive effect.

b. Likeness

The second question is whether failure to comply with labour rights could constitute a reason to distinguish products.[73] Both the outward direction of such regulation and the possibility of what could be perceived as protectionist

---

[70] See further Cullen (n 41).

[71] P Alston, "Resisting the Merger and Acquisition of Human Rights by Trade Law: A Reply to Petersmann" *European Journal of International Law* 13 (2002) 815–844 at 830.

[72] AB report in *United States-Import Prohibition of Certain Shrimp and Shrimp Products*, AB-1998-4 WT/DS58/R (98-0000), 12 October 1998, (1998) 38 *International Legal Materials* 121.

[73] See text accompanying n 25.

exploitation of the labour standards would render such distinction controversial. This would remain the case even if it were based on rights contained within the ILO Core Conventions due to their lack of universal binding effect (although the question may be raised as to what extent such a measure could easily be dismissed as protectionist). Therefore, it appears that notwithstanding the close relationship between labour rights and trade liberalisation, and the very tangible impact which non-compliance with internationally recognised labour right might have upon the competitiveness of products, it is unlikely that Article III would have significant traction in this particular instance unless the distinction between labour standards and labour rights offered above were applied. In that case, it might be possible to determine that products produced in compliance with labour rights are not like those in the production of which labour rights were abused.

c. Labour Rights and the GATT General Exceptions (Article XX)

The third question is whether it is possible to invoke Article XX for the protection of labour rights. While specific labour rights might come within the scope of the public morality or public health exceptions, any invocation to protect the rights of workers in another state would be problematic unless the distinction between labour rights and labour standards suggested above were applied. That distinction offers a non-relative baseline of protection for a given category of fundamental rights.[74] It would be difficult to argue that the sale of a carpet, produced by child labour in another state, is damaging to the public morality of the importing state, as it is the production method (and not the product itself) which raises questions of morality. Thus, it is the background knowledge concerning the production which is potentially damaging rather than the product itself.[75] This may readily be contrasted with a restriction on the import and sale of pornography or even blow-up dolls,[76] where it is the product itself which is allegedly damaging to public morals within the importing state. This raises the same product/process distinction that has been drawn in relation to environmental objections, and it arises in this context for similar reasons. To seek to protect public morality in the exporting state engages the question of extra-jurisdictional competence. In the context of environmental protection, states make choices as to the standard of protection they wish to enjoy and the balance to be drawn between environmental and other interests. These differ from state to state. Similarly, states make judgments as to what is morally acceptable

---

[74] See Cullen (n 41).

[75] The measure may be introduced in order to protect the 'morals' of the exporting state or of the producers within the exporting state. Whether a convincing 'morality' argument may be made on such grounds is arguable, however, and will be dependent largely upon whether there is an international core of 'morality' which can be related to.

[76] For which the exception of public morality was invoked before the Court of Justice in Case 121/85 *Conegate Ltd. v Commissioners of Customs and Excise* [1986] ECR 1007.

in their particular society, and these will differ not just from state to state, but also within states over even relatively short periods of time.[77] Thus, morality is also a relative issue. Arguably, in fact, the product/process distinction is more acceptable in relation to labour standards or human rights issues than environmental issues, as the effects of the choices that a state makes in this field are generally restricted to within the state, whereas the effects of environmental choices spread beyond the borders of the acting state.[78] Again, however, if the distinction between labour standards and labour rights suggested above were applied, this would offer a non-relative baseline which could form the basis of an Article XX justification and quite possibly also the basis of a determination that products are or are not like.

The relative nature of public morality makes it difficult to justify the imposition of import restrictions on the basis of the manner in which a product has been made, particularly where the product itself poses no threat to morality. Thus, prima facie, it is difficult to include a restriction enacted to protect certain labour standards within the general exception of 'public morality'. There is also, as Charnovitz observes, a high potential for protectionist abuse in the characterisation of a measure as a 'moral' issue. Charnovitz, however, concludes from an analysis of the history behind the 'public morality' clause that it could, indeed, potentially be used in this way. He concedes that there would be considerable pressure upon the WTO, were any dispute to arise concerning a public morality exception, to rule out any 'outwardly directed'[79] protection of public morality, but holds that given the historical application of such clauses, 'outward protection' would be justifiable.[80] The difficulty in relation to import bans to protect the population of the exporting country arises if comparison is made to the cases involving environmental exceptions,[81] where the import ban could be viewed as being intended to change the policy of the exporting state, thus interfering with sovereignty. The evolutionary approach by which the WTO panel shifted from its restrictive approach to the consideration of Multilateral Environmental Agreements in *Tuna Dolphin*[82] to its wider interpretative approach in *Shrimp-Turtle*[83] must, however, be relevant

---

[77] A UK example can be seen in the liberalisation in laws concerning the 'age of consent' in the latter half of the twentieth century.

[78] The exception to this arises in relation to gross violations of human rights, which can impact upon the stability of a region, and thus have effects outwith the state committing the abuse.

[79] Protection directed at those outside the acting state, for example, the labour force in the exporting state.

[80] Charnovitz (n 39).

[81] Panel Report, *United States-Restrictions on Imports of Tuna*, BISD 40S/155 (DS21/R) (1991) 30 ILM 1594.

[82] ibid.

[83] Panel Report, *United States-Import Prohibition of Certain Shrimp and Shrimp Products*, WT/DS58/R (98-1710), 15 May 1998; Appellate Body Report AB-1998-4 WT/DS58/R

here. In *Shrimp-Turtle*, the panel indicated that extra-jurisdictional action *may* be permissible where it is applied in compliance with the Article XX chapeau; that is, where the measure is applied in a manner that is not indiscriminate or arbitrary, it may be permissible, even where its effects would be extra-jurisdictional. If this development in the context of environmental protection also applies to human rights protection, it is possible that fundamental rights, including labour rights, may fall under the Article XX(a) (public morality) general exception to the GATT, even where the measure is intended to change practice in another state. Yet the Appellate Body was careful to refer to the nexus established between the US and the resource conserved—the US measure may have been intended to change behaviour in other states, but it was with regard to conservation of a shared resource. Such a nexus would be more difficult to establish in relation to public morality. Where the 'morality' exception is on strongest ground in relation to 'outward', or 'extra-territorial', protection of morals is where the morals to be protected reflect universally accepted norms or, better still, *jus cogens* obligations.[84]

In view of its history, Charnowitz concludes that the 'public morality' clause would appear to cover, inter alia, 'slavery, weapons, narcotics, liquor, pornography, compulsory labour and animal welfare'.[85] The question of whose morality may be protected would be considered under the issue of 'necessity'. In Charnovitz's view, 'import measures to safeguard the morals of the domestic population would probably receive the lightest scrutiny'. Export bans to protect a foreign population would probably also be accepted where the domestic population was similarly protected, but are less likely to be successful where there is no equivalent domestic protection. Howse, like Charnowitz, also looks explicitly to 'public morality' to justify trade measures to address 'labour practices which violate human rights',[86] since the evolution of human rights forms 'a core element of public morality' and consequently 'the concept of public morals extends to include disapprobation of labour practices that violate universal human rights'.

On this basis, a violation of labour standards which constituted a violation of human rights may be more securely acted against on the basis of violation of customary international law. However, this would be premised upon a determination that the right at issue constituted customary international law, which is by no means a given. This would be a stronger argument, since rather than invoking a general exception to the GATT,

(98-0000), 12 October 1998, (1998) 38 ILM 121, both available online at www.wto.org.

[84] It appears, however, that there may be a stronger case for such interests, according to which public morality itself may tie into the second level of argument (concerning human rights and the WTO), which will be returned to below.

[85] Charnovitz (n 39) 729–30.

[86] R Howse, 'The World Trade Organization and the Protection of Workers' Rights' (1999) 3 *Journal of Small and Emerging Business Law* 131.

the basis of action would be the rules of international law, which bind the WTO and its members. Human rights thus constitute the underlying law which free trade may not infringe rather than forming the exception to the GATT rules. However, as noted above, establishing that any labour rights comprise customary international law is far from straightforward.

It has been suggested that Article XX(e)[87] indicates that the WTO does not preclude 'outwardly directed' measures to protect foreign nationals in other states. This could suggest that outwardly directed measures may be acceptable in relation to the other exceptions, as they are not inherently precluded in the WTO. However, consideration of the purpose of Article XX(e) weakens this argument as this provision was included on strictly economic, competitive grounds, and therefore was not originally focused upon outwardly directed measures. It would require an evolutionary rather than purposive approach to the interpretation of Article XX(e) to permit an exception, for example, in relation to products of forced labour (as one of the core rights). The argument could also be made that as provision is expressly made for exception in relation to the products of 'prison labour', any other labour rights to be excepted would have been explicitly mentioned. This argument may gain force in light of the fact that labour rights were referred to in the Havana Charter, but were not included in the GATT/WTO. Alternatively, it is possible that the Article XXIX incorporation of the provisions of the Havana Charter protects labour issues without the need for an explicit public policy exception.

It has also been proposed that the explicit inclusion of an exception for the products of prison labour (a provision relating expressly to process methods) implies that public morality cannot be interpreted to include process methods, since if it could, the prison labour exception would be superfluous. (An extension of this argument was made to support the argument that the other exceptions should explicitly not be interpreted to include process measures, or indeed wide social measures; however, it has been seen in *US-Shrimp* that it may be possible to invoke Article XX in support of process measures.)[88] Yet again, however, since the prison labour exception was included on competitive grounds rather than as an issue of public morality, it is difficult to accept that any conclusions should be drawn about the scope of the public morality exception from the mere existence of the prison labour exception. It appears that, notwithstanding doubts as to its scope, the 'public morality' exception would be the most

---

[87] The exception relating to products of prison labour.
[88] See C McCrudden, 'International Economic Law and the Pursuit of Human Rights: A Framework for Discussion of the Legality of "Selective Purchasing" Laws under the WTO Government Procurement Agreement' (1999) 2 *Journal of International Economic Law* 3; CT Fedderson, 'Focusing on Substantive Law in International Economic Relations: The Public Morals of GATT's Article XX(a) and "Conventional" Rules of Interpretation' (1998) 7 *Minnesota Journal of Global Trade* 75.

likely justification for restriction on the basis of labour rights. There are, however, problems with its application, especially in relation to whether it may be used to protect the labour rights of workers in another state or engaged in the production of a morally neutral end product.[89]

Thus it is difficult to see how even labour rights, which are closely connected to trade, to which the WTO has made a commitment, and regarding which there is an internationally recognised body of core law, might do more than inform the interpretation of WTO law in a particular dispute. This is without prejudice to the fact that the DSB has, so far, reserved its position on any entitlement to refer to international treaty provisions by which all parties to a particular dispute (but not all WTO Members) are bound. In conclusion, it appears that the 'general exceptions' are not particularly useful in relation to finding an appropriate balance between the protection of human rights (or labour standards) and trade liberalisation.

III. CONTRASTING APPROACHES: THE EU AND WTO APPROACHES COMPARED

In view of the conclusions above regarding the EU experience, given that human rights are now embedded in the EU legal order (notwithstanding its economic origins) and the WTO is frequently criticised for its impact upon national (human rights) regulation, it is interesting to transpose the facts of *Schmidberger* and *Omega*[90] to the WTO context, with a view to exploring the extent to which the WTO legal order would be capable of handling similar issues.

Schmidberger concerned a restriction on free movement of goods caused by an environmental demonstration (an exercise of the rights of freedom of expression and freedom of assembly) which closed a major trans-European route for 30 hours.[91] The broader relevance of *Schmidberger* arises from the fact that the human rights at issue in this case are rights which apply

---

[89] It is worth recalling that in *Asbestos*, it was indicated that consumer differentiation of products, eg, on their health effects, may distinguish otherwise like products. If consumer preferences regarding labour standards could also be viewed in this way, it is possible that regulation against products made from child labour may not breach national treatment (if consistently applied). In such a case there may be no breach of GATT and recourse to Article XX would not be necessary. However, in *Asbestos*, the public health concerns were supported by international standards, and it is possible that without this support, consumer preferences may not be held to be relevant. Panel Report European Communities, *Measures Affecting Asbestos and Asbestos Containing Products* WT/DS/135/R, 18 September 2000; Appellate Body Report WT/DS/135/AB/R, 12 March 2001.

[90] Case C-112/00 *Schmidberger v Austria* [2003] ECR I-5659; Case C-36/02 *Omega Spielhallen und Automatenaufstellungs-GmbH v Oberbürgermeisterin der Bundesstadt Bonn* [2004] ECR 614, whch are both discussed in ch 3.

[91] It is established EU law that a failure to act to prevent a restriction can constitute a precluded state measure, which is a violation of Article 34 TFEU; Case C-265/95 *Commission v France* [1997] ECR I-6959.

beyond the EU context. They are found in many international human rights instruments;[92] therefore, the issues arising in this case could arise outside the EU.[93]

As *Schmidberger* concerned a restriction on free movement of goods, it would fall within the scope of the GATT. Within the context of the GATT, the central question would be whether the state's failure (to prevent the restriction on trade in goods) constituted a violation of either Article XI (the prohibition of quantitative restrictions on imports) or Article III (the requirement of national treatment). The restriction on movement was internal and could not come within the scope of Article XI. Turning to Article III, the question is whether there is a 'law, regulation or requirement' which accords less favourable treatment to imported products. In view of the fact that generally the GATT does not apply where there is no element of mandatory government action, albeit that GATT norms may extend to indirect mandatory action,[94] it is unlikely that there would be a 'law, regulation or requirement'. Even if the state's failure to prevent the restriction could constitute a 'law, regulation or requirement', there would be a violation only if imported products are treated less favourably, which was not the case in this instance. Therefore, it appears there would be no breach of GATT rules. As such, the trade restriction posed by the particular exercise of human rights would not be questioned in the WTO context.

Omega[95] primarily concerned services and so would hypothetically come within the ambit of the GATS (assuming that the relevant activities were covered by the schedule of the restricting state). Germany had invoked the (German Constitutional) right to human dignity in order to ban Omega from 'facilitating or allowing in its ... establishment games with the object of firing on human targets ... thereby, "playing at killing" people'.[96] Human dignity and human rights fall within the public policy derogation (from freedom of provision of services) provided for in Article 46 EC. This case invites comparison with the GATS *Internet Gambling*[97] dispute, in which public morality was invoked under Article XIV to justify a restriction to the provision of gambling services. The Appellate Body ruled that the very existence of a restriction banning a particular type of provision of services constituted a restriction under Article XVI: 2(a) (a numerical quota), since

---

[92] See, inter alia, Articles 10–11 ECHR, Article 21 UDHR and Article 21 ICCPR.

[93] How the situation would be considered under WTO law will be examined below.

[94] Such as 'informal guidance' by governments to industry, regarding which they may implicitly face various kinds of informal sanctions for failure to comply. See M Trebilcock, R Howse and A Eliason, *The Regulation of International Trade* (4th edn) (London, Routledge, 2012).

[95] *Omega* (n 90).

[96] ibid [5].

[97] *US-Measures Affecting the Cross-border Supply of Gambling and Betting Services*, DS285, Report of the Panel, 10 November 2004, Report of the Appellate Body, adopted 20 April 2005.

it had the effect of restricting supply.[98] The measure thus required justification by reference to Article XIV GATS, including the chapeau requirement precluding arbitrary or unjustifiable discrimination.[99]

Applying this to *Omega*, the key issue under the GATS would have been the existence of a 'form of numerical quota' which, in view of the total ban, would have been present. The next question would be whether the measure would come within the Article XIV exception on the grounds of public morality. Again arguing by analogy, it is likely that the maintenance of human dignity, based upon constitutional rights and human rights, would have been a legitimate exercise of the public morality exception. Finally, the measure would be tested for compliance with the chapeau,[100] which it should satisfy as the restriction also applied to domestic service suppliers.

The WTO has been criticised for unduly restricting the ability of Member States to protect human rights, and the EU has been suggested by some as a model for the integration of human rights and economic liberalisation. However, application of WTO law to the facts of the two seminal EU cases on this issue indicates that regarding the first, there would be no GATT issue arising (and thus no restriction on the Member State's ability to exercise its regulatory autonomy in this context). Regarding the second, the WTO system would likely accommodate fundamental rights through the application of the GATS Article XIV public morality exception. The application of the Article XX GATT and Article XIV GATS exceptions requires what both the panel and the Appellate Body have explicitly characterised as a balancing approach.[101] This 'balancing' approach is, on paper, similar to the EU's 'proportionality'-based approach, which can, as seen above, be characterised as constituting an applied sustainable development-based approach.[102]

---

[98] AB Report, ibid, at paras 221–65 (but note that this is limited to contexts in which a commitment to liberalise has been inscribed in the Schedule of Specific Commitments). The Appellate Body in this ruling caused concern regarding the extent to which the GATS could restrain national regulatory choices. See J Pauwelyn, 'Rien Ne Va Plus? Distinguishing Domestic Regulation from Market Access in GATT and GATS,' (2005) 4 *World Trade Review* 131; and J Pauwelyn, 'WTO Softens Earlier Condemnation of U.S. Ban on Internet Gambling, but Confirms Broad Reach into Sensitive Domestic Regulation', *ASIL Insight*, www.asil.org/insights/2005/04/insights050412.html; E Reid, 'Regulatory Autonomy in the EU and WTO: Defining and Defending its Limits' (2010) 44(4) *Journal of World Trade* 877.

[99] See ch 6 above.

[100] The chapeau to Article XIV GATS applies in the same way as the chapeau to Article XX GATT; see above.

[101] Although this characterisation has been the subject of some criticism. See, inter alia, DH Regan, 'The Meaning of "Necessary" in GATT Article XX and GATS Article XIV: The Myth of Cost–Benefit Balancing' (2007) 6 *World Trade Review* 347.

[102] There is, however, little evidence of the Appellate Body in fact engaging in a balancing exercise; see ch 7 above.

IV. CONCLUSIONS

It is beyond doubt that the fragmentation of international law contributes to tension in the pursuit of different objectives. The relationship between WTO rules and human rights protection has been perceived to be particularly problematic, yet there is some reason to question this perception. In any manifestation, the resolution of tension between different objectives of different bodies of international law requires consensus among those affected; without consensus, questions of legitimacy will arise.

There is some evidence of the emergence of consensus that human rights should be engaged with in the WTO legal order. This has been seen in the very objectives of economic liberalisation and of the WTO itself (as expressed in the Preamble). Recognition of sustainable development as an objective indicates acceptance of the integrated nature of economic and social (and human rights) development: that these are mutually reinforcing is consistent with the wider objectives of economic liberalisation.

A. The Significance of Consensus

It has been demonstrated that the fragmentation of international law raises complex legal issues, albeit that for the most part, the separate bodies of law should be able to exist and operate in parallel. In the event of a dispute, the panel and the Appellate Body would, insofar as it were possible, interpret the GATT consistently with other international law. However, if a fundamental conflict were observed, they must apply the GATT rules.

The most problematic area might be if it were indeed possible to invoke the general exceptions with regard to products produced in a particular manner, or to justify a finding that products were not 'like'. This would mean that the national treatment obligation would not apply. If such a restriction was not based upon universal standards, and the public morality issue had no direct relation to the product within the import market or impact upon consumers, it would be pertinent to question whether such exception to or restriction of the international (WTO) commitments is appropriate. If, however, such a restricting measure were based on universal standards or rights, the position would be, appropriately, rather different, since these may be taken into account.

Pursuit of the protection of human rights, with any degree of certainty or legitimacy, within the current WTO framework appears to require the identification of a body of universal standards, concerning which there is both consensus and universal (or near-universal) recognition. The UDHR, although non-binding, may provide a core as it is undoubtedly representative of the will of the international community. The ICCPR and the ICESCR also provide bodies of binding law which have widespread acceptance. The

ILO Conventions indicate international recognition of a body of rights. These bodies of laws could certainly provide the basis for a body of rights which might legitimately be recognised within the WTO framework, escaping the charge of protectionism.

It is clear from the above analysis that not all 'human rights' have the same status or command the same recognition and accommodation with regard to other branches of law or competing rights: different categories of rights, and different instruments, carry different weights. Furthermore, it is evident from the EU experience that consensus regarding the existence and value of particular rights was crucial to their eventual recognition in the EU legal order. This is reinforced by the findings of the analysis testing the potential accommodation of labour rights in the WTO legal order. Thus, to talk of 'trade and human rights' as one single issue is misleading: the content and definition of specific rights is crucial to their recognition and the status they are accorded vis-a-vis other rights (including trade rights).

It is argued that, notwithstanding acknowledged difficulties concerning the definition of human rights, the principle of sustainable development offers an integrative conceptual framework which can usefully be applied to the relationship between WTO law and human rights. Moreover, by reference to the EU experience, it has been demonstrated that this is not merely an abstract conceptual approach: it is possible to operationalise the commitment expressed through the emergence of the principle of sustainable development. Analysis of the EU experience also confirms the significance of the existence of consensus as to rights to be protected in order to realise the commitment to sustainable development.

Analysis of the GATT and WTO case law indicates that customary international law and other rules of international law applicable between the parties should and can (respectively) be taken into account in the application of WTO rules. Thus, while it is important to recognise and engage with the *limitations* of the WTO regime, the possibilities should equally be recognised.

Internal non-discriminatory measures to protect the rights of those within the regulating state, as arising in the context of Article III GATT, should not be held to violate WTO rules, although problems arise regarding the WTO's (lack of) sensitivity in the characterisation of products as 'like'.[103] However, it is arguable that recognition of justification for national regulatory measures on the grounds of particular product characteristics is not currently sufficiently contextually sensitive.[104] There can be little doubt that justification based on international law would be more likely to be accepted.

---

[103] See ch 7 above.
[104] GATT Panel Report, *Thailand-Restrictions on Importation of and Internal Taxes on Cigarettes*, DS10/R 37S/200, adopted 7 November 1990, BISD 37S/200.

These factors apply equally in the event that a state seeks to invoke an exception to justify a restriction, under Article XX GATT, on the grounds of public morality or public health. In ruling upon the exercise of a public policy exception, a balancing process must be carried out between the objective of economic liberalisation and the public policy exception in question. Questions inevitably arise as to the legitimacy of the panel and the Appellate Body to engage in such a balancing process (such questions have arisen in the context of Article XX(b)).[105] A degree of prima facie legitimacy is provided by the WTO's commitment to sustainable development and labour rights, and also by the objectives of economic liberalisation itself. The key to addressing the legitimacy questions is to apply a consistent, transparent, contextually sensitive mechanism which recognises that varying standards are an inherent consequence of national public policy exceptions. EU experience indicates that proportionality is central to such a mechanism.[106] However, recognition that there may be ways to mitigate legitimacy concerns is not to suggest that it has consistently achieved this, but rather that it might be possible. There are clear limits in place as regards outwardly directed action to protect human rights. Just as there should be sensitivity to particular values within a regulating state, so too should there be sensitivity to another state's choices insofar as these do not violate customary international law or *jus cogens*. Once again, measures based on universal standards will be less likely to breach WTO rules.

The relationship between economic liberalisation and human rights is indeed a complex one. Although on many levels mutually supportive, a tension exists between global (economic) standards and regional or national human rights choices and standards. Sustainable development offers a conceptualisation which highlights the mutually reinforcing nature of these objectives, but recognises the need to balance them in particular contexts. Finding a balance or establishing a mechanism to appropriately balance these interests in particular contexts is crucial. This is possible within the WTO context, in light of the whole of its objectives. However, it is also crucial to note the limits of what the WTO can or should do. The broader questions of prioritisation are political questions, which it is not the place of the DSB to determine. Any conclusions on the protection of non-economic interests within WTO law are complex, not least in recognising the significant difference in status of environmental as opposed to human rights interests. It appears that the environment is protected through Article XX GATT; however, such protection is less certain in relation to human rights. While the extent to which environmental protection has been realised in the disputes brought before the GATT and WTO panels is negligible, there are

[105] See, inter alia, ibid.
[106] See ch 3. See also Reid (n 98).

two provisos to the extent to which generalised conclusions may be drawn from this. First, there has been a shift in the argument used in weighing up the competing interests in trade/environment disputes. The fact that this has not, as yet, led to a change in outcome of disputes belies the significance of the developments in principle.

Second, the fact that an environmental measure has not yet been held to be a legitimate restriction on trade tells us little about the cases which have not been brought as a consequence of the existence of the exception. Many of the 'environmental' measures which have been the subject of complaint have indeed had an air of protectionism rather than genuine environmental concern. There are instances in which genuinely environmentally inspired measures are not being challenged, in all likelihood as a result of recognition of the exception. This should equally be borne in mind in considering the degree of protection which may be offered to human rights without violating the GATT. First and foremost, the WTO and its members are bound by their other commitments of international law and by *erga omnes* and *jus cogens* obligations. Consequently, if a state violates a universal human right, it will be liable for this violation under the rules of state liability. This will not, however, give rise to any GATT obligation (or competence) to protect human rights. One explanation why a human rights exception, under for example 'public morality', has not been tested or invoked before the WTO is that the state which is subject to a genuine public morality/human rights measure would be unlikely to complain against the measure, knowing that its human rights responsibility would in any case arise in other jurisdictions.

Whatever the scope of the potential exception under public morality, there are limitations even upon its applicability (for example, whether it may be used to protect the public morality in another state). Although there are signs that extra-jurisdictional measures may be permitted under certain circumstances in relation to environmental protection, it is easier to conceive of the effect upon the state imposing the trade restriction, as environmental effects do not recognise state borders. In the event of an outright conflict between the protection of human rights and the operation of WTO rules, there is no means by which the WTO DSB may disapply WTO rules in order to give precedence to the human rights objective.

In relation to both human rights and the environment, there remains a significant issue—that is, the process by which the dispute settlement panel interprets the 'conflicting' interests and then balances the non-economic with the economic interest. Thus, at the heart of the resolution of the relationship between economic and non-economic interests is the balancing act to be performed: who should perform this act? How should they go about interpreting the 'conflicting' interests? Arguably, in order to do so, the 'panel' performing this balancing act should be expert in all the relevant fields, and certainly it should bring an element of objectivity to the issue.

Under the present international institutional structure, it is questionable whether this is the case, or is even possible. The only forum within which the balance may currently be assessed has a specific interest and mandate: the pursuit of trade liberalisation.

This raises an issue requiring further scrutiny: both environmental and human rights protection may conflict with WTO law. In order to be protected within the context of international trade, both are currently largely reliant upon the interpretation of 'exception provisions' by the WTO.[107] Can the WTO fulfil its responsibility in relation to compliance with labour/human rights standards by merely ensuring that it does not inhibit action to enforce (by acting passively rather than actively)? Even if this is possible, is the WTO the appropriate body for this task? This is more pressing if the potentially normative effects of WTO rulings are considered, which mean that any lack of objectivity in balancing the different international obligations and interests is significant.[108]

The Court of Justice has found a means by which to reconcile economic and non-economic objectives, and it is worth considering what elements of that approach may be transferable. However, such a comparison must be handled with caution, as there are different objectives and institutional structures in place that affect the extent to which the WTO could apply the EU's approach. But in any event, the comparison of the case law undertaken above raises doubts as to whether the assumption that a European Court of Justice-type approach would enhance the protection of non-economic interests within the WTO legal order is indeed well founded.

There are therefore two related questions which need to be addressed in the following chapter. The first concerns whether an alternative conceptual approach to the interpretation of the WTO rules could facilitate the balancing of economic and non-economic interests within the existing legal and institutional framework: whether an alternative conceptual lens could mitigate the incoherence in the interaction of different systems of international law. The second question concerns what may be learnt from the EU experience in seeking to reconcile these competing interests.

---

[107] Setting aside the suggestion discussed above that a consumer preference for environmentally sound products can render to otherwise like products 'unlike', which would mean there was no breach of national treatment, and therefore no need to apply the Article XX exceptions. This could be applied to differentiate between products on the basis of the use of, for example, child labour in their production or not. See *Asbestos* (n 89) in which ruling a difference in health effects was considered in this way. See RL Howse and DH Regan, 'The Product/Process Distinction—An Illusory Basis for Disciplining Unilateralism in Trade Policy' (2000) 11 *European Journal of International Law* 249; Jackson (n 25).

[108] See ch 6 above.

9

Effecting the Reconciliation of Competing Interests: Reconceptualising the Legal Framework

T HIS BOOK IS concerned with how the relationship between economic and non-economic objectives and interests is managed in the regulation of international trade. The developed nature of WTO law, notably including its binding dispute settlement process, means that the WTO legal order occupies a unique space in terms of both its potential to engage with and its influence upon the management of the relationship between trade liberalisation and non-economic objectives. Contemporary global challenges, such as climate change, which engage economic and non-economic interests ask questions of the existing legal architecture, actors and institutions; yet, to take WTO law as a starting point carries a risk of subordination of the non-economic interests to economic objectives, including trade liberalisation.

The previous chapters have examined the interaction between WTO law and other international law (specifically relating to the protection of non-economic objectives and interests, notably environmental and human rights protection). While some capacity of the WTO to engage with other international law has been recognised, it has been seen that this is subject to significant limitations. Thus, for example, with regard to environmental protection, the impact of WTO law upon members' capacity to introduce measures to tackle climate change or ensure energy security has been shown to be problematic. Similarly, it has been seen that the relationship between WTO law and human rights is complicated from the very point at which we seek to define 'human rights'.

I. THE EU EXPERIENCE

The first part of this book examined the considerable EU experience in managing the inter-relationship between economic and non-economic interests. This analysis allowed the conditions which drove the EU approach to be identified and unpacked; the significance of a holistic approach, built around sustainable development, became apparent.[1] The question is what, if anything, can the international community learn from this experience?

The identification of the conditions which enabled, or even drove, the EU to develop fundamental rights protection as a constitutional principle and facilitated the emergence of environmental protection in the EU is important. The conditions identified include the particular characteristics of the EU legal order, including the role of the Court of Justice and the principle of supremacy of EU law, and consensus on the very value of these interests, including, in the case of human rights, their substantive content. These conditions do not exist in the WTO; therefore, the suggestion made by some that the WTO might somehow replicate the EU's approach is unrealistic. The EU does not provide a model which can be picked up and applied in the international context, notwithstanding its export of the issue, and elements of its approach, into its external relations. What the EU does offer is an approach to governance, and recognition of the inter-dependence of interests, which can be carried forward 'domestically' and may have application globally. In particular, it represents a move away from a sub-stantively compartmentalised approach. The EU experience demonstrates that economic and non-economic issues must be engaged with holistically, and that sustainable development provides a context for this. Both the EU's internal and external experiences highlight the significance of alternative regulatory mechanisms and decision-making processes.

In this chapter, drawing from the analysis of the global position under-taken in earlier chapters and extrapolating from the EU experience, three propositions are made. The first is that the WTO objectives should be reconceptualised in the light of the international commitment to 'sustain-able development'. Second, it is proposed that alongside this reconceptuali-sation, it is necessary to develop a substantive adjudicative method which operationalises the commitment to sustainable development; it is argued that this combined approach, comprising the reconceptualisation, given teeth by an accompanying adjudicative mechanism, effectively reframes the status and potential of non-economic interests and their relationship to trade liberalisation rules. This in turn should support more effective responses to contemporary global challenges. Third, I explore the lessons which may be drawn from the EU experience and the extent to which they support such an approach.

---

[1] See ch 2 above.

II. RECONCEPTUALISING THE OBJECTIVES OF THE WTO THROUGH THE LENS OF SUSTAINABLE DEVELOPMENT

A. Unpacking the Objectives of the WTO Rules

The immediate objective of the WTO rules is trade liberalisation. Fundamentally, it has to be asked whether this is pursued as an end in itself or in pursuit of an underlying objective. Traditionally, trade liberalisation has been seen as a means by which to pursue 'welfare enhancement' and economic development.[2] The GATT was originally conceived within the Bretton Woods settlement as a means of engendering better relations between states, facilitating peace as well as economic well-being. This is reinforced in the WTO Agreement, the Preamble to which provides that the Members recognise:

> [T]hat their relations in the field of trade and economic endeavour should be conducted with a view to raising standards of living, ensuring full employment and a large and steadily growing volume of real income and effective demand, and expanding the production of and trade in goods and services, while allowing for the optimal use of the world's resources in accordance with the objective of sustainable development, seeking both to protect and preserve the environment and to enhance the means for doing so in a manner consistent with their respective needs and concerns at different levels of economic development.

In this it is apparent that trade liberalisation is indeed pursued as a means to an end. This raises a question concerning the nature of that end—what are the objectives of the trade liberalisation regime? In addressing this question, Jackson takes the texts of the WTO Charter, the GATT and the Havana Charter as his starting point and identifies:

> [F]ive prominent goals of the WTO system: keep the peace, promote world economic development and welfare, work towards sustainable development and environmental protection, reduce the poverty of the poorest part of the world, and manage economic crises that might erupt partly due to the circumstances of globalization and interdependence.[3]

Jackson views 'world economic welfare' as being probably fundamental to the objectives of the regime and refers to the dominant view that free markets facilitate economic development, 'which in turn increases the probability of individuals satisfactorily pursuing their own chosen goals'. However, as

---

[2] See ch 7; Adam Smith *An Inquiry into the Nature and Causes of the Wealth of Nations* (The Strand, 1776) Book IV, ch II; David Ricardo, *On the Principles of Political Economy and Taxation* (London, 1817).

[3] JH Jackson, *Sovereignty, the WTO and the Changing Fundamentals of International Law* (Cambridge, Cambridge University Press, 2006) 84.

Jackson recognises, this does not *necessarily* maximise satisfaction.[4] Dillon further observes that economic welfare enhancement pursued through trade liberalisation, consistent with the 'law' of comparative advantage, focusing as it does on wealth *maximisation*, does not engage with *redistribution* of wealth.[5] Trade liberalisation can be seen to create both winners and losers. Consequently, it makes sense that there be a possibility for action to mitigate the detrimental individual effects of free trade where they occur in order to ensure the wider objective of welfare gain. Returning to Jackson, 'substantial arguments are made in favour of some sort of mixture of policies, perhaps to temper the perceived negative effects of "too pure market approaches"',[6] notwithstanding the need to respect market forces. This is a point that was recognised 200 years earlier by Smith.[7] Cho characterises the underlying issue in relation to linkage as being 'the tension between free markets and social regulation'[8] with the real question being 'how', rather than 'what', to link. Dillon also focuses on the question of how to draw these interests together, but more explicitly highlights the need for balance between trade law and social, environmental and labour policies.[9]

There is thus both historical and contemporary recognition that trade liberalisation is not an unqualified 'good', even on its own terms: that trade liberalisation may make a substantial contribution towards, but can require further governmental intervention to achieve, economic welfare gain. This highlights the need to seek approaches which appropriately balance trade liberalisation and social and environmental interests, and, in so doing, challenge the discourse and practice which reinforces the predominance of trade liberalisation as an end in itself. To this end, the framework of sustainable development provides a significant departure point.

The WTO is clearly mandated to pursue the economic element of sustainable development through trade liberalisation. The preamble to the WTO Agreement commits the organisation and its members to 'sustainable development' itself.[10] Despite a lack of clarity as to the nature of this objective,

---

[4] ibid.

[5] S Dillon, 'A Farewell to Linkage: International Trade Law and Global Sustainability Indicators' (2002–03) 51 *Rutgers Law Review* 87, 112, referring to Michael H Davis and Dana Neacsu, 'Legitimacy, Globally: The Incoherence of Free Trade Practice, Global Economics and Their Governing Principles of Political Economy' (2001) 69 *University of Missouri-Kansas City Law Review* 733, 753–62.

[6] Jackson (n 3) 86.

[7] Smith (n 2). Such provision can be seen in the 'General Exceptions' provisions of the GATT.

[8] S Cho, 'Linkage of Free Trade and Social Regulation: Moving Beyond the Entropic Dilemma' (2005) 5 *Chicago Journal of International Law* 625, 639.

[9] Dillon (n 5) 137. Similarly, Hilpold observes the need that an 'equilibrium line' between these two sets of goals which are mutually supportive, partially competing, has to be found': P Hilpold, 'WTO Law and Human Rights: Bringing Together Two Autopoietic Orders' (21 October 2010) 57. Available at: http://ssrn.com/abstract=1695505.

[10] See chs 6 and 7.

sustainable development has been recognised by Pascal Lamy as a 'goal' of the WTO.[11] However, since the latter decades of the twentieth century, the dominant perspective applied to the objectives of the WTO in general, and to the pursuit of 'trade liberalisation' in particular, has been essentially neoliberal.[12] Under this perspective, trade liberalisation appears to be pursued essentially for its own sake, with little sense of a broader or more contextual purpose. Yet addressing contemporary global challenges such as climate change requires a contextual approach. It requires engagement with a range of interests, including economic, environmental and social interests, insofar as it requires behaviour change (in mitigation and adaptation).

B. The Impact of the Narrow (Neoliberal) Interpretation of the WTO Objectives

The neoliberal narrowly conceived pursuit of 'trade liberalisation', without consideration of such wider objectives and interests, is at odds with contemporary needs and undermines the ability of the WTO to engage with contemporary global challenges. It is also at odds with the body of case law (both WTO and EU) which demonstrates the interaction between trade liberalisation and non-economic interests (including environmental and human rights protection).[13] The question of the relationship and the line to be drawn between the pursuit of trade liberalisation and non-economic interests is one which has been explored in the 'trade and ...' linkage discourse.[14] In that context, it is frequently framed as a question of competing objectives. It is, however, pertinent to ask whether this is a fruitful or even appropriate conceptualisation of the relationship between trade liberalisation and non-economic interests.

Such narrow understanding of the objectives and purpose of the WTO, and of trade liberalisation itself, inevitably shapes the decisions of the DSB, whose function it is to ensure the application of WTO rules. These

---

[11] P Lamy, 'Trade Can Be a Friend, and Not a Foe, of Conservation', *WTO Symposium on Trade and sustainable Development within the framework of paragraph 51 of the Doha Ministerial Declaration*, speech available at: www.wto.org/english/news_e/sppl_e/sppl07_e.htm.

[12] See A Lang, *World Trade Law after Neoliberalism: Reimagining the Global Economic Order* (Oxford, Oxford University Press, 2011); R Howse, 'From Politics to Technocracy—And Back Again: The Fate of the Multilateral Trading Regime' (2002) 96 *American Journal of International Law* 94, 97.

[13] See chs 2, 3, 6, 7 and 8 above.

[14] See, inter alia, ATF Lang, 'Reflecting on Linkage: Cognitive and Institutional Change in the International Trading System' (2007) 70(4) *MLR* 523; JL Dunoff, '"Trade And": Recent Developments in Trade Policy and Scholarship—And Their Surprising Political Implications' (1996–97) 17 *Journal of International Law and Business* 759; Alvarez et al, *Symposium—The Boundaries of the WTO* (2002) 96 *AJIL* 1; Dillon (n 5); Cho (n 8).

prevailing assumptions have also shaped understanding of how it might act; in so doing, these assumptions limit the DSB's potential to respond to global challenges such as climate change. Recently, the Appellate Body in particular has sought to engage with other bodies of international law and to accommodate that within the WTO legal order.[15] There is also evidence of a willingness to embrace national regulatory choices; this is explicit in the SPS and TBT Agreements.[16] However, as long as the starting point for determination of the relationship between economic and non-economic interests is the pursuit of 'liberalisation of trade', and so long as the question asked concerns the extent to which other, non-economic (loosely defined) objectives may be accommodated within the pursuit of 'trade liberalisation', a narrow definition of the purpose of trade liberalisation is likely to subordinate the other interests. It would be easier for the panels and the Appellate Body to engage effectively with other interests, and they would have more legitimacy and credibility in doing so if the purpose of trade liberalisation was re-examined and contextualised. Looking forward, therefore, in order for the international community, and the WTO in particular, to respond effectively to contemporary global challenges, it is necessary to recognise, examine and contest the assumptions brought to the definition of the purpose of the WTO rules. The dominance of the neoliberal perspective must be recognised as being contestable and be challenged: the objectives of the WTO must be revisited and reviewed.

C. The Need for a Holistic Approach

The proposal that the objectives and purpose of the WTO be revisited and reviewed has been made by a number of commentators proposing a range of approaches, some of which will be discussed below. These include that a more holistic interpretation is necessary. What is suggested here specifically, however, is that the objectives of the WTO are reconceptualised through the lens of sustainable development.

The operational relationship between trade liberalisation and the protection of non-economic interests has been seen in the examination of the EU experience.[17] National social regulation, human rights or environmental protection can restrict trade, the corollary being that trade liberalisation obligations restrict a state's capacity to regulate according to its national policy choices. To treat such national policy considerations as being separate from and at odds with the pursuit of trade liberalisation allows for the

---

[15] See chs 6–8 above.
[16] See chs 7 and 8 above.
[17] See ch 3.

pursuit of 'trade liberalisation' for its own sake, without regard for other considerations. Lang criticises the approach whereby:

> Critics of the trade regime again and again find themselves forced by the terms of the debate into arguing for exceptions or qualifications to the pursuit of international trade liberalisation, rather than a rethinking of its fundamental contours.[18]

Such an approach impedes the realisation of the underlying objectives of the trade liberalisation regime. Pragmatically, the existing trade regime must be engaged with in any exploration of the relationship between trade liberalisation and human rights protection; however, it is crucial that in engaging with that regime, a holistic view is adopted of its objectives.[19]

It is almost 20 years since Schoenbaum observed that:

> There is no fundamental conflict between protection of the environment and an open, multi-lateral trading system, and reform can be accomplished largely within the framework of current WTO/GATT rules and agreements as well as the jurisprudence of GATT and WTO dispute resolution panels.[20]

However, the dynamic nature of the trade-environment relationship and the fact that what is an appropriate balance in one context may not be suitable in others mean that there is no single universal solution to the balance to be struck between environmental interests and trade. What is required is a mechanism through which a balance may be arrived at on a case-by-case basis. Schoenbaum saw this as being possible within the existing WTO legal framework, although to this end he proposed some amendment to Article XX GATT. To achieve a consensus on amendment to Article XX, however, would be immensely difficult: the tortuous process of the Doha round demonstrated the near-impossibility of achieving consensus on reform. In light of that difficulty, the pragmatist's question is what can be achieved within the existing rules. It has been observed above that a narrow understanding of the objectives of the WTO is problematic. One lesson which may be drawn from the EU context is that a 'holistic' or non-compartmentalised approach is constructive. There are therefore a number of reasons to support the proposition that it would be helpful to apply a holistic approach to the interpretation of provisions of the WTO, going beyond the economic perspective. Exploration of this possibility is premised upon recognition of the inherent contingency of the narrow contemporary understanding of WTO objectives.

---

[18] Lang (n 14) 540.

[19] See further Cho (n 8) 627; Lang (n 14) 541.

[20] TJ Schoenbaum, 'International Trade and Protection of the Environment: The Continuing Search for Reconciliation' (1997) 91 *American Journal of International Law* 268, 312.

D. Embedded Liberalism

Ruggie characterised the establishment of the original GATT as an agreement of 'embedded liberalism'—an agreement in which the pursuit of trade liberalisation is part of a broader compact bringing together the desirability of non-discrimination in trade relations and state intervention in order to secure domestic stability.[21] Such characterisation would support an approach such as the EU's, based upon sustainable development. Notwithstanding Lang's concern that 'embedded liberalism' may simply enhance trade lawyers' support for domestic social measures, rather than developing the ability of governments to adopt such measures,[22] this characterisation of the trade regime has been influential.[23] Howse expresses trade liberalisation under the GATT as 'embedded within a *political* commitment, broadly shared among the major players in the trading system, to the progressive, interventionist welfare state'.[24] However, as Howse observes, through the latter part of the twentieth century, the compact of embedded liberalism was challenged as a consequence of the emergence of a 'technocratic elite', trade specialists, who sought rather successfully to 'depoliticise' the operation of the trade regime.[25] This group of 'insiders' ultimately 'moved from free trade as an economic ideology to free trade as embedded in a broader liberal economic ideology'.[26]

E. The Integration of Non-economic Interests into the WTO Legal Order?

The challenge which faces the international community is how to move forward from this in a context in which contemporary challenges require responses drawing from and protecting a range of interests. A significant number of commentators have advocated the integration of non-economic

---

[21] JG Ruggie, 'International Regimes, Transactions, and Change: Embedded Liberalism in the Post-war Economic Order' (1982) 36 *International Organization* 379, 398. See further JG Ruggie, 'Taking Embedded Liberalism Global: The Corporate Connection' in D Held and M Koenig-Archibugi (eds), *Taming Globalization: Frontiers of Governance* (Cambridge, Cambridge University Press, 2003); A Lang, 'Reconstructing Embedded Liberalism: John Gerard Ruggie and Constructivist Approaches to the Study of the International Trade Regime' (2006) 9 *Journal of International Economic Law* 81.
[22] Lang (n 12).
[23] ibid.
[24] Howse (n 12) 97.
[25] ibid.
[26] ibid 104.

interests into the WTO legal order; thus, Schoenbaum concludes his analysis by suggesting that:

> Environmental interests, in turn, must learn to work within the context of the legal framework for international trade to achieve their goals, albeit within a context in which 'environmental considerations should become a continual concern at the WTO'.[27]

It has been suggested by Petersmann that human rights be integrated into the WTO legal order. [28] The integration of non-economic interests into the WTO legal order recognises the inter-relationship between economic and non-economic interests, and recognises the need to address that relationship. So why not pursue that approach? Why instead seek to recast the very objectives of the trade regime within the frame of sustainable development?

The integration of non-economic interests into the WTO legal order does indeed hold some initial appeal: it appears constructive to build human rights considerations into the operation of the WTO. Moreover, it has been suggested that it could be possible to put human rights on the level of underlying principles, as they are in the EU, rather than exceptions. In this context it may be recalled that human rights were also initially not seen as being relevant to the operation of EU law.[29] It is too simplistic, however, to suggest that the WTO dispute settlement panels should, or even could, incorporate recognition of human rights in the WTO in the same manner as the Court of Justice has done within the EU. To do so would ignore the particular legal and political history which led to recognition of fundamental rights as a general principle of EU law.[30] Thus, as was shown in chapter two, the analysis of the emergence of human rights in the EU[31] demonstrated that the existence of a set of common values, shared by the EU Member States, was highly significant. In addition to the shared constitutional principles, each of the Member States had already adhered to the ECHR. That relative homogeneity, exemplified by shared values and obligations, has no equivalent among the membership of the WTO.[32] Although it is possible that the ILO fundamental rights, for example, may constitute an accepted set of rights, there is no binding mechanism through which they may be enforced, or even a consensus that they should be.[33] Consequently, there is nothing that impinges upon the WTO legal system in the manner that the ECHR, the shared principles of the (then) EC Member States and

---

[27] Schoenbaum (n 20).

[28] EU Petersmann, 'Time for a United Nations "Global Compact" for Integrating Human Rights into the Law of Worldwide Organizations: Lessons from European Integration' (2002) 13 *European Journal of International Law* 621.

[29] See ch 2 above.

[30] See ch 2 above.

[31] See ch 2 above.

[32] See ch 8 above.

[33] See ch 8 above.

the position of the national constitutional courts affected the EC legal system. Without such factors, there is no reason why the WTO legal system would pursue this development even if it could (which is doubtful), unless a consensus to do so can be achieved among the Members. Indeed, were it do seek to do so, this would raise significant questions regarding the legitimacy of such a development.

i. The Dangers of Integrating Non-economic Interests into the WTO Legal Order: Reinforcing Existing Hierarchies

Setting aside the question of whether the EU could serve as such a model, there are a number of dangers inherent in integrating non-economic interests into the trade liberalisation regime. The first, quite fundamentally, is that any discourse which takes as its starting point the existing trade regime and explores how environmental protection may be 'linked' to that regime, or how human rights may be mainstreamed or integrated into the pursuit of trade liberalisation, risks appearing to accept the narrow conception of the trade regime. According to this conceptualisation, 'non-trade' concerns are 'add-ons'[34] to the realisation of the objectives of trade liberalisation. 'Trade', thus conceptualised, acquires a pre-eminence over wider societal interests.[35]

There is a further danger, evident in Petersmann's proposal to integrate human rights into the WTO legal order, which concerns the definition of rights to be integrated. As seen in the previous chapter, the breadth of definition of 'human rights' means that to discuss 'the approach' to be taken to 'trade and human rights' is virtually meaningless. Petersmann's approach is built around the centrality of market rights, the individual's right to trade as guarantor of their right to dignity. Thus, market rights are placed at the top of, essentially, a rights hierarchy; the argument is that once these rights are secured, the enjoyment of other rights follows. However, an approach such as this, which recognises the centrality of human rights but takes a narrow market-based hierarchical view of those fundamental rights, does little to address the problems identified as a consequence of the uncertain relationship between different systems of international law. It will not necessarily address the failure of the international community to develop a mechanism by which, in any context, these difficulties may be resolved. Thus, to prioritise market rights in the WTO risks perpetuating the current problems which arise from the lack of mechanism to balance 'conflicting' interests.

---

[34] Gathii similarly uses the term 'add-ons' to describe the manner in which 'free-traders' characterise 'social issues' in relation to the 'free-trade agenda': JT Gathii, 'Re-characterizing the Social in the Constitutionalization of the WTO: A Preliminary Analysis' (2001) 7 *Widener Law Symposium Journal* 137.

[35] See Dunoff (n 14) 768–70; Dillon (n 5) 89–91.

While the issue identified so far has concerned the need for developments in one field of international law to be recognised and taken account of in overlapping areas, this evolution must address not just the language through which overlaps are addressed, but should also reflect substantive developments. The need to address the questions surrounding the relationship between, for example, human rights and the WTO is not satisfied by redesignating the freedoms guaranteed by the WTO as fundamental rights and integrating these within the WTO legal order. Rather, it should assess the protection given to the diverse rights at issue in any given circumstances. Just as in the shift from labour standards to labour rights,[36] a mere shift in the terminology will not achieve any change in the substance of how these 'standards' or 'rights' should be protected. Similarly, incorporating the language of rights into the WTO system will not per se achieve adequate protection of other rights. In fact, it may be more damaging if it serves to reinforce one particular set of values or has the effect of introducing a new requirement before an exception may be invoked.[37] Alston clearly expresses such concern in his observation that: 'In a form of epistemological misappropriation [Petersmann] takes the discourse of international human rights law and uses it to describe an agenda which has a fundamentally different ideological underpinning.'[38] A parallel concern, arising from the lack of consensus regarding the definition of human rights, is felt particularly by developing states: that the pursuit of 'human rights' protection could be used for protectionist purposes. Even if the starting point for a WTO panel or the Appellate Body to draw the line between pursuit of trade liberalisation and 'conflicting' non-economic objectives is 'welfare enhancement', and even if 'human rights' are integrated into this decision making, the outcome will inevitably be shaped by the conceptualisation of both 'welfare' and 'human rights'. This is better pursued on the basis of a reframed conceptualisation of the objectives of the WTO—that is, in pursuit of sustainable development.

---

[36] Discussed in ch 8 above.

[37] Recalling that Petersmann (n 28) believes that the liberalisation of trade is the best mechanism by which to enhance welfare, and among others social rights, it is inevitable that he should conclude that the 'fundamental market rights' should only be limited by what is 'necessary' to pursue the protection of social and other rights. Thus, Petersmann observes that: 'The universal recognition of human rights requires us to construe the numerous public interest clauses in WTO law in conformity with the human rights requirement that individual freedom and non-discrimination may be restricted only to the extent necessary for protecting other human rights' (at 645). Yet, as Howse observes, this may not serve the general exceptions of the GATT well, notably because in addition to introducing a dubious human rights requirement to, for example, Article XX(g) (conservation of natural resources), it also introduces a 'necessity' test which is not present in that particular requirement for exception. See R Howse, 'Human Rights in the WTO: Whose Rights, What Humanity? Comment on Petersmann' (2002) 13 *European Journal of International Law* 651–659.

[38] P Alston, 'Resisting the Merger and Acquisition of Human Rights by Trade Law: A Reply to Petersmann' (2002) 13 *European Journal of International Law* 815, 842.

F. Integrating the WTO Legal Order into the Context of Sustainable Development

Consequently, in order to effectively support the recognition and protection of non-economic interests in their interactions with the WTO legal order, it is necessary that rather than non-economic interests being integrated into the WTO legal order, the WTO legal order, and conceptualisations of welfare and non-economic interests, should be seen within the wider context of the international commitment to sustainable development. Thus, it is necessary to reframe the WTO objectives from that perspective.

G. The Theoretical Framework

Any proposal to reframe the WTO objectives in the light of the international commitment to sustainable development engages questions concerning the theoretical framework of international law. To what extent would a reframing be possible within the existing legal and theoretical framework? Can the existing framework successfully address the current incoherence of international law relating to the reconciliation of economic and non-economic issues,[39] or is it necessary to modify it to deal with the difficulties?[40] Kingsbury argues that it is essential to establish a theoretical framework to explain the international legal system in order to understand the behaviour and outcomes of the trade-environment interface.[41] This would apply equally to the interface between trade and human rights. Having considered the frameworks he views as being the most influential (political realism,[42] international cooperation theory[43] and liberal theory),[44] Kingsbury concluded that political realism is the dominant theoretical paradigm. However, he argued that the evaluation of trade-environment controversies is most effectively approached from liberal theory because that comprises norms of

[39] See DM Driesen, 'What is Free Trade? The Real Issue Lurking Behind the Trade and Environment Debate' (2001) 41 *Virginia Journal of International Law* 279.

[40] This chapter does not seek to deal comprehensively with these questions, but to raise further thoughts on these issues for consideration elsewhere.

[41] B Kingsbury, 'The Tuna Dolphin Controversy, the World Trade Organization and the Liberal Project to Reconceptualize International Law' (1994) 5(1) *Yearbook of International Environmental Law* 1.

[42] According to political realism, states are essentially homogenous units, each concerned primarily for its own survival, and restrained in its actions only by the equal actions and concerns of other states.

[43] International cooperation is founded on essentially the same premise as political realism, but attempts to explain the large number of instances of international cooperation (and non-cooperation) which political realism views as aberrations.

[44] The liberal theories, in contrast to political realism and international cooperation theory, are founded upon the interests of individuals and groups within states, which influence state actions, interactions and preferences.

interaction of individuals and groups in transnational society, rather than viewing the international legal system as being best modelled upon laws made by states to regulate their inter-relations. The enforcement of liberal norms of transnational action relies upon international organisations and international courts as well as on states, both through national courts and before the supranational bodies.

i. Would a Liberal Theoretical Framework Be Helpful?

The strength of the liberal theoretical approach is that it recognises both the impact of market influence and wider transnational pressures on the development of legal rules and institutions, and also the regulatory power of non-state bodies such as transnational industrial groups, which are unaccounted for by the state-based theories. Kingsbury proposed that it would be easier to resolve the difficulties concerning the trade-environment interface (exemplified in the jurisprudence of the GATT and WTO panels) if this approach were applied to the WTO. This liberal theoretical approach is also entirely consistent with the broader trend, highlighted by Petersmann, towards deregulation, market economies, protection of human rights and democracies. According to Petersmann, this reflects 'increasing recognition that individual freedom, non-discrimination and rule of law are the best conditions for promoting individual and collective self-determination and social welfare'.[45] Petersmann also finds traditional state-based (democratic) theories of little assistance in the achievement of a liberal global order. However, he finds evidence in the EU that international economic law is now one of the most important instruments of foreign policy, both for the promotion of the rule of law and democracy as well as for economic welfare.[46] It has been seen in the first part of this book, in particular in chapter two, that there are limits to the extent to which the EU experience may be generalised.[47] However, as has been seen, the centrality of Petersmann's thesis concerns deregulation, focusing primarily upon market rights. This, he observes, is consistent with the traditional theory of liberal trade as maximising welfare.

If this approach were combined with Kingsbury's, the risk is that actors would single-mindedly pursue liberal trade at the cost of all other interests. The foundation of liberal trade lies in the pursuit of broader welfare gains, so it should be pursued as a means to an end, not as an end in itself. The dangers in the pursuit of liberalism through existing institutions are particularly apparent if this simply perpetuates a given set of interests and actors,

---

[45] EU Petersmann, *The GATT/WTO Dispute Settlement System International Law, International Organizations and Dispute Settlement* (London, Kluwer Law International, 1997) 1–2.

[46] Petersmann (n 28).

[47] For criticism of Petersmann's view of the EU, see Alston (n 38).

endowing them with new force: this was seen above in discussion of the argument for integration of human rights into the WTO. The weaknesses inherent in allowing the unchecked pursuit of liberal trade are demonstrated clearly by, in particular, the GATT panel findings.[48] The dangers of transnational (or supranational) organisations operating unchecked with a single agenda are apparent. Thus, the danger of the adoption of a 'liberal' theoretical approach is that it could permit the replacement of the operation of single-state interests with single-interest actors and tribunals.

Fundamentally, whatever the theoretical framework applied or employed, the current difficulties in managing the relationship between economic and non-economic interests in the regulation of international trade cannot be addressed without revisiting the interpretation of the objectives underpinning their respective regulatory regimes, as well as the actors involved. Thus, the conclusion is reached once more that if the WTO is to be able to engage meaningfully and effectively with contemporary global challenges, it is necessary that the dominant neoliberal understandings of the WTO objectives be recognised as contingent and be contested. It is suggested that this be done in light of the overarching objective of sustainable development.

ii. The Need to Unpack the Pursuit of Trade Liberalisation: Non-discrimination or a Right to Market Access?

The interpretation of WTO rules in light of sustainable development essentially engages the underlying tension between the desire of states to liberalise trade and their desire to maintain the regulatory autonomy to protect interests of particular concern. This is a tension familiar to all those who have examined the EU internal market rules.[49] The core question in that context concerns the purpose of the internal market rules: are they to create a single market to which there is unfettered access (an economic freedom or market access-based approach) or a market free from nationality-based barriers to trade (a discrimination-based model)?[50] As shown in chapter eight, the latter provides a greater degree of national regulatory autonomy. This question concerning the purpose of the rules manifests a tension which has given rise to a body of complex and apparently conflicting case law and which has not been fully resolved, even in the relatively homogeneous context of the EU.

In the global context, Driesen has similarly attributed divergent results in cases concerning the interpretation of free trade agreements to differing

---

[48] See ch 7 above. See also R Howse, 'Adjudicative Legitimacy and Treaty Interpretation in International Trade Law: The Early Years of WTO Jurisprudence' in JHH Weiler et al (eds), *The EU, the WTO and the NAFTA* (Oxford, Oxford University Press, 2001).

[49] See chs 3 and 4 above.

[50] Discussed in ch 8 above.

concepts of free trade.[51] The dominant account of Smith and Ricardo's theories is that they propounded a 'laissez-faire' approach to free trade. However, as Driesen observes, both Smith and Ricardo's work includes elements suggesting support of a non-discriminatory rather than strictly laissez-faire view of liberal trade.[52] This can be seen in Smith's advocacy of compensatory taxation and general taxation for legitimate public purposes. Similarly, Ricardo views taxation as a necessary rather than an unacceptable trade restriction. This is consistent with the recognition discussed above that trade liberalisation brings costs and benefits, and states may wish to forgo some of the benefits of trade liberalisation in order to mitigate some of the costs.

According to Driesen, examination of the GATT text and jurisprudence supports non-discrimination as the GATT-compliant approach to be pursued to free trade. He argues that this would remove the legitimacy problems facing WTO panels in balancing free trade and restrictions upon it. However, as Driesen acknowledges, the GATT offers no definition of discrimination, notwithstanding that the preamble and Article III appear to support a definition of free trade as trade free from discrimination. Article XI, in contrast, appears to be more closely related to 'laissez-faire'. Article XX permits national regulatory exceptions, but has been construed narrowly.[53] While recognising the possibility of non-discriminatory coercion, Driesen also recognises that trade which is free from international coercion is not necessarily the same as trade free from discrimination. He thus proposes that anti-coercion may be equated to 'laissez-faire'. However, the relationship between non-discrimination and non-coercion is more complex than suggested by this analysis, which concerns only direct discrimination. This reflects the WTO concern with directly discriminatory measures in line with the national treatment principle (as in Article III GATT). So-called 'indistinctly applicable' measures cannot, prima facie, be described as 'discriminatory' because they apply to all states' products.[54] However, the effect may be discriminatory where it constitutes a 'dual burden' (that is, a burden whose effect does not weigh equally upon the imported and domestic products): this 'dual burden' effect is familiar to the EU, in which context the Court of Justice developed the concept of 'mandatory requirements' as a means of handling indistinctly applicable, dual-burden measures.[55]

Yet, the WTO is a classic contract-based organisation of international law rather than a supranational organisation. The Members seek to maintain

---

[51] Driesen (n 39) 284.

[52] ibid 290.

[53] Article III is the national treatment rule, Article XI is the prohibition on quantitative restrictions and Article XX is the general exceptions. See further ch 6 above.

[54] Discussed in ch 3 above.

[55] Case 120/78 *Rewe-Zentral AG v Bundesmonopolverwaltung für Branntwein* [1979] ECR 649.

their freedom to regulate their internal domestic affairs. There are lacunae in the provisions of the WTO, for example, those which have been seen in relation to the interpretation of the exceptions and, even more so, regarding its relations with other non-economic interests. However, the WTO Agreement, unlike the EU Treaties, is not a 'framework treaty' and the dispute settlement panels, and even the Appellate Body, cannot be expected to 'fill the gaps': such an expectation would be, as Jackson observes, tantamount to requiring that the panels and the Appellate Body engage in 'law-making rather than law applying, arguably more appropriate for a legislature which does not exist, or negotiations which substitute for legislation'.[56]

There is thus a conflict between the sovereignty-based system and the necessary evolution of the international trading system.[57] However, as Jackson explores, what is needed is a step away from traditional concepts of international law, international organisations and sovereignty, with new consideration of 'allocation' of power, along the lines of the approach taken through the application of the principle of 'subsidiarity'.[58]

If a broad definition of 'discrimination' were adopted in the WTO context, encompassing both direct and indirect discrimination, there is no reason why discrimination should not be central to the assessment of restrictive national regulatory measures. Driesen considers that this would be an extension of 'discriminatory', which would give rise to legitimacy problems. Yet, extension or not, the potential for legitimacy problems cannot remove the fact that such indistinctly applicable measures do exist and can have discriminatory effects.[59] Such indistinctly applicable measures are manifest in states' exercise of national regulatory autonomy. Recognising this tension between the desire to protect and uphold values of particular national significance on the one hand and the desire to establish and participate in an international organisation committed to the liberalisation of trade on the other, Howse and Nicolaides have developed an approach of 'global subsidiarity'.[60] Pursuant to this approach, the trade regime would only engage with the domestic choices of more democratic actors

---

[56] JH Jackson, 'International Economic Law in Times that are Interesting' (2000) 3(1) *Journal of International Economic Law* 3, 8. *Cf* N Notaro, who maintains that the WTO Appellate Body should play a similar role to that played the Court of Justice in response to political crises and blocked decision making, but does not suggest a basis or source of legitimacy for this: N Notaro, 'The EC and WTO Trade and Environment Case Law' (2001–2002) *Cambridge Yearbook of European Legal Studies* 327, 347.

[57] See ch 6 above.

[58] Subsidiarity is the principle according to which, in the EU context, decisions are taken as close to the citizen as possible, and in the case of a shared competence, the Member State will exercise the competence unless the EU could better achieve the desired objective; this is discussed in ch 2 above. Similarly, R Howse and K Nicolaidis propose a subsidiarity-based approach in 'Enhancing WTO Legitimacy: Constitutionalization or Global Subsidiarity?' (2003) 16 *Governance* 73.

[59] Driesen (n 38) 349–50.

[60] Howse and Nicolaides (n 58).

to the extent necessary to avoid a slide into protectionism. Their starting point on this is the national treatment principle.[61] As the national treatment principle is essentially concerned with discrimination, this suggests a framework of rules based upon the removal of nationality-based barriers to trade rather than upon constituting a right to market access (or economic freedom). This discrimination-based approach, to that extent consistent with Driesen's, contrasts sharply with the 'constitutionalised' visions of the WTO put forward by Petersmann and others. It is proposed here that the reframing of the WTO rules in the light of sustainable development should occur within the context of a discrimination-based rather than a market access or constitutionalised approach to trade liberalisation.

The conclusion that it is necessary to re-evaluate the purpose and objectives of the WTO may be reached through many routes, as is evident in the various perspectives discussed. In the principle of sustainable development we have the basis for a conceptual framework through which this can be done. This is not inconsistent with either 'embedded liberalism' (the original theoretical context of the GATT) or indeed the WTO's own preambular commitment to sustainable development. It would therefore be a relatively small step to unpack that preambular commitment and to interpret the purpose of the WTO in light of the international commitment to sustainable development. That sustainable development has been recognised as a 'goal' of the WTO is relevant to the legitimacy of this proposal. This is therefore a relatively small step, but it could have quite radical implications.

iii. The Consequence of Reconceptualising the Objectives of the WTO in the Light of Sustainable Development

Sustainable development carries international recognition and indeed wide support and endorsement. Its key characteristics have been explored above: it constitutes three pillars of commitment and objective—economic, social and environmental—none of which, crucially from the perspective of its potential for the WTO, take absolute priority. It inherently recognises the mutual dependency of economic, social and environmental interests and, in so doing, it recognises that these must be balanced against one another when they come into contact. Interpreting the WTO rules from this perspective would move the organisation and its rules away from the pursuit of trade liberalisation for its own sake. It would allow concerns represented by the non-economic pillars to be seen as equally important and pursued as such. It would require the application of WTO rules to be carried out in this light. As a result, it would add legitimacy to the engagement with non-economic objectives in

---

[61] It is worth recalling at this point that the TBT and SPS Agreements go beyond the national treatment requirement with regard to national regulatory measures.

the interpretation and application of WTO rules, without suggesting the 'constitutionalisation' of WTO rules. This would in turn reframe the terms of engagement from a question of the extent to which non-economic interests may be accommodated within the trade regime, and thus inherently subordinate to pursuit of trade liberalisation, to a more genuinely balanced relationship. However, even if such a perspective were accepted for the interpretation of the WTO Agreements, the question remains as to whether it could have any practical relevance and whether it is capable of implementation. In this regard, the experience of the EU is, once again, informative.

III. OPERATIONALISATION OF THE SUSTAINABLE DEVELOPMENT-BASED APPROACH

In order to assess the potential of the sustainable development-based approach, and indeed whether this may be operationalised in the WTO, it is helpful to first unpack the starting point: what has been the WTO approach to the relationship between economic and non-economic interests? It was seen in chapter seven that the Appellate Body, in the last 15 years or so, has moved well beyond the early GATT panel approach to the relationship between trade and environment, which was much criticised for its failure to effectively take account of environmental interests. The broad trends are, first, as in *Korea Beef*,[62] to refer to a 'weighing and balancing' of competing interests and, second, to shift the basis of its decisions (and judicial scrutiny) from substantive review of regulation to review of the process employed by Members introducing regulatory standards, as in *US-Shrimp*.[63]

As regards the first, while the Appellate Body has referred to 'weighing and balancing', there is little evidence that it has in fact substantively engaged in such a process. It can be criticised for this, suggesting as it does a decision-making process which has not then been applied. However, the Appellate Body would also be subject to criticism if it did 'weigh and balance' competing interests and, ultimately, without a clear mandate or jurisdiction to do so, imposed its own decision over that of a national regulator, whose decision may reflect democratic choices. 'Weighing and balancing' suggests a degree of subjectivity in the decision making which it would be right to subject to careful scrutiny.

Regarding the second trend, to shift its focus from a substantive review of the Members' regulatory choices to a process-based review—which is on

---

[62] Panel Report, *Korea-Measures Affecting Imports of Fresh, Chilled and Frozen Beef (Korea-Various Measures on Beef)*, WT/DS/161/R, adopted 10 January 2001, para 673 and Appellate Body Report, *Korea-Various Measures on Beef*, WT/DS161/AB/R, adopted 10 January 2001.

[63] *United States-Import Prohibition of Certain Shrimp and Shrimp Products*, AB-1998-4, WT/DS58/R (98-0000), 12 October 1998 (1998) 38 ILM 121.

its face attractive—it avoids the charge that the Appellate Body is imposing its view of the appropriate balance between competing interests over that of the national regulator. In this trend towards process review, the Appellate Body has effectively held that a proportionate measure which pursues a legitimate objective, within the Article XX exceptions, will still breach Article XX if due process is not observed in its adoption. Cremona has observed that in so doing, the Appellate Body sees the right to invoke an Article XX exception as being in direct competition with the rights of other WTO members to benefit from its provisions. This itself demonstrates a lack of common global interest or polity.

The Appellate Body held in *EC-Asbestos*[64] and in *Brazil-Retreaded Tyres*[65] that it is for Members to select their own desired levels of protection, but the process of the implementation of that protection will be scrutinised. This right is written into the SPS and TBT Agreements.[66] Yet there is a question, which is particularly evident in the context of SPS risk assessment and the Appellate Body's reliance on science in that context. This concerns whether a clear distinction may be really drawn between review of the substance and review of the process in the way suggested.[67] The review of the reasoning upon which a decision is based which was undertaken by the Appellate Body in *Continued Suspension*[68] and confirmed in *Australia-Apples*[69] may itself be affected by the starting perspective of the reviewer.

More recently again, in *Clove Cigarettes*[70] the Appellate Body has indicated that when reviewing a national regulatory measure, the purpose of that measure is relevant to the extent that it impacts upon the competitive relationship between the products affected. This indicates a shift back to a more market-based analysis, away from what possibly had been a resurgence of the 'aims and effects' test. Similarly, as seen above, in the *US-Tuna II* case, the Appellate Body referred once again to the need to weigh and

---

[64] Panel Report, *European Communities-Measures Affecting Asbestos and Asbestos Containing Products*, WT/DS/135/R, 18 September 2000; Appellate Body Report WT/DS/135/AB/R, 12 March 2001.

[65] *Brazil-Measures Affecting Imports of Retreaded Tyres*, WT/DS332/AB/R, 3 December 2007.

[66] Article 3 SPS; Article 2 TBT. See ch 7 above.

[67] See ch 7 above and E Reid, 'Risk Assessment, Science and Deliberation: Managing Regulatory Diversity under the SPS Agreement' (2012) 2 *European Journal of Risk Regulation* 535.

[68] *US-Continued Suspension of Obligations in the EC-Hormones Dispute*, Report of the Appellate Body WT/DS320/AB/R, adopted 14 November 2008, DSR 2008:X 3507; *Canada-Continued Suspension of Obligations in the EC-Hormones Dispute*, Report of the Appellate Body WT/DS320/AB/R, adopted 14 November 2008.

[69] *Australia-Measures Affecting the Importation of Apples from New Zealand*, Report of the Appellate Body, WT/DS367/AB/R, 29 November 2010.

[70] *United States-Measures Affecting the Production and Sale of Clove Cigarettes*, Panel Report WT/DS406/R, 2 September 2011; Appellate Body Report WT/DS406/AB/R, 4 April 2012, para 119.

balance: '(i) the degree of contribution made by the measure to the legitimate objective; (ii) the trade-restrictiveness of the measure; and (iii) the nature of the risks at issue and the gravity of the consequences that would arise from non-fulfillment of the objective(s)'.[71] But, once again, the Appellate Body did not in fact engage in any such weighing and balancing, focusing instead upon whether Mexican proposed alternative measure would meet US objectives.[72] On the other hand, the conclusion which can be drawn from these recent rulings (*Clove Cigarettes* and *Tuna Dolphin II*) is that regulation which applies more broadly, and is arguably therefore more restrictive, may by virtue of its comprehensiveness (and lack of discrimination) be more likely to withstand panel or Appellate Body scrutiny.[73]

What these cases together demonstrate is that there remains a lack of clarity about how the Appellate Body will approach the relationship between trade liberalisation and national regulation pursuing 'non-economic' objectives. Given that the Appellate Body itself emphasises the need for due process on the part of the domestic regulator, it is evidently unsatisfactory if it does not apply consistent and transparent approaches to its review of these measures. Therefore, it is desirable that the Appellate Body find an adjudicatory mechanism which delivers transparency and predictability. In order to achieve this it is first necessary that the international community articulate more clearly the relationship between trade liberalisation and non-economic interests. If this is done as suggested above, through the lens of sustainable development, then that creates a policy space in which the sustainable development-based approach may be implemented.

A. Sustainable Development as the Basis of an Adjudicative Mechanism

The analysis of the EU experience presented in chapter three indicates that a sustainable development-based approach can be given effect.[74] It is worth reiterating that it is not suggested here that the WTO can simply adopt the approaches of the EU or that the Appellate Body could (or should) seek to replicate what the Court of Justice has achieved. However, one crucial achievement of the Court of Justice, which could be adopted by the WTO panels and the Appellate Body, is the development of a substantive adjudicative mechanism which has been characterised in chapter three as a ground-up application of sustainable development.[75]

---

[71] *US-Measures Concerning the Importation, Marketing and Sale of Tuna and Tuna Products (US-Tuna II (Mexico))* WT/DS381/AB/R, paras 321–22.
[72] See ch 7 above.
[73] Discussed in ch 7 above.
[74] See ch 3 above.
[75] Discussed in ch 3 above.

B. Applying the Sustainable Development-Based Approach: The Role of 'Proportionality'

This sustainable development-based adjudicative mechanism requires that where trade liberalisation comes into contact and conflicts with environmental or social protection, the extent of the trade restriction is balanced against the extent of restriction of the other interest which would be imposed through unencumbered application of the trade (liberalisation) rule. The test which is applied to achieve this is one of 'proportionality', which the European Court of Justice has defined as requiring that the regulatory measure must be appropriate to achieve its objectives and that the restriction must be the least possible in order to achieve the desired objective.[76] This is thus framed in very similar terms to the Article XX WTO 'necessity' test. However, what is crucial under the sustainable development-based approach is that at the same time as the trade restriction is tested for its proportionality, so too is the restriction of the non-economic objective posed by trade liberalisation. Thus, it is a two-way application of proportionality.

The advantages of this test are that it is essentially objective: the two questions asked are whether the measure is appropriate to achieve its (legitimate) objective and whether there is a less restrictive alternative which will achieve equivalent results. It should be noted that the Court of Justice, like the Appellate Body, has steered away from ruling a measure out on the basis of the relative value of the objective pursued (thus, it studiously avoids superimposing its subjective judgment of the object pursued). However, the two-way balancing process it has adopted squarely connects and reinforces the inter-relationship between trade liberalisation and non-economic interests, and it also removes a crucial degree of primacy of a narrow construction of 'trade liberalisation'. This combined approach, reinterpreting the objectives of the WTO in the light of 'sustainable development' and adopting an adjudicative mechanism which operationalises this, would, moreover, effectively reframe the status and potential of non-economic interests and their relationship to trade liberalisation rules.

C. The Benefits of this Approach

If the WTO continues to be shaped and determined by the neoliberal agenda, its role will become increasingly narrow and marginalised as it fails to adequately engage with contemporary challenge and values. Or, to the extent that it (through the panels or the Appellate Body) *does* respond to contemporary global challenges and engage with non-economic interests,

---

[76] See chs 1 and 3 above.

it will be dogged by questions of legitimacy which will affect not only the institutions themselves, but also the status of non-economic interests as they interact with trade liberalisation. In providing a lens through which to approach the relationship between economic and non-economic interests, a sustainable development-based approach would enhance the legitimacy of consideration and protection of non-economic objectives within the WTO legal order. This opens up the potential for redefining the relationship between economic and non-economic objectives.

It is therefore argued that without a reframing of the purpose and objectives of the WTO, the move to a more process-based approach to the relationship between trade liberalisation and non-economic interests will not provide a satisfactory basis for the WTO to engage with contemporary global challenges. However, a reframing of the objectives and purpose of the WTO and trade liberalisation alone will not be enough to ensure the integrated approach to responding to global challenge: while necessary, it is not sufficient. It is essential that this reframing be accompanied by a refinement of the adjudicative mechanism employed by the panel and the Appellate Body. Both this necessary reframing and refinement of the adjudicative mechanism can be realised through reference to the principle and objectives of sustainable development. If the WTO through the panels and Appellate Body were to take such a lead, it has the potential to open up space for a broader (international) redefinition and refinement of the relationship between economic and non-economic interests. Crucially, however, this is just a starting point and it is premised upon the WTO as it is currently constituted, and the international legal order and principles currently existing.

The WTO is currently the only global 'international' body which can adjudicate on the balance to be drawn between trade liberalisation and non-economic interests, yet its effectiveness in doing so is questionable. The measures referred to above would render the WTO better equipped, but would not provide the perfect mechanism for responding to global challenges. This would require a reconsideration of the nature of international legal governance. Real questions can and should be asked of the international legal order and its continuing state-based focus.

IV. RECONCILING THE PURSUIT OF ECONOMIC AND NON-ECONOMIC INTERESTS: LESSONS FROM THE EU

It is apparent from the EU experience that a reconciliation of the pursuit of economic and non-economic interests is possible, but that this requires both a will and a consensus. There is no inherent conflict between pursuit of trade liberalisation and the protection of non-economic interests; they are mutually dependent. However, in particular instances, they collide, which requires a balancing exercise between the long-term gain and short-term cost. This is a process which is achieved within states which are small-scale liberal markets and it is a process which has been shown to be possible within the EU. As such, it should be possible within the international legal framework and community. Yet such a process requires common interests and shared perceptions of the costs and benefits: these are less likely to be the case on a global scale. The requisite policy choices are easier to make within a smaller, more homogenous bloc, such as the EU, than in the global context.

It has, however, proved possible to achieve a common policy choice in relation to international trade and its benefits: it has also been possible to achieve consensus around the significance of sustainable development. It should therefore be possible to build on that to achieve common policy choice in the wider context, particularly if the common objectives of liberal trade and non-economic interests are recalled. The achievements in the context of liberal trade should be built upon and applied to broader contexts, without necessarily using trade sanctions to promote non-economic interests, but using the universal consensus on the common objectives of trade liberalisation and international law.

A. EU Lessons: The Internal Perspective

As was demonstrated in Part I of this book, the EU has found its own balance in the relationship between economic and non-economic interests, however imperfect or incomplete that may be. In relation to fundamental rights, there are lacunae with regard to the approach taken to the rights of third country nationals within the EU, but there have also been problems in relation to the disparities between the rights declared in the Charter of Fundamental Rights and the lack of protection of certain of these in practice.[77] The problem of the lack of effective protection for these rights is a serious one, as has been evidenced by the EU experience relating to environmental protection. On the other hand, the very development of the Charter, and of secondary legislation under Article 13, does suggest that the EU has progressively developed a more mature and complete conception of fundamental rights; it is clear is that this is an ongoing process.

In relation to environmental protection in the EU there is, again, evidence of a developing polity. Whereas protection initially developed as a byproduct of market integration, there is increasing evidence of the growing strength of environmental policy per se. This can be seen in the efforts to give effect to the duty of integration, as well as in the approach

---

[77] See ch 3 above.

of the Court in *PreussenElektra*. Despite ongoing problems in relation to access to justice (notwithstanding efforts to resolve these), there is evidence, once again, of the development of a genuine EU environment policy. Thus, notwithstanding their evident differences, the policies in relation to the protection of fundamental rights and of the environment share some underlying characteristics. The explicit EU focus upon sustainable development will ultimately strengthen the interests pursued through human rights and environmental policy. That these have been linked together with economic development provides indisputable evidence of a growing European governance which is far removed from the original European Economic Community. This sense of an emerging governance and polity is reinforced by the increasing emphasis upon stakeholder and citizen participation in decision making.

The EU experience has also shown us that the sustainable development-based approach can be, and has been, operationalised. As it is a process-based approach, it recognises and accommodates different outcomes. It is therefore an approach which can be transferred and applied beyond the EU in the international context. The EU experience has also demonstrated the significance of consensus regarding the values and interests to be protected. There is considerable international recognition of sustainable development and, indeed, this is reflected in the inclusion of sustainable development in the EU's agreements with third states. This observation invites consideration of the broader lessons that can be learnt from the experience of EU external relations.

B. EU Lessons: The External Perspective

The development of EU external competence, and its manifestations, demonstrates the complexity in establishing which actor should act at which point and in which context. Here the key issue concerns the transfer of competence and its consequent impact upon sovereignty. Again, therefore, it is evident that for the EU to pursue particular interests in its external relations, there must be a will and a consensus to do so. Originally, human rights in the EU's external relations developed largely as a result of the need for the EU to avoid inadvertently breaching its obligation to uphold human rights in all its activities, and the implementation of external human rights policy has been shown to be far from perfect. While this imperative, to avoid breaching its internal obligations, remains and is in fact if anything strengthened under the Lisbon Treaty, there is also evidence, particularly since the Treaty of Nice and consolidated in the Lisbon Treaty, of a shift to a broader perspective and a more active human rights policy extending beyond the context of development cooperation. The EU's external environmental policy clearly reflects its internal competence and addresses the pragmatic reality that many environmental challenges require an international approach. However, it is also worth noting that the EU's external environmental and development cooperation competence is concurrent rather than exclusive, recognising the continuing competence of Member States in these areas.[78] It is clear that the EU's human rights and environmental competence have evolved from matters which are incidental to its economic policy and activity, and now constitute distinct policy areas and objectives. However, albeit recognised as distinct policy areas, the EU's internal approach is increasingly premised upon sustainable development and is therefore integrated. This is mirrored in its external relations. Yet the resistance of some partner states to the inclusion in trade agreements of clauses relating to non-economic interests reinforces the significance of consensus, not just European but also that shared with the partner state.[79]

The emphasis upon international instruments as reference points is significant, for this mitigates the criticism that the EU is imposing its values upon partner states. The fact that the human rights clause has evolved into an explicitly reciprocal commitment helps to negate the charge of EU paternalism. Similarly, the focus upon the development of dialogue regarding in particular human rights obligations and within the GSP is also significant, for it reinforces the cooperative element rather than compulsion. In this context, the EU has demonstrated its willingness to act (albeit in limited contexts) to enforce compliance, but has reinforced the significance of the incentive-based approach, the carrot rather than the stick: the EU's approach to Sri Lanka demonstrates a desire to maintain cooperation if at all possible.[80]

The very inclusion of environmental and human rights commitments in trade and other cooperation agreements is significant. That their inclusion has evolved as it has, towards dialogue and away from sanction, towards reciprocity, referencing international instruments and engaging civil society is consistent with the EU's emerging emphasis upon good governance and democracy. It recognises the need for consensus and it extends the consideration of non-economic interests in economic agreements to the broader international legal order. The EU approach, both internal and external, reinforces the sense of an emerging EU polity: this is a global actor with an identifiable presence. As such, it is contributing to the shape of the international agenda with regard to how the relationship between economic and non-economic interests should be developed. As the WTO Members have accepted sustainable development as an objective, the EU approach could be followed in respect of the interpretation and application of the WTO rules. Were this to be done, it would assist in the internal legitimacy

---

[78] See ch 4 above.
[79] See ch 5 above.
[80] See ch 5 above.

of WTO recognition of non-economic interests. In so doing, it would also have spillover effects into the broader international regulatory order.

V. CONCLUDING COMMENTS

These final comments regarding the lessons from the EU experience have not sought to reiterate the detailed analysis of the relationship between economic and non-economic interests in international trade. Rather, they seek to draw out some key strands running consistently through this complex issue. The Court of Justice has proved itself willing to balance economic and non-economic interests, even with some legitimacy, yet its function (in relation to a body of law which pursues a variety of objectives, which are increasingly being integrated) is very different from that of the WTO DSB. The same expectations which exist in relation to the function of the Court of Justice simply cannot be made of the WTO DSB.

The evolving nature of international values and international law is crucial here. The EU has clearly developed its protection of non-economic interests from being 'add-ons' dealt with where they interact with economic interests to being objectives pursued in their own right. In contrast, the WTO rules remain primarily targeted upon the removal of restrictions on trade. While the international community is moving on, and international law has moved on in many contexts, the WTO has not yet adjusted. This presents a challenge: the WTO remains the only 'international' body which can adjudicate on the balance to be drawn between economic and non-economic interests, yet it remains ill-equipped to do so in the light of current values. Thus, it leaves the international community with a problem, given the development of international environmental law, the shift from the concept of labour standards to labour rights, the declaration of fundamental labour rights and the commitment to sustainable development evident in the UN Summit in Johannesburg in August 2002.

If we can learn anything from the EU in relation to the reconciliation of economic and non-economic interests, it is that this is only possible where consensus exists as to the values to be pursued, the extent to which they may be pursued and the means by which they should interact with other interests. The necessity of consensus can be seen in the EU's approach to human rights in its external relations—for example, reference to different rights is included in different contexts. The necessity of a common will to pursue the values included within the common consensus is demonstrated by the failure of the EC-Australia negotiations with respect to the human rights clause.

That the EU has managed to establish such a consensus internally is a reflection not only of the relative homogeneity of its Member States, but also, in relation to fundamental rights, of the fact that those Member States were all already bound by the ECHR. The fact that that consensus is in the process of deepening is a reflection of the nature of the EU, its suprana-tionality and developing polity. All of these render the EU experience very different from that of the WTO, and all contribute to the extent to which the EU can develop, balance and pursue potentially conflicting objectives. This does not, however, mean that the EU experience offers no practical assistance to this issue. It demonstrates, for all its imperfections, that the pursuit of economic and non-economic interests may be reconciled within the context of regulation of international trade, and that it is possible to develop the necessary consensus to do so. Yet, to establish consensus, there must be political will, which must reflect democratic choice. The short-term interest, however, may not be conducive to the establishment of a necessary consensus of common values and interests. Thus, it may be difficult for governments to take the electoral risk of putting long-term interests ahead of short-term interests.

In addressing this issue, it is useful to consider one of the weaknesses of the EU approach: the very lack of consistency of definition of rights in what is intended to be a policy ensuring the universality of its rights protection in its relations with third states. This highlights that 'rights' (in this context) is not a particularly useful term. Just as in relation to international labour standards/rights, it may be more beneficial to try and work towards a definition of core values and objectives which can be accepted as universal and which would be consistent with the pursuit of sustainable develop-ment, stemming perhaps from the Brundtland definition. It goes without saying that any measures taken in these contexts should avoid protection-ism. Thus, consistency and universality are essential. So too, however, is a recognition from developed states that any values agreed (with developing states) as core or universal must be supported—thus, where standards are to be attained and maintained, this cannot be achieved in a vacuum, but will almost undoubtedly require support in terms of technical and material aid and cooperation (incentives rather than sanctions). This reflects the reality that 'trickle-down' will not effectively (or efficiently) occur unless the trickle is assisted. It is equally imperative that any such agreed standards should be consistently applied.

The current framework of international law in which this 'conflict' operates is not altogether satisfactory. There can be little doubt that the institutional framework is a weakness and that the dominant interpretation of the primary objective of the WTO (liberalisation of trade) hampers the pursuit of non-economic interests, and will continue to do so at least until the pursuit of trade liberalisation is reframed within a more holistic, sus-tainable development-based conceptualisation. This remains a significant problem for an international community bound by the WTO, but which in other contexts has demonstrated a serious commitment to the pursuit of non-economic interests.

Yet hope for the future may be drawn from the achievements of the EU. The identification of prima facie conflicting objectives need not lead to a breakdown of the international legal system. These interests may be reconciled, facilitating balanced, sustainable development. However, this will only be possible if there is a genuine consensus as to the direction of future development and a common vision of priorities for that development.

Index